Palgrave Studies in Prisons and Penology

Shadd Maruna
School of Criminal Justice
Rutgers University
Newark, USA

Jonathan Simon
Law
University of California Berkeley
Berkeley, USA

Michael Welch
Shreveport, USA

This is a unique and innovative series, the first of its kind dedicated entirely to prison scholarship. At a historical point in which the prison population has reached an all-time high, the series seeks to analyse the form, nature and consequences of incarceration and related forms of punishment. Palgrave Studies in Prisons and Penology provides an important forum for burgeoning prison research across the world.

Kate Gooch

Prison Violence

The Search for Recognition and Respect

palgrave
macmillan

Kate Gooch
Department of Social and Policy Sciences
University of Bath
Bath, UK

ISSN 2753-0604 ISSN 2753-0612 (electronic)
Palgrave Studies in Prisons and Penology
ISBN 978-3-031-91364-8 ISBN 978-3-031-91365-5 (eBook)
https://doi.org/10.1007/978-3-031-91365-5

Cover illustration: xijian / Getty Images

This Palgrave Macmillan imprint is published by the registered company Springer Nature Switzerland AG.
The registered company address is: Gewerbestrasse 11, 6330 Cham, Switzerland

In memory of Irene.
For Matt and Joshua.

Foreword

I remember the Deputy Chief Inspector calling me after he concluded the first inspection (I had been leading another inspection elsewhere). He sounded shocked, angry, appalled distressed ... all of these. And he was not normally someone given to displays of emotion. He described frightening levels of violence, the squalor, and the broken windows. He spoke of the 'learned helplessness' of the management and staff—a phrase the author of this book uses.

This Young Offender Institution (YOI) for young adults was the worst prison we had ever inspected, and it was this place, the young men and staff within it, how it had got to the state the inspectors found, and the efforts by the new governor to turn it round before we inspected it again, that this book describes. It is a hard but important story.

The book is bracketed by that first inspection and an account of the follow-up inspection I led when we returned 18 months later, but it is not really about the inspection process itself. Nevertheless, as I have this platform, I will mention three insights about the inspection process that the book reveals.

First, my experience was that most people thought the inspectorate had done a good job when we turned up somewhere, revealed things that had gone badly wrong and made recommendations about how they should be put right, which the prison then duly implemented. There is some truth in that, but I felt success was when we arrived somewhere and found it was working well, the prison knew we would be coming (if not usually when), the standards we would be inspecting against, and so had worked to meet those standards before we came. In this case it was the knowledge we would be coming back and what we would be looking for when we arrived that drove improvement, not particularly the recommendations we made. The book describes a degree of theatre that accompanied this approach—something I always felt a bit uncomfortable with—but it seemed to work.

Second, in the excellent methodology chapter, the author describes her research as 'loitering with intent'—which is pretty much how I would describe my own inspection approach. Of course, all the inspection team had areas they had to work through, but I asked them not to allow a checklist approach to prevent them from paying attention to their hunches and spending the time necessary to follow up concerns as they emerged. I or the Deputy Chief Inspector would join the last day of every week-long inspection. When I started in the role, I would use this time to do a tour of the prison accompanied by a junior prison officer to help me find my way around before joining the inspection team to discuss our findings. I would try to see as much of the prison as possible and so inevitably I ended up 'seeing' very little. As I became more experienced, I changed my approach. I would often start in the segregation unit and ask the staff there which wing provided most of the men they held. Then I would go to that wing and 'loiter with intent' for an hour or two—and saw more than I did on any tour. Prison governors all had a prison workshop they were particularly proud of—bicycle repairs were a favourite—and would suggest I went there. I did, to be polite (they were often empty I found which did not create the impression the governor hoped). Then I would make a point of going to the recycling workshop. Almost all prisons had one and they were always working. You could tell a lot from how a prison was treating the men who cleaned the yoghurt pots I found. It seems to me that the research methodology the author describes has something to teach anyone whose job it is to find out what is really happening in an institution—be it a prison, school, hospital, or elsewhere: Loiter with intent.

Third, the author powerfully locates the dreadful situation of the YOI she describes in the wider context of the political and policy context of the period. 'Catastrophic and wide-ranging reforms to the staffing, resourcing, and management of public sector prisons' she rightly calls out. Local leadership is important—as the example described in this book powerfully demonstrates but however good that leadership:

> Governors had little influence over but would deal with the fallout from sentencing policy, constant penal policy change, the privatisation of facilities management, restricted autonomy over budgets, the removal of local organisational support (e.g. finance and HR), population pressures, and the incarceration of people with acute mental health needs for whom there were no secure beds.

So I regarded my inspection findings not as an assessment of the leadership of a prison but as an assessment of the outcome for the prisoners it held. Responsibility for those outcomes extended far beyond the walls of the prison.

There is horror in the outcomes described here.

> When we encountered him at midday, Craig was banging his head against a wall and the metal cell door, but with new faces and no uniforms, the arrival of James and I gave him sufficient pause and he shouted out to us. Tears rolled down his cheeks as he lamented that he had nothing to lose or live for. His body bore the scars and injuries of just a few short days in custody and the weight of a short life exposed to frequent hardships. The marks of a ligature pulled tight around his neck were pink and visible—a haunting reminder of how close he had come to death. He pulled up his sleeves to show us where he had scratched his arm, seemingly trying to convey something of the depths of his despair. Craig was keen to tell us he had only fought harder when officers had tried to restrain him but complained that his thumb was still throbbing. Handcuffs had been used and he rubbed his wrists as he was talking, but as he shrugged off the pain he added, "I've been tortured and felt worse pain." Being restrained had stirred an incensed reaction from Craig. For all his claims of hardness and physical prowess, and his attempts to impress upon us that "he didn't show emotion," Craig frequently became overwhelmed and struggled to contain his distress. Prison staff were faced with the difficult task of deciding where to hold and what to *do* with a young man who might both seriously assault someone and attempt suicide.

The horror here is not the description of the physical marks of Craig's distress—but what the author, citing Liebling (2004), describe as the moral outrage of human beings treated in this way. Why did no one notice (or care) what was happening in this YOI? How could these young men matter so little that they were treated in this way? Central to the reform effort described was the idea that they were 'worth' something—that they did matter.

The idea of a 'moral' standard is a thread which runs through the book. I am not sure if this is what the author intended but it is appropriate in my view. The book is unflinching in its descriptions of the violence it describes and recognises that the pain, fear, and humiliation that arises from it is not just a consequence of its physical manifestation, but even more so of the threats and tension that envelop the daily life of the YOI. This actual and threatened violence is contextualised by recognition of the life-stories of the young men involved but their own 'agency and responsibility' is not denied nor are the difficulties in managing it.

Too much of the academic and policy literature I read shies away for this. Losing the individual cruelty, harm, and fear of prison violence in clouds of data or making too easy a distinction between perpetrator and victim. Here these things are addressed head on and so the conclusions the author comes too are all the more credible. She exposes deep rooted fallacies about prison 'gangs,' misunderstandings of the connection between the increased availability of new psychoactive substances and the rise in prison violence, over-managerialism that disempowered governors and focusing too much on the individual prisoner rather than the context. These misunderstandings have real impact, influencing both wider prison policy and the assessment and treatment of individual prisoners.

To reveal too much about the conclusion of the book would be a spoiler in a foreword but no one who reads the book now several years after the events it describes should be unaware that the neglect it describes are now commonplace. Many prisons and YOIs have 'been left to crumble—morally and physically' as this YOI was. There are some answers here in this powerful account, should anyone be looking.

London, England, UK Nick Hardwick

Prologue: An Inspector Calls, Again

This Friday was like no other. Normal routines and rhythms had been disrupted. On any other day, the 'morning meeting' with the senior management team would start the day. In any other week, Friday was characterised by contradictory rhythms. The gradual emptying of classrooms and idleness of workshops contrasting with a sharp focus on two key potential flashpoints for prison violence: the Islamic prayer service and the distribution of 'canteen.'[1] One hundred prisoners walking to the Chapel for the Islamic prayer service caused prison officers to be especially vigilant for any signs of 'trouble.' Whilst 'Friday prayers' was for many a moment of spiritual importance, a small number had used these occasions to assault others, to negotiate drug deals, or organise the physical assault of others. Once everyone had returned safely from Friday prayers, prison officers would distribute canteen—items that would be quickly consumed, sold, stolen, or used to repay debts. Those young men who failed to repay their debts were punished by their peers, leading prison officers to dub Fridays as 'Black eye Friday.' Whilst Friday prayers and canteen distribution would continue, there was a different feel to this Friday. Today, the senior management team would finally hear whether

[1] 'Canteen' included items such as food, toiletries and stationery, and could be ordered on a weekly basis.

their efforts to create a more hopeful, just, safe, and decent prison had proved successful.

The countdown to this moment had begun 16 weeks earlier when the date of the inspection was announced. The Governing Governor regularly reminded their senior team how many weeks remained before the re-inspection. As weeks turned to days, the focus and intensity had increased, as had the number of visits from senior figures within the Prison Service. In truth, though, the countdown began more than a year before when Her Majesty's Chief Inspector of Prisons declared the young offender institution (YOI) the worst prison in England and Wales. Last time, the findings had been so damning that the Inspection team did not return on the Friday to offer the customary verbal feedback or a summation of the report. The YOI had failed against every measure of a 'healthy prison,' the criteria developed by Her Majesty's Inspectorate of Prisons (HMIP) to assess prisons, YOI's, and other custodial settings. The Inspectorate focused on four measures: safety, respect, purposeful activity and (at the time) resettlement,[2] scoring prisons against a sliding scale of 'good,' 'reasonably good,' 'not sufficiently good' and 'poor.' In prison vernacular, this scoring system was translated into numerical readings; 'good' being '4' and 'poor' being '1.' For Governing Governors and their senior management teams, HMIP inspection narratives and scores can 'make or break careers.' Governing Governors can be moved to other roles and postings and, as in this case, the YOI or prison may become the focus of local and national media attention. Within the YOI, the phrase 'worst prison in the country' would linger in the minds of the staff long after it was printed in the national and local press.

When HMIP had last visited, young men were living in 'squalid' conditions in cells unfit for human occupation. Windows were not just cracked, but broken and missing panes of glass, leaving occupants exposed to the elements in the depths of winter. The broken windows facilitated illicit trade since 'lines' could be passed from strips of bed sheets strung between cells. Curtains were fashioned from whatever materials could be found. Graffiti covered dingy cell walls. Once painted in magnolia, but now stained with blood, dirt, and grime, the cell walls told the stories of

[2] The 'resettlement' test has now become 'rehabilitation and release planning'.

in-cell assaults never revealed in official statistics. Young men had graffitied the walls with messages about postcode affiliations, peer groups associations, injunctions to 'Fuck the system' and 'Fuck' certain individuals, and more philosophical declarations such as 'I'm on my own when it goes down.' Litter piled up beneath cell windows. Under each torched, damaged, and jagged hole to the outside world was a number; this number serving as a very faint reminder that the residential buildings contained people—young men who were still growing, maturing, and developing. For them, the YOI was quite simply a 'shit hole.' Mouldy apple cores and rotting half-eaten sandwiches abandoned on the floors and window sills spoke of a shared hopelessness. None of the young men had recently killed themselves, but the scars of the assaults and despair were often hauntingly visible. The squalor and injustices moved the incoming, experienced Governing Governor to tears. If prisons can be 'moral communities' (Liebling 2004: 474), the reverse was clearly true.

High levels of violence—the focus of this study—was a symptom, not the cause, of the inhumanity, indecency, and immorality. The chaotic living conditions were matched with a volatile, chaotic, and insecure prison. As the Chief Inspector would later remind us, 'it was one of the most violent places' he had visited. To the young men concerned, it was a 'war zone.' Imprisonment had been reduced to an act of survival. All pretence of rehabilitation had disappeared, succumbing to the pressure of accommodating too many young men without the necessary financial resources. Some would survive—damaged, scarred, marked by their own self-harm and suicide attempts. For those who would graduate to adult prisons, their time in the YOI had effectively prepared them for the instability that increasingly characterised the adult prison estate.

Penal reformers called for the immediate closure of the prison, and the fate of the YOI remained precarious even up until the re-inspection. The scrutiny was intense. The senior management team felt the 'eyes of the world upon them.' The Prisons Minister had visited mid-week and, and in conversation with the Chief Inspector, had asked why the poor conditions at the YOI had gone unnoticed for so long, and why action had not been taken earlier. These questions hung in the air unanswered. De-sensitised and unable to effect change, prison staff and managers—even very senior managers—admitted they had 'stopped seeing things.' It might have been tempting to criticise or vilify staff and managers for the prison's shortcomings, but they too were bruised. What might be perceived as apathy or indifference was in fact a consequence of helplessness and hopelessness. They too needed redemption. They too desired change.

The Chapel usually served as a multi-faith setting, but was also the site of awards ceremonies, presentations on drug recovery, the reading of poems, and full staff briefings. It was a place for intimate family connections, permissible emotional expression, spiritual fulfilment, and operational briefings. Today, it was the setting for the formal feedback from HM Chief Inspector on the progress of the jail over the preceding year. How long it seemed from Monday morning when the Inspection had begun and the reality of this 'big week' had loomed large, shaping every interaction and conversation. At the start of the week, there was an air of nervous tension. The rallying call to the senior team was to 'be confident and proud of the journey so far,' be 'honest but not undersell' themselves, and remember that whatever happened they had 'put pride back into the Prison Service.' The young men themselves were also aware of the significance of the inspection and were keenly interested in the outcome. They knew what it meant for staff seeking to present their best, issuing threats when it served their interests: 'you don't want me smashing my cell while the Inspectors are here.'

As the senior team now waited for the feedback, they twitched nervously, periodically turning in their seats to see if the Chief Inspector and his team had arrived. The pensive faces of Monday morning were replaced with anticipation and excitement. Nods of acknowledgement passed between colleagues. Custodial Managers who were on 'rest days' came into work dressed in 'civvies'[3] to hear the feedback first-hand. The charged atmosphere of Inspection week had lifted. For the first time since the research began, there was lightness in the air, reminiscent of years gone by when the school year was ending and all that awaited was the unfettered freedom of the summer holidays. In this case, a good inspection would free the YOI from the threat of closure and intense scrutiny. The senior management team waited. Waited for the scores. Waited for the

[3] 'Civvies' are everyday civilian clothes (as compared with prison uniform).

feedback. Waited to see whether their efforts, strategy, and vision had proved right. Surely, they had done enough. Surely.

Bath, UK Kate Gooch

Reference

Liebling, A. (2004). *Prisons and their moral performance*. Oxford University Press.

Acknowledgements

A project of this length and nature inevitably incurs a great debt. It would not have been possible without the young men and prison staff who offered James (my co-researcher) and I a glimpse into their lives and trusted us with their stories, their fears, their pain, and their hopes. Writing these words several years on, those people remain deeply imprinted in my mind. They have shaped the writer and researcher I have become. I have always felt a great weight of responsibility to capture their experiences and narratives accurately—I hope I've done them justice here.

My deep gratitude goes to James Treadwell with whom I conducted the empirical research. James was and is an exceptional ethnographer. His companionship during the research, and his willingness to allow me to test ideas out with him in the conversations that followed, have meant a great deal. Since leaving the YOI, I've taken responsibility for data analysis, report writing, book writing, and sharing the findings with practitioners. James read and commented on some book chapters, adding helpful notes and sharing fieldnotes that might be relevant.

I have been fortunate enough to be surrounded by colleagues who have supported and encouraged me but also nourished my intellectual development and curiosity. My thanks go to: Kate Doolin, Erika Rackley, Richard Young, Marie Fox, Claire McIvor, James Lee, Martin George, Rob Cryer, Adrian Hunt, Neil Chakraborti, Sarah Moore, Pete Manning, and Alison Liebling. Draft versions of the book were read by several colleagues who generously offered thoughtful feedback and suggestions. I am grateful to: Ian O'Donnell, Simon Winlow, Kimmett Edgar, Jamie Bennett, Sarah Moore, Omar Khan, Jack Spicer, Kate Doolin, David Maguire, Eamonn Carrabine, Ben Crewe, and Yvonne Jewkes. To Ben Crewe, I extend particular thanks. Over more than a decade, he has mentored, coached, and encouraged me to be a better writer, scholar, and empirical researcher. He helped me work through the 'knotty' parts of prison research and stretched me to think harder and deeper about what I was observing. I also extend my thanks to Yvonne Jewkes who helped me discover, and gave me the confidence to pursue, a writing style that could help me realise my ambition to offer readers an insight into the smells, sights, and sounds of prisons—not just what they are like but how they *feel*.

Several prison governors and frontline staff have continued to be a source of enduring encouragement and wisdom. Special mention goes to Rob Luxford, Mark Greenhaf, Tom Wheatley, Pia Sinha, Emma Dunkerley, James Lucas, Jo Geoghegan, Russ Trent, Steve Hodson, PJ Butler, Debbie McKay, and Ed Borgman. I'm also grateful to Jenny Rees, Ed Cornmell, Richard Vince, Alan Scott, and Sarah Coccia for not only generously supporting my research but also wholeheartedly engaging with the findings.

To my church family at HCC, your love, generosity, grace, and prayers have sustained me in more ways than I can explain. Special thanks go to Chip and Sarah Kawalsingh, Stuart and Nittah Coles, Tate and Wendy Kandi, Dan and Tiffany Hussain, Daniel and Bianca Ndlovu, Jen Goffin, and Paul and Tanya Goffin, all of whom have walked with me in every season and whose examples of great faith continue to inspire me.

This book would not have been possible with the love, support, and encouragement of my family. To my wonderful mum and dad, to Daniel and Hannah (and their growing families), and to Ian and Jen—thank you! Most importantly of all, my love and deepest gratitude go to Matthew—for his steadfast love, for enduring my endless conversations about prisons, and for accommodating my growing piles of books—and to Joshua—who is a constant joy and has enriched my life in every way.

Competing Interests The author has no competing interests to declare that are relevant to the content of this manuscript.

Contents

About the Author

Kate Gooch is a Senior Lecturer/Associate Professor in Criminology at the University of Bath. Prior to this, she worked in the Law Schools of the University of Birmingham and the University of Leicester. She is interested in crime and criminal justice but has a particular focus on youth custody and prisons. Drawing on ethnographic and qualitative methods, she not only analyses the causes, forms, and dynamics of harmful and criminal activity within prison (including violence, homicide, self-harm, suicide, and organised crime), but also the moral, social, cultural, environmental, and leadership contexts that prevent or support harm and continued criminality.

1

Introduction

At 7.30 pm, the wait for Jevon to arrive was finally over. It was a dark, wet, cold Winter's night just a few days before Christmas, and the 'sweatbox'[1] was now exiting the vehicle lock and approaching Reception. The YOI was eerie at night. Corridors that had a few hours earlier been filled with young men jostling and chatting now lay empty, silent, and dark. Those youthful voices could only be heard in the distance as the conversations, laughter, threats, and demands echoed from the cell windows. In Reception, however, the day was not yet over.

Earlier that day, Jevon had been unlocked by three officers in full personal protection equipment (PPE) but had decided to leave the London prison of his own accord without being forced onto the van. Brought alone in the sweatbox, it was now many hours after Jevon's expected arrival time. He had spent most of the journey stuck in a small box travelling tediously down a crowded and partially closed motorway and would arrive at the new prison tired and hungry. To smooth over any potential frustration, the Supervising Officer (SO) had arranged for hot food to be kept warm for him, but the SO remained concerned that Jevon might

[1] Cellular escort vans used to transfer prisoners to and from court and/or to other prisons were dubbed 'sweatboxes.'

K. Gooch, *Prison Violence*, Palgrave Studies in Prisons and Penology,
https://doi.org/10.1007/978-3-031-91365-5_1

'come straight off the bus ready to fight.' 'Is it likely?' James Treadwell, my co-researcher, asks. The SO shrugs. 'The Dep [Deputy Governor] wants us to greet him with a cup of tea,' the SO tells us, 'I am not doing that, don't fancy a hot tea in my pretty face.' He gently laughs. 'I've got this.' He gestures with the small plastic bottle of water he is holding in his hand. 'Can't do much harm with this!' He chuckles. He begins to walk towards to the escort van, turns to us and calmly but seriously adds: 'If anything does kick off, just get out the way.' Familiar advice we had long learned to heed.

The Reception officers were prepared for trouble. Jevon's prison record included a long list of violent incidents and rule violations. He had been flagged as a potential risk to staff, having seriously assaulted several prison officers and slashed another prisoner with an improvised weapon.[2] 'Nothing we can't handle,' the SO confidently told us. Yet the Reception officers had maintained a careful vigil all afternoon, periodically checking the clock and re-assessing when their shift might end. As the hours had passed, they were increasingly aware that their colleagues would soon finish their shifts and would not be rushing to their aid if needed. Some officers had already decided to 'stay back' after their shift—a demonstration of solidarity and support for their colleagues. Others declined the overtime pay: 'A few quid in overtime payments is not worth a bust jaw.' For officers, the possibility of violence structured their working lives. To say, 'it seems quiet today' was deemed bad luck, often prompting officers to touch the closest wooden furniture or item. A good day was a safe day.

As Jevon stepped out of the sweatbox and shuffled the handful of steps to Reception, he was flanked by officers. Handcuffs bound his wrists. At 18 years-old, Jevon was already a tall, broad, and muscular young man who looked much older than his age. Jevon approached the desk and the Reception Officers relieved the escort staff of their duties. 'You aren't going to give us trouble when they come off?' The SO nods towards the handcuffs as he poses the question. Jevon shakes his head. 'We have one rule here,' the SO continues as he takes off the handcuffs, watching Jevon and assessing his demeanour, 'You be alright with us, and we will be

[2] An 'improvised weapon' refers to those weapons fashioned within prison from items such as toothbrushes and razor blades.

alright with you.' Jevon nods. The water bottle is passed to Jevon as he frees his wrists and his hands adjust to their newfound freedom. 'Have you eaten lad?' another officer asks, although he already knows the answer and promptly leaves to fetch a plate of hot food. Clear plastic bags containing Jevon's property are dragged in behind him and recorded one at a time by the desk officer. Jevon is just as interested in checking his property has safely arrived as the officer is in recording it. A move between prisons means a different set of rules about what property can be kept (and in what quantities) within cells—small details that can quickly become the big issues.

Jevon is only a few months into a lengthy sentence for a serious violent offence, and the transfer was just one of many transitions that he will make as he matures from a teenager to a young man, and then to a man in his 30s and 40s. 'Is it bad here?' Jevon asks. 'Lad like you will be fine,' the officer responds, 'You know the score: keep your head down, stay away from drugs.' Although the officers assumed that Jevon would adjust easily, his trepidation is clear as he scans the room, his hands tremble and his foot repeatedly taps the floor. Jevon might be familiar with prison, and some details about his violent capabilities had preceded him, but he would still have to establish himself in a new prison and amongst a new group of peers drawn from Liverpool, Manchester, Birmingham, Wolverhampton, Nottingham, Stoke on Trent, and beyond. Violence was troubling not just to prison staff, but even those who appeared to use it most. No one wanted to succumb to injury even if they found pride and dignity in defending themselves. With the initial checks complete, James asks Jevon, 'You heard about this place?' He smiles. 'Pen is Pen, same rules,' he replies, before picking up a clutch of possessions and preparing to be escorted through the locked gates and doors to the First Night Centre, and then whatever future challenges this 'Pen' held.

Seven months earlier, James and I had entered the Young Offenders Institution (YOI) seeking to understand the nature and dynamics of prison violence, bullying, and victimisation. Our interest in violence amongst young men (aged 18–21 years old) fortuitously aligned with those of the Governing Governor who was keen to reduce the high levels of bullying and violence explicitly criticised by Her Majesty's Inspectorate of Prisons during their inspection. What began as a study of a single

English YOI soon exposed the depths of the crisis across the English and Welsh prison system where the broken windows (and the moral malaise it embodied) were ignored or reluctantly accepted for too long. I saw how a committed and passionate leadership team energetically sought to arrest this decline and breathe hope into a hopeless place, earnestly embracing one of the most demanding leadership challenges in the face of unrelenting organisational and external scrutiny. A prison may decay, rot, and even grow malignant, but a prison can also heal, be restored, and find its own form of rehabilitation. It was here that I found myself, observing the metamorphosis of what had been dubbed the 'worst prison' in England and Wales. This is not to detract from the point that prisons are inherently and structurally places of pain, coercive force and violence (also see Scott, 2015; Scraton et al., 1991), but to recognise that the extent and severity of that harm is a matter of choice. We have the prisons we create.

Although prison violence has attracted sustained academic interest (Bottoms, 1999; Wooldredge, 2020), very few studies have specifically focused on violence by young men aged 18–21 years old (note, by way of exception, Edgar et al., 2003) or indeed on YOIs for young adults (note Harvey, 2007; Liebling, 2012). This paucity of research is concerning. Although young adult men represent a relatively small proportion (less than 4%) of the overall prison population (Ministry of Justice, 2025a), they are disproportionately involved in recorded assaults (Ministry of Justice, 2025b), more likely to experience poorer staff-prisoner relationships, and more likely to be restrained, segregated, and experience restricted daily 'regimes'[3] (Her Majesty's Inspectorate of Prisons, 2021). This occurs at precisely the time when young men are still maturing and still forming their identities as young *men.* Too often, imprisonment is less a disruption to experiences of violence, indignity, and tragedy experienced in childhood and early adulthood than a perpetuation and intensification of them. Those young men with the most 'intense vulnerability' (Liebling, 2012) and complex needs are 'managed,' and not cared for, and

[3] This rather vague term is typically used to refer the daily schedule, including when prisoners are locked in and unlocked from their cells, when meals are served, when medication is distributed, when showers can be taken, when phone calls can be made, when prisoners may use the gym or exercise yard, and when activities such as employment, education, visits, faith services and health appointments can occur.

too easily dismissed by prison officers as a 'drain on resources.' Typically, prison violence is seen by policy makers and practitioners as the 'pathological manifestation of abnormal otherness' (Sim, 1994: 105), diverting attention from the physical, policy, economic, cultural, and relational context that is not only conducive to violence but generates it.

The aim of this book is to analyse the anatomy, aetiology, culture, and dynamics of contemporary prison violence and victimisation by young adult men aged 18–21 years old. It explores why some young men hurt others, why some are repeatedly victimised, and how others who witness such harm avoid direct involvement. It analyses the cultural (Chaps. 3, 8, and 9), economic (Chap. 4), relational (Chap. 5), individual (Chaps. 6 and 7), normative (Chap. 8) and situational (Chap. 9) features of prison violence and victimisation. Rather than identifying a single cause of prison violence, this book articulates the ways in which these individual, situational, relational, economic, and cultural features interact. In so doing, it illustrates how the moral qualities of the prison structured the role, form, and function of prison violence and victimisation. Moral order begets social order. This is not to excuse or minimise the agentic actions and decisions of individuals, or overlook the influence of prior experiences, but to recognise that our understanding of prison violence and victimisation cannot be divorced from its setting. Context matters. This book therefore not only seeks to re-assert the critical importance of justice, hope, humanity, integrity, and compassion, but also the importance of recognition and respect. Crucially, it is the narratives, experiences, and lives of the young men within the prison that remain 'centre stage' because it is for these individuals that prison violence has its most tragic consequences.

The Winters of Discontent: The Research in Context

> The biggest change, which has hit us for six, is 'Benchmarking' and 'New Ways of Working.' It just isn't working. I think it's changed prisoners' lives drastically. (Dave, Supervising Officer)

This study began at a time when prisons across England and Wales were experiencing a period of unabated decline caused, in part, by the imposition of severe austerity measures. On 8th November 2012, Chris Grayling, then Secretary of State for Justice, announced the introduction of a 'benchmarking project' across public sector prisons. Prisons, he said, should be 'cheaper not smaller' (Ministry of Justice, 2012). This benchmarking project introduced the most catastrophic and wide-ranging reforms to the staffing, resourcing, and management of public sector prisons. It was also accompanied by the 'Fair and Sustainable' initiative—or 'Unfair and Unsustainable' as it was dubbed by some prison officers—which sought to 'modernise' contract terms and conditions (National Offender Management Service, 2012).

Although the benchmarking programme subsequently generated a profound sense of loss and grief amongst prison staff, at the time, 'both the Prison Governors' Association and the Prison Officers' Association welcomed the decision … [and] worked closely with NOMS [the National Offender Management Service][4] to implement it' (House of Commons Justice Committee, 2015: para 62). The contracting out of new prisons in the 1990s, and the loss of HMP Birmingham to the private sector in 2011,[5] had generated anxiety within the public sector about the possibility of future prison privatisation. Set against the possible competition of a further four public sector prisons,[6] the explicit intention of the benchmarking project was to determine whether the same 'benefits' as competition could be realised at greater speed by 'streamlining what prisons do,' increasing efficiency and 'driving down' costs (House of Commons Justice Committee, 2015; National Offender Management Service, 2013: para 66). Economic rationalisation was tolerated if it temporarily stalled plans to privatise more public sector prisons. However, these measures were anything but rational.

---

[4] In April 2017, the National Offender Management Service (NOMS) was rebranded as Her Majesty's Prison and Probation Service (HMPPS).

[5] In July 2019, HMP Birmingham formally returned to public sector management following the publication of a highly critical report by Her Majesty's Inspectorate of Prisons in the aftermath of two high profile riots in December 2016 and August 2017.

[6] HMPS Coldingley, Durham, Onley, and Wolds were all named as public sector prisons whose operational deliver might be subject to competition.

The benchmarking programme was based on four critical fallacies. First, that you could simultaneously reduce costs and improve performance (House of Commons Justice Committee, 2015). Second, that you could 'preserve a focus on real work and purposeful activity' (House of Commons Justice Committee, 2015: para 69) whilst reducing the number of staff available to facilitate such activity. Third, that you could make very little contact between staff and prisoners 'matter.' It is a long-held maxim that strong staff-prisoner relationships are at the heart of 'what matters' in prison life (Home Office, 1984; Liebling, 2004; Liebling et al., 2011; Sparks et al., 1996), and that effective prison officer work underpins critical functions such as prison security and safety. The 'every contact matters' rhetoric that evolved—which stressed the 'importance every contact every member of staff has with prisoners' (National Offender Management Service, 2013: para 10)—served to justify, but could never compensate for, the loss of prison officers. Fourth, that you could remove layers of line management and leave prison officers feeling equally well supported.

Between 2011 and 2014, a total of £369 million was saved from public sector prisons (National Audit Office, 2015). Later spending reviews led to further commitments to reduce costs, with the effect that resource savings of 34% was required by 2015–2016 (ibid.). Much of the initial cost savings was realised through staff redundancies (the Voluntary Early Departure Scheme (VEDS)), and it was hoped that VEDS would eventually save £300 million a year (Hansard, HC Deb, 7 March 2016). Over a five period (2010–2015), the number of prison officers decreased by 5000 (more than 25%) through a combination of VEDS and natural attrition (National Offender Management Service, 2017). Prisons were left with fewer officers, and those that remained not only had less experience, but also felt over-stretched and under-valued. As the prison population expanded to nearly 85,000 people, the prison estate was quickly bulging at the seams (with less than 1000 spaces to spare), putting the remaining officers under greater pressure and forcing the Ministry of Justice to—somewhat embarrassingly—re-hire more than 2000 prison officers who had left under VEDS. Some prison governors were forced to rely on the deployment of prison officers from other prisons (on 'detached duty') to stem the problem (House of Commons Justice Committee,

2015). However, this would prove insufficient to stave the serious problems that were unfolding.

Unsurprisingly, prison governors could not operate their prisons as they would wish, with many forced to 'accept the unacceptable.' Governing Governors were frequently forced to restrict 'the regime' and reduce the number of prisoners permitted to engage in activities (including employment or educational opportunities). Even pre-pandemic, 31% of prisoners in Local Prisons (i.e. those receiving men from court) and 37% of young adults (aged 18–21 years old) were locked in their cells for more than 22 hours a day (Her Majesty's Inspectorate of Prisons, 2017). The 'decency agenda' that had defined prison policy in the 2000s (for further analysis, see Liebling, 2004) was aborted as prisons became overcrowded and too many prisoners were housed in accommodation unfit for human occupation (Gooch, 2022; Her Majesty's Inspectorate of Prisons, 2017). A combination of ongoing austerity measures, the contracting out of prison maintenance—in one case, to a company that subsequently collapsed (House of Commons, 2018)—and poor contract management left the prison estate in a general state of disrepair. In the worst cases, some prisoners were living in squalid, graffitied cells with no running water, with no electricity, with broken windows, and accompanied by vermin (Her Majesty's Inspectorate of Prisons, 2017, 2019, 2022). Nearly half of the prison estate needed major repair or replacement (National Audit Office, 2020: 7). However, much of the investment in prison buildings has been on building new, large prisons rather than replacing crumbling buildings.

If the 2010s have proved anything it is that 'cost saving' and 'efficiency' measures do not produce prison reform, and that the price of too cheaply run prisons is disorder, violence, death, staff sickness and staff attrition. The number of prison homicides doubled, and the rate[7] of prison violence trebled between 2010 and 2019 (Ministry of Justice, 2025b). Taking all physical assaults together, there were at least three assaults every hour in 2019. When the hours prisoners spend confined are considered, this figure increases to an assault every 7 minutes. In addition, the number of sexual assaults increased threefold between

[7] The rate represents the number of incidents per 1000 prisoners.

2009 and 2019 (ibid.). Prisoner protests were frequent, with the number of incidents of 'concerted indiscipline,' 'incidents of height' and 'barricades' increasing eight-fold (Ministry of Justice, 2025c). As further evidence of the profound distress amongst prisoners, the rate of self-harm and self-inflicted deaths by male prisoners doubled (ibid.). This statistical data would appear concerning enough, but it was only the tip of the iceberg and failed to include the much larger dark figure of harm, drug use, and criminality that went unreported, unrecorded and/or unattended to. Although not all prisons were suffering the same levels of harm, overall the prison system had breached a moral threshold where most prisons could not be described as 'good enough' or 'minimally safe' (Auty & Liebling, 2024).

What followed was a series of announcements from consecutive Secretary of States regarding plans to reform and modernise the prison estate and 'design out' the 'dark corners of prison bullying, drug-taking, and violence' (Ministry of Justice, 2015). The Government committed to recruit new prison staff (Ministry of Justice, 2016). It was not, however, sufficient to reverse the damage. Prison officers were (and are) leaving just as quickly as they are recruited and trained (Ministry of Justice, 2020, 2024a, b). At the end of the decade, the House of Commons Justice Committee observed that the prison system was 'in the depths of an enduring crisis in prison safety and decency that has lasted 5 years' (2019: 6). Claims of a 'crisis' within prisons are far from unique and appear as contemporaneous as the prison itself (Chamberlen & Carvalho, 2019). However, even if the crisis was not novel, it has proved intractable.

It was against this background that this study of a YOI facing some of the worst problems began. As the outset, I had many questions in mind: Why had violence and bullying become such a regular occurrence within the YOI? Why were young men disproportionately experiencing and perpetrating harm against others, sometimes serious harm? Who or what was responsible for the rapid decline in prison safety during the 2010s? Why were prisons—like this YOI—beginning to fail HM Inspectorate of Prisons' healthy prison test, but also witnessing unprecedented numbers of suicides, homicides, and drug-related overdoses? Quite simply: Why had prisons become so violent? In seeking to answer these questions,

I was confronted with one immediate problem: namely, that the existing research on prison violence could not take me very far in understanding why violence had increased, both within the YOI or more generally.

Understanding Prison Violence, Escaping the Echo Chamber

There is no shortage of research on prison violence. Even a cursory glance of the existing academic literature reveals a pre-occupation with various forms of violence, including physical assault (Bottoms, 1999; Bowker, 1980; Edgar et al., 2003; Fuller & Orsagh, 1977; Wright, 1991), sexual assault and rape (Hensley et al., 2003, 2005; Lockwood, 1980; O'Donnell, 2004; Struckman-Johnson & Struckman-Johnson, 2000, 2006; Struckman-Johnson et al., 1996; Tewksbury, 1989), and, to a lesser extent, the collapse of order in the form of collective riots and protests (Carrabine, 2003, 2005; Rynne et al., 2008; Useem & Piehl, 2006; Useem & Reisig, 1999). Surprisingly, though, our understanding of prison violence is still 'pixelated' (Reiter, 2014: 417), primarily due to the perpetual, even compulsive, return to a quantitative analysis of importation and deprivation factors. Those familiar with prison scholarship may anticipate a faithful rehearsal of these models; this chapter returns to these theories to argue that the problem is not that the 'first principles' enshrined within the importation and deprivation models have ceased to be relevant, but it is the application of those principles that has stifled research. In so doing, this chapter not only makes the case for ethnographic research, but also the importance of returning to subjects (such as prison victimisation) that might—at first glance—appear well rehearsed.

Originally conceptualised by Sykes, the deprivation model approaches a reading of the prison that focuses on the 'pains,' burdens, and losses experienced in prison and how they structure prison life, prisoner adaptations and prisoner society. Unsurprisingly, Sykes' seminal text *The Society of Captives* (1958) has much to say about prison violence. Coining the phrase 'the deprivation of security,' Sykes acknowledges that close confinement with other criminals, some of whom have committed violent offences, is ‘far from reassuring’ (1958: 77). Sykes ties the ‘threat’ to questions of ‘manhood,’ arguing that prisoners are aware that sooner or later their manhood will be ‘tested,’ often in full view of others (1958: 77–78). Whilst Sykes proposes that inmate solidarity offers a collective adaptation to the ‘pains of imprisonment,’ he recognises that some prisoners respond by extorting, assaulting, and threatening others. The ways in which they do so imputes several ‘argot roles,’ including: the ‘real man’ who ‘does his time’ with dignity; the ‘ball busters’ (who are openly deviant); the ‘toughs’ (those who are quick to quarrel) and ‘hipsters’ (who lack the requisite bravery); the ‘rats’ and ‘centre men’ (informers); the ‘gorillas’ and ‘merchants’ (those who rob or exploit others); and, the ‘wolves, punks and fags’ (those who are homosexual or effeminate). Notably these argot roles denote different relationships with prison violence, from the emotional outbursts of the ball-buster, the ‘calculated use of violence’ by the ‘gorilla’ for material gain, the sexually motivated violence of the wolves, the quarrelsome and explosive ‘toughs,’ and the inauthentic toughness of the ‘hipster’ (Sykes, 1958: 102–105). However, this lexicon characterises a particular social world at a particular time in a specific prison and jurisdiction. Sykes’ analysis is not, and was probably never meant to be, a description of all prisoner societies (for further analysis see O’Donnell, 2023). That said, Sykes’s lexicon illustrates an important feature of prisoner society: namely that categorising fellow prisoners, and attaching status and reputation to some at the expense of others, contributes to social order. The prisoner hierarchy, then, is a functional response, as is the inmate code and culture.

Irwin and Cressey (1962) contested Sykes’ argument that prison norms and adaptations arose from the conditions of imprisonment, arguing that prisoners import values and a latent criminal subculture into prison. Irwin and Cressey suggested that any ‘prisonisation’ or ‘assimilation’ within prison (Clemmer, 1940; Goffman, 1961) did not completely remove these external influences, and prisoners may draw solutions to the problem of imprisonment from prior experiences and community criminal cultures. The appeal of the ‘importation model’ is not only in recognising the ‘symbiosis’ (Wacquant, 2001) between prison and community normative ‘codes,’ strategies, and cultures (see Anderson, 1999; Brookman et al., 2011; Gambetta, 2009; Maguire, 2021; Matsuda et al., 2013;

Mears et al., 2013; Mitchell et al., 2021), but also how these earlier experiences of street and criminal cultures frame 'interpretations' (Athens, 1997) of, and adaptations to, prison settings. Whilst Irwin and Cressey were essentially questioning the genesis of the prison culture, they agreed with Sykes that prisoners did not flawlessly follow the espoused precepts and may act in defiance of them. It was also clear, though, that prisoners still evaluated each other's behaviours in accordance with the code of conduct. Thus, the lapses in conduct only served to reinforce the prison code of conduct not nullify it.

The importation-deprivation framework has stimulated a wealth of research studies focusing on the specific factors (or the combination thereof) that cause or increase the likelihood of violence (for a summary, see: Bottoms, 1999; Fleury-Steiner & Wooldredge, 2020; McGuire, 2018). Whilst numerous (and far too numerous to list here), this ever-growing body of research on prison violence typically relies on quantitative measures of prison violence generated from administrative records and/or self-report surveys. The dominance of quantitative studies appears to arise from difficulties securing prison access to conduct qualitative and ethnographic research (see, for example, Simon, 2000; Skarbek, 2014; Trammell, 2009; Wacquant, 2002) and an erroneous belief by some that positivist methods are superior and hold a greater claim to objective and 'scientific' endeavour (Young, 2011). Quantitative studies are instructive, but it is their dominance in the study of prison violence that is problematic, producing three critical shortcomings.

First, quantitative research typically seeks to test and establish the relationship between pre-determined variables but lacks the necessary *explanatory power*. Gleaning quantitative data regarding the possible relationships between certain variables and prison violence might tell you *what* matters but not necessarily *why* it matters. For example, one of the most consistent findings is that youth (i.e. those under the age of 21) is associated with increased prison violence (McGuire, 2018). However, studies often say very little, if anything at all, about why this is the case. It is less clear, for example, whether higher rates of youth prison violence are partly explained by greater visibility (and the likelihood that assaults are more likely to be noticed, reported, and recorded), and whether adult prisoners are more sophisticated, more strategic, more likely to ruminate, better able to 'bide their time' and better able to evade detection. Volatility is not the same as severity or sophistication but is often conflated in assessments of 'risk.' Indeed, homicidal violence is primarily committed by adult prisoners, as are more serious assaults and attempted murders within prison. By focusing on visibility rather than severity, the danger is both misdiagnosing true 'dangerousness' but also failing to appreciate the (largely negative) lessons young men are learning about how to successfully navigate prison life (a theme taken up in Chap. 7).

Second, more than 50 years of research has not produced any real consistency regarding the factors—or combination of factors—that increase or prevent prison violence. It is often difficult to establish the strength of any one variable, either because researchers employ different definitional or methodological approaches, or because studies simply do not agree with each other. For example, 'racial or ethnic differences in rates of violence misconduct' have not been found 'uniformly' (McGuire, 2018). In other cases, the proxy measures used lead to misleading results. For example, Klatt et al. (2016) sought to test the relevance of pre-prison substance misuse (alongside other importation factors) to prison violence. In so doing, they (incorrectly) relied on pre-prison substance use as a proxy measure for prison substance misuse—thereby overlooking the ways in which prison substance misuse can be a situational response to the existential problems experienced during confinement (Gooch & Treadwell, 2020). Klatt et al. subsequently conclude that drug use is a strong predictor of physical and sexual violence, however, as this book shows, the relationship between drug misuse and physical violence is more nuanced, and it is more typical for drug users to be either victims or victim-perpetrators of violence (a theme taken up in Chaps. 4 and 5).

Third, quantitative studies are often undertaken at a distance, leading to *limited vision* and introducing the problem of 'ecological fallacy' (Cicourel, 1982; Wacquant, 2004: 6). In designing questionnaires, the researcher(s) pre-determines what variable(s) and question(s) will be relevant, failing to adequately allow for the emergent and unprecedented. Bourgois goes so far as to say that surveys 'collect fabrications,' arguing that:

> Only by establishing long-term relationships built on trust can one begin to ask provocative personal questions and expect thoughtful, serious answers. Ethnographers usually live in the communities they study and they establish long-term, organic relationships with the people they write about. In other words, in order to collect 'accurate data,' ethnographers violate the canons of positivist research; we become intimately involved with the people we study. (2003: 13)

The 'bogus of positivism' (Young, 2011) is that it assumes that society is static. Young argues (2011: 82) that 'the positivist dream of a scientific sociology of crime, which attempts to objectively relate cause and effect, becomes all the more impossible in late modernity.' He adds: '…social predicaments give rise to much more pluralistic vocabularies of motive ('causes') while the meanings of outcomes ('effects') are fiercely contested' (ibid.). Prison violence is equally susceptible to this diversity of motives, meanings, interpretations, and cultural sensibilities. Prisons, too, are not inert institutions; they are communities of people whose social norms, behaviours, attitudes, and practices evolve.

The ecological fallacies introduced by an over-reliance on administrative or quantitative analysis have significant consequences. For example, the rhetoric within the Prison Service was that 'volatile, disengaged and resource intensive' young men were primarily responsible for the increase in prison violence. Endorsing this view, the *Prison Safety and Reform* White Paper stated:

> Our analysis identifies a number of personal and situational factors that have driven this increase in violence, self-harm and self-inflicted deaths since 2012. We know that younger, male prisoners are more likely to be involved in violent incidents, as are those with a history of violent offending as well as current or previous drug use and gang membership. (Ministry of Justice, 2016)

This view is pervasive but holds little empirical weight. For reasons discussed in Chaps. 3, 4, and 5, gang membership and drug use are poor predictors of prison violence in England and Wales. Equally, whilst there is a disproportionate number of assaults and fights amongst young prisoners, the increase in prison violence was predominantly caused by older prisoners (Ministry of Justice, 2025), mirroring patterns in the community (Billingham & Irwin-Rogers, 2022). Official explanations were not only erroneous, but also conveniently distracted attention from the disintegrating and deteriorating prison estate. The explanations were also illogical: there was no evidence that gang activity or membership had increased so significantly that it could have stimulated such a dramatic rise in prison violence or disorder. Indeed, the prevalence of gang activity within the community was contested (Hallsworth, 2011; Hallsworth & Young, 2008; Pitts, 2008) and research suggested that urban youth street groups were becoming increasingly entrepreneurial and individualistic (Densley, 2012, 2014; Robinson et al., 2019; Windle & Briggs, 2015).

The reliance on quantitative research has contributed to a dilution of the importation model from its original aim of better explaining the importation of 'belief systems that are conducive to violence' (Mears et al., 2013: 696) to identifying the specific characteristics of individuals who are more likely to commit prison violence. In this way, the importation model has become reductionist. The ability to 'score' individuals (as is now the case in English and Welsh prisons[8]) to predict who are most likely to assault others is attractive. For scholars, identifying and assessing the strength of importation factors is much easier when administrative records or surveys are used as the primary data source. For practitioners, there is some 'political purchase' (Haggerty & Bucerius, 2020) in being able to displace the problem of prison violence and recast responsibility on individuals. As King and McDermott (1990: 449) note:

> The official discourse on control problem, while it sometimes pays lip-service to the capacity of the system to generate its own trouble, falls back time and time again on a model that locates trouble primarily in the disposition of individual prisoners. Thus, repeated attempts are made to identify individual 'troublemakers' and 'subversives' by references to some more or less easily recognisable and classifiable characteristics.

[8] For example, VIPER (violence in prison estimator) is used to determine who is most likely to be implicated in prison violence. It produces a score for each individual and estimates how violent they are likely to be. This can stimulate more intensive supervision in the form of CSIP (challenge, support, or intention plan).

The fallacy of such an approach was quickly apparent when confronted with posters in the security corridor of the YOI that identified those who was most likely to involved in violence or disorder based on their sentence length, index offence and age. For reasons that are more fully described in Chaps. 5 and 6, involvement in prison violence (and other forms of rule violations) was far more fluid, dynamic and diffuse, defying the kind of reductionist approach that such criteria dictate. Even if an individual satisfied the criteria, this did not guarantee that they were or would be violent with any sort of regularity (or even at all). Prisoners 'behave differently in different prison settings' (Adams, 1992: 315) and they behave differently over time.

Much of the research on prison violence focuses on importation rather than deprivation factors (for notable exceptions, see Bryne et al., 2007; McCorkle et al., 1995; Steiner & Wooldredge, 2008, 2018; Wooldredge, 2020), with the effect that the precise relationship between individual and situational is 'difficult to gauge' (McGuire, 2018: 4). Deprivation is relative. Some prisons are 'more survivable than others' (Liebling, 2011: 530). Even within the same jurisdiction and between prisons with the same function, the form and frequency of safety and security problems varies for reasons unrelated to importation factors. Each prison has its own personality, history, organisational memory, culture, peculiarities, leadership style and philosophy. These differences influence individual prisoner adaptations, particularly in relation to behaviour that is designed to seek staff attention, and in the nature of the 'control problem' (Kruttschnitt & Gartner, 2005; Liebling, 2022; Sparks et al., 1996). For example, in their comparative study of two High Security prisons (HMP Long Lartin and HMP Albany), Sparks et al. (1996) found institutional differences in prisoners' freedom of movement, the prison regime, the framing and quality of staff-prisoner relationships, the nature and degree of prison officer supervision, the exercise of discretion and the enforcement of the rules. Consequently, whilst Long Lartin appeared to have avoided major disturbances, and there were fewer assaults on staff, Albany was better able to reduce 'opportunities for trouble,' had a less developed prison economy and better protected more vulnerable prisoners (Sparks et al., 1996: 316–322). The deprivation model largely focuses on what is taken away and what pain is caused, not on the range of factors that are less about what the prison fails to offer and more about the daily practices, norms and routines of prison life—(i.e. culture)—that vary between prisons.

This critique of the existing literature is not designed either to suggest that the first principles of Sykes's and Irwin and Cressey's texts should be abandoned (although, for further critique, see Haggerty & Bucerius, 2020; O'Donnell, 2023), or that quantitative studies have little utility. Rather, it is to illustrate the importance of retaining a qualitative and ethnographic sensibility. That researchers must 'venture into the immediacy of crime' and 'be there in the criminal moment' (Ferrell, 1998: 28) is a maxim that is true for prison violence not just community-based illegality. Had I been tempted to rely on quantitative measures, I would have quite simply missed the myriad ways prison life and society in England and Wales had fundamentally changed during the 2010s, and how the anatomy, aetiology, culture, logic and dynamics of prison violence and victimisation had evolved. I might have missed not just what was happening, but also crucially *why*. Something as complex as prison victimisation cannot be understood from afar and, as others have shown, necessitates a sociological analysis of prison conditions, culture, configurations of penal power, leadership styles, penal philosophy and the interpretation of prison policy at a local level (Crewe, 2009; Crewe & Liebling, 2017; Hamm, 2013; Jacobs, 1977; Kruttschnitt & Gartner, 2005; Liebling, 2004; Liebling, 2022; Skarbek, 2014; Sparks et al., 1996; Williams & Liebling, 2023).

Ethnographic research was necessary for another crucial reason. Prison violence is often recorded as a series of isolated incidents; however, these moments of violence hold wider sociological purchase. Viewed both collectively and individually, the instances of violence paint a portrait of a social world that extends beyond the prison—one that was (and is) influenced by technological, pharmaceutical, economic, political, policy, legislative, and cultural change. Fassin argues (2017: 13), '[p]rison worlds are simultaneously a reflection of society and the mirror in which it sees itself. … Life on the outside intersects with life on the outside. Prison is not a separate from the social world; it is a disturbing shadow.' For example, Jacobs (1977) demonstrates that the dominance of street gangs within Stateville penitentiary was related to economic instability, political influences (including the civil rights movement), the 'intrusion of the courts' and the emergence of central 'professional administration' of the prison (and greater bureaucracy), which in turn led to declining staff morale, greater conflict between staff, a frustration of the prison's ability to meet 'basic control and maintenance goals,' and ultimately an 'organisational crisis' that gangs could exploit. Prisoner behaviour has sociological and ecological explanations; prisons are shaped by their social environment in ways that influence prisoner behaviour (Hamm, 2013; King & McDermott, 1995; Kruttschnitt & Gartner, 2005; Liebling, 2022; Skarbek, 2020; Sparks et al., 1996; Toch, 1977; Williams & Liebling, 2023). As I quickly discovered, prison violence could only be understood when viewed within the wider political, economic, policy, sociological, cultural, legal, and penal context. Unlike purely quantitative research, ethnography is 'supple and emergent' (Ferrell, 2018: 190), able to account for the sociological change and situate such change within its historical context (Fassin, 2017).

The Structure of This Book

This book begins and ends with the two inspections, 15 months apart and each a watershed event. During that time, the high levels of violence within the YOI would reduce, and the violence that did occur became less severe. When the research began, there were 411 prisoner assaults in preceding 12-month period, a figure that far exceeded nearly all other YOIs (Ministry of Justice, 2025). This had reduced to 247 prisoner assaults by the following year. However, prison violence was not being effectively recorded at the time of the first inspection, so it possible that the reduction is more marked than these figures suggest. That said, violence continued to 'run like a bright thread through life' (Sykes, 1958: 102) within the YOI and, however reduced in frequency, there was still too much violence and victimisation, and too many young men were harmed by their imprisonment. By witnessing the changes within the

YOI first-hand, I was able to analyse whether it was to truly possible to 'transform' the violent YOI, how improved moral practices could prevent prison violence, and how the multifaceted changes happening within and beyond the YOI were influencing prison violence and victimisation. This book continues in the rich tradition of single site prison ethnographies that have become the 'hallmark' of sociological analysis and where examining the particular can reveal the general (Crewe, 2009; Fassin, 2017; Jacobs, 1977; Sykes, 1958). In this case, ethnographic research revealed a series of transformations that were not only overtaking the YOI but the wider prison estate (as my continued research confirmed).

This book begins in Chap. 2 with an analysis of the methodological approach. Often such methodological notes are demoted to an Appendix, but since the argument here is that close, immersive research was necessary to understand the complex dynamics of prison life and prison victimisation, this methodological discussion has been elevated. Much is written about the practice, emotions, and ethics of undertaking prison research (Drake et al., 2015; Jewkes, 2014; Liebling, 1999, 2001); Chap. 2 does not offer a final word on such matters but focuses on how James and I conducted sensitive research on illicit prison behaviour. I have not sanitised individual 'wrongdoing or excuse[d] the pain they cause[d] others' (Stuart, 2020: 216), nor have I concealed the realities of living in a prison that had for a long time failed these young men. Whilst the sustained efforts to improve the prison was consistently evident, imperfections remained; I witnessed both to the redemptive efforts and to the flaws. My aim is to present an authentic and careful account, neither romanticising nor vilifying our participants nor sensationalising or minimising violence or its antecedents.

Chapter 3 analyses the anatomy, dynamics, and culture of prison victimisation. The analysis goes beyond prison violence to explore the multifaceted forms of victimisation, how they overlap, and how they become culturally engrained. It is argued that the perceived jeopardy and volatility of prison life is judged by young men not only in the number of assaults but also in the threats, verbal abuse, thefts, robberies, coercion, extortion, and intimidation—actions that are omitted from official statistics but reveal a much 'darker' figure of prison victimisation. Moreover, technological advancements had created new forms of 'global humiliation,' allowing young men to broadcast the victimisation of their peers far beyond the prison. In analysing the anatomy of prison violence, I challenge two key myths, namely that prison violence was gang related and that prison bullying was a useful concept for explaining prisoner behaviour. Whilst earlier research has suggested that prison bullying is a distinct, recognisable, and pronounced problem within YOIs (Beck, 1995; Connell & Farrington, 1997; Ireland, 2000, 2002, 2005), there has been a tendency for some scholars to conflate 'bullying' with other forms of victimisation and expand the definition beyond what is meaningful. In practice, 'bullying' was an 'unreliable concept' (Edgar et al., 2003: 60) for understanding the fluidity, social structure, and anatomy of prison victimisation. Equally, the 'gang trope' (Phillips, 2012) proved an inaccurate description of harmful group behaviour and the ways in which conflict was imported into the YOI.

Violence and victimisation have always featured as a 'resource' within criminal markets (Hall et al., 2013; Winlow, 2001; Winlow & Hall, 2006); this is no less true for criminal enterprise in prison. Chapter 4 focuses on the appeal of the prison illicit economy and the ways in which economic activities were intimately connected to prison victimisation. Whilst the illicit economy has always been a feature of prison life, a new drug economy and a 'debt economy' has emerged, stimulating prison victimisation to sustain criminal enterprise, punish infractions of the 'social contract' (Shortland, 2019), to preserve control of the economy, and punish the loss of goods. Violence has often been regarded as explosive, uncontrolled expressions, yet these young men could be deliberate, intentional, and controlled in their use of violence. These young men were 'learning to graft,' with varying degrees of sophistication and connection to wider criminal networks. The consumeristic, hedonistic, and capitalistic culture within the prison represented an extension of street cultures and identities (Hall et al., 2013), but for those who could profit from it, they acquired social and economic power within prison.

Chapter 5 provides an account of contemporaneous *young* prisoner society, and the varied ways that victimisation structured prisoner social roles. Perversely, some of the most domineering and intimidating characters could orchestrate and co-ordinate assaults without direct involvement, thereby avoid detection and punishment. Although a proportion of young men were largely regarded as 'uninvolved,' prison victimisation was an enduring possibility and threat. Even for those who seemed to avoid incidents of prison violence, they were never far away from someone who might test them, assault them, seek to usurp them, or seize control of the illicit economy. That said, some were far more confident in their ability to overcome aggressors, and some were far less likely to be threatened or tested in the first place. For these young men, whether someone was a 'victim' was not necessarily determined by whether they were involved in an incident, but whether the label became a permanent stain and social signifier. Victimhood, therefore, was determined not by whether you were challenged, but whether you failed to meet the challenge. Such failure was noticed, attracted disdain, and believed to justify further and sustained victimisation.

Chapter 6 situates prison violence within the life-courses of these young men. Despite the largely feminised 'trauma turn' (Auty et al., 2022) in prison practice and wider criminological research, the relationship between 'adverse childhood experiences' (Craig et al., 2017; Felitti et al., 1998; Fox et al., 2015) and prison violence is underexplored. Importation studies of prison violence tend to focus on discreet characteristics—such as age and ethnicity—rather than interrogate the importance of experiences of violence, loss, and abuse prior to and during imprisonment. This neglect is surprising given the well documented prevalence of such experiences amongst male prisoners (Hosser et al., 2007; Maschi et al., 2011; Weeks & Widom, 1998; Williams et al., 2012) but may arise from the reliance on administrative records to analyse prison violence and the absence of reliable information about men's pre-prison lives within those records. Chapter 6 considers how experiences across the life-course inform how young men frame, interpret and make sense of violence. It analyses why young men convicted of violence in the community were not always violent in custody but also challenges the tendency to categorise young men engaged in harmful behaviour as either 'vulnerable' and 'poor copers,' or 'violent' and 'disruptive.' For some young men, violence was as much a symptom of crisis and distress as self-harm, fire-setting, and suicide attempts were.

Whilst young men recognised that they were not yet in 'deep end custody' (King & McDermott, 1995: 89), the experience of imprisonment within the YOI during 'key formative years' came at 'great cost for many' (Maguire, 2021: 155, 161). Chapter 7 traces the formative lessons that these young men were learning about the men that they should or would become. The YOI very effectively prepared them for time that many would serve in adult prisons, either during their current sentence or in subsequent sentence. Chapter 7 explores the ways in which these young men were learning to 'graft,' learning to fight, learning to 'play the game' (and navigate the rules of the system), and learning to become 'real men.' They were ultimately 'learning to jail.' Thus, the prevention of young adult violence required a systemic approach, one that focuses on not only improving the quality of custodial provision for young adults, but also the structure, culture and quality of youth custody.

Violence is typically perceived to be 'disorderly;' yet for these young men, violence could not only restore order but conformed to logical, predictable, and explicable norms and rules. Violence was meaningful, but it was also critically tied to the pursuit of social recognition, respect, and justice. What was seen as morally 'right' (Fiske & Rai, 2015) was culturally embedded and socially structured. Chapter 8 therefore explores the rationality of prison victimisation. It analyses the prisoner normative code and the relationship between victimisation and social identity. Prison violence and victimisation is frequently understood through the lens of gendered performance, with the performance of hegemonic masculinity (i.e. the dominant or privileged form of masculinity) (Connell, 1995) within prison typically tied to the use of physical violence (Michalski, 2017). This emphasis on the actuality of violence overlooks the extent to which the threat of violence can be as, if not more, important in structuring social relations. This raises questions about when and why threats are taken seriously, and in this book, the concept of 'carceral capital' is proposed to explain how young adult prisoners acquire status, credibility, gravitas, and social recognition.

Chapter 9 focuses on the social, organisational, and environmental context of prison violence. The possibility that a prison may be violent is largely taken for granted and it is typically this aspect of prison life that is sensationalised in media portrayals of prison life. However, Chapter 9 argues that frequent and severe victimisation between prisons is structured by the morality of the prison, and the extent to which prisoners feel that their humanity and dignity is recognised by the State. Although prisoner culture may emphasise strategies and norms supportive of prison violence, *high* levels of prisoner victimisation are a symptom of moral malaise *by the State*. As Liebling notes (2004: xviii), 'prisons differ significantly in their moral practices' and it is these moral practices that not only become the background against which prison violence occurs, but that structures the 'moral grammar' (Honneth, 1995: 166) of prisoner behaviour (and the perceived necessity of harmful behaviour to meet physical and psychological needs).

Ultimately, this book argues that high levels of prison violence were (and are) not inevitable, nor were the routine ways in which young men exploited, intimidated, and extorted their peers. Increased prison violence often leads to calls for more sentencing options, longer custodial sentences, stricter and more punitive regimes, and more 'tools' for prison officers (e.g. tasers, pepper spray, stab vests) (Bulman, 2017; Prison Officer Association, 2019) and to 'screw everything down.' To prevent prison violence, moral and legal boundaries did need to be re-established within the YOI, and the Governing Governor 'had to put the law back into the place.' Yet, somewhat counterintuitively, the senior leadership team also had to let the prison 'breathe' by: prioritising stronger relationships; developing a culture of care and compassion; meeting physical and psychological needs; offering positive reinforcement, second chances and adopting a fundamental belief in the possibility of young men 'making good' (Maruna, 2001); taking seriously the needs and views of individual prisoners; responding robustly, proactively and proportionately to harm when it occurred (including the unlawful, corrupt, inappropriate, or unwanted behaviour by staff); and maintaining a resolute belief in the possibility of 'hope' and 'redemption' (Maruna, 2001) for the young men and the prison. To improve the YOI—and in turn prevent and reduce prison violence—the senior leadership team had to re-set the moral foundations and re-establish justice, humanity, hope, dignity, recognition, respect, and the 'law*full*ness' of YOI. This book therefore introduces a moral vocabulary to the study of prison violence, but it does so in such a way as to move the discussion (and research) from the identification of 'rotten apples' and 'wicked people' (Maruna, 2023) to the underpinning desire for recognition and respect. It is the absence of social recognition by the State and by their peers that underpins much youth prison violence.

References

Adams, K. (1992). Adjusting to prison life. In M. Tonry (Ed.), *Crime and justice: A review of research* (Vol. 16, pp. 275–359). University of Chicago Press.

Anderson, E. (1999). *Code of the street: Decency, violence and the moral life of the inner city*. W.W. Norton.

Athens, L. (1997). *Violent criminal acts and actors revisited*. University of Illinois.

Auty, K. M., & Liebling, A. (2024). What is a 'good enough' prison? An empirical analysis of key thresholds using prison moral quality data. *European Journal of Criminology, 21*(5), 725–753.

Auty, K. M., Liebling, A., Schliehe, A., & Crewe, B. (2022). What is trauma-informed practice? Towards operationalisation of the concept in two prisons for women. *Criminology & Criminal Justice, 23*(5), 716–738.

Beck, G. (1995). Bullying among young offenders in custody. *Issues in Criminological & Legal Psychology, 22*, 54–70.

Billingham, L., & Irwin-Rogers, K. (2022). *Against youth violence: A social harm perspective*. Bristol University Press.

Bottoms, A. E. (1999). Interpersonal violence and social order in prisons. *Crime and Justice, 26*, 205–281.

Bourgois, P. (2003). *In search of respect: Selling crack in El Barrio*. Cambridge University Press.

Bowker, L. H. (1980). *Prison victimisation*. Elsevier.

Brookman, F., Bennett, T., Hochstetler, A., & Copes, H. (2011). The 'code of the street' and the generation of street violence in the UK. *European Journal of Criminology, 8*(1), 17–31.

Bryne, J., Hummer, D., & Taxman, F. S. (2007). *The culture of prison violence*. Pearson.

Bulman, M. (2017). Prison officers 'need tasers and tab vests to cope with rising violence in jails'. *The Independent*.

Carrabine, E. (2003). *Power, discourse and resistance*. Ashgate.

Carrabine, E. (2005). Prison riots, social order and the problem of legitimacy. *British Journal of Criminology, 45*(6), 896–913.

Chamberlen, A., & Carvalho, H. (2019). The thrill of the chase: Punishment, hostility and the prison crisis. *Social & Legal Studies, 28*(1), 100–117.
Cicourel, A. V. (1982). Interviews, surveys, and the problem of ecological validity. *The American Sociologist, 17*(1), 11–20.
Clemmer, D. (1940). *The prison community*. Holt, Reinhart and Winston.
Connell, R. W. (1995). *Masculinities*. Polity Press.
Connell, A., & Farrington, D. P. (1997). The reliability and validity of resident, staff and peer reports of bullying in young offender institutions. *Psychology, Crime & Law, 3*(4), 287–300.
Craig, J. M., Piquero, A. R., Farrington, D. P., & Ttofi, M. M. (2017). A little early risk goes a long bad way: Adverse childhood experiences and life-course offending in the Cambridge study. *Journal of Criminal Justice, 53*, 34–45.
Crewe, B. (2009). *Prisoner society: Power, adaptation and social life in an English prison*. Oxford University Press.
Crewe, B., & Liebling, A. (2017). Reconfiguring penal power. In A. Liebling, S. Maruna, & L. Mcara (Eds.), *Oxford handbook of criminology* (pp. 889–913). Oxford University Press.
Densley, J. A. (2012). The organisation of London's street gangs. *Global Crime, 13*(1), 42–64.
Densley, J. A. (2014). It's gang life, but not as we know it: The evolution of gang business. *Crime & Delinquency, 60*(4), 517–546.
Drake, D. H., Earle, R., & Sloan, J. (2015). *The Palgrave handbook of prison ethnography*. Palgrave Macmillan.
Edgar, K., O'Donnell, I., & Martin, C. (2003). *Prison violence: The dynamics of conflict, fear and power*. Willan.
Fassin, D. (2017). *Prison worlds: An ethnography of the carceral condition*. Polity.
Felitti, V. J., Anda, R. F., Nordenberg, D., Williamson, D. F., Spitz, A. M., Edwards, V., Koss, M. P., & Marks, J. S. (1998). Relationship of childhood abuse and household dysfunction to many of the leading causes of death in adults: The Adverse Childhood Experiences (ACE) Study. *American Journal of Preventive Medicine, 14*(4), 245–258.
Ferrell, J. (1998). Criminological verstehen: Inside the immediacy of crime. In J. Ferrell & M. S. Hamm (Eds.), *Ethnography at the edge: Crime, deviance and field research* (pp. 20–42). Northern University Press.
Ferrell, J. (2018). *Drift: Illicit mobility and uncertain knowledge*. University of California Press.
Fiske, A. P., & Rai, T. S. (2015). *Virtuous violence: Hurting and killing to create, sustain, end and honor social relationships*. Cambridge University Press.

Fleury-Steiner, B., & Wooldredge, J. (2020). *Understanding and reducing prison violence: An integrated social control-opportunity perspective*. Routledge.
Fox, B. H., Perez, N., Cass, E., Baglivio, M. T., & Epps, N. (2015). Trauma changes everything: Examining the relationship between adverse childhood experiences and serious, violent and chronic juvenile offenders. *Child Abuse & Neglect, 46*, 163–173.
Fuller, D. A., & Orsagh, T. (1977). Violence and victimization within a state prison system. *Criminal Justice Review, 2*, 35–55.
Gambetta, D. (2009). *Codes of the underworld: How criminals communicate*. Princeton University Press.
Goffman, E. (1961). *Asylums: Essays on social situations of mental patients and other inmates*. Penguin.
Gooch, K. (2022). "Just don't wear prison issue!": Material deprivation, material machismo and the illicit economy. In B. Crewe, A. Goldsmith, & M. Halsey (Eds.), *Power and authority in the modern prison: Revisiting the society of captives* (pp. 193–212). Oxford University Press.
Gooch, K., & Treadwell, J. (2020). Prisoner society in an era of psychoactive substances, organized crime, new drug markets and austerity. *British Journal of Criminology, 60*(5), 1260–1281.
Haggerty, K. D., & Bucerius, S. (2020). The proliferating pains of imprisonment. *Incarceration, 1*(1), 1–16.
Hall, S., Winlow, S., & Ancrum, C. (2013). *Criminal identities and consumer culture*. Willan.
Hallsworth, S. (2011). Anatomizing gang talk. *Más allá de las pandillas: violencias, juventudes y resistencias en el mundo globalizado, 1*, 25–46.
Hallsworth, S., & Young, T. (2008). Gang talk and gang talkers: A critique. *Crime, Media, Culture: An International Journal, 4*(2), 175–195.
Hamm, M. S. (2013). *The spectacular few: Prisoner radicalization and the evolving terrorist threat*. New York University Press.
Harvey, J. (2007). *Young men in prison: Surviving and adapting to life inside*. Willan Publishing.
Hensley, C., Tewksbury, R., & Castle, T. (2003). Characteristics of prison sexual assault targets in male Oklahoma correctional facilities. *Journal of Interpersonal Violence, 18*(6), 595–606.
Hensley, C., Koscheski, M., & Tewksbury, R. (2005). Examining the characteristics of male sexual assault targets in a southern maximum-security prison. *Journal of Interpersonal Violence, 20*(6), 667–679.

Her Majesty's Inspectorate of Prisons. (2017). *Life in prison: Living conditions.* Her Majesty's Inspectorate of Prisons.

Her Majesty's Inspectorate of Prisons. (2019). *HM chief inspector of prisons for England and Wales: Annual report 2018–2019.* Her Majesty's Inspectorate of Prisons.

Her Majesty's Inspectorate of Prisons. (2021). *Outcomes for young adults in custody.* Her Majesty's Inspectorate of Prisons.

Her Majesty's Inspectorate of Prisons. (2022). *HM chief inspector in prisons for England and Wales: Annual report for England and Wales 2021–2022.* Her Majesty's Inspectorate of Prisons.

Home Office. (1984). *Managing the long term prison system: The control review committee.* Home Office.

Honneth, A. (1995). *The struggle for recognition: The moral grammar of social conflicts.* Polity Press.

Hosser, D., Raddatz, S., & Windzio, M. (2007). Child maltreatment, revictimization, and violent behavior. *Violence and Victims, 22*(3), 318–333.

House of Commons. (2018). *The collapse of Carillion* (Briefing paper 8206). House of Commons.

House of Commons Justice Committee. (2015). *Prison planning and policies: Ninth report of session 2014–2015, HC 309.* The Stationery Office Limited.

House of Commons Justice Committee. (2019). *Prison population 2022: Planning for the future.* The Stationery Office Limited.

Ireland, J. L. (2000). Bullying among prisoners: A review of the research. *Aggression and Violent Behavior, 5*(2), 201–215.

Ireland, J. L. (2002). *Bullying among prisoners: Evidence, research and intervention strategies.* Brunner-Routledge.

Ireland, J. L. (2005). Bullying among prisoners: The need for innovation. In J. L. Ireland (Ed.), *Bullying among prisoners: Innovations in theory and research.* Willan.

Irwin, J., & Cressey, D. R. (1962). Thieves, convicts and the inmate culture. *Social Problems, 10*(2), 142–155.

Jacobs, J. B. (1977). *Stateville.* University of Chicago Press.

Jewkes, Y. (2014). An introduction to "doing prison research differently". *Qualitative Inquiry, 20*(4), 387–391.

King, R. D., & McDermott, K. (1990). 'My geranium is subversive': Some notes on the management of trouble in prisons. *British Journal of Sociology, 41*(4), 445–471.

King, R. D., & McDermott, K. (1995). *The state of our prisons*. Oxford University Press.
Klatt, T., Hagl, S., Bergmann, M. C., & Baier, D. (2016). Violence in youth custody: Risk factors of violent misconduct among inmates of German young offender institutions. *European Journal of Criminology, 13*(6), 727–743.
Kruttschnitt, C., & Gartner, R. (2005). *Marking time in the golden state: Women's imprisonment in California*. Cambridge University Press.
Liebling, A. (1999). Doing research in prison. *Theoretical Criminology, 3*(2), 147–173.
Liebling, A. (2001). Whose side are we on? Theory, practice and allegiances in prisons research. *British Journal of Criminology, 41*(3), 472–484.
Liebling, A. (2004). *Prisons and their moral performance*. Oxford University Press.
Liebling, A. (2011). Moral performance, inhuman and degrading treatment and prison pain. *Punishment & Society, 13*(5), 530–550.
Liebling, A. (2012). Young adult offenders in custodial institutions. In F. Lösel, A. E. Bottoms, & D. P. Farrington (Eds.), *Young adult offenders: Lost in transition* (pp. 65–73). Willan.
Liebling, A. (2022). The changing "regime of the custodians": Visions of order and authority in high-security prisons in England and Wales, 1988–2020. In *Power and pain in the modern prison* (pp. 253–271). Oxford University Press.
Liebling, A., Price, D., & Shefer, G. (2011). *The prison officer*. Willan.
Lockwood, D. (1980). *Prison sexual violence*. Elsevier.
Maguire, D. (2021). *Male, failed and jailed: Masculinities and the 'revolving door' imprisonment in the UK*. Palgrave Macmillan.
Maruna, S. (2001). *Making good: How ex-convicts reform and rebuild their lives*. American Psychological Association.
Maruna, S. (2023). Wicked problems, not wicked people. In A. J. Tamatea, A. J. Day, & D. J. Cooke (Eds.), *Preventing prison violence: An ecological perspective* (pp. xii–xiii). Routledge.
Maschi, T., Gibson, S., Zgoba, K. M., & Morgen, K. (2011). Trauma and life event stressors among young and older adult prisoners. *Journal of Correctional Health Care, 17*(2), 160–172.
Matsuda, K. N., Melde, C., Taylor, T. J., Freng, A., & Esbensen, F.-A. (2013). Gang membership and adherence to the "code of the street". *Justice Quarterly, 30*(3), 440–468.
McCorkle, R. C., Miethe, T. D., & Drass, K. A. (1995). The roots of prison violence: A test of the deprivation, management, and "not-so-total" institution models. *Crime & Delinquency, 41*(3), 317–331.

McGuire, J. (2018). *Understanding prison violence: A rapid evidence assessment*. Her Majesty's Prison and Probation Service.
Mears, D. P., Stewart, E. A., Siennick, S. E., & Simons, R. L. (2013). The code of the street and inmate violence: Investigating the salience of imported belief systems. *Criminology, 51*(3), 695–728.
Michalski, J. H. (2017). Status hierarchies and hegemonic masculinity: A general theory of prison violence. *British Journal of Criminology, 57*(1), 40–60.
Ministry of Justice. (2012). *Rehabilitation revolution: The next steps*. Ministry of Justice.
Ministry of Justice. (2015). *The treasure in the heart of man—Making prisons work*. Ministry of Justice.
Ministry of Justice. (2016). *Prison safety and reform, cm 9350*. Ministry of Justice.
Ministry of Justice. (2020). *HM Prison & Probation Service workforce quarterly: December 2019*. Ministry of Justice.
Ministry of Justice. (2024a). *HM Prison & Probation Service staff equalities report: 2023–2024*. Ministry of Justice.
Ministry of Justice. (2024b). *HM Prison & Probation Service workforce quarterly: September 2024*. Ministry of Justice.
Ministry of Justice. (2025a). *Offender management statistics quarterly: July to September 2024*. Ministry of Justice.
Ministry of Justice. (2025b). *Safety in custody statistics: Quarterly update to September 2024*. Ministry of Justice.
Ministry of Justice. (2025c). *HMPPS annual digest: April 2023–March 2024*. Ministry of Justice.
Mitchell, M. M., Pyrooz, D. C., & Decker, S. H. (2021). Culture in prison, culture on the street: The convergence between the convict code and code of the street. *Journal of Crime and Justice, 44*(2), 145–164.
National Audit Office. (2015). *A short guide to the Ministry of Justice*. National Audit Office.
National Audit Office. (2020). *Improving the prison estate*. National Audit Office.
National Offender Management Service. (2012). *Fair and Sustainable: Revision to proposals for working structures in HM Prison Service following consultation with trade unions*. National Offender Management Service.
National Offender Management Service. (2013). *Public sector benchmark*. National Offender Management Service.
National Offender Management Service. (2017). *National Offender Management Service annual workforce statistics bulletin*. Ministry of Justice.

O'Donnell, I. (2004). Prison rape in context. *British Journal of Criminology, 44*(2), 241–255.
O'Donnell, I. (2023). *Prison life: Pain, resistance and purpose.* New York University Press.
Phillips, C. (2012). 'It ain't nothing like America with the bloods and the crips': Gang narratives inside two English prisons. *Punishment & Society, 14*(1), 51–68.
Pitts, J. (2008). *Reluctant gangsters: The changing face of youth crime.* Cullompton Willan Publishing.
Prison Officer Association. (2019). General Secretary: PoA members need protection. Published online: https://www.poauk.org.uk/news-events/news-room/posts/2019/april/general-secretary-poa-members-need-protection/.
Reiter, K. (2014). Making windows in walls. *Qualitative Inquiry, 20*(4), 417–428.
Robinson, G., McLean, R., & Densley, J. (2019). Working county lines: Child criminal exploitation and illicit drug dealing in Glasgow and Merseyside. *International Journal of Offender Therapy and Comparative Criminology, 63*(5), 694–711.
Rynne, J., Harding, R. W., & Wortley, R. (2008). Market testing and prison riots: How public-sector commercialization contributed to a prison riot. *Criminology & Public Policy, 7*(1), 117–142.
Scott, D. (2015). Eating your insides out: Cultural, physical and institutionally structured violence in the prison place. *Prison Service Journal, 221*, 58–62.
Scraton, P., Sim, J., & Skidmore, P. (1991). *Prisons under protest.* Open University Press.
Shortland, A. (2019). *Kidnap: Inside the ransom business.* Oxford University Press.
Sim, J. (1994). Tougher than the rest? Men in prison. In T. Newburn & E. A. Stanko (Eds.), *Just boys doing business? Men, masculinities and crime* (pp. 100–177). Routledge.
Simon, J. (2000). The 'society of captives' in the era of hyper-incarceration. *Theoretical Criminology, 4*(3), 285–308.
Skarbek, D. (2014). *The social order of the underworld: How prison gangs govern the American penal system.* Oxford University Press.
Skarbek, D. (2020). *The puzzle of prison order: Why life behind bars varies across the world.* Oxford University Press.
Sparks, R., Bottoms, A. E., & Hay, W. (1996). *Prisons and the problem of order.* Oxford University Press.
Steiner, B., & Wooldredge, J. (2008). Inmate versus environmental effects on prison rule violations. *Criminal Justice and Behavior, 35*(4), 438–456.

Steiner, B., & Wooldredge, J. (2018). Prison officer legitimacy, their exercise of power, and inmate rule breaking. *Criminology, 56*(4), 750–779.
Struckman-Johnson, C., & Struckman-Johnson, D. (2000). Sexual coercion rates in seven Midwestern prison facilities for men. *The Prison Journal, 80*(4), 379–390.
Struckman-Johnson, C., & Struckman-Johnson, D. (2006). A comparison of sexual coercion experiences reported by men and women in prison. *Journal of Interpersonal Violence, 21*(12), 1591–1615.
Struckman-Johnson, C., Struckman-Johnson, D., Rucker, L., Bumby, K., & Donaldson, S. (1996). Sexual coercion reported by men and women in prison. *Journal of Sex Research, 33*(1), 67–76.
Stuart, F. (2020). *Ballad of the bullet: Gangs, drill music and the power of online infamy*. Princeton University Press.
Sykes, G. (1958). *The society of captives*. Princeton University Press.
Tewksbury, R. (1989). Fear of sexual assault in prison inmates. *The Prison Journal, 69*(1), 62–71.
Toch, H. (1977). *Living in prison: The ecology of survival*. The Free Press.
Trammell, R. (2009). Values, rules, and keeping the peace: How men describe order and the inmate code in California prisons. *Deviant Behavior, 30*(8), 746–771.
Useem, B., & Piehl, A. M. (2006). Prison buildup and disorder. *Punishment & Society, 8*(1), 87–115.
Useem, B., & Reisig, M. D. (1999). Collective action in prisons: Protests, disturbances and riots. *Criminology, 37*(4), 735–760.
Wacquant, L. (2001). Deadly symbiosis: When ghetto and prison meet and mesh. *Punishment & Society, 3*(1), 95–133.
Wacquant, L. (2002). The curious eclipse of prison ethnography in the age of mass incarceration. *Ethnography, 3*(4), 371–397.
Wacquant, L. (2004). *Body and soul: Notebooks of an apprentice boxer*. Oxford University Press.
Weeks, R., & Widom, C. S. (1998). Self-reports of early childhood victimization among incarcerated adult male felons. *Journal of Interpersonal Violence, 13*(3), 346–361.
Williams, R., & Liebling, A. (2023). Do prisons cause radicalization? Order, leadership, political charge and violence in two maximum security prisons. *British Journal of Criminology, 63*(1), 97–114.

Williams, K., Papadopoulou, V., & Booth, N. (2012). *Prisoners' childhood and family backgrounds: Results from the Surveying Prisoner Crime Reduction (SPCR) longitudinal cohort study of prisoners*. Ministry of Justice.
Windle, J., & Briggs, D. (2015). Going solo: The social organisation of drug dealing within a London street gang. *Journal of Youth Studies, 18*(9), 1170–1185.
Winlow, S. (2001). *Badfellas: Crime, tradition and new masculinities*. Berg.
Winlow, S., & Hall, S. (2006). *Violent night: Urban leisure and contemporary culture*. Berg.
Wooldredge, J. (2020). Prison culture, management, and in-prison violence. *Annual Review of Criminology, 3*(1), 165–188.
Wright, K. N. (1991). The violent and victimized in the male prison. *Journal of Offender Rehabilitation, 16*(3–4), 1–26.
Young, J. (2011). *The criminological imagination*. Polity Press.

2

'Loitering with Intent': The Philosophy, Politics, and Practice of Prison Ethnography

'About yesterday, you won't be snitching to the Governor, will you?' came the softly spoken question from Mikey, a Custodial Manager. He was blocking my path as we walked to the Board Room for Thursday's morning meeting, his imposing tall frame overshadowing mine. His hushed and earnest question at odds with his normal confident, self-assured, and outspoken demeanour. Ethnographic research requires delicacy and discretion. It is political, not only in the sense that prison ethnography can generate unrivalled perspectives on the social reality of government prison policy and ministerial decisions, but also in the sense that it involves immersion in a social world where there are multiple interests at stake (and sometimes in conflict). Mikey's question betrayed something of the power structures and inequalities that exist even between those typically characterised as power holders. The classic question 'whose side are we on?' (Becker, 1967)—which at times would be reinterpreted by others as 'who do you believe?'—would frame my relationships with young men, officers, managers, and governors. Just as the young men might be guarded with prison officers, and vehemently (if only verbally) uphold the injunction against 'snitching' (informing), so too did prison officers and custodial managers draw boundaries—relational boundaries and

K. Gooch, *Prison Violence*, Palgrave Studies in Prisons and Penology,
https://doi.org/10.1007/978-3-031-91365-5_2

boundaries of knowledge—between each other and with senior managers. However, Mikey's question came as a surprise, not least because I had been clear about the boundaries of confidentiality and had hitherto not made any disclosures to the Governing Governor, but also because Mikey's question was framed in such a non-threatening manner that it made me reflect upon where and with whom he felt power lay. My mind raced to recall what he had said on Wednesday that he might now be concerned about.

Wednesday morning had not started well. The atmosphere was tense and the frustration amongst the senior management team ebbed barely beneath the surface. The morning meeting was one way in which the Governing Governor could be briefed by the senior management team, and communicate key messages, (re)set standards and reinforce priorities. It was our first meeting of the day too, and although James and I might have already visited the wings or stood observing 'free flow,'[1] we always arrived in time to attend morning meeting. Several months into their tenure, the Governing Governor was irritated that the preferred practices were taking time to establish, that relationships between the officers and young men were not yet as good as they wanted, and managers were not 'asking the right questions' despite the enduring and considerable efforts of the senior management team to instil in them what those questions should be. Transforming established and problematic prison culture(s) takes time. It requires relentless effort and is beset with missteps and seemingly backwards steps. Inevitably, the senior management team wanted change to be quicker, not least of all because they were keenly aware of the looming return of HM Inspectorate of Prisons (HMIP).

Over the course of the past 24 hours, a young man had been slashed in the showers, and another had barricaded himself in his cell for a short period. One of the young men in the segregation unit (dubbed the 'CSU' or 'Care and Separation Unit') had proceeded to jump over the railings and stand on the 'netting'[2] until he could be coaxed off. Another, Phillip, was still declining to eat and had also been moved back to the segregation

[1] 'Free flow' was when the young men moved from the residential units to work, education classes, the gym, healthcare, the library and the chapel. The corridors were lined with prison staff, as were the entrances to the different units and areas of the prison.

[2] The 'netting' was a metal grid separating the first and ground floor.

unit. He was now refusing to speak to anyone other than healthcare staff. Phillip ultimately wanted to be transferred to a Category B Local Prison near his family; his 'hunger strike' an effort to force prison staff into transferring him. Jayden had smashed his cell observation glass in the First Night Centre, and was still shouting rhythmically and loudly as he kicked his cell door and hit his head against it. The clash of metal against his body punctuated the air. This self-harm was borne out of frustration that his personal clothes had been taken and replaced with 'prison issue' clothes. There had been several fights throughout the day, with the effect that general alarms had been 'constant.' It was not yet clear how the various incidents may or may not be related, but things were already 'bubbling' as the young men were unlocked for work and education at 8:30 am.

After Wednesday's morning meeting, James and I walked to Res C (Residential Unit C) to interview several young men. When we arrived, there were already several people gathered, unusually so, including the 'Oscar 1' (a custodial manager who was on 'duty' to respond to operational matters), another custodial manager (CM), a nurse, and several prison officers who were joined in slightly hushed but earnest conversation. Something was afoot. The wing was pensively quiet, but neither calm nor tranquil. Unknowingly, we had walked into a hostage situation and would not move from the unit for the rest of the day. Two young people had barricaded themselves and a bystander in the small room normally used by DARS (the Drug and Alcohol Recovery Service). The two instigators were now refusing to open the door or release the 'hostage' who was sat at the back of the room. They claimed to have Valium, Mamba (a psychoactive substance, see Chap. 4), medication prescribed for nerve pain, and cans of tuna (seemingly innocuous but often placed in socks to create weapons). Throughout the day, their behaviour edged between aggressive protests and compliant negotiation.

All three young men had recently arrived at the YOI, two from a large Category B prison in the North West of England and a third from a YOI holding boys aged 15–18 years old. They were all from Manchester and, after completing induction, asked to move to Res D (Residential Unit D). This request was refused, and the young men were moved to Res C only to find that the cells were not ready. All three young men were left in the DARS room until they could move to their cell. For whatever reason, the DARS room also had a Cross-Trainer machine in it. It was unclear what motivated the young men to use the Cross-Trainer to barricade themselves, but two of the young men were seen as the primary instigators with the third (Peter) playing a very passive role. Peter later explained:

> They just barricaded themselves in the room because one of the officers had said to them, 'Right you are all going to Res D tomorrow. Take our word for it you are going to Res D.' … So they walked us on to Res C and they [the other two young men] said, 'This isn't Res D.' … They [the two young men] thought [the officers] were stitching them up because they were putting them on a different wing where they didn't know anyone.

It was quickly clear that none of the young men had given any serious consideration to the consequences of barricading themselves in a room. At approximately 3:30 pm in the afternoon, five hours into the hostage situation, one of the instigators asked the negotiators whether the incident would be regarded as a hostage situation since he had heard the word hostage mentioned and was nervous about what this would mean for his 'record.' He also confided in the officer standing at the door that he had mental health issues and that he had previously been sectioned under the Mental Health Act. The officers seemed uncertain about the veracity of these claims and no serious consideration was given to them.

Very soon after our arrival, a screen was erected around the room where the hostage situation was ongoing. Trained negotiators were briefed and replaced the officer who had been stood at the DARS room door. More people arrived. The command suite was opened, and the gate 'frozen' so that no one could enter or leave the prison. Several prison officers were asked to put on PPE (personal protection equipment, including helmets, padded arm and leg guards, and shields). Those in the equipment described themselves as 'power rangers.' Once 'kitted up,' the prison officers sat in one large group in a staff restroom in the centre of the residential unit. Whilst they waited for the call to action, food and drink were brought to them. Conversation and laughter bubbled out of the offices as prison officers discussed earlier occasions when NTRG (the National Tactical Response Group) had arrived to provide specialist support.

The subsequent arrival of NTRG and prison officers from the neighbouring prison required the YOI's own C&R (Control and Restraint) team to stand down, much to their great disappointment and frustration. With their egos bruised, one officer lamented that the decision to 'pull staff out of PPE gear' demonstrated that the 'Prison Service was lacking in the values of honesty, integrity and decency.' The rationale for the decision was that the barricading young men might feel resentful of any prison officers involved in the 'entry, extraction and relocation.' The prison officers dismissed this and were vexed by the decision, as if something had been taken away from them or they were being punished. One Supervising Officer (SO) was asked to remove his PPE gear due to his back problems, causing considerable disquiet between him and his colleagues. The prison officers commented that he was 'either fit for duty or he wasn't, and if they were expecting him to be on normal duties, he should be allowed to put on PPE.' In protest, the SO walked off the wing and eventually off duty.

A hostage situation is a rare event; there had only been one other hostage incident in the previous 6 years. The incident was resolved without injury to the young men who, after the door was blown off, were dragged from the room. The importance of such rare events is not simply in how they punctuate everyday prison life and how the prison finds its equilibrium again (or does not as the case can be), but the norms that underpin, and the meaning attached to, the associated operational decisions and actions. Throughout the hostage situation, James and I were not only privy to the events as they unfolded but were asked to step into offices with the SO and CM's so they and others could share stories. As and when they deemed necessary, they would close the door so others could not hear their disclosures or told us 'This is not for your notes' (instructions that I faithfully honoured). They needed to trust us and we needed to trust them too. Even with Mikey's subsequent desire for reassurance, Wednesday had been a turning point in terms of our relationships with the staff on Res C and the CM's within the prison. I would later understand that our presence on the wing that day demonstrated a commitment to the research that they had not expected. Their experience of researchers had been that they were 'in and out in less than two weeks.' Conversely, the knowledge that James and I were prepared to 'do our time' (King, 2000: 298), 'loiter with intent,' and remain within the prison for many months—including late into the evening, at weekends and even at the point of operational complexity—solidified in their minds our trustworthiness and authenticity.

Prison ethnographies are surprising endeavours. They are never quite what you expect them to be, but always something remarkably more. From the outset, it was impossible to predict what might be observed or discovered—even when examining seemingly familiar topics such as prison bullying, violence, and victimisation. The prison always reveals more of itself than anticipated, even by those who manage and govern them. We tend to think about 'the prison' as an imposing physical, immovable, and inert structure, but the prison is more ecological, more organic, and more dynamic than the physical security and architecture betrays. It breathes. It smells—anchoring memories of prison life with the smell of laundry detergents or, conversely, with the potent, unmistakable, and distinctly sour 'prison' smell (a unique combination of the smell of stale smoke, unclean and unkept men who have spent too many hours locked in small cells with too little ventilation and too little access to showers). Prisons produce sound—sometimes of laughter, cell bells, general alarms, music, banging doors and gates, and at other times a cacophony of the discordant, piercing, and jarring sounds that signal human distress, tragedy, and disharmony. Time is the defining feature of imprisonment, but it loses its regularity and essential rhythms as each prison (often absent of clocks) produces its own internal rhythms, habits, and routines. Time also has a fluid quality in prison—hard to grasp, sometimes passing slowly and other times quickly. Whilst prison ethnographic research is intellectually stimulating, it is also monotonous (or 'fucking boring' as it was described) at times (for further discussion on boredom, see Fassin, 2017a).

This chapter describes our ethnographic and qualitative approach. As Adler (1985: 11) notes, 'direct personal observation, interaction, and experiences is the only way to acquire accurate knowledge about deviant behaviour' and this observation extends to harmful and violence behaviour within a prison. Had James and I chosen—as might have appeared reasonable—to interview or survey prisoners in relatively sterile areas (such as the visits hall or legal visits), or to omit an ethnographic approach, we might have failed to fully appreciate the context or significance of prisoner's accounts or be more vulnerable to partial narrations. Ethnography can reveal the hidden and veiled (also see Rhodes, 2013). The ethnographic research was more than a familiarisation exercise. James and I had to look closely and fully invest ourselves (also see Liebling, 2014). Whilst it was impossible for us to adopt an 'insider' role, through quiet and continual observation it was possible to see, sense and make sense of the prison. It was this presence that also allowed us to establish 'long-term organic relationships with the people [I] write about' (Bourgois 2003: 13) and develop the necessary trust that allowed for fuller conversations about illicit, harmful and violent interactions within the prison. That James and I witnessed the incidents that were described in interview, and knew the characters involved, or could discern between what appeared and what was *really* happening assisted us in interviews, particularly with those who were more dominant, more controlling, and more intimately connected with illicit activity inside the prison and out. Such conversations inevitably confronted us with the best and worst features of humanity. This chapter therefore describes our 'research morality' (Ferrell, 1998: 25), our approach to the 'field' and how we navigated the political and ethical dilemmas that we inevitably encountered in a prison world that—like the criminal world outside—was in a state of change and flux.

Gaining Access

Gaining access to prison is often precipitated by a quagmire of administrative processes and, at the point of entering the prison, applications to conduct the research had already been considered by multiple gate keepers. As James and I set foot in the prison that first day, and learnt how to collect and use keys, it would have been easy to assume that the problem of gaining access had long been resolved. However, gaining access would be under constant negotiation as we moved throughout the prison and sought to interview young men and prison staff, some of whom were (understandably) suspicious about our motives or cynical about what difference the research could make. Establishing credibility in the complex prison social world where the interests of different social groups and power holders can vary is crucial but by no means guaranteed. It is possible to be in a prison but miss the 'action' because, for example, researchers are skilfully manoeuvred away from such knowledge. Ethnography is essentially relational and collaborative; it is, as Erickson and Stull (1998) argue, 'a joint venture' with those who host the research and those whom we seek to understand.

The research project reflected a meeting of minds between us as researchers and the new Governor. I had visited the prison before the landmark inspection and had been invited to conduct research within the prison by the (unbeknown to me) soon to be outgoing Governor. Shortly after the inspection that had cast such doubt on the future of the YOI, I received a phone call from the Head of Residence explaining what had happened and asking, 'You've seen the prison, it really isn't as bad as they've said is it?' In that moment, I had no reassuring reply to offer. It was as bad as the Inspectorate had concluded. Initially, I thought that this might be the end of our relationship with the prison, concluding that the new Governing Governor was unlikely to welcome research at a time when so much reform was needed. However, on the encouragement of a colleague, I rang the Governor's management co-ordinator to see if there was any appetite for the research to continue. To my surprise, the 'Number One' (Governing) Governor answered, and I was able to speak to them directly. That they were open to research is testament to their commitment to making decisions based on data and evidence, the appetite for input from a variety of people (including academics), and the desire to improve the prison.

I am, and have always been, grateful for the trust that the Governor initially showed in James and I, and their willingness to embrace the research. There was an openness even to findings that might have been uncomfortable to hear, and I found I was able to speak freely with the Governor and senior management team. This was not achieved without grace, understanding, and investment on both sides. I had been rigorously tested before even holding the first meeting. During the first telephone conversation, I was asked questions about my previous research experience. When I was explicitly asked where I had conducted my doctoral research, I declined to jettison the anonymity I had promised the senior management team of that YOI. The decision not to name the prison—I later learned—had secured a degree of trust that initially served to open the possibility of a meeting with the Governor, and then with members of their wider team and colleagues within HM Prison and Probation Service. I would also later learn that had James and I proved unable to work effectively with the senior management team, we would have been asked to conclude the research within two weeks. Senior managers understandably valued discretion. During the research, and subsequently, we deliberately avoided media coverage or social media posts; we did not name the prison and we did not talk about what we were seeing or doing.

James and I took seriously the task of supporting the YOI in better understanding the problem of prison violence and in helping the senior team to think carefully about how to prevent and reduce its incidence. It was not open to us to simply rest in the theoretical or conceptual and resist the need to think about the practical—indeed the stakes were too high. We accepted invitations to attend management meetings, contribute at senior management team away days, and socialise with the team during the Christmas festivities and for other celebrations. Some may argue that such social proximity might have endangered any claim to objectivity, but we did not ascribe to the notion that any social science researcher can ever truly be 'outside' the research. Indeed, Fassin (2017b: 296) argues, 'subjectivity was the necessary condition for objectivity.' This is not to say that we could, or indeed needed to be, a prisoner or prison manager to understand their perspectives. Rather, our role as ethnographers was to understand the prison social world and to 'grasp the facts observed in the entirety, to understand the rationales of all protagonists, to give an account of the diversity of points of view' (Fassin, 2017b: 299).

The Governor's explicit endorsement of the project during morning meetings led to further offers of help and support from the senior management team. Over time, as prison officers saw our commitment to spend time in the prison and with them (either on the landings or with a cup of coffee in an office), they too became increasingly open with us. This gave us a range of perspectives on some of the same problems. For example, on Res D, the officers had divulged (without prompting) the details of a recent incident where an officer had punched a prisoner twice—an incident caught on CCTV. The officer's arrogant confidence that he would not be caught was soon unsettled as the invitation to the Governor to 'check on the CCTV' served to reveal his guilt not his innocence. As the officers were explaining what had happened, an officer tried to google the individual to see if he had been sentenced yet. The conversation was interrupted by the arrival of the SO who told James and I that a young man had been taken to the segregation unit for punching an officer and encouraged us to go to the segregation unit to observe what happened next and discover why the young man had punched the officer. There was an element of serendipity about this (also see Wolcott, 2010). James and I often found that we needed to follow our gut instincts about where to spend our time on a particular day. This might appear less strategic or 'scientific' than is necessary, but these instinctive reactions were a result of accumulated knowledge about how to make sense of the prison, how to anticipate where problems might be, how to appreciate the ebb and flow of daily life, and our growing ability to sense the factors that indicated when the prison was becoming disorderly.

Becoming 'Part of the Furniture'

Ethnographic research requires long-term immersion and is distinguishable from short-term observations (e.g. over a matter of days or weeks) or research that does not involve being 'where the action is' in prisons (e.g. research through correspondence). This is not to privilege ethnographic research or dismiss the importance of other methodological approaches which time, resource, access, and the research questions may dictate. Rather, it is to say that ethnographic research has a particular meaning: it is 'immersive, in-depth research with subjects of study' (Ferrell, 2018: 189). It is a 'way of seeing' (Wolcott, 2008). As an ethnographer, I sought to be a keen observer, 'trying to detect and articulate … the social universe' of the YOI (Liebling et al., 2021). Prisons are 'pervaded by an interpersonal opacity that thwarts even those who govern, manage or live in them' (Rhodes, 2001: 76)—an opacity that can only be (even if always partially) revealed with time and close observation. Crewe argues (2009: 147) that certain forms of penal power have moved away from the prison wings and landings with the effect that 'it would be insufficient to assert that life in prison is essentially on the landings' (2009: 147). Whilst his central point—that penal power has dispersed and prison officers have less power over critical decisions—remains accurate, the prison wings and landings are still 'where the action is in prison' (McDermott & King, 1988). It is on the landings where violence, self-harm, drug dealing and drug use occurs, where officers make decisions about who to unlock (or not), where essential decisions are made about who can have what 'rewards' and prized jobs, and where the politics of prison life are ironed out.

To understand the everyday life of prisons is to 'take the mundane seriously and ask what is at stake in our daily encounters' (Back, 2015: 821). I paid close attention to the habits, routines, slang, rituals and the rules regarding social etiquette (e.g. shouting 'coming through' if someone was holding a gate open and knowing when it was time to make a cup of coffee). An immersive approach also revealed how low-level protests were staged (e.g. refusing to go into cell), how issues such as 'plugging' were dealt with ('I'll ask the nurse to bring down the laxatives') and what was understood as a threat (e.g. kicking a mop bucket in the general direction of an officer). Some of these interactions seemed trivial but revealed complex moral, ethical, and political dilemmas. For example, the decision by a senior manager to move a young man who had assaulted a prison officer from the segregation unit to the wing was contested in ways that revealed the multiple interests at stake and how values such as 'justice' were subject to diverse interpretations. Prison officers were incredulous and cynical about the motives for the decision whilst senior managers were keen to ensure that segregation was used as a last resort and for the shortest minimum period. Ethnographic study, then, reveals 'something of values—or even more precisely—values in action' (Engelke, 2017: 94).

Whilst references to prison ethnography abound, and complete volumes have been given to the method (Drake et al., 2015), the precise mechanics of such research are often illusive. Those describing prison ethnography may make opaque references to 'hanging around on the wing'—it is necessarily more deliberate and systematic than this implies. James and I did a great deal of 'hanging around,' often leaving with prison officers at the end of 'A shifts' at 7:30 pm–8 pm at night. We stood on the wings as men cleaned. We chatted with young men and prison staff in the association rooms and exercise yards. We walked with prison staff and young men around the prison to collect items from the 'stores.' We waited in staff offices for the roll check to be deemed correct, at which point officers could leave. We chatted with nurses in the Healthcare centre, met those from the Independent Monitoring Board (IMB), and talked about television programmes preferred by officers in First Night Centre (Love Island). We stood on 'free flow' as young men walked to and from education and work. We went to the gym with prison staff (at lunchtime) and with the young men. We observed all the wings closely, regularly, and over time. With permission, we attended GOAD reviews (meetings to determine whether continued segregation was justifiable), security meetings, safety meetings, and adjudications,[3] and did so more than once. We saw the prison in every season and at every point in the day, and at times left with the officers as the night shift started. Weekends were different to weekdays but showed a degree of commitment: 'you are here, and you are not locked up' and 'you are here and you are not being paid' was said to us more than once. We learned when to speak and when to keep quiet, when to stay and when to 'get out of the way.' We simply tried as much as we could to be there and being there mattered (Ferrell, 1998: 32).

As the weeks and months rolled by, prison officers would 'tip us off' to things we needed to see. For example, on arriving one day, we were told by one of the SOs that we 'needed' to go to a particular Residential Unit where he thought there were 'problems.' There were. The same thing would happen with prisoners: 'you should talk to my mate, I have told them you are sound.' Young men would approach us and initiate conversation during association[4] or whilst walking around the prison. We were also familiar with who the wing cleaners, 'Red Bands'[5] and orderlies[6] were, as well as who the more dominant individuals were on each wing. Young men would ask to be interviewed. It was difficult to conclusively

[3] A prison disciplinary hearing convened by a governor to establish whether an alleged violation of Prison/Young Offender Institutions Rules had occurred.

[4] The period in the prison schedule when prisoners are unlocked from their cells and can informally socialise with one another, play pool, walk around the exercise yard, and speak to prison officers about any queries.

[5] Young men who had more extensive access to the prison and could remove around more freely.

[6] Orderlies largely performed a range of low level tasks in places such as the gym, library, and chapel.

confirm but the fact that certain key people on each wing knew us—and were referring other people to us—seemed to have 'thawing' effect with others.

James and I had to overcome the suspicion of young men that we were 'FEDs' (police officers), psychologists, journalists or 'grasses,' and instil a confidence that we could appreciate and understand what they were describing, lamenting or praising. We were openly asked about our role—'Where are you from? Are you from X?'—as young men tried to place us. We could tell the prisoners to google us, which would elicit a laugh. In the early days, young men assumed James was a police officer, partly because he wore a Superdry jacket, and declined to disclose his previous employment as a probation officer to prisoners, even if he sometimes did so with staff. James quickly dropped a Superdry jacket for Stone Island Denims and Lacoste polo shirts. It later transpired that the young men were not unreasonably suspicious—whilst entering the prison, we saw a police officer had arrived for a meeting wearing a Superdry jacket. Most of the time, though, we were relatively casual in our appearance (a practical decision for days spent largely on the wings) and only dressed in smarter business attire when our days were spent with the senior management team.

Over time, the senior management team, wider prison staff group and prisoners themselves seemed to grow increasingly confident in our ability to 'call it.' Three months into the project, the Deputy Governor returned from annual leave to a series of incidents on Res D. She later relayed to me that she had told others: 'Staff think they know what's happening, but James and Kate will know what's happening.' I was also told that the running joke was that if the senior management team wanted to know something, they should ask us and not the staff. James and I were regarded as 'part of the furniture.' The compliment was returned to us by prisoners: 'you know more about the main players in here than the staff know—you aren't daft and we know it.' On another occasion, a wing cleaner told another young man that I 'knew stuff' and that he could freely talk to me about his 'nicking'[7] and 'added days.'[8] This was reassuring, but also increased the weight of responsibility—not just about the importance of rigorous data collection for the sake of reliable findings, but because others were relying on us in very real ways to identify what was happening and help them think about how to address it. At all times, we sought to protect the confidentiality of participants and avoid any sense that we had exposed individuals.

James and I were committed to conducting ourselves with integrity and being transparent with others about the scope of our research, the nature of their involvement, and the extent to which informal exchanges were part of the 'data set.' Inevitably, this required a considerable amount of judicious discretion on our part. Staff and prisoners were often very aware of our role—staff might check 'you're not going to tell the governor' or ask how much they could say to us. Yet, our research role was also precisely why they brought us into conversation or suggested there were certain things we ought to see. Staff and prisoners alike were as keen as we were to ensure that we had a full and accurate picture of the prison. In some cases, this meant dealing with the variation between the narrative and the facts. For example, one interviewee, Robert, described an elaborate car chase involving a police helicopter and multiple cars whilst he was on an expensive stolen motorcycle. The reality was that he was convicted of stealing a pedal bicycle. Of course, it was less important that Robert had embellished his criminality as why he felt it necessary to do so. Equally, we did not naively accept explanations such as 'falling in the shower' when young men presented with black eyes or injuries. A slightly jovial 'Now we both know that's not true' was often met with a wry smile or served to open discussion about the incident. Sometimes James was more direct: 'Oh fuck off Danny, we know that's bollocks because we already know why it happened.'

[7] A 'nicking' is when a prison officer reports a violation of Prison/YOI Rules (see Prison Act 1952, Prison Rules 1999 and Young Offender Institution Rules 2000). The person who is alleged to have committed the offence is required to attend an Adjudication where a Governor Grade will either accept a guilty plea or, in the event of a not guilty plea, determine whether the charge has been proved. Sanctions can be imposed if the charge is proven.

[8] The Independent Adjudicator (a District Judge) can award a maximum of 42 days for a serious violation of prison rules.

Ethnographic research requires considerable social dexterity and an ability to both 'take more than one side seriously' (Liebling, 2001: 473). For each of the parties concerned—prisoners, prison officers, custodial managers, senior managers—they were concerned that you understood *their side* and, in some cases, that we adopted their side. Thus, the 'whose side are you [and we] on?' (Becker, 1967) question never left us. Although ethnography may depend 'on the establishment of ongoing empathetic relationships with others' (Liebling, 2014), there was a tendency for some to not only want us to empathise with them but also identify with them. In this sense, the research was political whether we wanted it to be or not. We were conscious that no one person knew the 'truth of prison' (Fassin, 2017b: 299) but that it was important for us to treat all parties with equal seriousness, respect and neutrality. In soliciting a diverse range of perspectives, we were able to compare the multiple explanations as to the 'facts.' We could 'note their similarities and their differences but also identify the context and the position from which were put forward' (Fassin, 2017b: 299). Sometimes ideas about what should be 'done' were in conflict—we tried to be attentive listeners, rather than explicitly express a particular normative position, but this required some diplomatic responses on our part.

Ethnography at 'the Edge': Understanding Harmful and Illicit Activities in Prison

It is well established that official statistics tend to 'substantially understate' the true level of violence (Bottoms, 1999). Understanding illicit behaviours and activities required some tact, subtlety, and discretion. James and I would not learn anything by being too forward with questions about violence and victimisation, or the associated problems of drug dealing, possession of contraband, and the crafting of weapons. The answers would be revealed in time, or volunteered without prompting, if we were willing to be patient. The strength of such an approach was confirmed in Nibbs' nod of approval:

> You want to know what is happening here? Don't talk, watch. Watch who talks to who. Watch people's hands, what gets passed. You want to understand what it is like here, don't come in with all your questions straight off, watch and learn. Who talks to who. Yes, some people will tell you some stuff, but you can learn a lot from doing what you were doing the other day.
>
> James: I know. That is why I know who sent you to find out who we were when we first came on the wing.
>
> [Nibbs smiles] You know it then; you know what you are doing. [Nibbs turns and walks away]

It took time to build this sort of candour and openness from our participants. They had to see us being in and around 'the action.' It also necessitated a confidence from prisoners that you could at least understand—if not agree with—why they might assault others, the norms that underpinned such behaviour, and the structural strains that often meant that they felt that they had few choices *but* to respond violently. We had to be careful not to rush to judgement. We had to prove we could handle ourselves within the prison and were not intimidated either by the environment or by the buoyancy of prison social life. Although this partly meant not showing fear, it was about far more. For example, Nibbs explained:

> First time I seen you, I could tell you both knew jail.
>
> James: *Is that why you came to talk to us*?
>
> Why did I come and talk to you? Lads wanted to know who those govs[9] were. Someone else says, 'They ain't govs, they're police.' Another says nobody knows them, if they was police or screws,[10] people would know them. I didn't know, but I could tell how you carried yourself, you know prison, you weren't fearful. Most people, you can see fear, you can even see it off new lads here. One look, I can tell who knows jail, who knows the score and who is out of place.

For us, any emotional reactions might have offered pause for reflection in terms of what it might say about the world we encountered. However,

[9] An expression used for prison governors but also variously to describe prison officers and custodial managers.

[10] A term normally used for prison officers.

had we been very emotional, fearful, or sensitive individuals, it would have been almost impossible to complete a research project on the very cruel, callous, and gratuitous violence that some people inflict on each other or be taken seriously by those who valorised nerve, resilience, bravery, and courage, whether that be prison staff or prisoners.

Equally, trying to understand crime and harm in prisons sometimes felt more like detective work, piecing the various jigsaw pieces together and then triangulating those observations with interview data, survey data, management information, informal conversation, what was recorded in wing observation books, and discussed in various meetings. As Amil reminded us, 'It's not about what people can see, it's more about what's going on underneath.' The various 'jigsaw pieces' and 'clues' to what lay beneath the superficial were a host of little details, all of which revealed the rich tapestry and portrait of a prison social system: who is connected with who; who meets and greets who; who pushes the trollies to and from the kitchens; which prisoners are given additional responsibilities; when do prisoners use distraction techniques; what have security found or confiscated this week; were complaints pouring in; who has fallen out with whom and why; who has just left or just arrived; what high profile offences have happened in the community; who owes who and for what; who is self-harming; who is staying in their cell instead of collecting a meal or making a phone call; who is on the wing when they should be at work; who is on the wrong wing during association; which staff have been arrested; which staff are unhappy; and so on.

Long-term prison research sub-consciously changed my behaviour in ways that were unanticipated. I became accustomed to standing with my back to the wall (not in front of cells or open doors) and from vantage points that allowed me the largest vistas—routines that stayed with me at conference, in cinemas, and restaurants. I developed an instinct for 'sensing' when the atmosphere was changing, when things were 'bubbling,' and when a fight was about to ensure—a 'gut reaction' that stayed with me even when, for example, navigating the night-time economy on the streets of Chicago (when my bemused husband couldn't understand why he was asked to cross the street away from a brawl that would fall out of a bar just a minute or two later). Other innocuous things would become habitual: checking the contents of bags and pockets, choosing mints over chewing gum, wearing clothes that could accommodate belts, and the occasional dream about accidentally bringing a mobile phone into a prison. I was never naïve, never complacent, and never dropped my guard fully. As an ethnographic researcher, I was working within a complex moral framework. I was a 'moral dualist' (also see Gooch, 2021; Liebling & Crewe, 2013), carefully balancing compassion and realism; vigilance and ease; a belief in the capacity to change with an awareness that people may not change; an appreciation of first impressions with a willingness to look beyond the superficial.

Prison violence may be 'morally inexcusable' but it is 'intelligible' (Mihut, 2013, cited in Liebling, 2014). The challenge, though, was to make sense of violence and criminality without dehumanising or vilifying participants (Liebling, 2014). Nor could I romanticise participants (whether prisoners or prison staff). Some young men would revel in the violence they caused. At other times, young men would describe gratuitous violence callously and with little empathy for the victim. Others, though, expressed regret, if only for the impact upon themselves. At other times, their anger was reserved for the prison staff and system they felt had failed them. Like Adler acknowledges (1993: 20), it was sometimes the case that 'people were up to more than they would ordinarily admit,' but it was also true that many were inclined to be open and honest. It is possible that some may have withheld some details, either because it would reflect poorly on them or their peers, or because they knew James and I were under an obligation to report any harmful or criminal conduct the authorities were unaware of, and/or where there was an immediate risk of harm. It also true that some details of their lives were too painful to revisit. This veiling of the things we fear might expose, embarrass or distress us is a fairly normal feature of human behaviour and although I recognise that ethnographic study is always 'partial' (Rhodes, 2001), I remain content that the account presented here is authentic and accurate.

Ethnographic research is messy and, at times, unflattering. As Bourgois (2003: 18) points out, 'Under an ethnographic microscope everything has warts and anyone can be made to look like a monster.' Whilst I have written this account 'without censoring even the goriest details' (Bourgois, 2003: 18), I took little pleasure in violence and saw little need either to valorise it or sensationalise it. Winlow et al.'s (2001: 536–537) remarks regarding their ethnographic study of bouncers, the violent night-time economy and professional organised crime resonated with my own position: 'Rather than glorifying male violence or losing oneself in 'edgework' (Lyng 1990, 1997), we sought to uncover a culture of male expression heavily reliant on physicality and violence … [but] we were never in the business of thrill seeking.' One of the reasons why James and I were a particularly effective research team was that our differences in personality and professional experience complemented each other but we were both prepared to 'graft' and work long hours within the prison. This came at a cost. Regularly leaving a prison at 7.30 pm or 8 pm, only to return in time for morning meeting at 8:30 am the following day meant many a missed bedtime story, many long hours of late-night email traffic, creatively finding ways to complete University administrative tasks and—faced with the realities of an academic environment that stressed continued productivity—the space for 'deep work' (Newport, 2016). We were frustrated when taxi firms declined to take us from the train station to the prison. We made difficult telephone calls to spouses explaining why we were late home (again). However, laborious though, we were not bruised or scarred like so many of the young men had been. It would be self-indulgent to dwell on our labours which paled in significance to the 'anguish of imprisonment' (Fassin, 2017b: 297). As Winlow et al. (2001) illustrate, we did not have the luxury of choosing less demanding research if we truly wanted to understand prison violence—but nor did we seek it. This study was both a privilege and responsibility.

Interviews

James and I triangulated our ethnographic observations and conversations, and the analysis of management information and security reports, with semi-structured interviews. We deliberately delayed the interviews until a couple of months had passed and we had a better understanding of the specific dynamics of the YOI. Using intelligence reports and adjudication records, we began by identifying prisoners who had reportedly been involved in an incident of bullying or violence (as either a victim or a perpetrator) or where there were suspicions of such activity over the four-week period prior to the research and over the 2 month period we had already been in the prison. Where possible, we interviewed both the perpetrator and victim to assess different parties' interpretations of the same incident. As Toch (1969: 142) notes: 'Every conflict between two parties is in reality two conflicts: one, the contest as seen by the aggressor, and two, the situation as perceived by the victim.' Interviewing all parties helped us better understand how violence and victimisation were interpreted, explained, and rationalised by all of those involved. It also enabled us to explore any differences between official accounts and the explanations by the young men themselves (which were often missing in institutional reports). It generated 'more complete explanations of why the violence occurred' and 'produced clear explanation of how a conflict escalated into physical violence' (Edgar et al., 2003b: 20, 77). Our approach also meant that often one interviewee could provide information that was lacking in another person's perspective (also see Edgar et al., 2003a: 20).

In addition to interviewing those known to be involved in prison victimisation, we conducted a second wave of interviews including those who were not officially implicated in any incidents. We were particularly interested to learn why some prisoners were rarely or infrequently involved in violence and victimisation, as well as the extent to which incidents might be under-reported. None of those who were approached for interview declined. Sometimes we interviewed together, sometimes separately. There were a couple of instances where an individual preferred to specifically talk to one of us (and not the other), and we were amenable to such requests. In total, we interviewed 53 young men and 8 prison staff. With informed consent, all interviews were digitally recorded and subsequently transcribed. Pseudonyms have been used for all participants.

Interviewing young prisoners was a demanding exercise frequently inflected with human emotion—anger, guilt, shame—as well as a search for meaning and existential clarity. In some cases, these young men struggled to complete an interview without dissolving into tears. Our immediate efforts to suggest we could pause or halt interviews and seek additional support for them was regularly met with the expressed desire to continue, typically on the grounds that the interview constituted their first opportunity to describe and disclose their feelings. Whist we honoured their requests to continue, it did not give any comfort that the interviews were serving that function and we always endeavoured to ensure that we were not doing harm to people in interviews. In other cases, young men posed questions seeking reassurance that we couldn't always honestly give. For example, Danny ended the interview by volunteering the details of a murder and then strongly denying his active involvement in the offence. He then asked James, 'do you think I did it?' James' response was an honest 'I don't know.'

There were occasions where young men reported intentions to harm themselves or others that James and I had to report. Indeed, having told the young men that we had a duty to report imminent or actual harm, some disclosures were made with the express purpose that we would raise their concerns with prison staff. Whilst we declined to be an advocate in other ways and would not take up grievances with, for example, aspects of custodial life (e.g. retrieving property) or criminal justice processes (e.g. offering legal advice), we did take seriously our responsibility to safeguard participants. Neither of us felt comfortable leaving the prison with the 'guilty knowledge' that there was a high likelihood that harm was imminent and we could have acted to prevent it. For example, Amil revealed to James and I that he was unable to tolerate his 'pad mate'[11] any longer and was intent on smashing his TV over him when he returned to his cell. We walked with Amil to the SO's office, where Amil relayed his desperation and his threat to bludgeon his pad mate with the TV to the SO. At first, the SO was unconcerned and, seemingly out of busyness, told Amil to return to his cell, much to Amil's agitation and anger. It was only when we indicated that we would stand with Amil until she had finished her tasks did she give any indication that she would re-assess Amil's cell allocation. The risk was obvious to us, and the murder of Zahid Mubarek at HM YOI Feltham never far from our minds (see Keith, 2006), but such misalignment between our immediate concerns and the seeming indifference of the SO caused us to reflect on how 'risk' was assessed, whether young men were taken seriously, and the extent to which sustained exposure to violence and threats of violence served to de-sensitive staff to obvious danger. Whilst I never assumed that our assessments were necessarily right, or

[11] Prison slang to refer to the person they were sharing a cell with.

that we could make more informed operational decisions, interactions such as the one between Amil and the SO were important cultural clues and prompted me to think carefully about what was indicative of a more general pattern and what was an isolated incident.

Deciding what to report, and when, did not end with potential harm by prisoners. Prisoners also reported instances of staff corruption, including someone bringing items into the prison (and that the activity was ongoing) and instances where prison officers deliberately revealed to prisoners who was a sex offender (and ensured they had sight of paperwork) so that the individual would be assaulted (also see Chap. 8). Thus, as researchers, our commitment to creating a safe environment (and not endangering those who live and work in the YOI) was twofold. Whilst it is typical for researchers to acquire ethical approval prior to conducting research (as I did), the commitment to ethical research is necessarily enduring and far less straightforward than the paper processes infer. As Ferrell (1998: 25) states, ethnography 'unavoidably entangles those who practice it in complex and ambiguous relations to subjects and situations of study, to issues of personal and social responsibility, and to law and integrity.'

A Man's World?: Team Ethnography, Gender Politics, and Researcher Identities

Data collection was a joint endeavour. This proved advantageous not only in terms of efficiency, but also in improving the quality and experience of immersive research. At times, James and I observed the same incidents from different positions in the room, or were able to speak to different people in the same room at the same time, giving us multiple viewpoints on the same events. At other times, we deliberately visited different areas of the prison. Essentially, team ethnography offered us what Erickson and Stull (1998) describe as 'plural gazes.' James and I frequently travelled to and from the prison together, and although there were days when we visited alone and interviews we conducted separately, we were able to move seamlessly between planning the day ahead, decompressing after an interview or visit, to analysing what we were discovering as we moved through the weeks and months of the research. We asked each other questions, discussed our findings and tested whether there were alternative explanations for what we were seeing. This process allowed us to become 'more overtly aware of what was and was not 'there' in the field' (Liebling et al., 2021), and indeed how our findings corresponded with the existing literature.

This 'field team' worked because our 'skills and capacities, temperaments and interests' were 'complementary, asymmetrical and non-competitive' (Mead, 1970, 326). We were very obviously a mixed gender team and it was inescapable that our gendered identity—coupled with our age, class, profession and interests—structured how we encountered the YOI and were encountered by prisoners and prison staff. The increase in the number of female prison officers and senior leaders has changed the composition of the prison workforce in ways that claims that 'prisons are amongst the most male dominated of modern institutions' (Newton, 1994: 193) may appear outdated. However, the YOI remained a 'crucible of masculinity' (O'Donnell, 2004: 241) in which some were counted amongst the 'men' and the 'lads,' and others were despised and rejected. Although there was evidence of caring practices from both men and women, prison officers typically reinforced the necessity of masculine traits both with each other and in the young men. Officers might joke with young men about their ability to 'cope' (and suggest they might not be able to 'hack it')—quips that young men often felt compelled to rebuff. Officers too also engaged in the play fighting, 'piss taking' and jostling with each other and the young men—something that some young men enjoyed but risked further entrenching the inability of others to 'perform' idealised forms of masculinity (also see Gooch, 2019).

Immersed within this same social context, we too were subject to the same gendered expectations. As Erickson and Stull (1998) argue, 'fieldworkers are more than mere collectors of data … team members are expected to behave in ways that are linked to local notions of role and identity.' James was 'boss' (a term used for prison officers) and I was 'miss' (despite attempts to encourage young men to use my name). We both fielded multiple questions about our relationship status from prisoners and prison staff alike (i.e. whether we were dating each other or had in the past—we had not and were both married to different people). Early on our first day, Bob had warned me to expect 'a lot of grief' from the young men. Flirtatious behaviour—whistling, the 'Hi beautiful' and the enduring 'So when do I get your number?'—was frequent and often harmless. It often opened up conversation and could be met with humour if James responded, 'Why would I give my phone number to you?' Mostly, I remained relatively tolerant of such behaviour, recognising that it was often a performance for the benefit of the other young men and only challenged such behaviour when it was too explicit or inappropriate. It would have been difficult to do otherwise since prison officers were just as guilty of positioning me in respect of my sexuality or engaging in flirtatious behaviour (e.g. 'those boots would look good on my bedroom floor').

Whilst working as a team helped us better understand the possible relevance of gender, it was always unclear how much our gender substantially changed the data. On one occasion, Joshua and Dean engaged James in conversation about boxing, fights, tattoos, and scars (see Chap. 6). Whilst boxing and martial arts was something James could talk freely about, and some of the young men had seen the same fights or been to the same gyms, I knew little. The somewhat competitive conversation allowed Joshua and Dean to stress and advertise their courage, strength, and bravery. Yet, in a quiet moment later that day, Joshua would later reveal to me that he was struggling with death of his son (see Chap. 6). An obvious conclusion is that Joshua felt compelled to stress his masculine credentials with James but felt relieved of such expectations with me. However, perhaps the fundamental difference was that there was no audience for Joshua to perform to whilst sweeping an office. Would Joshua have revealed his grief to James if afforded time and privacy? If I had been interested in boxing and martial arts, would the exchange have been different? It was almost impossible for us to establish to extent to which our gender influenced the data or if participants would have responded differently had we been an all-male or all-female team (also see Damsa & Ugelvik, 2017). It was also possible that there were other factors that were more important—age, class, experience, professional identity, interests, and crucially, our integrity. What was often more important to our participants was not whether we were male or female, but whether we were trustworthy, compassionate, discreet, honest, credible (in the sense that we could understood their norms, strains, and experiences) and whether we had the nerve and confidence to spend long periods of time on prison wings.

Getting In, Getting Out

Many of the questions received at conferences have been about access negotiations. Less is said or was asked about how to leave the 'field,' which can be especially tricky for immersive studies. However well embedded James and I were, we could have easily overstayed our welcome. It is of course always necessary 'to terminate the research at a given date, however rich the data' (Sparks, 2002: 578). I wanted to 'finish well' but also ensure that I had conducted myself in such a way that the prison, in the broadest sense, would be open and receptive to further prison research by others. Somewhat fortuitously, a natural conclusion to the project came with the departure of the Governing Governor at a time when James and I were more than nine months into the ethnographic study and beginning to sense that we were reaching saturation point. As we left the field, I continued analysing and making sense of the data, and then began writing.

As promised, I prepared a lengthy and detailed research report and held a series of events with practitioners across HM Prison and Probation Service to discuss the research findings. This in turn led to further invitations to continue my research on prison violence in other sites (research that includes Category A, Category B Local, Category B Training, and Category C prisons) and internationally (in Australia and Aotearoa New Zealand). My ongoing dialogue with representatives from the Home Office, Ministry of Justice, Youth Justice Board and HM Prison and Probation Service has given confidence that what is recorded in this book was neither isolated to the YOI, nor to YOIs more generally, but the embodiment of trends across the closed male prison estate in England and Wales. That said, there are important differences between YOIs and closed male adult prisons, and where necessary, distinctions are made to indicate such. However, this account remains that of a particular prison at a particular time. As Fassin states: 'The anthropologist must restrict himself to an account of the facts, what he has seen and heard, what he has understood, and what he can offer to render the meaning of what he has witnessed' (2017b: 297). Here I have sought to do just that.

References

Adler, P. A. (1993). *Wheeling and dealing: An ethnography of an upper level drug dealing and smuggling community*. Columbia University Press.

Back, L. (2015). Why everyday life matters: Class, community and making life livable. *Sociology, 49*(5), 820–836.

Becker, H. (1967). Whose side are we on. *Social Problems, 14*(3), 239–247.

Bottoms, A. E. (1999). Interpersonal violence and social order in prisons. *Crime and Justice, 26*, 205–281.

Bourgois, P. (2003). *In search of respect: Selling crack in El Barrio*. Cambridge University Press.

Crewe, B. (2009). *Prisoner society: Power, adaptation and social life in an English prison*. Oxford University Press.

Damsa, D., & Ugelvik, T. (2017). A difference that makes a difference? Reflexivity and researcher effects in an all-foreign prison. *International Journal of Qualitative Methods, 16*(1), 1–10.

Drake, D. H., Earle, R., & Sloan, J. (2015). *The Palgrave handbook of prison ethnography*. Palgrave Macmillan.

Edgar, K., O'Donnell, I., & Martin, C. (2003a). *Prison violence: The dynamics of conflict, fear and power*. Willan.

Edgar, K., O'Donnell, I., & Martin, C. (2003b). Violence in prison. In R. M. Lee & E. A. Stanko (Eds.), *Researching violence* (pp. 69–87). Routledge.

Engelke, M. (2017). *Think like an anthropologist*. Pelican.

Erickson, K. C., & Stull, D. D. (1998). *Doing team ethnography*. Sage.

Fassin, D. (2017a). Boredom: Accounting for the ordinary work of policing (France). In D. Fassin (Ed.), *Writing the world of policing* (pp. 267–292). University of Chicago Press.

Fassin, D. (2017b). *Prison worlds: An ethnography of the carceral condition*. Polity.

Ferrell, J. (1998). Criminological verstehen: Inside the immediacy of crime. In J. Ferrell & M. S. Hamm (Eds.), *Ethnography at the edge: Crime, deviance and field research* (pp. 20–42). Northern University Press.

Ferrell, J. (2018). *Drift: Illicit mobility and uncertain knowledge*. University of California Press.

Gooch, K. (2019). 'Kidulthood': Ethnography, juvenile prison violence and the transition from 'boys' to 'men'. *Criminology & Criminal Justice, 19*(1), 80–89.

Gooch, K. (2021). "You've got a hard edge!": The gender politics, complexities and intimacies undertaking prison research at the "edge". In J. A. Schlosser (Ed.), *Prison stories: Women scholars' experiences doing research behind bars* (pp. 173–192). Rowman and Littlefield Publishing Group Ltd.

Keith, B. (2006). *Report of the Zahid Mubarek inquiry*. The Stationery Office.

King, R. D. (2000). Doing research in prison. In R. D. King & E. Wincup (Eds.), *Doing research on crime and justice*. Oxford University Press.

Liebling, A. (2001). Whose side are we on? Theory, practice and allegiances in prisons research. *British Journal of Criminology, 41*(3), 472–484.

Liebling, A. (2014). Postscript. *Qualitative Inquiry, 20*(4), 481–486.

Liebling, A., & Crewe, B. (2013). Prisons beyond the new penology: The shifting moral foundations of prison management. In J. Simon & R. Sparks (Eds.), *The SAGE handbook of punishment and society* (pp. 283–307). Sage.

Liebling, A., Schmidt, B. E., Beyens, K., Boone, M., Johnsen, B., Kox, M., Rokkan, T., & Vanhouche, A.-S. (2021). Doing team ethnography in a transnational prison. *International Criminology, 1*(2), 123–134.

McDermott, K., & King, R. D. (1988). Mind games. *British Journal of Criminology, 28*(3), 357–375.

Mead, M. (1970). The art and technology of fieldwork. In R. Naroll and R. Cohen (Eds.), *Handbook of method in cultural anthropology*. Natural History Press.

Newport, C. (2016). *Deep work*. Piatkus.

Newton, C. (1994). Gender theory and prison sociology: Using theories of masculinities to interpret the sociology of prisons for men. *Howard Journal of Crime and Justice, 33*(3), 193–202.

O'Donnell, I. (2004). Prison rape in context. *British Journal of Criminology, 44*(2), 241–255.

Rhodes, L. A. (2001). Toward an anthropology of prisons. *Annual Review of Anthropology, 30*(1), 65–83.

Rhodes, L. A. (2013). Ethnographic imagination in the field of the prison. *Criminal Justice Matters, 91*(1), 16–17.

Toch, H. (1969). *Violent men: An inquiry into the psychology of violence*. Penguine Books Ltd.

Winlow S., Hobbs, D., Lister, S., & Hadfield, P. (2001). Get ready to duck. Bouncers and the realities of ethnographic research on violent groups. *British Journal of Criminology, 41*(3), 536–548.

Wolcott, H. F. (2008). *Ethnography: A way of seeing*. Altamira Press.

Wolcott, H. F. (2010). *Ethnography lessons: A primer*. Left Coast Press Inc.

3

'They'll Do Harsh Shit in Here': The Anatomy and Culture of Prison Victimisation

Everyone—including me—was asking themselves the same question: will a prison officer be assaulted? It was Saturday morning, and the atmosphere was tense, heavy, and charged. It had been a difficult week for both the young men and prison officers on Res D (Residential Unit D). On Tuesday, at 5 pm, Rhys had taken a metal chair and hit Carter with it several times, prompting two groups of young men to intervene—one group to defend Carter and another group to support Rhys' efforts to punish Carter. A large fight between the two groups ensued or, as the staff inaccurately described it, an incident of 'concerted indiscipline.' Various weapons had been stockpiled, including improvised weapons, mops, and brooms. More officers were called, running from other wings to support their colleagues. Batons were used by prison officers after Rhys refused to drop the metal chair or cease his attempts to hit Carter. Now with a full complement of staff, the young men were swiftly separated and returned to their cells. Rhys was taken to the segregation unit in handcuffs. Others would soon join him in the days that followed. Both wings on Res D were placed in 'lockdown.' Those who remained on the wing spent the remainder of the week 'banged up' in their cells unable to enjoy normal activities, partly because the

K. Gooch, *Prison Violence*, Palgrave Studies in Prisons and Penology,
https://doi.org/10.1007/978-3-031-91365-5_3

investigation was ongoing, partly because the possibility of further violent reprisals remained, and partly to allow weapons and contraband to be recovered by the 'dedicated search teams.'[1]

The cause of the unrest was the seizure of a 'throwover'[2] by the Security team. Although outside his control, the seizure prompted reprisals against Carter who had been appointed to collect the package (in this case a swift, visible, and serious beating with a chair). Tensions between the two groups remained heightened, partly due to the way the groups had divided according to ethnicity and then directed racist abuse at each other: the Black and Asian young men standing in opposition to the White young men. Initially, prison staff assumed the assault and subsequent fight was prompted by racial tensions. However, this was a dispute over disrupted business transactions that had quickly escalated.

The air was thick with the sour prison smell of unkempt men. No one was shouting and no music was playing. Unusually, the bins were overflowing with litter and the wings looked unclean and neglected. As the wing cleaner, John, walked steadily into the association room from his cell, he complained to an officer that he did not have any cleaning equipment. The immediate response was, 'So you're saying that you don't want a landing job anymore?' John, now angered by the response, answered, 'No!' and continued to litigate for the missing cleaning items. The officer simply replied, 'So you're retiring as the landing cleaner then?' Infuriated but powerless, John simply moved away, mumbling something inaudible under his breath. John's compliance was 'pragmatic and fatalistic' (Crewe, 2009). Losing his highly esteemed and much sought-after wing cleaner job was too great a loss and John recognised that any further challenge or perceived resistance was unwise and self-defeating. Whilst some—like John—would begrudgingly accept the 'legitimacy deficits' (Carrabine, 2003), others were less willing.

Shortly after, Liam walked past an officer, the officer whispered something indiscernible in his ear prompting Liam to turn on his heel, 'square up' to him, and start walking towards him. 'Come on then,' he bellowed.

[1] The dedicated search teams were regionally based and typically visited the YOI at the request of the Governing Governor to conduct searches of the cells and wing.

[2] A 'throwover' is a package containing contraband quite literally thrown over the fence and wall.

A couple of officers and young men instinctively moved towards the pair, the latter getting in between Liam and the officer and succeeding in persuading Liam to 'just leave it, it's not worth it.' After staring at the officer a few seconds longer, Liam turned to walk away with the other young men, shaking himself as he did, angry and conceding defeat only very reluctantly. A conversation between Carl and another officer about the limited time unlocked was concluded by the officer simply saying, 'Keep complaining and I simply won't unlock you tomorrow. I won't give you a nicking,[3] I just won't unlock you tomorrow. I'll just keep you banged up.' Carl—shocked and powerless—simply gave up the fight and walked away. The possibility that prison officers could use their discretionary power in ways that usurped formal rules was not a surprise to these young men. Such clumsy and authoritarian expressions of power by officers did little to prevent protests or possible assaults; rather, it only served to fuel frustrations. Like a tidal wave rolling in and then retreating, the rising tension and palpable sense that an assault was imminent would come and then roll away just as quickly.

As association turned into lunchtime, I breathed a sigh of relief, catching myself as I did. Somehow, more by default than design, a staff assault had been avoided. All the circling and conspiring amongst the young men had come to nothing. Without explanation, they had swallowed their anger and decided against violent protest. One by one they collected their lunch and returned to their cells. Saturday's lunch was chips, nuggets, curry sauce, a chocolate donut, and slices of bread—the precise amounts of each depending on an individual's social position. Those who were respected or feared collected double portions of chips and half a loaf of bread (not just the allotted two slices). I stood with my back to the wall near the entrance to the wing, watching as the young men collected their food and returned to their cells for the rest of the day. Quite inexplicably it seemed, as Yasir turned the corner, he launched a full plate of food at an officer standing nearby, and then kneed the officer in the genitals.

[3] A 'nicking' is when a prison officer reports a violation of Prison/YOI Rules (see Prison Act 1952, Prison Rules 1999 and Young Offender Institution Rules 2000). The person who is alleged to have committed the offence is required to attend an Adjudication where a Governor Grade will either accept a guilty plea or, in the event of a not guilty plea, determine whether the charge has been proved. Sanctions can be imposed if the charge is proven.

Within seconds, Yasir was face down on the floor and being restrained by three officers. Wrist and thumb 'locks' were applied as Yasir's screams and protestations sounded.

In the flurry of activity, the officers had missed the fight breaking out behind the servery. None of the officers had been observing the young men as they continued to collect their meals. Two young men had jumped over the servery and started punching Charlie, the servery[4] worker. I shouted to the nearest officer and the pressing of the general alarm[5] brought officers from other wings. The fight was broken up, and the two assailants were led back to their cells. As was Yasir. The assault by Yasir served a dual purpose, communicating his frustration with staff and serving as a distraction to allow another target to be assaulted without staff intervention. Turning to the Custodial Manager (CM), the officer says that Yasir needed an ice pack. 'He needs an ice cube,' was the response from the CM. The officer and CM laughed, breaking the tension. Meanwhile, Charlie remained behind the servery trying his best to resume his composure. His pride was the only thing seriously hurt—an injury that would be just as significant as any bruise. He continued to serve lunch, periodically shrugging his shoulders and readjusting his clothes, as if trying to get something, or someone, off his back. Keen to show he had 'given as good as he got,' Charlie mocked his assailants but was unable to conceal how shaken he was. His peers humoured him, chuckling a little but without offering any reassurance that he had in fact fought back. He hadn't.

Violence is notable in its absence, not just its presence. It is the possibility, not just the actuality, of physical violence that structures social interactions, shapes the emotional texture of prison life, and informs how power is used and with what techniques. As McVicar (1972: 224) argues, 'social relations shape ideology.' Statistical data may record the end result—the moment where the assault or fight finally occurs—but it inevitably fails to capture the crescendo, the way tension builds, the occasions when a prisoner changes their mind, or when prisoners or prison

[4] The servery was where hot meals were served.

[5] Alarm buttons are located around the prison and when pressed, prompt other prison officers to hastily move from their current position to the area where the alarm was initially pressed.

staff intervene to prevent an assault or fight occurring, or how rational words persuade an individual to take an alternative course. All these things shape prison life. The near misses not just the events. The threats not just the punches. Physical violence can become routine and part of the everyday framework of daily prison life (Bottoms, 1999) but without being mundane (c.f. O'Donnell & Edgar, 1998). This is not to detract from Toch's point that daily prison life is not 'continually suffused with imminent violence' (Toch, 1997: 168), but to recognise that the threat or potential for physical violence structures social interaction even when no fight or assault occurs.

This chapter has two principal aims. First, it analyses the anatomy of prison victimisation. Official statistical data record physical assaults, fights, and sexual assaults (see Ministry of Justice, 2025) but overlook the multifaceted nature of prison victimisation and the ways in which physical and sexual violence occur within a wider context of threats, verbal abuse, coercion, theft, robbery, exploitation, exclusion, and bullying. Focusing on violence alone runs the risk of misunderstanding the culture, process, and experience of prison victimisation. In some cases, it is the threat of violence (Gambetta, 2009), rather than the assault itself, that is just as effective—perhaps more so—in controlling others (whether prisoners or prison staff). Severe assaults undoubtedly do cause physical harm, but the psychological harm caused by ongoing, relentless abuse and humiliation can be just as damaging (O'Donnell & Edgar, 1999).

Very few studies focus on the spectrum of prison victimisation (for notable exceptions, see Bowker, 1980; Edgar et al., 2003), possibly due to the over-reliance on administrative data and survey measures that typically isolate and focus on violent incidents. However, as Bowker argues (1980: 31), 'All … forms of victimisation are related so that each becomes a causal factor in the other, forming an insane feedback system through which prison victimisation rates are under constant pressure to increase.' This chapter builds on this earlier work by Edgar et al. (2003) and Bowker (1980) by re-examining the contemporary culture of prison victimisation and how different forms of victimisation coalesce and with what effects. It describes the cultural aspects of prison victimisation that remain a consistent feature of prison life as well as their contemporary (re)interpretation. In so doing, it explores the emergence of 'global humiliation' within prison and sets the foundations for the analysis of 'economic victimisation' (Bowker 1980) in Chap. 4.

Secondly, and linked to the above, this chapter explores the extent to which 'bullying' remains a critical problem within Young Offender Institutions (YOIs). It is often said that bullying is an 'enduring and worsening problem' in YOIs (House of Commons Justice Committee, 2016: 28). However, in practice, it was often far more difficult to discern a specific series of incidents that constituted bullying. Whilst prison bullying was well defined in policy documents, the turbulent, volatile, and dynamic social relations within the YOI made it far harder to identify when victimisation was repeated by the same person or people. The argument here is not that bullying did not occur, but that it was easy to overestimate the frequency of bullying. Paradoxically, the focus on bullying had the effect of overlooking the very deliberate, intentional, and financially profitable exploitation—and its links to wider criminal networks—that was far more frequent. As wider youth and criminal culture had become more consumeristic and hedonistic (Hall et al., 2013; Winlow, 2001; Winlow & Hall, 2006), so too had young prisoner culture and these cultural imperatives structured prison victimisation.

'Window Warriors,' Verbal Abuse, and Threats

Prisons are often noisy places. Much of that noise is a chorus of domestic activities (e.g. the sound of young men showering), the peculiar features of custodial institutions (doors and gates banging, shutting and being locked or unlocked), leisure activities (music playing from a radio, pool bools being hit, a guitar playing), and the sounds of young men as they come together with each other and with officers—sometimes harmoniously and at other times bumping up against each other, confronting each other and shouting at each other. The sounds of prison life continued even when young men were locked within their cells, creating different sorts of warning signals. Like much of prison life, those sounds were often mundane as young men continued conversations out of windows. Such verbal exchanges allowed news and gossip to spread (e.g. who had just arrived, who was being moved, where the search team were), and deals to be arranged. Even when physically separated, though, young men would goad, test, accuse, humiliate and manipulate others with the effect that many were unable to drop their 'defensive postures' (c.f. Jewkes & Laws, 2021).

Verbal abuse included insults, racist slurs, and labels that signalled contempt and were associated with the violation of prison social norms, including 'nonces,'[6] 'nerds,'[7] and 'snitches.'[8] It also included direct challenges to someone's authenticity and criminal credentials. For example, Martin noted some young men were accusing others of 'dirty charges,' but added that they were:

> Just talking shit, and that, through the doors. Trying to say people are in on a rape charge, trying to get you in trouble with people, trying to make shit up. It's what people are like in here. Everyone's an instigator and everyone likes to see a fight go off. They all spark stuff.

False accusations were common and formed part of a pattern of verbal abuse that was deliberately designed to test, isolate, and humiliate others. Such accusations needed little evidentiary basis; the label itself was often sufficient to alter another's perceptions of the victim (Edgar et al., 2003: 34). Crucially, once imposed, such labels were difficult to shed but could justify further abuse and victimisation.

Verbal abuse that was directed at mothers, grandmothers or partners was particularly provocative and could lead to beatings, slashings and stabbings (Clemmer, 1940; Edgar et al., 2003; Harvey, 2007; Phillips, 2012a). 'Mums' and 'Nans' were permanently valorised with visible tattoos and remained highly esteemed even by those young men who had stolen from, or hurt, family members. Some young men deliberately antagonised those who had lost a parent to suicide, illness or as part of local authority child protection proceedings. Even as relatively young men, these men were quick to identify sensitive topics and deliberately re-open raw emotional wounds. For example:

---

[6] Those 'not on normal courtyard exercise' and typically sex offenders or those committing offences against children, women, and the elderly.

[7] Those who were seen as inadequate, weak, or unable to socially integrate.

[8] Those informing staff about prisoner affairs and/or wrong doing.

> Some geezer's shouting, mouthing, and that. Saying things about my family, and that. I just went mad, like. I battered him! (Kyle)

> Well, my fiancé passed away like three weeks ago and, basically, I've been having like notes put under by door saying, 'Ha ha your fiancé's dead, I hope you're next. I hope you die of AIDs,' and stuff like that. Basically, pathetic little things but when I'm on the edge, the littlest thing pushes me straight over. (Oliver)

The magnitude of these verbal insults was not just the public exposure and potential embarrassment, but the way in which verbal abuse served to 'provoke and precipitate' (Gilligan, 1996: 112) unwelcome feelings, de-stabilise any sense of 'social and psychological recovery' (Halsey, 2018: 27), and remind young men of events, experiences and losses that they struggled to repress (also see Ellis et al., 2017). When locked in their cells, it was impossible for young men to avoid verbal abuse should it continue beyond what they could bear. They could shout back, but they could not respond physically until they were unlocked, which could be many hours later.

For some, verbal abuse was easily dismissed by some young men as 'nothing' or 'minor'—these young men could be antagonised without being emotionally distressed. For others, there was immediate psychological damage. Verbal abuse could be destructive, especially if it extended to demoralising demands to sing nursery rhymes or infantilising songs (e.g. 'I'm a Barbie girl'). These instances of verbal abuse were designed to 'break the other person's spirit' (Edgar et al., 2003: 33). It was a perverse power play, reinforcing the social hierarchy and the aggressor's elevated position within it. That some young men complied with such requests illustrated something of the fear some young men inspired. Of course, others who were uninvolved in the incident could also hear these exchanges, reinforcing the power of the perpetrators and increasing the 'pliability' of those listening (Toch, 1992b: 202). When the instigators were more than one in number and their identities unknown, this heightened the distress, shame and humiliation (Katz, 1988: 26). In the worst cases, victims were instructed to kill themselves:

> They'll do harsh shit in here. Like, I've heard people shout out of doors, 'Try to kill yourself or I'm going to kill you tomorrow,' and the kid will actually try and kill himself. They found him hanging in his cell. (Harry)

Such behaviour clearly had the potential for catastrophic consequences, especially since prior experience of victimisation is known to elevate suicide risk within prison (also see, for example, Biggam & Power, 1999; Blaauw et al., 2001; Bowker, 1980; Favril et al., 2020; Harris, 2015; Liebling, 1992). However, verbal abuse was rarely taken seriously by prison officers, many of whom simply suggested that they could not possibly identify who was responsible. Yet officers were quick to 'place on report' anyone who threatened or verbally abused them. In many ways, this dismissal of the 'window warriors' was misguided; a more proactive response to the catalysts of violence might have enabled officers to intervene and prevent assaults.

Threats

Threats were common and more frequent than the use of physical violence itself. Threats took a variety of forms: (1) 'coercive threats' (Edgar et al., 2003: 40)—where demands were made to assault an individual, handover property, or to prevent an individual reporting victimisation to prison staff; and, (2) 'retaliatory threats'—where conflict led to threats to assault someone later and/or upload videos to YouTube and other social media sites. Threats were not always verbal but could be written on notes and passed under cell doors, through cell doors or via 'lines' between windows. Young men could also feel threatened when no words were said. Body language, tone of voice, facial expressions, and physical position (e.g. blocking someone's entry or exit) could all express an intent to harm. Calm but assertive demands to 'get off the phone,' serve larger portions of food at the servery, or handover items (e.g. trainers or canteen) could be perceived as threatening if it was assumed that non-compliance would lead to physical violence. Actions such as revealing a weapon, stepping forward to 'square up to the individual,' raising their fists or otherwise 'puffing up' their appearance further evidenced the intentions and capacity of the perpetrator. Thus, threats constitute a 'process in which perceptions and interactions work together to produce behaviour' (Decker & van Winkle, 1996: 21). They were situationally formed based on perceptions of the social setting and individuals within it.

Credible threats could obviate the need for physical violence. Threats were particularly effective in controlling individuals and patterning power relationships. Threats had the obvious advantage of reducing the risk of physical harm; '[t]hreatening violence persuasively is cheaper than resorting to it' (Gambetta, 2009: 78). Like wider criminal culture, the threat of violence not only has a constraining influence, but also served to coerce payments, enforce contracts for illegal enterprises, and consolidate and reinforce membership of criminal groups (Decker & van Winkle, 1996; Marsh, 2020; Pearson & Hobbs, 2003). Threats that were designed to prevent someone from 'grassing' to prison staff had an enduring quality, constraining behaviour many weeks or months after the threat was spoken. If a victim did report their fears to officers or teachers, they were heavily reliant on prison staff to make and keep them safe (and it was typically the victim, not the perpetrator, who was moved). If the threat was sufficient, it reinforced the reputation of the individual issuing the threat. If the warning was not heeded, the person issuing the threat either had to retreat, prove their resolve by putting out a 'contract' on the individuals' head (for a sum of money), rob them, or assault them.

Threats were most effective with prison officers, often inspiring fear, anger, and avoidance behaviour. Officers were threatened at a far greater rate than they were assaulted. Teachers too were not exempt. In one instance, for example, Aran threatened to shoot a teacher with a shotgun—a threat that appeared credible given his prior firearms offences. Some threats were idle and unlikely to eventuate in negative outcomes; in other cases, young men felt little compunction in assaulting prison staff:

> I've got his name in my pad. I wrote it all down. He said that I had threatened him with a flask. I didn't threaten him with a flask I threatened him with my fist. I told him that if he come back to my pad then I would punch him up. (Mark)

It was rare for some of the more vulnerable, least aggressive, and less well socially integrated young men to dare to threaten staff unless they were paid to do so or seeking to repay a debt. Rather, it was typically those young men who were also involved in peer violence that were more likely to assault officers. Once threatened, officers were understandably unwilling to take unnecessary risks, such as unlocking the individual or responding to their cell bell. The threat had a polarising effect, severing the relationship and often leading to disciplinary sanctions. Officers proactively reported any threats made against themselves but were far less committed to 'nicking' prisoners for threatening their peers. Whilst threats were alarming, it was not wholly a surprise that young men sought to negotiate power in this way. Prison officers' attempts to encourage compliant behaviour amongst young men were often based on threats (e.g. 'if you don't do X, you'll be dropped to basic,' 'you'll get a nicking if you do X'). Thus, however inappropriate, young men were responding to the terms prison officers set for their relationships.

Physical Victimisation

Physical victimisation included fights, assaults, and assaults involving weapons. There were at least 1–2 recorded assaults per day, however, these 'official statistics' did not account for the assaults and fights that happened in cells and showers (where there was no CCTV), or the assaults officers failed to see or record. Whilst young men would punch, kick and stamp on each other, weapon use was common. It was atypical for weapons to be appropriated from other areas of the prison or brought into the prison, rather weapons were typically fashioned by inserting objects into socks (e.g. tuna cans) or using items available to them (e.g. attaching a razor blade to a toothbrush). Injuries varied from cuts to black eyes, bruises, bleeding noses, stabbings, slashings, and broken bones. In some cases, the greater injury was to the victim's pride, image, social standing and 'ontological security' (Giddens, 1991). Yet, violence could just as easily bolster a reputation and give the individual 'a name,' deter exploitation and victimisation, be reassuring, generate pride, offer relief, assuage anger, cause economic gain, restore justice, punish perceived or actual wrongdoing, and prove entertaining (also see Chaps. 5 and 8), The prevailing myth is that prison violence is 'disorderly,' but violence could create order by settling power dynamics, resolving a dispute, addressing injustice, or restoring an internal sense of self. Physical violence was therefore both feared and admired, avoided and desired, punished and honoured.

Physical assaults were not all alike. The circumstances could vary significantly and evolve dynamically. Variables such as the number of perpetrators and victims involved, the location of the incident, the use of weapons, how long the incident continued for, the presence of an audience, and whether the assault was filmed all changed the experience, severity, visibility, and impact of the incident. Physical violence may be more or less frequent, more or less visible, involve more than one person, and be more or less severe, but all these things—frequency, severity, complicity and visibility—reflect (and inform) the relational, cultural and environmental context. To all the young people we met, the YOI was perceived to be a turbulent and volatile environment, particularly on Res C and D. It was not uncommon to find these Residential Units to be described as 'the jungle,' 'the lion's den,' 'Beirut,' and 'the war zone.' For example:

> It's a war zone. Fights every single day. Officers getting kettled, hot water thrown over them, getting smacked with pool balls in socks and you just get smacked round the head with them, people make knives. So, they'll get, like, a razor, they'll break it up, get the blade, melt down the end of their knife or their fork and put it in their toothbrush, then when it's gone solid, you've got yourself something to slice someone's face open. It's crazy. That's why I love it over here. (Cory)

Notably the reputation of Res C and D attracted young men such as Cory. Whilst some were keen to avoid those wings, others would prefer them and congregate there with associates, co-defendants, or people whom they had formed an acquaintance within custody.

Violence could validate or confirm masculine credentials, but this was only true if the violence was not seen as 'sly' or cowardly. More experienced young men—particularly those who were comfortable with the use of violence—lamented the absence of 'straighteners' believing that being assaulted from behind or with a weapon was 'unmanly' violence:

> Because these aren't like men in here. They won't fight you face to face. They will see you from behind and wrap a fucking bottle or a brick round the back of your head. I have seen a lad get a brick from bricklaying, put it in a sock and ran up to this kid behind him and hit him three of four times whack whack whack whack with a house brick in a sock. Then I have seen lads getting hit with tuna cans. I have seen people getting hit with a speaker, like the back of it is pretty heavy, sharp. Seen people get hit with that over the head in a sock. People getting hit with mop sticks and that been snapped over their backs. (Joshua)

Contrary to earlier assumptions about the link between the use of violence and the performance of masculinity (Michalski, 2017; Sloan, 2016; Toch, 1998; Sim, 1994), violent assaults in and of themselves were insufficient to prove, validate, or perform 'masculinity.' Rather, assessments of the 'manliness' of individuals were predicated on much finer calculations regarding strength, courage, and competence. The 'sneaky' assaults created a tense, 'edgy' atmosphere:

> The only worries you have got is who is going to jump you. Anywhere where they have got the chance to prove their point and make a mark. That's all it is. Once someone has done that that's it. You have to look behind you. It's not nice. I don't even look behind me on road,[9] when I am at home and that. I don't look behind me because you don't need to. But in here you have to. You feel vulnerable. You don't know who is going to do it but it's going to happen. It's not a nice feeling being on edge. (Jack)

Even for individuals capable of defending themselves, an assault from behind was difficult to defend and could allow others to establish their reputation at their expense. Since these 'Judas assaults' were often to the head, or involved the use of weapons, they also risked more serious injury. Thus, however good their 'anticipatory strategies' (Jones & Schmid, 2000), however well-established their social standing, and however well

[9] 'On road' referred to time in the community, but particularly on the 'streets'.

proven their capabilities, immunity from victimisation was by no means guaranteed.

Violence that occurred between 'pad mates'[10] in a cell could be well hidden and difficult for officers to recognise unless an individual reported such or had obvious bodily injury that they were prepared to explain the causes of. Whilst some would share cells with people they knew (however loosely), others were compelled to share with whomever the prison allocated. Amil, for example, complained about his pad mate:

> It's the littlest things that annoy me, driving me to think things that I shouldn't. My pad mate will sit up all night ripping bits of paper. I don't know if you can imagine how annoying it is to sit there and just hear rip, rip, rip, rip, all night. He just sticks a wallet of envelope down on the side at about 2.00 am in the morning then goes to sleep, and it just makes me feel like I want to pick up the television set and smash it on his head in the middle of the night.

Long periods of time with someone you neither admire nor respect could prove challenging and lead to poorer health and wellbeing (Muirhead et al., 2021). Disagreements and frustrations could build quickly. It was the small things that mattered: quirky habits, theft, disputes over television viewing, controlling the remote control, banging on the pipes, and behaviours that were symptomatic of distress or mental ill health. Prison officers largely expected young men to endure such frustrations and rarely intervened unless serious harm was imminent, but there was always a risk that such intervention could come too late.

Historically prison-based victimisation could only be observed by prisoners and prison staff, but the ability to record, upload and disseminate photographs and videos to social media and internet sites via illicit mobile phones created a new form of public humiliation. These sites (including YouTube, Facebook, Instagram and Twitter) allowed a distant audience (in the U.K. or abroad) to view the victimisation of young prisoners, and then share, 'like,' comment on, and re-distribute to their own networks.

---

[10] The person they share a cell with.

It was 'global humiliation' to an unknown audience. This behaviour was not an everyday occurrence but still an embedded practice. For example:

> This one lad had a phone with a camera on recording, and this one lad cutting [another] lad behind him. I just said leave him alone, you've done enough. And then they started shouting stuff out the window that night and I said, 'Are you going to shut the fuck up because no one likes you, you're a fucking idiot and you're a big bully.' And he was like, 'Why didn't you say that to me earlier?' and I said, 'I'll say it to you in the morning to your face if you want?'
>
> Left it a bit and then the day before he got out, he shouted at me out the window that, 'You're going to be on YouTube in less than 48 hours and your face is getting cut,' and I said, 'Alright I'll send you home with two black eyes you prick.' (Joshua)

Social media and the uploading of video or pictorial content expanded the performative stage in unpredictable and enduring ways. Whilst Goffman describes a 'performance of self' occurring within a highly temporally and spatially bounded region (1969: 106), social media and internet platforms have stretched and disrupted those boundaries in elusive ways. Those who were exposed in and by the footage had 'no control over the future dissemination of the footage. Not only must they 'cope with the effects of the assault, but also the humiliation of the assault being shared over and over again, in a temporal extension of the assault' (Sandberg & Ugelvik, 2016: 1030). The online content could be available indefinitely. It could also be downloaded and saved by consumers of the content. It created 'artefacts' (Hogan, 2010: 384). Producing social content created 'new forms of self-presentation and interaction' (Stuart, 2020: 79). For the victims though, this online content undermined any efforts to present themselves as social successes within the prison. Exposing their peers online reinforced the prison normative code, including how contemptible sex offenders were. This was not accidental behaviour, but intentional and deliberate.

Groups, Not Gangs

During the fieldwork, James and I were periodically asked whether prison bullying and violence was linked to gang activity within the prison. Such questions were understandable for two reasons. First, there has been a tendency in the academic literature to attribute responsibility for prison violence to gang members and associates (Byrne & Hummer, 2007; Delisi et al., 2004; Fleisher & Decker, 2001; Gaes et al., 2002; Pyrooz & Decker, 2019; Winterdyk & Ruddell, 2010; Worrall & Morris, 2012). Typically, such North American scholarship suggests that prison gangs tend to operate with a formal constitution and leadership structure, dominate 'the yard,' control the illicit economy, and provide 'governance institutions' in the absence of 'legal governance' by prison staff (Pyrooz & Decker, 2019; Skarbek, 2014, 2020). There is, however, an 'obvious danger' (Phillips, 2012a: 54) in importing US centric explanations for prison violence into a context that is socially, politically, culturally and physically different—a danger we were particularly alive to.

Second, the interest in the relationship between gang activity and prison violence within the YOI was also a consequence of local legacies. The YOI was located a short distance away from a large Metropolitan city that had, certainly in the 1980s–2000s, been the site of high profile and fatal gun violence between two rival gangs. The murder that would give the two gangs national media attention also led to the imprisonment of four individuals for life (with sentences of 18–24 years). 'Turf wars' and shootings would continue, but in the absence of the 'elders' (many of whom were serving long or life sentences), the two gangs became less cohesive. Splinter groups began to form but without the same sophistication and leadership. Other diffuse and informal street groups gained some reputation, but primarily through the use of social media rather than as more serious criminals (Stuart, 2020; Thapar, 2021).

Within the prison, young men had historically been asked to identify which gang they were affiliated with and separated according to their answer, reinforcing the need to join a gang in order to gain some degree of protection within the prison. This practice had ceased when our research began, but its legacy remained in the minds of some officers who questioned whether such a practice ought to be re-introduced. It was the young men themselves who had the greatest insight into the redundancy of the 'gang' as a simple heuristic for understanding contemporary crime. It was not uncommon for young men who had an identifiable peer group within the community to quickly discredit the gang label. Whilst they admitted being involved with 'guns, knives, robberies, the usual,' they saw these affiliations as a natural consequence of their social proximity and shared experiences growing up in the same neighbourhoods and schools rather than gang behaviour:

> Just people that had grown up in the same area. If you cause a problem, then obviously the problem's going to get, you know, something's going to happen, but as far as, 'Oh, you can't come here because you're from this area,' that didn't happen in my area. So, it wasn't a gang, it was just, like, everyone was just united, innit? Everyone was just close to each other. Like, everyone had everyone's back, innit? (Daniel)

Young men might have been keen to dismiss or minimise their gang affiliations to, for example, avoid more intensive surveillance and civil gang injunctions (Treadwell & Gooch, 2015). However, the durable, highly structured gangs described elsewhere (Pitts, 2008) were not pervasive. Whilst criminal activity could be affiliated with identifiable peer groups, the gang label was easily '[mis]attributed' (Hallsworth & Young, 2008: 180).

Since urban street violence was infrequently related to entrenched gang membership, it was also true that prison violence was rarely connected to gangs. Some young men imported conflicts from the community and would continue to remain antagonistic to those from rival areas or groups (Phillips, 2012a). However, imported conflict more often represented a specific dispute between two individuals rather than representing attempts to reinforce territorial ownership of areas they were geographically divorced from. Equally, these young men were not actively recruiting people to their peer groups and gangs (c.f. Skarbek, 2014). Within the YOI, and like adult prisoners (Crewe, 2009: 319), young men would develop peer groups along shared regional or ethnic identities. Regional and geographic affiliations united young men through a shared history, shared familiarity with specific places, a similar accent, a common and readily understood colloquial language, and—in many cases—prior experience of specific local authority care homes and alternative education settings (e.g. pupil referral units). Connections might also be forged based on shared cultural backgrounds, ethnicity, kinship ties, and other forms of shared identity (e.g. being from a Traveller community). Divisions could form between groups based on little other than being from a different area, and this could contribute to prison violence:

> Sometimes I just fight on my own. When I was on Res D like as a cleaner, and there's about five Manchester kids and they tried to like surround me, and the biggest one come at me like, tried to hit me and I ducked. I banged him and broke his nose and that. We just don't really like the Manchester kids. Like two of them moved on here and we all battered them and got them off the wings. We just don't like them. We get on with the [London lads] and the Scousers. (Paul)

The loyalties forged between men from different localities were susceptible to whim rather than any sort of predictable rules (e.g. the 'London lads' could just as likely be in conflict with the Scousers as they could be in solidarity). If young men were in the minority, they typically felt vulnerable and isolated. Thus, regional affiliations performed both a social role and a crucial psychological security function.

Despite the 'seductive imaginary of prison gangs' (Phillips, 2012b: 135), the gang was therefore a particularly vacuous description of social behaviour and ongoing criminality within the YOI. Like Phillips, we found that there was 'no recognisable equivalent of the US gang' (Phillips, 2012a: 56). The absence of prison gangs in the English context reflects a wider pattern across the adult prison estate (Gooch & Treadwell, 2020, 2021, 2025). Whilst the association between youth gangs and prison violence was (and is) weak, violent assaults committed by multiple assailants were common.

Being 'jumped' by a group of young men could cause serious physical, psychological and social injury. If an assault happened in a cell or shower, the inability to decisively respond was compounded by the lack of space. The odds were most unevenly stacked when weapons were used, either as a threat or as part of the assault, but it was not uncommon to find some severe attacks involving a group of young men stamping on the head or body of the victim. Being 'jumped' was described as 'the worst thing to happen here' and a 'violation.' For example:

> I've already been jumped in here. Some guy ran his mouth, said my girlfriend's a slag, I told them to shut the fuck up, and he didn't like it. He came in my pad, when all my mates were in the pad. Quite funny, that was, he shit himself. He thought he was going to get a good hiding from the six of us in the cell. There was no chatting; he came in, threw all in. He was holding me under an arm, bombing my face with the right arm. I says, 'Do you really want to do this?' He hit me, and I said, 'Do you really want to do this, then?' And at that point, got him! (laughing) I just swished and bombed him in the jaw – and he looked like a twat. All the lads were laughing and joking at him, telling everybody else on the wing that day.
>
> So, his mates from sosh[11] decided they were going to wrap me, at least six of them. I got a broken nose and everything … I still turned around, 'You bunch of pussies didn't even knock me out.' (Harry)

Harry was taken to hospital, and the primary perpetrator and instigator of the conflict subsequently admitted the offence. Harry's experience was not uncommon:

> I had about eight lads run in the pad started booting me, kicking me in the face, jumping on me. Same happened about four days ago, just down there. Had two lads jump in the pad with work boots on. I just covered myself up. And like I've clocked on, I've sat down on the bed and then the next thing I know I've seen his boot just hit me in the face, and then erm, I've sort of dropped. You cover you head more than you cover your body. And then like he's started just jumping on my head, booting me in my ribs. (Daniel)

At the time of the interview, Daniel was anticipating another assault later that day but did not know from whom. In the scenarios above, he had simply curled up and tried to cover himself. At other times he had fought

[11] Prison slang used to refer to 'association,' the period in the day when young men could socialise or use the exercise yards.

back. Some victims had associates who were prepared to 'back them'; others did not have identifiable acquittances whom they could rely on and the effect of the group assault was to render them socially isolated.

Theft and Robbery

Cell theft was largely seen as sly and cowardly, leading victims to question how trustworthy their acquaintances really were. As Peter mentioned: 'You end up not trusting anyone.' Cell theft was largely opportunistic behaviour. Theft was relatively easy and required little direct confrontation with the victim since cell doors were often left unlocked by prison staff when prisoners were showering, cleaning their cells, washing clothes, or collecting their meals. Even those young men like Luke, who were more self-assured, did not risk leaving their cell doors open:

> Even now I know that I can leave my door open and go out onto sosh, but I choose not to. I know these kids won't rob me I know this for a fact but I can't trust them. To leave my door open and hope that everything is there when I come back. I can't do that bruv.

It was often difficult to identify thieves and some victims could consequently feel 'fatalistic about cell theft' (Edgar et al., 2003: 35). This provided fertile ground for malicious allegations. Joel, a trusted prisoner, suggested stealing items from someone you disliked, and planting them in another's cell, was an easy way to sow discord, avenge slights, or create entertainment. He also stated that anyone caught stealing from cells should have their hand slammed in the cell door, because 'that's the way that sort of thing is dealt with,' utterly missing the contradictory nature of his own narrative. Others would punish any thefts with little concern as to whether they had accurately identified the perpetrator—the revenge serving a communicative and symbolic function.

Theft could also be achieved through the misuse of canteen sheets (an A4 menu page of items that can be ordered via the prison), either completing the canteen sheet by hand on behalf of the true owner or modifying their entries after it had been completed. Once the items were delivered to the individual's cell on canteen day (Friday afternoons), the items were seized. For example:

> He used to take my canteen sheets, and because he kept doing it and doing it, he kept thinking he could take drugs and that. And I was listening to it go up £40, £50 and that. I was like, yeah, he'll get a banging now if I was to get off this wing. And I'm saying to myself, he's put me through a lot of shit, he fucking deserves it, boom. (Ollie)

Ollie asked to move wings, and when he did, his pad mate was assaulted because his pad mate inherited the debt. However, the example also illustrates multiple layers of exploitation, and the ways in which victims could seek their own revenge surreptitiously and without directly confronting their aggressor.

Robbery was common. Once only one person could benefit from the theft, there were frequently occasions when groups of young men would surround the victim in the cell or showers. Newcomers were particularly vulnerable to robbery. For example:

> I have robbed people because like I said it's the lads who have the nice pads are the ones that are earning it. That's our circle kind of thing. We won't rob each other. But if someone comes in and they have nice shower gels, we will offer to buy them off them first, but if they don't want to sell then we will rob them. (Adam)

> That happens a lot. They walk in your cell, 'What have you got for me?' 'I've got shit, you bastard. What the fuck are you on about? What have I got for you? I don't even know you! Never spoken to you in my life!' (Harry)

Such robberies were relatively routine, but it was the victim who was blamed for their failure to defend themselves and their property. Whilst 'pad thieves' were generally regarded as repugnant; those who robbed others were not necessarily excluded from positions of status. They may not be afforded respect, or liked, but such behaviour often sent the message to others that the perpetrator was a 'game lad' whereas the victim was simply 'a mug.'

Sexual Victimisation

Sexual assaults were an aberration: rare and noteworthy when they did occur. When asked about sexual assault, most young men were 'almost incredulous that such questions were being asked seriously' (McGurk et al., 2000: 17). James and I were mindful that young men might find it difficult, uncomfortable, or distressing to discuss or report sexual violence (Stevens, 2017). The triangulation of all data, however, led us to the same conclusion. There were no prosecutions, almost a negligible number of recorded incidents in morning meetings, limited intelligence reports referencing a sexual component or assault, only very specific conversations about sexual activity and assault (see below), rare reports in interview, and, almost no patterning in social roles or the prison vernacular. The absence of a prison 'argot' (Sykes, 1958) that reflects widespread coercive sexual activity further illustrated that sexual violence was relatively uncommon (also see O'Donnell, 2004). Consistent with earlier research (Edgar et al., 2003; O'Donnell, 2004), the argot within the YOI referenced sexual offenders whose offences were committed within the community, homosexual and transgender prisoners, but there were no other references to roles that individuals may play in either consensual or non-consensual sexual activity. This contrasts sharply with North American research where the linguistic culture describes forms of coercive and consensual sexual activity (such as 'gorillas,' 'players,' 'fish,' 'booty bandits,' and 'punks'), and men dressing in feminine clothes ('queens') (see, for example, Bartollas et al., 1976a; Donaldson, 2001; Lockwood, 1980; Sykes, 1958; Toch, 1992a). Moreover, the tendency towards group physical violence within the YOI did not lead to group sexual assaults. There were no 'gang rapes' as described by North American prison researchers (Struckman-Johnson et al., 1996).

Few young men feared sexual assault, marking a notable contrast with recorded experiences of North American prisons (Lockwood, 1980). New arrivals quickly realised that televised and cinematic portrayals of prison rape and sexual abuse (typically within North American prisons) bore little relation to the English YOI:

> That old 'drop the soap' rumour is a load of bullshit! It is absolutely the biggest [myth]. I don't know if that happens in man's jails but in YOIs it is never going to happen. It never is. I think that is more of a joke than anything to be honest. (Robert)

Most prisoners believed that being implicated in sexual assault would mark them as homosexual and therefore were keen to distance themselves from such behaviour:

> You get no points for that. (Tyrone)

The infrequency within which sexual victimisation occurred underscores how values, culture, and social relations tightly structured prison victimisation (Lockwood, 1980: 154). In the YOI, sexually assault was dishonourable and disgraceful.

Of the small number of incidents, there were three specific forms of sexual assault that occurred: (1) sadistic serious violence; (2) instrumental and exploitative (including 'spooning' where contraband was forcibly removed from newcomers); and, (3) non-consensual 'sexual favours.' It was the serious, sadistic assault of Jon that was unusual for its brutality and cruelty. Jon had moved to a double cell with Steve. For his part, Steven had been asking for a single cell, or, alternatively, to decide whom he shared with. These demands were given short shrift by the wing officers: 'He will go where we fucking put him.' Jon and Steven were unlikely pad mates. Whilst Jon was shy, slight, and unimposing, Steven was confident, boisterous, and stocky. One officer described Steven as having eyes 'full of malice' and added, 'He is cold. There's nothing behind his eyes.' Steven was drawn from one of the most notorious, deprived, and violent estates in a nearby large Metropolitan city. Convicted of street robbery and involved in community drug dealing, Steven had quickly begun to feature prominently in violent incidents within the prison. Conversely, Jon was serving a short custodial sentence, nearing release, and had less custodial experience. He was easily overlooked during the normal hustle and bustle of the wing. Neither Jon nor Steven was judged 'high risk' for cell sharing, and Jon was moved into Steven's cell on a Friday morning.

Consequently, they would spend many unstructured hours together over the weekend, allowing Steven to establish his power and control.

Steven quickly assumed dominance of the cell. He demanded that they switch beds and at times would force Jon to sleep on the floor. He took possession of the television. He regularly 'teased' Jon, but later in interview would dismiss this as mere play, 'just a joke.' At times he grew incensed that Jon had been 'chatting shit,' 'thinking he is bad' and that Jon had not given him the deference and respect he was owed. Steven took Jon's possessions. The cell was far from 'a place of safety and relaxation' (Sloan, 2016: 95)—Jon was trapped. The persistent, routine, and sometimes violent abuse would culminate in a humiliating sexual assault where part of a broken broomstick was forced into Jon's rectum. Steven had also forcibly tattooed Jon, branding him with his name and physically assaulting him. Sexual victimisation 'seemingly complet[ed]' the physical domination (Johnson et al., 2017: 154), and was exacerbated by Jon's inability to exit the cell. It was days later when, at breaking point, Jon reported the assault to prison officers and revealed the tattoo marks and injuries. Jon was quickly separated from Steven and the matter referred to the police. The police referral did not ultimately end in prosecution or conviction, and after Jon had left the prison, Steven would glory in his assault and joke about it.

Standing idly with the wing cleaners, Steven boasted, 'I owned him, little queer.' 'Why would you fucking do that man, why would you take it?' Steven asked, laughing as he did. Whilst Steven was not homosexual, he found it funny that his former cell mate undeniably was, both in his own eyes and (as Steven assumed) in the eyes of anyone who heard the story. For Steven, the very act of humiliating and emasculating his victim was a source of entertainment. He appeared to derive a degree of pleasure from the physical and sexual violence. It was not an act 'done simply to relieve sexual frustration' (c.f. Bartollas et al., 1976a: 261), but an act of physical intimidation reproducing 'men's domination of women in the social world behind the walls' (Sabo, 2001: 64). Steven was unashamed; it was 'better to be hard than soft in prison' (Sabo, 2001: 64) and to Steven's mind, this was further proof that he was hard and manly. To others, the incident, and Steven's retelling, confirmed his reputation as someone who was viscous and not to be 'fucked with.' He was feared and avoided by some, but largely continued good relations with the more senior young men on the landings. Of course, the vernacular of being 'hard' and someone who should not be 'fucked with' had obvious sexual connotations (also see Sabo, 2001), but rather than suggesting that Steven was homosexual—something that was culturally 'taboo'—the incident was 'psychologically heterosexual' (Donaldson, 2001: 125). Somewhat bizarrely, Steven did not consider himself—and did not appear to be considered by the wing cleaners and servery workers—as someone who might be guilty of a sexual offence and did not 'incur the stigma that such an offence would attract if perpetuated outside the walls' (O'Donnell, 2004: 241).

Bullying

Prison bullying has been described as an 'endemic' in young offender institutions (Dyson et al., 1997; Her Majesty's Inspectorate of Prisons, 1997), and in their predecessor Borstals, Detention Centres and Youth Custody Centres (McGurk & McDougall, 1991). Not only is bullying associated with physical, emotional, social, and psychological harm (Ireland, 2002a; Ireland & Qualter, 2008), but it is also a contributory factor in self-harm, suicide ideation, suicide attempts and self-inflicted deaths (Blaauw et al., 2001; Harris, 2015; Prison and Probation Ombudsman, 2011, 2013, 2014). However, the term 'prison bullying' has been developed and applied without precision and with insufficient empirical grounding.

As a concept, prison bullying is largely a construct of psychological research and was not 'discovered' until the 1990s. Until then, the term was loosely used to describe a diverse range of behaviours including: initiation ceremonies, verbal harassment, demands to perform humiliating and demeaning acts (e.g. drinking urine), sexual assault, shaving intimate areas, physical beatings, shoving, pushing, 'taxing' (taking items) and 'baroning' (charging high rates of interest for borrowed items) (Beck, 1995; Dyson et al., 1997; Ireland, 2005; McGurk & McDougall, 1991). However, it is difficult to establish the relative presence of bullying in these studies since distinctions between single and repeated acts are not clearcut. To confuse matters further, North American scholars prefer the term 'victimisation' to describe consistent predatory behaviour (see, for example, Bartollas et al., 1976b; Maitland & Sluder, 1998; Mutchnick & Fawcett, 1991). It was only in response to the burgeoning interest in school-based research that both British prison scholars (Beck, 1995; Connell & Farrington, 1997; Dyson et al., 1997; Ireland, 2000) and the English and Welsh Prison Service developed prison-based definitions and strategies (Ireland, 2002a).

Bullying is a slippery concept, partly because the very behaviour that can form part of a bullying relationship can occur independently of it. For example, bullying may include theft, robbery, assault, verbal abuse, threats or seemingly low-level taunts and aggressive behaviour (including giving smaller portions of food or denying access to the pool table). However, the presence of such behaviour does not automatically signify a bullying relationship. Her Majesty's Prison Service (2004) originally opted for a relatively clear and concise definition:

> Conduct motivated by a desire to hurt, threaten or frighten someone. It can be physical, verbal, psychological, emotional or economical and often very subtle. It is usually repeated behaviour, unprovoked and intended to cause fear or harm to the victim. Bullying cannot be mutual: it always involves a power imbalance. This distinguishes bullying from fights and assaults.

The definition retains three distinguishing elements of bullying: (1) intention; (2) persistence (i.e. the behaviour should continue over time); and, (3) an imbalance of power. Taken together, these three elements distinguish bullying from victimisation more generally and violence more specifically, neither of which require all three elements to be present. However, the Prison Service definition has flaws—a problem that may stem from the fact that anti-bullying strategies 'evolved in conjunction with the literature' (Ireland, 2002a: xv) rather than in response to it.

Quite what constitutes sufficient frequency is difficult to meaningfully establish, leading to seemingly arbitrary suggestions such as a minimum of weekly incidents (Connell & Farrington, 1996; Ireland, 2002b). This problem has prompted some to refer to the presence of fear rather than frequency or actual incidence (Ireland, 2005), but this risks encapsulating large numbers of individuals who have experienced no direct or indirect harm. The reference to 'unprovoked' aggression in the Prison Service definition is problematic given the overlap between perpetrator and victims, the mutuality of some victimisation, and the ways a victim may contribute to their own victimisation (e.g. by misjudging whom they had aimed verbal abuse, threats or physical violence at) (see Edgar & O'Donnell, 1998). The more problematic efforts to define bullying arise from efforts to unduly widen the definition to acts that are better described as victimisation rather than bullying. For example, Ireland (2002a) suggests that bullying could be accidental. I disagree and found no evidence of 'accidental' bullying with the YOI. Generally, those who could be described as bullying others knew that what they were doing was harmful, even if they were disinclined to use the term bullying.

There was very 'little consensus' (Edgar et al., 2003: 56) amongst prison officers or young prisoners regarding the true definition of bullying. It was universally agreed that bullying happened, but no one could agree on who was involved or what bullying entailed. Any such discussions quickly slipped into descriptions of other forms of victimisation that occurred independently of a bullying relationship (e.g. retribution for non-repayment of debt). It was often implied that there was a repetitive element to such behaviour. However, it was sometimes difficult for officers to evidence the persistence of such behaviour even if they were broadly aware that an individual might be repeatedly targeting certain young men. Officers were primarily concerned about assaults and security breaches, and often lacked the time to forensically assess seemingly disparate incidents and/or accurately identify the bullies.

The only element with which there appeared to be any agreement amongst officers and young men on what constituted bullying was its psychological impact. This was believed to be the primary purpose of bullying and introduced a subtlety to the behaviour that could be easily missed if done 'on the sly' or away from an officer's hearing or sight. For example,

> They get constantly reminded: you are a nerd, you are a nerd, you are a nerd. Every single day. It is bad, you know what I mean? Like some of the

> things people do like walking past someone and barging them out of the way, or taking his cake, or if he is on the pool table taking his pool cue and telling him to sit down and telling him how shitty his trainers are or whatever. Just to reinforce that you are down there. You are a nerd so we will treat you as such. Just to reinforce that you are down there. (Tyrone)

Undoubtedly, there were some young men who were relentlessly targeted by the same individual and/or group of individuals. When it did occur, bullying reinforced the lowliness of the victim's position and sought to break their will and resolve. The purpose was to 'make people feel small' and 'break them down until he reaches breaking point.' If the victim believed that perpetrators would make good on threats to assault them if they 'grassed,' victims could quickly feel that they had no recourse to support and no avenue of escape. It was this coupling of psychological harm and social isolation that appeared most likely to increase distress and could become especially heightened if the victim was already burdened by feelings of shame, regret, guilt, low self-worth, rejection, and hopelessness (as some were).

Conclusion

Official statistics are merely the 'tip of the iceberg' (Thapar, 2021) in terms of the everyday experience of prison victimisation and the ways in which victimisation punctuates and structures the routines of everyday prison life. Threats, demands, verbal abuse, theft, robbery, extortion, 'bullying' (for want of a better term) and coercion are all excluded from the Ministry of Justice data, but constituted distinct forms of harm and became the backdrop against which physical and sexual violence occurred. Thus, the 'dark figure' of prison victimisation is not only explained by individuals declining to report victimisation or prison staff choosing not to record (Byrne & Hummer, 2008; Cooley, 1993) but the structural omissions that mean a significant number of incidents are deliberately omitted from statistical data.

This chapter has shown that two common conceptions of youth prison violence lack empirical weight. First, youth prison violence is not gang violence. Group assaults did occur, but they were not gang assaults. This illustrates the fallacies of importing findings from North American research into the English and Welsh context. If there was any connection with harmful group behaviour and criminal network, it was much more closely linked to the illicit economy and to 'crime that was organised' (Reuter, 1983; Schelling, 1971)—a theme explored in Chap. 4. The danger of the gang mythology is that erroneous 'evidence' becomes the basis of Government discourse and policy making (see, for example, Ministry of Justice, 2016), including decisions to 'transform the management of young adult custody' (Ministry of Justice, 2013) or to attribute increases in prison violence to 'gangs' where no such evidence supports that assertion.

Second, it is often assumed that bullying is frequent and systemic within YOIs. However, in practice, it was almost impossible to identify bullying that met the Prison Service definition. This is not because the definition needs revising, or because young men did not engage in behaviours that constitute bullying—such as verbal abuse, relentless humiliation, violence, sexual assault, theft, robbery, extortion—but because there was considerable fluidity to such behaviour. Some young men were victimised by the same individual(s) consistently over time, but prison victimisation was often far more dynamic. Timelines were difficult to establish. Moreover, once someone was perceived to be a 'victim,' their sustained victimisation may be at the hands of a changing group of people. I therefore echo Edgar et al.'s observation (2003: 60) that:

> The problem here is not that a more precise definition of bullying is required. Rather, because bullying is susceptible to diverse interpretations, it is an unreliable concept for characterising a range of harmful behaviours between prison inmates.

It is notable that the bullying descriptor often falls away in adult prisons. This is not because the behaviours in adult prisons are different—adult prisoners also verbally abuse, exploit, threaten, exclude, and assault others. That young men did not see their behaviour as bullying was partly borne out of a desire to avoid additional surveillance, the loss in social esteem and forfeiture of freedoms that such labels attracted, and partly borne out of a resistance to their infantilisation. Those who might be regarded as bullies were keen to distance themselves from school like behaviour—as the terms implies and is often understood—and define themselves men who prized 'toughness,' courage, bravery, and strength, and had little time for fragility and frailty. The 'logic' of violence is explored in terms of the economic imperatives (Chap. 4), its social value (Chap. 5), its relationship to life-course (Chaps. 6 and 7), and moral rationality (Chaps. 8 and 9).

References

Bartollas, C., Miller, S. J., & Dinitz, S. (1976a). The exploitation matrix in a juvenile institution. *International Journal of Criminology and Penology, 4*, 257–270.

Bartollas, C., Miller, S. J., & Dinitz, S. (1976b). *Juvenile victimisation—The institutional paradox*. Halstead Press.

Beck, G. (1995). Bullying among young offenders in custody. *Issues in Criminological & Legal Psychology, 22*, 54–70.

Biggam, F. H., & Power, K. G. (1999). A comparison of the problem-solving abilities and psychological distress of suicidal, bullied, and protected prisoners. *Criminal Justice and Behavior, 26*(2), 196–216.

Blaauw, E., Winkel, F. W., & Kerkhof, A. J. F. M. (2001). Bullying and suicidal behavior in jails. *Criminal Justice and Behavior, 28*(3), 279–299.

Bottoms, A. E. (1999). Interpersonal violence and social order in prisons. *Crime and Justice, 26*, 205–281.

Bowker, L. H. (1980). *Prison victimisation*. Elsevier.

Byrne, J. M., & Hummer, D. (2007). Myths and realities of prison violence: A review of the evidence. *Victims & Offenders, 2*(1), 77–90.

Byrne, J. M., & Hummer, D. (2008). The nature and extent of prison violence. In J. M. Byrne, D. Hummer, & F. S. Taxman (Eds.), *The culture of prison violence* (pp. 12–25). Pearson Education.

Carrabine, E. (2003). *Power, discourse and resistance*. Ashgate.

Clemmer, D. (1940). *The prison community*. Holt, Reinhart and Winston.

Connell, A. E., & Farrington, D. P. (1996). Bullying among incarcerated young offenders: Developing an interview schedule and some preliminary results. *Journal of Adolescence, 19*(1), 75–93.

Connell, A., & Farrington, D. P. (1997). The reliability and validity of resident, staff and peer reports of bullying in young offender institutions. *Psychology, Crime & Law, 3*(4), 287–300.

Cooley, D. (1993). Criminal victimization in male federal prisons. *Canadian Journal of Criminology, 35*(4), 479–495.

Crewe, B. (2009). *Prisoner society: Power, adaptation and social life in an English prison*. Oxford University Press.

Decker, S. H., & van Winkle, B. (1996). *Life in the gang*. Cambridge University Press.

Delisi, M., Berg, M. T., & Hochstetler, A. (2004). Gang members, career criminals and prison violence: Further specification of the importation model of inmate behavior. *Criminal Justice Studies, 17*(4), 369–383.

Donaldson, S. (2001). A million jockers, punks, and queens. In D. Sabo, T. A. Kupers, & W. London (Eds.), *Prison masculinities* (pp. 118–126). Temple University Press.

Dyson, G. P., Power, K. G., & Wozniak, E. (1997). Problems with using official records from Young offender institutions as indices of bullying. *International Journal of Offender Therapy and Comparative Criminology, 41*(2), 121–138.

Edgar, K., & O'Donnell, I. (1998). Assault in prison: The 'victim's' contribution. *British Journal of Criminology, 38*(4), 635–650.

Edgar, K., O'Donnell, I., & Martin, C. (2003). *Prison violence: The dynamics of conflict, fear and power*. Willan.

Ellis, A., Winlow, S., & Hall, S. (2017). 'Throughout my life I've had people walk all over me': Trauma in the lives of violent men. *The Sociological Review, 65*(4), 699–713.

Favril, L., Yu, R., Hawton, K., & Fazel, S. (2020). Risk factors for self-harm in prison: A systematic review and meta-analysis. *The Lancet Psychiatry, 7*(8), 682–691.

Fleisher, M. S., & Decker, S. H. (2001). An overview of the challenges of prison gangs. *Corrections Management Quarterly, 5*(1), 1–9.

Gaes, G. G., Wallace, S., Gilman, E., Klein-Saffran, J., & Suppa, S. (2002). The influence of prison gang affiliation on violence and other prison misconduct. *The Prison Journal, 82*(3), 359–385.

Gambetta, D. (2009). *Codes of the underworld: How criminals communicate*. Princeton University Press.

Giddens, A. (1991). *Modernity and self-identity: Self and society in the modern age*. Polity Press.

Gilligan, J. (1996). *Violence: Reflections on our deadliest epidemic.* G.P. Putnam's Sons.
Goffman, E. (1969). *The Presentation of self in everyday life.* The Penguin Books.
Gooch, K., & Treadwell, J. (2020). Prisoner Society in an era of psychoactive substances, organized crime, new drug markets and austerity. *The British Journal of Criminology, 60*(5), 1260–1281.
Gooch, K., & Treadwell, J. (2021). 'It doesn't stop at the prison gate': Understanding organised crime in prison. *Prison Service Journal, 252*, 15–30.
Gooch, K., & Treadwell, J. (2025). The prison firm: The 'transportation' of organised crime, the evolution of criminal markets and contemporary prisoner society. *Criminology and Criminal Justice, 25*(1), 245–264.
Hall, S., Winlow, S., & Ancrum, C. (2013). *Criminal identities and consumer culture.* Willan.
Hallsworth, S., & Young, T. (2008). Gang talk and gang talkers: A critique. *Crime, Media, Culture: An International Journal, 4*(2), 175–195.
Halsey, M. (2018). Child victims as adult offenders: Foregrounding the criminogenic effects of (unresolved) trauma and loss. *British Journal of Criminology, 58*(1), 17–36.
Harris, L. (2015). *Changing prisons, saving lives: Report of the independent review into self-inflicted deaths in custody of 18–24 year olds, Cm 9087.* Her Majesty's Stationery Office.
Harvey, J. (2007). *Young men in prison: Surviving and adapting to life inside.* Willan Publishing.
Her Majesty's Inspectorate of Prisons. (1997). *Young prisoners.* Her Majesty's Prison Service.
Her Majesty's Prison Service. (2004). *Violence reduction: Prison service order 2750.* Her Majesty's Prison Service.
Hogan, B. (2010). The presentation of self in the age of social media: Distinguishing performances and exhibitions online. *Bulletin of Science, Technology & Society, 30*(6), 377–386.
House of Commons Justice Committee. (2016). *The treatment of young adults in the criminal justice system.* House of Commons Justice Committee.
Ireland, J. L. (2000). Bullying among prisoners: A review of the research. *Aggression and Violent Behavior, 5*(2), 201–215.
Ireland, J. L. (2002a). *Bullying among prisoners: Evidence, research and intervention strategies.* Brunner-Routledge.
Ireland, J. L. (2002b). Social self-esteem and self-reported bullying behaviour among adult prisoners. *Aggressive Behavior, 28*(3), 184–197.

Ireland, J. L. (2005). Bullying among prisoners: The need for innovation. In J. L. Ireland (Ed.), *Bullying among prisoners: Innovations in theory and research* (pp. 3–23). Willan.

Ireland, J. L., & Qualter, P. (2008). Bullying and social and emotional loneliness in a sample of adult male prisoners. *International Journal of Law and Psychiatry, 31*(1), 19–29.

Jewkes, Y., & Laws, B. (2021). Liminality revisited: Mapping the emotional adaptations of women in carceral space. *Punishment & Society, 23*(3), 394–412.

Johnson, R., Roucheleau, A. M., Martin, A. B., Cullen, F. T., & Liebling, A. (2017). *Hard time: A fresh look at understanding and reforming the prison.* Wiley-Blackwell.

Jones, R. S., & Schmid, T. J. (2000). *Doing time: Prison experience and identity among first-time inmates.* Jai Press.

Katz, J. (1988). *Seductions of crime: A chilling exploration of the criminal mind from juvenile delinquency to cold-blooded murder.* Basic Books.

Liebling, A. (1992). *Suicides in prison.* Routledge.

Lockwood, D. (1980). *Prison sexual violence.* Elsevier.

Maitland, A. S., & Sluder, R. D. (1998). Victimization and youthful prison inmates: An empirical analysis. *The Prison Journal, 78*(1), 55–73.

Marsh, B. (2020). *The logic of violence: An ethnography of Dublin's illegal drug trade.* Routledge.

McGurk, B. J., & McDougall, C. (1991). The prevention of bullying among incarcerated delinquents. In P. K. Smith & D. Thompson (Eds.), *Practical approaches to bullying* (pp. 130–139). Fulton.

McGurk, B. J., Forde, R., & Barnes, A. (2000). *Sexual victimisation among 15–17 year old offenders in prison* (RDS occasional paper 65). Home Office.

McVicar, J. (1972). Postscript. In S. Cohen & L. Taylor (Eds.), *Psychological survival* (pp. 221–229). Penguin.

Michalski, J. H. (2017). Status hierarchies and hegemonic masculinity: A general theory of prison violence. *British Journal of Criminology, 57*(1), 40–60.

Ministry of Justice. (2013). *Transforming the management of young adults in custody.* Ministry of Justice.

Ministry of Justice. (2016). *Prison safety and reform, Cm 9350.* Ministry of Justice.

Ministry of Justice. (2025). *Safety in custody statistics: Quarterly update to September 2024.* Ministry of Justice.

Muirhead, A., Butler, M., & Davidson, G. (2021). Behind closed doors: An exploration of cell-sharing and its relationship with wellbeing. *European Journal of Criminology, 20*(1), 335–355.

Mutchnick, R. J., & Fawcett, M. (1991). Group home environments and victimization of resident juveniles. *International Journal of Offender Therapy and Comparative Criminology, 35*(2), 126–142.

O'Donnell, I. (2004). Prison rape in context. *British Journal of Criminology, 44*(2), 241–255.

O'Donnell, I., & Edgar, K. (1998). Routine victimisation in prisons. *The Howard Journal of Criminal Justice, 37*(3), 266–279.

O'Donnell, I., & Edgar, K. (1999). Fear in prison. *The Prison Journal, 79*(1), 90–99.

Pearson, G., & Hobbs, D. (2003). King pin? A case study of a middle market drug broker. *The Howard Journal of Criminal Justice, 42*(4), 335–347.

Phillips, C. (2012a). 'It ain't nothing like America with the bloods and the crips': Gang narratives inside two English prisons. *Punishment & Society, 14*(1), 51–68.

Phillips, C. (2012b). *The multicultural prison: Ethnicity, masculinity and social relations among prisoners*. Oxford University Press.

Pitts, J. (2008). *Reluctant gangsters: The changing face of youth crime*. Cullompton Willan Publishing.

Prison and Probation Ombudsman. (2011). *Learning from PPO investigations: Violence reduction, bullying and safety*. Prison and Probation Ombudsman.

Prison and Probation Ombudsman. (2013). *Learning lessons bulletin: Child deaths*. Prison and Probation Ombudsman.

Prison and Probation Ombudsman. (2014). *Learning lessons bulletin: Young adult prisoners*. Prison and Probation Ombudsman.

Pyrooz, D. C., & Decker, S. H. (2019). *Competing for control: Gangs and the social order of prisons*. Cambridge University Press.

Reuter, P. (1983). *Disorganized crime: The economics of visible hand*. MIT Press.

Sabo, D. (2001). Doing time, doing masculinity: Sports and prison. In D. Sabo, T. A. Kupers, & W. London (Eds.), *Prison masculinities* (pp. 61–66). Temple University Press.

Sandberg, S., & Ugelvik, T. (2016). Why do offenders tape their crimes? Crime and punishment in the age of the selfie. *British Journal of Criminology, 57*(5), 1023–1040.

Schelling, T. C. (1971). What is the business of organized crime? *The American Scholar, 40*(4), 643–652.

Sim, J. (1994). Tougher than the rest? Men in prison. In T. Newburn & E. A. Stanko (Eds.), *Just boys doing business? Men, masculinities and crime* (pp. 100–177). Routledge.

Skarbek, D. (2014). *The social order of the underworld: How prison gangs govern the American penal system*. Oxford University Press.

Skarbek, D. (2020). *The puzzle of prison order: Why life behind bars varies across the world*. Oxford University Press.

Sloan, J. (2016). *Masculinities and the adult male prison experience*. Palgrave Macmillan.

Stevens, A. (2017). Sexual activity in British men's prisons: A culture of denial. *British Journal of Criminology, 57*(6), 1379–1397.

Struckman-Johnson, C., Struckman-Johnson, D., Rucker, L., Bumby, K., & Donaldson, S. (1996). Sexual coercion reported by men and women in prison. *The Journal of Sex Research, 33*(1), 67–76.

Stuart, F. (2020). *Ballad of the bullet: Gangs, drill music and the Power of online infamy*. Princeton University Press.

Sykes, G. (1958). *The society of captives*. Princeton University Press.

Thapar, C. (2021). *Cut short: Youth violence, loss and hope in the city*. Viking.

Toch, H. (1992a). *Mosaic of despair: Human breakdown in prison*. American Psychological Association.

Toch, H. (1992b). *Violent men: An inquiry into the psychology of violence*. Penguin.

Toch, H. (1997). *Corrections: A humanistic approach*. Harrow and Heston.

Toch, H. (1998). Hypermasculinity and prison violence. In L. H. Bowker (Ed.), *Masculinities and crime* (pp. 168–178). Sage.

Treadwell, J., & Gooch, K. (2015). An ASBO for violent gangsters or just continuing criminalisation of young people? Thinking about the value of "Gangbo". *British Society of Criminology Conference*, 60–76. Papers from the British Society of Criminology Conference.

Winlow, S. (2001). *Badfellas: Crime, tradition and new masculinities*. Berg.

Winlow, S., & Hall, S. (2006). *Violent night: Urban leisure and contemporary culture*. Berg.

Winterdyk, J., & Ruddell, R. (2010). Managing prison gangs: Results from a survey of U.S. prison systems. *Journal of Criminal Justice, 38*(4), 730–736.

Worrall, J. L., & Morris, R. G. (2012). Prison gang integration and inmate violence. *Journal of Criminal Justice, 40*(5), 425–432.

4

'Grafting': Debt, Drugs, the Illicit Economy, and Prison Victimisation

As I stood near the cell door that was now flung wide open, Luke—or 'Risky' as I knew him—sat opposite us on a plastic chair, his back pressed against the cell wall. The cell curtains were drawn, creating shadows reflective of his sullen mood. At over six-foot-tall, his long limbs stretched out, overtaking the cell. Luke was both physically large and socially dominant. However, this 'King of the Wing' would shortly be unceremoniously dethroned. James and I had entered the wing just moments before, and we were quickly met with the enthusiastic invitation from Dave, the Supervising Officer, 'You need to see this!' He ushered us to follow him, his body worn camera already recording. As we obediently followed, he turned to announce, by way of explanation: 'We are breaking up the bullying ring!'

Earlier that morning, Dave had informed Luke and two others that they would be relocating to other wings. Two large trollies lined the 'spur'[1] in preparation, already overflowing with several bags of property owned by two other young men. 'Operation Shutdown'—as it had been dubbed by the young men—had begun. Luke had been deliberately left until last. Unusually, no one was showering or using the exercise yard.

[1] An expression used to describe a corridor of cells typically ending in a central space connected to other spurs.

K. Gooch, *Prison Violence*, Palgrave Studies in Prisons and Penology,
https://doi.org/10.1007/978-3-031-91365-5_4

Only one person was unlocked to clean, but he was maintaining a safe distance from Luke's cell, stealthily moving down the spurs to quietly whisper updates through the cracks in the cell doors. Shifting between cells, mop in hand, he was making no efforts to clean the floor or remove the litter. Both the prison officers and young men were waiting to see how Luke would react to this unexpected and unwelcome interruption to his business and social life.

Officers were keenly aware that other young men were lining up on 'canteen day' (Fridays) to repay Luke or deliver the demanded items. However, Luke was undeterred by the removal of his television or the threat of segregation, and simply resisted any attempt by officers to encourage or cajole him into desisting from his nefarious activities. He had spent much of his sentence on 'Basic regime,'[2] and was disinclined to engage in work that he found unappealing:

> Everyone needs a source of income whether it's legal or illegal; everyone needs a source of income. I haven't got time to be sitting on my ass with no money like a bum. And if no one is going to offer me the legal way.
>
> People haven't got anything to lose. The only thing you have to lose is your TV and most people don't care about their TV. Sometimes I sit in my cell with my TV off. I would rather read a book, write some music, read a magazine, than sit there and watch the TV.

Unable to access 'legal' money, Luke turned to 'grafting' on the wing—from which there was little to lose and much to gain. Luke pressured and threatened others on the wing to handover items, 'quadrupling people's debts' if necessary (even whilst spending long periods of time in his cell). He regularly demanded 'rent' from those young men whom he regarded as weak, inferior, or guilty of transgressing certain norms (such as being homosexual, effeminate, transgender, or a sex offender). 'Added days'[3] for

[2] The lowest level of the 'Incentives and Earned Privilege Scheme', a policy that set out the 'rewards' to which young men were entitled, including details such as how much association time they could have (free time out of cell), how much money they could spend, and whether they could have a television in their cells.

[3] For more serious breaches of Prison/YOI Rules and the criminal law, the Independent Adjudicator (a District Judge) may require a prisoner to serve additional time in prison, to a maximum of 42 days per infraction.

assaults within prison had already been added to the end of Luke's sentence but had seemingly done little to deter further victimisation at Luke's hand. Operation Shutdown was finally initiated when two young men found the courage to name Luke and four others (spread across two wings) for victimising them. All five perpetrators were being separated and dispersed across the prison.

James and I had previously met Luke many times. Normally, we enjoyed easy conversation with him, but on this occasion, we were met with stony silence. Barely concealed anger tightened across Luke's facial muscles and clenched jaw. He was visibly weighing up whether this was a battle worth fighting—whether his verbal protest was sufficient or whether he should take the opportunity to express his frustration with physical force. It was difficult to determine how much our presence was mitigating the likelihood of violent protest, but it was clear that Dave hoped that we would serve that function, relying on our social capital with Luke to avoid a staff assault or damage to the cell.

'This is very inconvenient for me,' Luke finally announced, allowing a large clear plastic bag to hang limply from his grasp. He scanned the officer's faces for any sign that his protest was proving persuasive. 'Why would I need to bully?' he continued. When this did not dissuade the officers, he escalated to implied threats: 'You don't want me smashing up my cell!' When threats failed, he then demanded evidence. Irrespective of his obvious rule violations, he expected and demanded due process. Justice was not only demanded by the innocent, but also the guilty. 'Stitch ups' were still 'stitch ups' even if officers' 'gut' decisions about guilt were not necessarily incorrect. Officers were unwilling to offer any details regarding the reports or intelligence that prompted transfers and interventions—often in the name of protecting the informant whom they rightly feared would be physically punished if their 'snitching' became obvious. No answers were given to Luke. He and Dave both implicitly understood that this was a fait accompli irrespective of any investigation that might occur (but did not in fact materialise).

Luke made no effort to move or fill the bag with the contents of his cell. Dave was, however, unmoved and undeterred. The proceeds of Luke's illicit activity were proudly displayed. At a quick count, the cell contained rows of shower gel (in equal quantities of 12 blue, 12 green and 12 cream shower gels), cereals, milk cartons, noodles, cleaning supplies, slippers, two extra pairs of trainers, a television, a PlayStation, a rug, an Arsenal bed cover and an Arsenal toilet seat cover. This was a stark contrast to the neighbouring empty cells that were barely softened by thin green prison curtains and with few if any supplies of food or toiletries. Luke had done all he could do ensure that he was 'living comfortably.' Staff had little interest in whether the property concealed contraband and no search occurred of the cell or property therein—the sole focus was to move Luke from one wing to another. Eventually, when his complaints, protestations, and angry threats proved futile, he slowly packed his bags. Six bags of property, each about two feet tall, would later be dragged from the cell; an amount far exceeding what was permitted under 'volumetric control'[4] rules.

His possessions now packed, Luke sat down, crossed his arms, glared at the officers, and refused to move. A stand-off ensued. Tom, the gym orderly and another young man also identified for a move, were utterly bemused by Operation Shutdown and now forcefully voiced their protestations and demands for evidence from behind their cell doors. The silence quickly replaced with thudding, banging, and shouting. Officers tried to reassure them that if the claims proved to be untrue, then they would be moved back to the wing. These promises were hollow, but briefly appeased the young men. Luke, however, said nothing. Rather than negotiate, officers suggested that Luke should take the lunch period to 'consider his next move,' sensibly de-escalating the situation and creating an opportunity for Luke to comply with their request whilst still 'saving face.' Later that afternoon, Luke was 'blocked off' having finally agreed to move to the CSU (segregation unit). The move was of such significance, that the Deputy Governor would accompany the officers in escorting Luke to the CSU. It was yet another example of just how a conflict that could have easily escalated to a staff assault could be resolved. In this case, the balance was tipped by skilful prison officer work but also the reality that Luke knew he would be fighting a pointless battle. Whatever he did, the outcome would still be the same: he would be

[4] A policy that specifies how much property and what kinds of property a prisoner can keep within their cells. Traditionally, the contents of their cell were required to fit within two property boxes.

sitting in segregation and would not be returning to that wing. He had no bargaining power. He could resist, but not overcome.

This example illustrates two important themes that are further developed in this chapter. First, victimisation was intimately connected with the prison illicit economy—something that has been significantly overlooked in previous studies of prison violence and victimisation, despite Sykes's (1958) early conceptualisation of the 'deprivation of material goods and services' as one of the five universal pains of imprisonment. To date, the illicit economy in English and Welsh prisons has largely been treated as a peripheral aspect of prison life (see as notable exceptions, Crewe, 2009; Kalinich, 1980; Sparks et al., 1996). This is less a criticism of earlier research than a recognition of how prison life has evolved. Sparks et al. (1996) allude to just such a possibility when discussing indebtedness amongst prisoners in the 1980's. Whilst noting that prisoners could 'get over [their] head' with debts of £20–£30, Sparks et al. found some debts were far larger (in the hundreds of pounds) and that this 'cash economy' was 'inherently likely to expand' (1996: 185–186). As this chapter illustrates, the prison illicit economy has indeed flourished, and the opportunities for pecuniary advantage increased, just as Sparks et al. speculated that it might. This chapter critically analyses the transformation of the drug economy, the emergence of a prison debt economy, and the factors that have increased the appeal and expansion of the prison economy for those who control it and those who rely on it, both inside the prison and out.

Second, the prison has become a key marketplace for criminal entrepreneurs. Thus, Crewe's observation that HMP Wellingborough's informal economy was 'vibrant but relatively limited' (2009: 367) no longer accurately captures prison life in contemporary English and Welsh prisons (also see Gooch & Treadwell, 2020, 2021, 2023, 2025). As Skarbek (2020: 4) argues, 'Surviving prison requires gaining access to necessary resources. Some prisoners overcome this challenge with ease; others fail to do so and suffer, or even perish.' Those who were able to overcome and resist their material impoverishment did so at the expense of others, creating greater social and economic inequalities than those imposed by the State. This chapter not only describes the multiple forms of extortion, exploitation and victimisation connected to the illicit economy, but also sets out a typology of indebtedness, distinguishing between 'convenience debtors,' 'habitual drug debtors,' 'desperate debtors,' 'naïve debtors,' and 'coerced debtors.' The chapter reveals something of the ruthlessness of those controlling the economy. It is argued that the 'violence of enterprise' (Hobbs, 1995) has contributed significantly to the rise in prison violence, primarily because the socially accepted 'terms and conditions' governing the economy are frequently enforced. In this way, the self-governance of the illicit economy by prisoners both stabilises and de-stabilises prison order (c.f. Skarbek, 2014, 2020). Notably, this enforcement extends the scope of 'prison' victimisation well beyond the prison walls.

The Appeal of the Prison Illicit Economy

The illicit economy was the lifeblood of the prison. Prisoners could, depending on their personal resources and 'privilege' level, legitimately order 'canteen' items such as food, writing materials, and tobacco (later, when the prison went 'smoke-free,' e-cigarettes and vapes). Clothing, trainers, CDs and games consoles could be ordered from catalogues, but required sufficient money in their 'spends' account[5] and, for items such as PlayStations, to on 'Enhanced' regime of the Incentives and Earned Privileges Scheme (IEP). This scheme also determined how much a prisoner could spend each week. For example, convicted young men on Enhanced could spend £25.50 each week, those on Standard could spend £15.50 and those on 'Basic' were limited to £4 per week. This was significant because one of the primary payment methods was canteen—items such as food, tobacco (later 'caps' and vapes) and toiletries that could be ordered each week and then used to repay debts, pay for services (e.g. a haircut), repay a gambling debt, barter or trade for more 'exclusive' and highly desired items, such as trainers and T-shirts. Canteen orders were delivered on Friday afternoons with the effect that 'canteen day' (or 'Black Eye Friday') became a peak period for the circulation of goods, for the settling of debts, and, for those who had not repaid their debts, threats and violent assaults.

[5] Prisoners did not have direct access to cash, but money could be transferred to the YOI and added to their 'private spends' account allowing young men to purchase more or higher value items.

The informal economy is illicit in the sense that the exchanging of almost all items is prohibited and typically viewed with suspicion by prison officers. Whilst some kinship or fraternal lending occurred, such altruistic exchanges were relatively rare. Exchanging materials goods was typically accompanied with the expectation of repayment (with interest). The prison economy was also illicit in the sense that it included items that were prohibited by law. Contraband included: drugs, alcohol, weapons, mobile telephones, SIM cards, mobile telephone chargers. Very rarely, alcohol was smuggled into the prison, but it was more common for 'hooch' to be brewed within cells, particularly during the Christmas period. Young men accessed the illicit economy to trade, purchase and broker additional items above the baseline provided by the State. For those without access to financial resources from family and friends, or for those who relied on tobacco (and later e-cigarettes and vapes) and drugs to manage daily life, accessing the illicit economy was often a necessity. In addition, some would pay the wing barber for a haircut or need to settle gambling debts. Essentially, everything in prison had a price.

Although the prison set a benchmark as to the minimum amounts of goods and services that young men could access, economic inequalities prevailed. Prisoners could earn a modest income through employment or educational activities. The most desired and highly paid jobs—cleaners and servery workers—were at the mercy of prison officer discretion. Other jobs that allowed the greatest freedom, such as 'Red Bands,'[6] Recycling work[7] and employment in the community,[8] required (the appearance of) compliant, 'good' behaviour. For most, though, prisoner pay was insufficient, and they relied on financial support from family members. As Steve put it: 'No one relies on the jail for money. If anyone told you they did, they're lying.' The extent to which young men benefitted from, or demanded, financial support from family members, partners, or friends defined the material impoverishment they endured:

[6] 'Red Band' prisoners were permitted greater freedom to walk around the prison and assigned more responsible work or peer support activities. They wore a red band with an ID card around their arms to visibly demonstrate that they had been assessed as suitable for the role and were allowed to enter certain areas.

[7] A number of young men were employed to recycle items, but this was normally regarded as more 'trusted' work.

[8] A small number of young men were released on temporary licence (ROTL) each day to undertake paid work in the community.

> I get them [family members] to send me money, man. I get my missus sending me in, my girl, and that. I make her just send money whenever I need money, but I'm alright. There are people in here that don't even get postal orders, or nothing. I've seen people in here like that. They haven't got money on their canteen. They have, like, £7. That's the jail's money. (Hussain)

The financial burden this placed on loved ones—coupled with the costs of visiting the prison—were considerable (Braman, 2002; Codd, 2008; Comfort, 2008) but was largely overlooked by young men who were primarily focused on their own interest. Whilst some prisoners had several hundred or thousand pounds available to them, some had no financial support. Amil, for example, had been disowned by his parents after marrying a British, white 'girl' whom they disapproved of. The marriage was brief, ending when Amil discovered his wife's affair and seriously assaulted his love rival with a metal bar. He regarded himself as 'socially destroyed' and had no one to turn to for financial assistance:

> If you haven't got any people on the outside to send any money, that's when you're in a hard situation. I mean you're really between a rock and a hard place, and where you're calling in a favour, or, you know you're stealing, or you're borrowing off someone that's going to want it back.

With empathy often lacking, the absence of external financial support was seen as a personal failing rather than a product of circumstances beyond the individual's control, even if the young men shared similar life experiences of disrupted or impoverished family life, estranged or strained relationships and local authority care. Constructions of 'manliness' were predicated on an ability to obtain and retain material goods, which extended beyond meeting basic needs (e.g. sufficient food and clothing) to include desired, stylish, and conspicuously displayed consumer designer goods (clothes, trainers, and soft furnishings). The consumerist culture of the streets (see Hall et al., 2013) was not only reproduced within the custodial context, but the stark deprivation only heightened the importance of possessing and displaying desired consumer items and symbols.

The use of postal orders[9] to send money to loved ones was—to some extent—reviewable by prison staff. Suspicion might be aroused if a young man received a postal order from a known associate or family member of another young man, or from an unusual address. However, the advent of online banking, social media, and mobile banking apps meant that prisoners could circumvent the surveillance of the prison and trade more freely via bank accounts in the community:

> Nowadays, it's all out on the outside. So, it's bank transfers, or it's cash on visits, or it's 'I'll give your family,' and they'll meet up after the visits, or he'll go to his house, collect the money like. (Peter)

The transition to online banking and mobile phone apps created new market opportunities. This was one of two significant factors transforming the appeal of the prison economy and its net worth. Hussain noted:

> You can make a lot of money in jail. People sell phones and everything in jail. A £10 Nokia phone, people sell it for £200 or £250. It's unbelievable. Some people can make more money in jail than they would make on the outside. My mate, he's making, like, £2,000 a week, £1,700 a week, on phones and Mamba,[10] and it's in bank transfers, and all that, you get me?

Using bank accounts greatly reduced the jeopardy of trading since 'following the money' through community bank accounts was (and remains) almost impossible for prison staff and local law enforcement agencies. The geographic spread of the networks sustaining these economic interactions could extend regionally and nationally to other prisons. Bank accounts could be accessed via illicit mobile telephones, but family members, friends, and associates were also involved in the movement of money between accounts. Dealers and creditors approached family members directly (via text or telephone call) to demand payment and/or threatened that their relative would be assaulted should they fail to acquiesce.

[9] Since concluding the research, HM Prison and Probation Service has replaced the use of postal orders with an online system for debit card payments. This has not, however, altered the practice of sending money via bank transfers to community bank accounts.

[10] 'Mamba' is prison slang for psychoactive substances (typically synthetic cannabinoids).

Thus, extraordinary pressure was applied, placing family members in an impossible predicament if they were reluctant or unable to repay. These considerable financial burdens may be coupled with requests to smuggle drugs during a visit—a request family members may interpret 'as a helpful act' (Codd, 2008: 56). Thus, prison victimisation was not just a 'prison problem,' and extended to the intimidation, threats and exploitation of family members outside.

'Mamba,' 'Mamba Muppets,' and 'Mambulances': A Transforming Drug Economy

Freddie is unresponsive. His eyes are rolled back in his head as he lies crumpled up on the cold cell floor. 'Well hasn't he been on the fucking Mamba?' asks the officer loudly, his voice betraying annoyance and frustration. From the door of the cell, James can see that Freddie is convulsing again. Just a few minutes ago, Freddie had waddled back to his cell with his trousers around his ankles and his buttocks exposed. Freddie had been hallucinating and shouting on the wing, much to the entertainment of the onlookers now stood at the cell door and fiercely mocking him. An officer pushes through the laughing young men and calls the cleaner over to the cell. When the convulsions cease, the cleaner pulls up Freddie's grey tracksuit trousers to give him some dignity. Freddie lies still whilst the young men try to push past each other and the officers to peer in. 'Let's film him for YouTube boss,' one shouts only half joking.

'Does he need an ambulance?' asks a second officer. 'Not now,' replies the first officer on scene, 'He is breathing,' he adds. The cleaner is trying to move Freddie, although this proves difficult because Freddie remains unresponsive and his limbs flop as the cleaner tries to lift them. 'Get him into the recovery position,' says the officer to the cleaner, before checking the cleaner has done so correctly. 'His airway is clear,' says the officer, 'He is breathing, fuck it, put him on the bed and we will keep an eye on him.' The other young men shout their (un)helpful suggestions: 'Throw a bucket of water on him.' They are growing impatient having realised that

Freddie's incapacitation will soon limit the officer's availability to deal with their own requests. 'He is fine now,' the officer concludes, 'Leave him in the recovery position and close the door,' the officer instructs the cleaner who does his best to push Freddie on to the blue plastic mattress. 'It [meaning Freddie] fucking stinks of that shit [Mamba],' the officer complains as the cleaner walks past him out of the cell. 'Why the fuck would you get like that?' the cleaner asks the officer. The officer does not answer and locks the door. With Freddie now taken care of, association[11] can continue as normal.

Of all items that can be trafficked into a prison, drugs and drug paraphernalia are by far the most common, accounting for approximately 40% of all seizures (Ministry of Justice, 2025). Drugs first emerged within the prison economy in the 1980s, rapidly becoming a central feature of prison life by the 1990s and a 'major concern' to successive Chief Inspectors of Prisons and Governments (Edgar & O'Donnell, 1998). Prior to our research, though, drug use within prison—as recorded through mandatory drug tests (urine tests)—had gradually declined (Ministry of Justice, 2017), but both the prevalence of prison drug use, and the nature of the drug economy, was about to change—both locally (within the YOI) and nationally. Until the 2010s, heroin and, to a lesser extent, cannabis had dominated the prison drug economy (Crewe, 2005, 2006). However, throughout the 2010s, psychoactive substances (PS)—synthetic cannabinoids typically known as 'Mamba' and 'Spice'—came to dominate the prison drug economy, even as use in the community declined (Office for National Statistics, 2020).

PS entered the prison drug economy seemingly unnoticed. In 2010, there were as few as 15 seizures of psychoactive substances; by July 2014, this number had increased to 436 seizures (Hansard, 2014) precipitating concern about this relatively unknown and non-detectable (what were then) 'legal highs.' By the end of the decade, the number of seizures of NPS had reached 6699—amounting to more than a 400-fold increase in just 10 years (Ministry of Justice, 2025). Since these figures only reflect the number of confiscated items, they are likely to be an underestimate. This

[11] Association is the period when young men could socialise, play pool, make telephone calls and use the exercise yard.

shift to PS surprised practitioners and policy makers. Her Majesty's Inspectorate of Prisons (2015: 9) found that 'the Prison Service and other relevant national bodies have found it difficult to keep pace with and respond to the unprecedented and rapid growth of [PS] use in male prisons.'

At the time of their introduction into prison markets, PS was excluded from the Misuse of Drug Act 1971. This had two key consequences. First, no penalties could be applied to any individuals supplying and/or in possession of PS in prison. Second, prisons could not test for any drugs that were not expressly listed in the Misuse of Drugs Act 1971. The possible jeopardy of importing or using PS within prison was greatly reduced because mandatory drug tests were unable to detect PS in urine and drug 'sniffer' dogs had not been trained to identify PS. Prisoners were keenly aware of the ambivalent legal status of PS and at first, the possibility of evading legal sanctions was one of several motivating factors for the sale of PS within prisons. However, this legal hiatus did not last. The Criminal Justice and Courts Act 2015 permitted the testing of drugs (such as PS) that were not expressly included within the Misuse of Drugs Act 1971 and the hastily introduced Psychoactive Substances Act 2016 prohibited the possession and supply of PS to and within prison. This did little to disincentivise supply or demand. In 2019, and despite the investment in drug testing, training of drug dogs, security apparatus and structures (Ministry of Justice, 2021a), HM Prison and Probation Service declared that 'the misuse of drugs in prison is one of the biggest challenges facing our criminal justice system today' (2019: 3). Prison drug tests were positive for PS in more than 50% of cases and far more frequently than for cannabis, opiates, or any other drug (Ministry of Justice, 2021b).

The continued dominance of PS within the prison drug economy might seem surprising. First, for nearly all consumers, it was a 'prison drug.' Few young men entered the prison as habitual users of PS and few intended to continue using PS on release (also see Criminal Justice Joint Inspection, 2021; Gooch & Treadwell, 2020; User Voice, 2015). The vast majority of young men in the YOI were using cannabis prior to imprisonment (Office for National Statistics, 2020) and simply switched to psychoactive substances because it was the most readily available drug.

Second, unlike cannabis and heroin, the effects of PS were unpredictable. Whilst it would make many lethargic and catatonic, it could just as easily cause seizures and cardiac arrest (Prison and Probation Ombudsman, 2019a, 2020). One interview was re-scheduled since it was quickly apparent that the young man was intoxicated—slurring his speech, stumbling, extremely lethargic and wearing a dazed and detached gaze. In some cases, the drug had a hallucinogenic effect. One young man, for example, tried to bite his tongue off because he thought it was on fire. This was not atypical:

> Their eyes are all fucked off it. I don't understand how they don't get caught. One that came on here the other day, he had smoked Mamba and the staff caught him on the wing, all dizzy and that, absolutely smashed he was. He walked up the stairs, he could barely stand up. They put him in the recovery position because they were not sure what would happen to him. (Pete)

> Listen, everyone smokes Mamba. … Mamba it makes everyone feel like it wrecks you. Mamba is not good. Don't smoke it. I wouldn't advise it. It's not the best. I have seen people fit on it. Stupid man. It's not the best that's what I would say. (Mark)

The variable and serious effects of PS were well known and easily observed. PS was quickly dubbed a 'dangerous' drug by the young men, but this did little to dissuade use. Nearly all the young men in the YOI had tried PS on at least on occasion and, despite experiencing and/or witnessing its more concerning effects, some continued to regularly use PS over time. For some, this was a consequence of their desperation for an 'escape' from the boredom or the realities of their current predicament. That some cared so little about their health was a sad reflection of their hopelessness and low self-esteem. It was clear, however, that these young men were less discerning drug users and were not motivated to test the quality of drugs in advance. This contrasts with adult prisons where the practice of testing batches of PS on 'Mamba muppets' and 'Spice pigs' had developed, either because dealers wanted to avoid the more problematic side effects of PS, wanted to maintain their status as reputable drug dealers of 'quality' drugs, or because they deliberately wanted to humiliate prisoners whom they deemed contemptible (see Gooch & Treadwell, 2020).

Against this background, the phrase 'Mambulances' soon emerged in prison vernacular, indicating something of the seriousness of the problem and the need for paramedic and hospital treatment for those prisoners who suffered serious and life-threatening effects. Ambulance calls out to English prisons doubled over a 4-year period between 2013–2014 and 2017–2018 such was the increase in drug use, self-harm, and violence (Bulman, 2018). Her Majesty's Inspectorate of Prisons noted (2015: 8) that 'some prisons have required so many ambulances that community resources were depleted.' In some cases, PS use proved deadly. Establishing the number of drug-related deaths each year is almost impossible given that toxicology tests are not always conducted and drug-related deaths can be recorded in multiple ways, including suicide, natural causes or 'other non-natural' causes (Prison and Probation Ombudsman, 2016, 2021a). However, it is estimated that each year at least 30 prisoners die accidentally from drug use (ibid.). These figures do not include those deaths where drug use is a contributory factor, such as a psychotic episode resulting from PS use or self-inflicted deaths prompted by debt, threats, pressure to hold or traffic drugs, or the 'mood altering effects of the drugs' (Prison and Probation Ombudsman, 2018, 2019a, b, 2021b).

Notably, young men in the YOI avoided the most serious consequences of PS use. There were certainly occasions when young men suffered effects that necessitated medical treatment, but none died as a result of PS use—a trend that has continued since James and I concluded our empirical research. This is in stark contrast to the neighbouring Category C and Category B Local prisons where there were recorded incidents of drug-related deaths, including deliberate attempts to kill themselves through drug use. There are two features of YOIs that partly explain these differences. First, compared to their adult counterparts, far fewer young adult prisoners use prescription medication and there is far less of an illicit market in diverted prescription medication. Secondly, in contrast to adult prisoners, young adults do not use opiate replacements to the same extent as adult prisoners. Thus, the relative absence of both prescription medication and opiates means that young adults were less likely to create the sort of fatal cocktails caused by mixing PS with other prescription and non-prescription drugs. Moreover, unlike our research in adult prisons, these young men did not report any attempts to deliberately affect their own suicide through a drug overdose.

For suppliers, the synthetic nature of the drug means that the composition of PS could be altered to create new strains undetectable to drug dogs or via mandatory drug tests. Herein lies part of the explanation for the continuing use of PS in prison. Decker and Townsend Chapman (2008: 151) note that drug 'smugglers try and find a comfort zone where the odds of getting away with a crime are in their favour.' With PS, drug suppliers not only had a product that could be modified to avoid detection, but both the consumption and ingress of PS could occur with comparatively greater ease. Unlike drugs such as heroin and cannabis, PS could be sprayed onto paper, with one A4 sheet of PS-dowsed paper could fetch as much as £1000. Thus, the sale of PS was lucrative. Once imprisoned, some felt uninhibited from drug dealing since there were few other restrictions that could be imposed:

> When you're outside you don't want to get caught because you can come to prison, but then when you're in prison, that problem starts to get eliminated, because you're in here. So, you're thinking, 'Right, if you do sell drugs, what's going to happen anyway because I'm going to stay here for longer?' So, that's the risk that people take, innit? (Kade)

The possible penalties were far outweighed by the financial gains. This is not to say that these young men were indifferent to the risks—they would of course minimise the extent to which they would personally be found holding or passing contraband if they could—but the prison economy was offering attractive financial rewards that some could not resist.

To explain the continued appeal of PS, commentators often mooted that the drug was odourless and therefore more difficult for prison staff to detect (Brown, 2014). However, it was quickly apparent that claims that prisoners were incentivised to use NPS because of its odourless quality were not borne out. Although not as potent as the smell of cannabis, PS did have a chemical odour. The primary appeal of PS for users was its ability to resolve the temporal problems of 'doing time' and/or their distress. Time remained the principal problem, especially for those on 'Basic regime' who spent long periods of the day confined to their cell.

> Saturday, I'm in my pad all day until, like, 3 pm or 4 pm. It's just something to smoke, like, to make the time go away on a Saturday, so it's alright. (Kade)

> … to relax. It's like when you are high, when you smoke weed and that, you don't want to sit down and fight you just want to chill out. The same as Mamba. You aren't looking to fight when you are high. Unless you have to. (Louis)

PS use was a way of 'having your day out of the prison' or 'melting the bars away.' It created a means of escape whilst young men remained secluded in their cells with little to do. If young men were able to avoid the most serious or disconcerting symptoms, they could spend several hours seemingly indifferent to their surroundings and predicament.

For others, drug use had already become the preferred strategy for 'blocking out' traumatic childhood experiences, pain and emotional turmoil. For example, Oliver was born in prison addicted to methadone owing to his mother's continued heroin and methadone use throughout pregnancy. His early years were 'chaotic,' marked by parental absence due to imprisonment, frequent changes in his living situation, occasions where he 'shoplifted' with his mother, and sexual abuse by a family friend. Before reaching his teenager years, Oliver was involved in drug misuse and prostitution. Somewhat fatalistically, Oliver explained that he 'expected' people to exploit and became involved in prostitution 'before they could force me to do it.' By 14, he was spending regular periods of time in custody. Within prison, he turned to drugs:

> I was sexually abused up until the age of 10. I was kind of taking drugs and drinking just to try and block it out. Like, when the drugs started taking hold, I was 13 and started like shoplifting, street robbery, robbing old people and then degrading myself to get drugs just to block the reality, so I could feel better. I've never really dealt with any of my issues. The only way I've dealt with them is drugs and drink. That's been my way of dealing. The drugs started getting more and more mad, and I started putting knives to people's throats and robbing them and stuff like that. … I've always used drugs as a blocker. Drugs have been my way of dealing with things. Drugs be like my counsellor. They block it all out and help me get on with it.

By the age of seven, drugs were an established part of his own life, not just that of his parents. Oliver described drugs as his 'counsellor' and 'emotional crutch.' Others too described how their drug use in and out of prison served to 'block a lot of shit.' Drugs therefore functioned as 'pain relief.' The normalisation of drug use was such that it was not those who were using drugs who were stigmatised, or indeed those who dealt drugs, but those who could not control their drug habits or manage their financial affairs.

'I Pass It Blatant': Grafting, Trading, and Dealing

As I stood at the end of the spur talking to the cleaners, a short, overweight young man poked his head around the corner to check where the prison officer was. Looking both ways, he then pulled his head back into the cell and disappeared for a few seconds. Re-appearing, with a wry smile, he waddled side-to-side as quickly as he could down the spur. In his hands was a TV very poorly concealed by a garishly green, prison-issued bed sheet. Ahmed was making good his theft of a TV. He turned the corner, and then proceeded to walk down the adjacent spur to a cell three doors down. The prison officer on duty was—fortuitously for Ahmed—walking towards the end of the spur unaware of what was happening behind him. It would only be a few seconds before he would reach the end of the spur and would then turn on his heels to retread his steps. His gaze was fixed ahead and if he heard the noise behind him, he didn't turn or move. Deftly, Ahmed turned into the cell and out of view just as the prison officer retraced his path along the spur. The TV was now safely deposited in the cell of two 'pad mates'[12] who were on Basic regime and not entitled to a TV. A few days earlier, Ahmed's television had been removed by prison officers and Ahmed's theft was a way of circumventing rules he was not intending to follow. It was likely that the officers would eventually notice the illicit TV in the cell, but Ahmed and his pad mate would be able to enjoy at least a few days of undetected

[12] Prison slang for the person they share a cell with.

viewing. The young man who had now lost his TV did not complain and was unlikely to do so. He had to content himself with a radio and simply hope that at some point an officer might notice the absence of the TV. In some ways, Ahmed's mischief was as much about 'seeing what you could get away with' (Parker, 1974: 48) as it was an attempt to remedy boredom. In other cases, it had an air of sophistication and seriousness. These mischievous 'games' (Kaminski, 2004; McDermott & King, 1988), though, left victims in their wake.

Contraband was always circulating. If someone was drug seeking, they knew that they had to go to the 'top dog on the wing,' and 'they'll send it to you if they've got it themselves personally or they'll send someone to you.' Drug dealers did not always need to advertise their wares; users had an instinctive knowledge about who was selling drugs. Drug dealers also carried themselves with confidence and authority because of the power and control they could and would exert amongst their peers (see Chap. 5). The 'passing' of drugs happened frequently and easily. An item shoved down the tracksuit trousers or socks. Lines created by bedsheets and then attached to the windows on the exterior wall allowed items to be moved between cells. CD's attached to lines flying across the floor and between, and then, under cell doors. A slight touching or shaking of hands. A hand reaching between the gates to the association room. Items stowed in trollies. Some young men enjoyed the 'thrill' and 'buzz' of such activities (Katz, 1988), including getting one over the officers:

> It's funny, I love doing that. It's fucking unreal mate. (Lewis)

Distraction techniques were used to facilitate the passing of items. These techniques ranged from a young man simply being noisy and shaking the gate, to verbal protests and challenges, refusing to obey an instruction, or staging a low-level fight.

Often, young men would give their best efforts to finding novel ways to conceal items (e.g. by wrapping drugs in cling film and kitchen foil) or obscure communications. For example:

> They wrap the cannabis up in cling film yeah, and then they roll it in Vaseline, roll it in pepper and coffee powder and wrap it up in cling film

> again. Roll it in Vaseline again and roll it in chilli powder and wrap it in cling film again and then shove it up their arse with a bit of baby oil or Vaseline. (Joshua)

> Ring off these [prison] phones in a different language. Before they even get someone to translate it has been done and dusted. I have put the phone down by then. End of conversation done and dusted. My boy will be out there with a blade. Cut all the bubble wrap off, put it in a pillowcase and it will go through the bars in the windows. It will come straight in and I'll grab it. (Mark)

Young men—like Mark—were bold enough to use the prison phones but smart enough to talk in a code and language the receiver would understand; others used illicitly held mobile phones. These ingenious methods could be diversified with relative ease and agility. The extent to which young men felt compelled to conceal their operations varied, and partly depended on the willingness of prison officers to tolerate drug dealing. For example, Matthew explained:

> The officers probably don't know the scale of what they're selling … but they know they are doing something dodgy, but it's either out of respect for them, or just because they get on with them, or just because they don't care about their job in general, they leave them alone. … When a certain officer's on, we can see them in the morning and you think, Fucking hell! Today's going to be a bad day for business! You just know straight away: Well, today's going to be a good day? You could even have a day where you could say to an officer, 'Open this door! I'm going to batter him!'

It was an open secret that some staff were involved in facilitating illicit trade, either in actively bringing contraband into the prison, turning a blind eye when people used or dealt drugs, or as noted above, giving freedom to those who would use it for nefarious purposes.

Of course, the efforts that young men made to avoid detection were matched by the considerable effort that the Prison Service (and Ministry of Justice more generally) invested in preventing drug supply. A plethora of different mechanisms exist to prevent 'ingress': walls and fences, searches, patrols, and careful (risk adverse) decisions regarding ROTL (release on temporary licence). In the general routines of prison life though, a 'find' by a prison officer was considered a mark of professional skill, but senior managers were often more tempted to take the long view and develop the 'intelligence' to discover who was financially benefitting from the contraband not just found in possession of it. Cell 'spins'[13]—regular or intelligence led—served as a way to check what was hidden in cells. The arrival of the dedicated search team always had a chilling effect on the wing. For example, an 'intelligence led' search was conducted following reports that a knife and other weapons had been taken and hidden on the wing, and 'something would happen on the servery tonight.' One prison officer responded by saying he intended to take the meals to the door rather than allow everyone out to collect their meals, but another pointed the inevitable problem this created, asking, 'Are you going to do that all weekend?' Several young men had been moved to the 'block' to 'disrupt' potential misbehaviour, including an individual—known as 'Shadow'—who had been putting out 'contracts'[14] for certain individuals on the opposite landing. The search eventually yielded a crop of four bottles of 'hooch,' improvised weapons, pieces of wire, pieces of metal, several pieces of wood with nails sticking out, and lines made from bed sheets. The search was viewed as a 'success' by prison staff, and likely prevented some harmful incidents that day or week. However, as long as demand remained and prison officers were directly or inadvertently complicit in facilitating drug supply, security operations and tactics could only have a limited impact on drug dealing within the prison.

The illicit economy was dynamic; including in the buoyancy of supply routes, the prices that contraband attracts, and the frequency and effectiveness of security tactics and strategies to 'disrupt' and abort illicit activity. Suppression of a particular supply route did not necessarily suppress supply routes as a whole nor the relative power of those who were responsible for supplying goods. Prison security tactics could cause disruptions to social order if, for example, a throwover was intercepted by staff. Those for whom the package was intended often penalised those young men who had failed to secure the package through a punishment beating. Yet,

[13] Prison slang for cell searches.

[14] A 'contract' on someone's head meant that payment would be made for assaulting the named individual.

young men—like their adult counterparts—diversify their supply routes to circumvent security tactics. Thus, as long as the relative benefits of drug dealing within the prison outweigh the costs, there remains an incentive for young men (and those within their networks) to continue trafficking contraband into the prison.

Dealers held the bargaining power and could largely take advantage of demand; they could be as 'greedy' as they wanted without suffering a diminution in status. For example:

> It's sort of all up to individuals, or how greedy he wants to be. Because, at the end of the day, the person that's in control has got it, because they know, regardless if you want it, your next door neighbour wants it, there's always going to be someone that wants it. The same thing with drugs. The same thing with phones. … Like, it's just the demands for it, innit? If somebody wants it that bad, they're going to have to pay for it. This is why there's so much drugs because obviously, there's so much people that want it. (Kade)

The costs of contraband—such as drugs, mobile telephones and chargers, SIM cards—were inflated in prison. As Ethan explained, 'A £10 phone (in the community) would be £500 in here.' The cost of mobile telephones varied depending on whether it was a Smart Phone or a small, easily concealable Xanax phone (approximately the size of two digits). PS was most widely available but small amount of cannabis might also be sold. Cannabis had an inflation rate of 10-fold compared with the community. Cocaine—which was rarely available—was costed at a hundredfold return (i.e. a package of cocaine worth £10 in the community was worth £1000 in prison, partly because it was mixed with a greater range of chemicals to bulk it out). Thus, there were 'serious profits' to be made from dealing contraband in prison, leading young men to conclude that they could 'make more money in jail.' Consequently, dealers could also tolerate some financial or contraband losses or delayed payments, and therefore would lend or deliberately extort those who in all other ways would not seem to be a financially secure investment. However, the failure to repay a debt was punished because it was disrespectful and represented an affront and 'violation.'

The Debt Economy

One of the simplest rules governing the illicit economy was: 'you borrow something, you pay double back'—a long-established practice known as 'double bubble' (Crewe, 2009; De Viggiani, 2012; Edgar et al., 2003). If payments were not repaid or items returned in a timely manner (i.e. the next time canteen was distributed), the amount owed would double each week until the debt was expunged. Thus, 'double bubble' could become 'triple, triple' and more besides. As Luke explained, 'I've had to quadruple people's debts before.' This practice was so engrained that it went unquestioned. None expressed any compunction about charging extortionate interest rates:

> I don't see as bullying or exploiting. I see that as fair in a way. I actually do see that as fair. Take the piss! Some of them do! So if I take it, you cannot snitch on me can you? It's like—say I really want this Renault Clio, I've only got £7,400, and it's £7,600 and it's not going down in price, lend me £200. I wouldn't come back to you and give you £200 back, I would come back to you and say here is £250 or here is £300. Thanks for that. So next time if I meet you, you are going to go, 'How much do you want?' Simple. That's the way it works. You cannot exactly say he has just robbed me. You know how the game works; I know how the game works. (Damien)

Prison officers typically likened 'double bubble' to pro-social behaviour in the community, stating, 'If you borrow something from a friend, you're expected to return it. This is no different.' There appeared to be little recognition amongst prison officers that the 'loansharking' (Bowker, 1980) behaviour was a form of exploitation. Consequently, extortion was normalised and only challenged if prison officers were directly confronted by young men asking for help (as in the case of the young men reporting Luke's extortion noted in the introduction).

Debt accumulated quickly and could become a perennial problem. Martin explained, 'Everywhere [in the prison], someone is in debt.' Even if debtors repaid the lender, some would incur further debts to sustain their smoking and drug habits or to have enough additional food and toiletries for the week. In other cases, payments were missed but the debtor continued to borrow more from others to survive another week in prison. It was not uncommon for young men who initially owed a very small amount (e.g. less than £10) to quickly owe amounts in the hundreds of pounds. This was far more pronounced where the demands for payment were in 'cash amounts.' However, the indebtedness of these young men rarely reached amounts in the thousands of pounds typical of older prisoners (Gooch & Treadwell, 2020). Although some kept a mental record of the amounts owed, it was not uncommon for careful written records to be maintained. These 'debt lists' would not only contain details of amounts owed, but also the details of bank accounts and dates when payments were required. Despite its seemingly informality and fluidity, it was a precise business. Repayment was expected and demanded. When repayment was not forthcoming, debtors were threatened or assaulted—actions that were seen as a rational and justifiable response to their infraction.

Debtors fell into five categories: (1) the convenience debtors; (2) the habitual drug debtors; (3) the desperate debtors; (4) the coerced debtors; and, (5) the naïve debtor. For a group of prisoners, the reliance on the prison economy was convenient, enabling them to improve their lot by acquiring 'exclusive' items (i.e. those only available in other prisons), purchasing contraband (e.g. borrowing a mobile phone to ring a girlfriend or updating social media content), pay for services (e.g. a haircut) and/or borrowing more canteen to satisfy their hunger. Any debts were manageable and unproblematic if they continued to receive external financial support and/or there were no security seizures. For example, at the time of the interview, Daniel owed £440 but was confident that he would 'be out of that come this weekend.' He explained: 'I always pay my debts, everyone knows … cause they've done me a favour, given it me, they've helped me so like I sort of see it as like my obligation to pay them back.' Young men like Daniel would move in and out of debt relatively freely throughout their sentence.

The second category of debtors were habitual drug users. With few exceptions, these young men had experimented with drugs in the community and were relatively desensitised to indebtedness. Habitual drug users were primarily focused on how to obtain more PS rather than how to finance their purchases (also see Marsh, 2020). More sophisticated young men very deliberately targeted those drug addicts with access to family credit and resources:

> People get addicted to it. That other circle [drug addicts], they will come to us. That's who we target to sell it to. They have got money coming in from their family but that's our money. We are making money. Like people on the out [in the community] come to us, that's our money to be made. (Adam)

The extent to which more active drug dealers sought to distinguish themselves from the drug addicts they sold to is not surprising (also see Crewe, 2005, 2006), but it is notable that there was an attitude of entitlement and ownership, that it was '*our* money to be made.' Adam was not unique in holding this view; others were like him and were seeking to not only survive, but also profit from their imprisonment.

The third category of 'desperate debtors' were those who simply lacked financial resources and/or could not manage their finances but also could not refrain from borrowing from others. These young men would quickly accrue large debts, and when they either felt disinclined or were unable to continue to borrow from their peers, would then seek 'emergency canteen'[15] from prison officers. The extent to which such provision was forthcoming varied, and largely depended on assessments as to the 'legitimacy' of the distress and how 'deserving' the prisoner was perceived to be. Of course, such emergency provision would only make the situation worse, since the young man would be compelled to repay this canteen the following week, leaving even less money available to sustain them. Often, the habitual drugs users and desperate debtors were highly visible because of their distress, their prison issue clothes, and the barrenness of their cells (the contents of which had been sold or stolen).

The 'coerced debtors' were those young men whose indebtedness was imposed upon them, rather than a consequence of their purchasing and borrowing habits. One of the most crushing forms of indebtedness was 'inherited debt,' which essentially involved the transfer of debt from the

---

[15] 'Emergency packs' were given at the discretion of prison staff to those who were deemed to have a particular need for canteen outside the normal order cycle.

original debtor to any associates or their current 'pad-mate.' This transfer of debt typically occurred when someone was released or 'shipped out'[16] to another prison rather than when transferred within the YOI since debts could still be recovered from other wings. Joshua explained:

> Say if me and you are padded up together and then you get shipped off, that's not your fault or my fault, but I would still have to pay your debt because it stays on with your pad mate.

Lenders cared little for the change in someone's circumstances; if they could succeed in pressuring someone else to repay, they would. For those on the receiving end of such demands, such demands caused frustration and resentment. Harry commented:

> Nick is a little prick. I know him from the out; my mum used to go out with his dad. Dickhead. When he first came in, he was telling everybody, 'Oh, here's my boy, here's my boy off-road,' and that. So, he caused me shit when he went to leave, because he was in debt. 'You're his boy, you're paying his debts, or you're getting wrapped.'[17] I had to [pay]. Fucking, the whole landing were like, 'Harry, we're sound with you and that, but he owes the person who runs the wing, he owes so-and-so. You've got to deal with it.' For fuck's sake, man! It really pissed me off, man.

Prison officers typically assumed that those who were in debt had brought this on themselves by, for example, borrowing more than they could afford and misusing drugs. Both activities were condemned by staff who often did not recognise that some prisoners were being victimised and the debts imposed on them. This lack of empathy only served to reinforce the prisoner normative code that demanded financial resourcefulness, the repayment of debts, and that valorised the ability to accumulate goods, but in so doing collapsed the distinctions between the 'prisoner' culture and staff cultures.

Coerced debt also included 'cell rent.' This practice was directed at those who were believed to be 'weak' and susceptible to pressure, or those

[16] Prison slang for being transferred to another prison.

[17] 'Wrapped' was slang for being beaten and could involve a group of assailants.

who had transgressed the normative code. For example, Jermaine explained that feminine or gay young men—who he described as 'moving funny'—would be charged rent:

> They get put on rent. They have to pay us things like buying canteen for us. When canteen comes, they have to give us our fair share of the canteen.

Canteen was demanded with the threat of being 'wrapped up' if they failed to comply. Not everyone was susceptible to demands to pay inherited debt or 'cell rent'—much depended on the perceived 'capital' (see Chap. 8), power and respect that young men were thought to have, and their ability to rebuff victimisation. Lewis—like other more formidable young men—simply refused: 'People charge you rent for your pad. They tried it to me before, but I don't pay shit man.' Others would choose to 'take the bang' (assault)—if it came at all—rather than pay the demanded sums, contenting themselves that further demands were unlikely.

The 'naïve debtors' were unwitting victims. More experienced young men took advantage of the naivety of newcomers and/or those young men who seemed too willing to please. In such cases, what first appeared to be a friendly gesture quickly became pernicious. Damien explained:

> You probably won't even know that it got doubled because you have just come in and you don't know the rules. You will be thinking so what is the deal with this then?

For the newcomer or unsuspecting victim, the demands for repayment could not only come as a shock but severed social support from those whom they had previously considered an ally. This could be especially unsettling and frightening. In the worst cases, more powerful individuals would also switch the tobacco (later 'caps' and vapes) requested for Mamba, not only leading the unsuspecting user to experience unpleasant and possibly life-threatening symptoms, but also increasing the amount of debt they owed. In one case, the deliberate switching of tobacco for Mamba led to Jake being hospitalised for a short period. He later commented that the experience of Black Mamba had left him very frightened: 'I thought I was going to die.' This incident came after he had been mercilessly bullied for his canteen and, when he returned from hospital, he was subjected to a prolonged assault by multiple individuals in his cell. Somewhat perversely, these incidents were not considered to be morally reprehensible by other young men but a 'normal, legitimised part of the taken for granted' (Sim, 1994: 103).

Conclusion

There is an inextricable link between prison-based illicit economies and prison violence. Violence is a critical 'resource' (Ellis et al., 2017) for governing illegal markets where other forms of social control are absent or inadequate (Hobbs, 2013: 171), and when formal governance institutions—such as prison officers—cannot be relied upon (Skarbek, 2014, 2020). Mirroring trends in the community (Durán-Martinez, 2018; Hobbs, 1995, 2013; Marsh, 2020; Winlow & Hall, 2006), credible threats, physical violence, and robbery were perceived to be legitimate responses to the non-repayment of debt, the loss of contraband or efforts to control and monopolise the illicit economy on a particular wing(s).

Earlier research studies (Copes et al., 2010) suggest that drug dealers are more at risk of victimisation. However, the growing appeal of the illicit economy—both for those who seeking access to goods and those selling them—has changed this relationship. Those who are co-ordinating financial transaction and contraband supply are more likely to inflict or orchestrate violent reprisals (Skarbek, 2020), rather than be a risk of victimisation themselves. Thus, although 'economic victimisation' (Bowker, 1980) has been an enduring feature of prison life, the structure of such activities, the way argot roles are framed, and the normative underpinnings of such behaviour has evolved—issues to which I turn in Chaps. 5 and 8.

In an overly simplistic way, the Ministry of Justice (2016) sought to explain the increase in prison violence by pointing to drug users who—they claimed—were more likely to be involved in violent incidents. This partly reflects the erroneous assumption that the use of PS was causing some prisoners to be aggressive, and it was this that was principally contributing to the increase in prison violence. Certain strains of PS did have this effect but, as noted above, PS use primarily caused young men to be lethargic, hallucinogenic and/or disconnected from reality. Klatt et al. (2016) found that drug use is a strong predictor of prison violence but based this assessment on drug use in the community not in prison. Equally, despite concluding that there was 'scant research' to conclude that drug use or dependency was linked to prison violence, Byrne and Hummer (2007: 82) argue that 'it is logical' that being incarcerated for drug-related offences will correlate with prison violence and disorder. Logic is not the same as evidence. The relationship between drug use and violence was more indirect than such assertions imply. Drug users were more likely to be victims rather than perpetrators of violence, particularly if they were regarded as weak and fragile, or were in debt. That said, drug users could become perpetrators if they were coerced to assault someone to expunge a debt or if they were both dealing and using.

The form and appeal of the prison economy has been altered by macro, micro, and meso factors. At a macro level, these changes included: the pharmaceutical development of synthetic drugs; technological developments to facilitate financial transactions, communication and conveyance; austerity measures; prison policies that constructed prisoners as less 'deserving'; deteriorating prison conditions; the democratisation of the drug economy that facilitated easier access for young men (Ancrum & Treadwell, 2017); post-industrialisation unemployment of working class men leading some to 'graft' through drug dealing (Maguire, 2021, also see Chap. 7); an increasingly consumeristic and hedonistic culture outside of the prison (Hall et al., 2013); and, the dynamic nature of criminal enterprise where the prison was increasingly seen as a financially lucrative market place (Gooch & Treadwell, 2020, 2021, 2023, 2025). At a meso level, within the prison, the economy was influenced by: security tactics; activity and boredom; the perceived ability to progress and be 'rewarded' for 'good' behaviour; styles of prison officer governance (i.e. how present and engaged officers were in their supervision of young men); and the extent to which the logic of austerity had been absorbed by those prison staff controlling the supply of basic items (see Chap. 9 for further discussion). At a micro level, the higher echelons of the prisoner hierarchy were reserved for those who held economic power and economic capital. The performance of 'hegemonic masculinity' (Connell, 1995) and the acquisition of 'carceral capital' was predicated on the ability to gain and retain consumer artefacts, not just on the advertised capacity for physical violence. This economic capital was converted into social capital (Bourdieu, 1986). The link between social recognition, status and 'carceral capital' is the subject of Chaps. 5 and 8.

References

Ancrum, C., & Treadwell, J. (2017). Beyond ghosts, gangs and good sorts: Commercial cannabis cultivation and illicit enterprise in England's disadvantaged inner cities. *Crime, Media, Culture, 13*(1), 69–84.

Bourdieu, P. (1986). The forms of capital. In J. Richardson (Ed.), *Handbook of theory and research for the sociology of education* (pp. 241–258). Greenwood.

Bowker, L. H. (1980). *Prison victimisation*. Elsevier.

Braman, D. (2002). Families and incarceration. In M. Chesney-Lind & M. Mauer (Eds.), *Invisible punishment: The collateral consequences of mass imprisonment* (pp. 117–135). New Press.

Brown, S. (2014). Synthetic cannabis causing serious health problems in English prisons. *The Guardian*, Thursday 15 May.

Bulman, M. (2018). Number of ambulance call-outs to English prisons almost doubles in four years, figures show. *The Independent*, Monday 3 September.

Byrne, J. M., & Hummer, D. (2007). Myths and realities of prison violence: A review of the evidence. *Victims & Offenders, 2*(1), 77–90.

Codd, H. (2008). *In the shadow of prison: Families, imprisonment and criminal justice*. Willan.

Comfort, M. (2008). *Doing time together: Love and family in the shadow of the prison*. University of Chicago Press.

Connell, R. W. (1995). *Masculinities*. Polity Press.

Copes, H., Higgins, G. E., Tewksbury, R., & Dabney, D. A. (2010). Participation in the prison economy and likelihood of physical victimization. *Victims & Offenders, 6*(1), 1–18.

Crewe, B. (2005). Prisoner society in the era of hard drugs. *Punishment & Society, 7*(4), 457–481.

Crewe, B. (2006). Prison drug dealing and the ethnographic lens. *Howard Journal of Criminal Justice, 45*(4), 347–368.

Crewe, B. (2009). *Prisoner society: Power, adaptation and social life in an English prison*. Oxford University Press.

Criminal Justice Joint Inspection. (2021). *A joint thematic inspection of the criminal justice journey for individuals with mental health needs and disorders*. Her Majesty's Inspectorate of Probation.

De Viggiani, N. (2012). Trying to be something you are not. *Men and Masculinities, 15*(3), 271–291.

Decker, S. H., & Townsend Chapman, M. (2008). *Drug smugglers on drug smuggling: Lessons from the inside*. Temple University Press.

Durán-Martinez, A. (2018). *The politics of drug violence: Criminals, cops, and politicians in Colombia and Mexico*. Oxford University Press.

Edgar, K., & O'Donnell, I. (1998). *Mandatory drug testing in prisons: The relationship between MDT and the level and nature of drug misuse*. Home Office.

Edgar, K., O'Donnell, I., & Martin, C. (2003). *Prison violence: The dynamics of conflict, fear and power*. Willan.

Ellis, A., Winlow, S., & Hall, S. (2017). 'Throughout my life I've had people walk all over me': Trauma in the lives of violent men. *The Sociological Review, 65*(4), 699–713.

Gooch, K., & Treadwell, J. (2020). Prisoner society in an era of psychoactive substances, organized crime, new drug markets and austerity. *The British Journal of Criminology, 60*(5), 1260–1281.

Gooch, K., & Treadwell, J. (2021). 'It doesn't stop at the prison gate': Understanding organised crime in prison. *Prison Service Journal, 252*, 15–30.

Gooch, K., & Treadwell, J. (2023). The 'screw boys' and the 'businessmen': Re-negotiating penal power, governance and legitimate authority through a prison violence reduction scheme. *British Journal of Criminology, 63*(4), 1219–1237.

Gooch, K., & Treadwell, J. (2025). The prison firm: The 'transportation' of organised crime, the evolution of criminal markets and contemporary prisoner society. *Criminology and Criminal Justice, 25*(1), 245–264.

Hall, S., Winlow, S., & Ancrum, C. (2013). *Criminal identities and consumer culture*. Willan.

Hansard. (2014). Prisons: Drugs. Questions for Ministry of Justice. HL7402, 24 April.

Her Majesty's Inspectorate of Prisons. (2015). *Changing patterns of substance misuse in adult prisons and service responses: A thematic review*. Her Majesty's Inspectorate of Prisons.

HM Prison and Probation Service. (2019). *Prisons drug strategy*. HM Prison and Probation Service.

Hobbs, D. (1995). *Bad business*. Oxford University Press.

Hobbs, D. (2013). *Lush life*. Oxford University Press.

Kalinich, D. B. (1980). *The inmate economy*. Lexington Books.

Kaminski, M. M. (2004). *Games prisoners play: The tragicomic worlds of polish prison*. Princeton University Press.

Katz, J. (1988). *Seductions of crime: A chilling exploration of the criminal mind from juvenile delinquency to cold-blooded murder*. Basic Books.

Klatt, T., Hagl, S., Bergmann, M. C., & Baier, D. (2016). Violence in youth custody: Risk factors of violent misconduct among inmates of German young offender institutions. *European Journal of Criminology, 13*(6), 727–743.

Maguire, D. (2021). *Male, failed and jailed: Masculinities and the 'revolving door' imprisonment in the UK*. Palgrave Macmillan.

Marsh, B. (2020). *The logic of violence: An ethnography of Dublin's illegal drug trade*. Routledge.

McDermott, K., & King, R. D. (1988). Mind Games. *British Journal of Criminology, 28*(3), 357–375.

Ministry of Justice. (2016). *Prison safety and reform, Cm 9350*. Ministry of Justice.

Ministry of Justice. (2017). *Annual National Offender Management Service digest: 2016 to 2017*. Ministry of Justice.

Ministry of Justice. (2021a). *Drug dogs to detect new versions of spice to stay ahead of criminals*. Ministry of Justice.

Ministry of Justice. (2021b). *HMPPS annual digest, April 2020 to March 2021: Finds in prison*. Ministry of Justice.

Ministry of Justice. (2025). *HMPPS annual digest: April 2023–March 2024*. Ministry of Justice.

Office for National Statistics. (2020). Drug misuse in England and Wales: Year ending March 2020. Available online: https://www.ons.gov.uk/peoplepopulationandcommunity/crimeandjustice/articles/drugmisuseinenglandandwales/yearendingmarch2020

Parker, H. J. (1974). *View from the boys*. David & Charles.

Prison and Probation Ombudsman. (2016). *New psychoactive substances play a part in yet more prison deaths. Speech by Nigel Newcomen CBE at Newbold revel, prison service training college*. Prison and Probation Ombudsman.

Prison and Probation Ombudsman. (2018). *Independent investigation into the death of Mr John Duffy a prisoner at HMP Liverpool on 16 July 2016*. Prison and Probation Ombudsman.

Prison and Probation Ombudsman. (2019a). *Annual report: 2018–2019*. Prison and Probation Ombudsman.

Prison and Probation Ombudsman. (2019b). *Independent investigation into the death of Mr Darren Williams a prisoner at HMP Woodhill on 4 January 2019*. Prison and Probation Ombudsman.

Prison and Probation Ombudsman. (2020). *Annual report: 2019–2020*. Prison and Probation Ombudsman.

Prison and Probation Ombudsman. (2021a). *Drug related deaths in prison*. Prison and Probation Ombudsman.

Prison and Probation Ombudsman. (2021b). *Independent investigation into the death of Mr John Taylor a prisoner at HMP/YOI Doncaster on 16 January 2020*. Prison and Probation Ombudsman.

Sim, J. (1994). Tougher than the rest? Men in prison. In T. Newburn & E. A. Stanko (Eds.), *Just boys doing business? Men, masculinities and crime* (pp. 100–177). Routledge.

Skarbek, D. (2014). *The social order of the underworld: How prison gangs govern the American penal system*. Oxford University Press.

Skarbek, D. (2020). *The puzzle of prison order: Why life behind bars varies across the world*. Oxford University Press.

Sparks, R., Bottoms, A. E., & Hay, W. (1996). *Prisons and the problem of order*. Oxford University Press.

Sykes, G. (1958). *The society of captives*. Princeton University Press.

User Voice. (2015). *Spice: The bird killer*. User Voice.

Winlow, S., & Hall, S. (2006). *Violent night: Urban leisure and contemporary culture*. Berg.

5

The 'King of the Wing,' 'Lads,' and the 'Nerds': Contemporary Young Prisoner Society, Prison Victimisation, and the Prison Illicit Economy

Mark and David were tightly knitted 'pad mates,'[1] preserving an unusual loyalty for one another and willingly sharing goods without demanding repayment with interest. They were an unlikely pairing. Mark was prone to angry outbursts if he felt disrespected and was well known for his willingness to use violence to express his frustration or communicate his dissatisfaction, whether with prison officers or his peers. He had been raised in a Traveller community, in what he described as a 'nasty family.' He proudly described both their propensity for violence ('we've been fighting for years') and the protection that afforded him: 'we stick together … There's an old saying which has been around for years is that if you stab one, you'll have 50 on your door—that's how we are.' Mark had been hired to 'kill a rapist' but attempts to stab, torture and drown the victim over several hours failed to kill him. Although he was paid £2000 for the attempted murder, he claimed that he 'didn't want the money anyway. Because my sister has been raped before … so in my eyes he needs to be killed.' He was not alone in sharing this view, but his profound distaste for 'rapist bastards' would later become acutely relevant. Conversely, David was quiet, meek, and mild mannered. Although relatively tall,

[1] The person they share a cell with.

K. Gooch, *Prison Violence*, Palgrave Studies in Prisons and Penology,
https://doi.org/10.1007/978-3-031-91365-5_5

muscular, and well built, he largely relied on Mark to be his spokesperson and defend their collective interests. They would frequently 'back each other on fights' and 'look after' one another. Mark had assumed a protective, caring role for David who struggled with depression, self-harmed and had set fire to their cell whilst they were both locked in it.

This alliance would come to a dramatic end when Mark discovered that David was accused of raping a minor, not just the two robberies he had disclosed. It was not until David appeared in court that his index offence became known to another prisoner (also in the court cells) who, in turn, informed others on the wing. Believing their continued alliance would bring his own reputation into question, Mark felt compelled to assault David:

> I was in shock. He was one of my best mates. He was one of the proper lads. It was heart-breaking. I didn't want to hit him, I really didn't, but I had to. I had no choice but to hit him. The fact is I would lose my respect on the wing and I would be taken for a mug by everyone and start fighting with everyone and I ain't having that. I had to keep my ratings up, you know what I mean. I'm quite a high rank in here. Everyone knows me. I have to keep my name up. I have to do what I have to do to get by. So I punched him up. We come through the door and we were scrapping here [indicates the entrance to the staff office]. And I went up to him and started banging him in his face and stuck a couple in his chest.

In the prison gossip mill, news of David's fall from grace spread quickly and soon became the subject of much conversation between prisoners and amongst prison officers—just as Mark intended and needed to preserve his social standing. Violence sent 'signals' (Gambetta, 2009), and in this case it communicated moral judgements about sex offenders and the inexcusable nature of dishonesty, betrayal, and humiliation. Mark took no joy in assaulting his best friend but regarded it as essential self-preservation. To his mind, had he not acted, people would have assumed he knew about David's index offence and that he considered such behaviour morally acceptable. In this way, social recognition was predicated not only on who you were, but also on who you were prepared to tolerate and socialise with. Violence demonstrated Mark's commitment to the normative code which regarded the punishment of sex offenders as legitimate and justifiable (also see Chap. 8, Lockwood, 1980). Mark had long absorbed the logic of violent punishment for sex offenders, but even when confronted with someone he knew and cared about, he still prioritised his own survival and reputation over the protection of his friend (who would be vulnerable to further assaults by others).

Whilst a move to the Supported Living Unit insulated David from further beatings, Mark soon experienced his own fall from grace. Just a few weeks later, Mark moved to the segregation unit (colloquially known as the 'CSU'[2] to staff or the 'block' to the young men) and refused to return to 'normal location' on a residential wing. Mark claimed that he was being threatened by a group of Black and Asian prisoners (although he declined to name them) for whom he was holding a mobile phone and was in £600 debt to. Mark, who had for so long been a dominant, aggressive, and powerful presence on the wing, was now 'running for cover' in the segregation unit. For all his bravado, Mark had found himself in a situation that he was unable to control and had armed himself with a Stanley knife. Without David, or anyone from the Traveller community, Mark found himself outnumbered by a group of young men whom he held deep-seated prejudices against:

> Like obviously, all the Asian and Muslim groups know that I am EDL, English Defence League. That's what I am. I am never going to change that. I have been this way since I was a kid. That's who I am. I don't go for race, I just go for outright supremacy. But these are going on a racial. You know when I was a kid, I did go on racial attacks against Muslims, you know what I mean. They are doing my head in. They're irritating.

His strategy of fighting indiscriminately against every threat had left him isolated in his time of need. There was no one to rescue him and no family to call on to expunge his debt. The staff whom he had fought against for so long were now his only route to safety. He would willingly accept more than 23 hours confined in segregation to avoid the retaliatory assault that he knew would be the fitting punishment for the loss of the

[2] Care and Separation Unit

mobile phone and financial negligence. Mark gave no thought as to where he would go after his short-lived respite in segregation; his immediate concern was a move from the residential units. The inevitable damage to his reputation was momentarily set aside and the battle to regain his status left for another day.

This chapter focuses on the structure, hierarchy and constitution of young prisoner society, and the relational context within which victimisation occurred. It provides a 'map' of the young prison social system (Sykes, 1958: 84). The depiction of 'argot roles' to classify and label prisoner behaviour and adaptations has long been a common feature of prison life (Sykes, 1958). The diverse ways in which young men were involved in the illicit economy and victimisation generated 'distinctive tags' (Clemmer, 1940) that indicated: approval and condemnation; power and powerlessness; inclusion and exclusion; (relative) wealth and poverty; and, honour and dishonour.

Prison records typically reinforce binary distinctions between perpetrators and victims. Prior research on prison bullying has, however, sought to distinguish between a wider range of roles, including: 'perpetrators' (or 'pure bullies'), 'victim-perpetrators' (or bully/victims'), 'pure victims,' and the 'not involved' (Ireland & Ireland, 2000; Ireland et al., 2007; South & Wood, 2006). This chapter expands this typology to make finer and more nuanced distinctions. First, it is argued that the 'perpetrator' role included those who orchestrate and co-ordinate drug dealing and assaults but without getting directly involved themselves (the 'King of the Wing'); the enforcers and 'middlemen'; and those young men who were responsible for violent incidents but without attaining wider power and control. Secondly, the victim-perpetrators were not just those who were both victims and perpetrators of violence (in single or disconnected incidents), but those who were coerced to assault others or hold and circulate contraband under duress. Third, nearly all had at one time been threatened or assaulted, but many did so without being persistently targeted or attracting the label of being a 'victim.' Thus, this chapter analyses why only some young men attracted the permanent stain of being a 'victim.' Finally, the reasons why young men were able to avoid prison victimisation varied, as did their motivation for any compliance.

The prisoner social system (and underpinning norms) creates predictability and order in a sometimes chaotic and volatile environment (see Sykes, 1958: 85–86). Whilst none felt (prison staff included) that you could ever 'let your guard down,' the reality that prison victimisation conformed to predictable patterns meant that those individuals who could successfully navigate social interactions were rarely consumed by fear. This partly explains the 'safety paradox' (Bottoms, 1999; Wolff & Shi, 2009) within prison—i.e. why some young men felt safe even when violence was frequent and even whilst living on wings described as 'Beirut' (common prison vernacular for volatile, turbulent, or violent wings), the 'Lion's Den' or the 'jungle.' This is not to say that social positions were rigidly fixed; 'individuals are never *always* a particular kind of prisoner' (Crewe, 2009: 151). Rather, social roles were dynamic and fluid and—as in the case of Mark and David—an individual's position within the hierarchy could swiftly change. As Anderson argues (1999: 87), 'Status in the group is constantly being adjusted.' Equally, the release or transfer of a powerful individual be transferred or released may cause uncertainty and instability until a new 'King of the Wing' takes his place.

Distinguishing the 'Lads' from the 'Nerds': Tests, Character Checks, and Initiations

Prisoner society was ordered by informal but readily understood social hierarchies. To the keen observer, these hierarchies were readily apparent and manifested in a host of daily interactions each seemingly inconsequential but all amounting to displays of power and social recognition (or its absence), including: how much food was served, whose cells people gathered in and around, who had the final say, who dictated who was on the telephones and for how long, who avoided conversation or stayed some distance from their peers. Naturally, some prisoners would rise to the apex of the hierarchies and others would suffer in their subordination:

> There are pecking orders on every wing. There's always someone that's top dog. All the time there's always someone that's a little fish on the bottom. (Martin)

Young men made crude separations between the 'lads' and the 'nerds'—a distinction that was based on commonly understood but informal criteria of whether you could 'hack jail,' had committed the right sort of crime, could handle yourself and avoid behaviour that was seen as irritating or indicative of fragility. The 'lads' were a loosely defined group, sometimes also described as 'our circle,' 'the mandem,' 'brethren,' or 'the boys.' In amongst the 'lads,' were the highest ranking 'Top dog' or 'King of the Wing'—young men who were respected, and at times feared, but to whom the rest of the lads gravitated. These social dynamics and alliances were highly visible. The 'lads' would typically congregate together, look out for each other, pass messages and gossip with one another, and enjoy easy conversation and mischief together (e.g. play fighting, 'messing around,' 'piss taking'). To be 'one of the boys' was a sign of social esteem and approval:

> And then you've got just the boys of the wing, the main mans, the ones that get on with each other and are all tight. It is mainly like the servery workers and the cleaners. I am on servery. [I'm one of] the mandem! (Robert)

For young men who sought social recognition and 'respect,' their social position was of some consequence. Whilst some were keen to avoid prisoner politics and 'keep their head down,' none wanted the indignity and stigma associated with being a 'nerd,' 'wrong 'un' or 'victim.'

Earlier research on prison bullying and victimisation (see Connell & Farrington, 1996; Grapendaal, 1990; Ireland, 2000; Kaminski, 2004; McGurk & McDougall, 1991), describes specific initiation ceremonies that prisoners were required to undergo. Contrary to these earlier studies, though, the young men in the YOI were not subject to formal initiation ceremonies. Rather, young men faced more informal testing. The first was one of criminal credentials. Young men were questioned about their index offence, primarily to eliminate them as possible sex offenders or 'nonces.'[3] Young men guilty by association if they befriended a 'wrong 'un.' When in doubt, demands were made to 'show your paperwork.' For those who were in fact charged or convicted of a sexual offence, the temptation was to remove all trace of such evidence (e.g. by destroying legal documents or letters from solicitors). However, even this would 'ring alarm bells' and would lead others to draw their own conclusions about the index offence.

Sex offenders were advised by staff and peer mentors to conceal information about their index offence and offer alternative explanations for their imprisonment. The success with which prisoners were able to do this varied. Some used other charges as a 'cover story.' Some individuals were prepared to admit to the charges but suggest that the girl had 'got it wrong' or that it did not happen in the way suggested. Such confessions would only be accepted if the person was viewed as credible in other ways and held good social standing with their peers. Those with more custodial experience had a sense of sentencing tariffs and quickly became suspicious if the described offence did not match the sentence. These young men had long memories and were attentive to inconsistencies. For example:

> You know when you get those dickheads that just tell you one little white lie that leads onto another lie and then leads onto another lie, and then two months down the line, after hearing it all, he slips up, and then you think, 'You dickhead.' Then it's like: No, I don't want to entertain you no more, I don't want to listen to you. (Jack)

For others, any attempt to conceal the true reason for their imprisonment was thwarted because their peers would undertake internet searches, ask family and friends to check, or would know someone from the community. As Ben summarised: 'It's a small world.'

On a small number of occasions, prison officers deliberately revealed individual's offences to other young men. Prison staff (including

[3] A phrase that is said to originate from HMP Wakefield where those who could not be unlocked for daily exercise due to fears for their safety were marked as 'not on normal courtyard exercise' ('nonce'). The term is often now used to describe sex offenders or those who commit offences against children and the elderly.

managers) often shared a dislike of sex offenders and would quietly admit to finding it difficult to work with sex offenders. Despite such misgivings, nearly all prison staff were able to maintain professional relationships with the young men. However, on one occasion, a prison officer deliberately delivered legal paperwork to the wrong cell knowing that it was likely that the young man charged with a sexual offence would be assaulted. Prison officers very rarely placed other young men in jeopardy, but further occasions were reported. For example, Stuart, who had been convicted of the rape of his sister complained:

> And then, same in here last week. The file had just gone, apparently. They've all found out, somehow. 'Cause apparently the guards have showed them. They've showed 'em what I'm in for. Like, the exact charges what I'm in for. Then on Tuesday I got two punches to the face for it.

Sometimes disclosures were made because of carelessness. For example, Logan showed me court documents specifying the details of a victim surcharge for a sexual offence against a child. The letters had been delivered to the correct cell, but there had been some cell moves and the letter was opened by the wrong person. News quickly spread amongst other young men on the wing and within a few days, Logan was assaulted by two young men in the showers. Logan questioned me as to why the prison officer did not check that he was delivering the letter to the correct person and why he did not know who was in which cell. It is possible that the mistake was entirely innocent, but it was costly. Such carelessness not only caused an assault, but also jeopardised Logan's confidence in staff.

In addition to establishing their criminal credentials, young men were tested to determine their fortitude, character, and willingness to defend themselves and their property. Young men were keenly aware that others might be unbridled in their aggression, appear odd or strange, or be suffering mental health crisis. Establishing the relative nerve, skill, and lucidity of newcomers was good sense and being a 'good judge of character' was seen as an important asset: 'I can look at someone and know if they are a donut or not.' No one wanted to be 'padded up' with a person with poor hygiene habits, irritating idiosyncrasies, or who was known to have been charged or convicted of sexual offences and/or crimes against children and the elderly. This 'deciphering' (Kaminski, 2004: 8) is a common feature across criminal communities. It served an important safety function; 'criminals have a lot to lose by misreading signs or emitting signals that are misread (unless they want them to be misread)' (Gambetta, 2009: x). No one wanted to miscalculate or misjudge a new arrival. Equally, as far as possible, young men only targeted those who they knew they could overcome and intimidate. Few were so unrestrained in their aggression that they would willingly provoke someone who was likely to defeat them or publicly expose their ineptitude. Thus, testing others was as much a form of self-preservation as it was an attempt to determine who could be influenced, exploited or should be ignored.

Consistently, young men concluded that the first few days and weeks were critical in establishing themselves amongst their peers:

> You're on surveillance from the first day you come to prison. (Matthew)
>
> If someone comes up to you to beat you up you can think what is going on here? If the first time someone comes to you and you let your guard drop even a little bit, someone is going to see. The best thing to do, even if it does end up getting yourself a few bruises or a few scratches, is to always play that front. Even if you're a person that doesn't like to, you have to always play that front. I always say that. (Damien)

Tests varied and included: verbal abuse, verbal challenges, requests to hand over property, simply taking property (particularly canteen, clothes, and trainers), questions about where they had come from, threats to assault them, demands to sing nursery rhymes, and demands to pay 'rent.' In addition, young men were quick to size each other up, which 'area' they were from, who they knew or were known by, their physical capability, the trainers they were wearing and the property they possessed. For example:

> When people come to jail people notice the vulnerable side of people: the way they act, the way they are, if they don't talk to anyone, if they stay in their cell. That's when people get targeted. (Paul)
>
> You have got a lot of what I would call opportunist bullies and when they see somebody, they pick out the right candidate and befriend him and say,

> 'Let's go and have a shower,' and he will walk in with his trainers and walk back out without them. That's just the way it is. (Tyrone)

The surest way for young men to establish themselves was to decisively rebut any attempts to intimidate, threaten, rob, steal from, or assault them. In some cases, as described above, simply being willing to fight was sufficient, as was a suitably abusive retort to verbal abuse, but in other cases, physical force was needed. The essential criterion was an advertised willingness to 'stand up' to others and quickly answer provocation with witty or condemnatory replies and insults. As Jacobs and Wright argue (2006: 47), 'Intolerance earns respect and makes you look strong. Strength is protective.'

Failure to 'stick up for yourself' was observed by all, not just the person initiating the challenge or abuse:

> Stick up for yourself, because the worst thing you can do is let someone take you for a mug, because if it happens, everyone will know that you've been a mug, so everybody will take you for a mug, and if you want that for your whole time in here, well, by all means, do what you're doing, but, if not, change the way you are. I came in, I had a fight within the first two weeks of me being in jail. (Cory)

For those with prior custodial experience or street capital (Mercan, 2022; Sandberg, 2008; Sandberg & Pedersen, 2009; Shammas & Sandberg, 2016), such testing was relatively easy to anticipate, recognise and answer. They knew and relied upon the same social cues to assess those around them, including facial expressions, how individuals carried themselves, what they wore, their accent, whether they could handle themselves in and around the prison (for further discussion, see Chap. 8). For naïve young men unfamiliar with prison life, it could be difficult to read what appeared to be friendly offers of goods—gestures that could envelope them within a cycle of indebtedness and exploitation. There were also 'costly signals' (Gambetta, 2009) related to sexuality, obvious and uncontrolled distress, a failure to rebuff victimisation, and an inability to cope with the daily demands of prison life (such as collecting meals, showering, or walking on 'free flow' to education or work). Living in close quarters meant that even the slightest misstep would be noticed and could easily tarnish an individual's reputation. As Robert observed: 'People notice the smallest things in here because you are with them every day.'

Testing one another with threats, demands and abuse could be costly. In some cases, the newcomer would neither submit to the demands nor accept the abuse, and the initial perpetrator could find themselves humiliated in front of their peers. For example:

> It was on the first day I went over to Res B [Residential Unit B] and this geezer come to my pad and says, 'Give me your burn.'[4] I said, 'Yo, shut the fuck up mate, you ain't having shit.' I'm going get you at dinnertime.' I said, 'Yeah, when it's dinnertime, I'll come out and we'll see what's happening.' When I walked off to dinner he went, 'Yeah, safe mate.' I told him, 'Don't talk shit man behind the door.' (Finlay)

Generally, those who were rebuffed by newcomers did not continue to press them; having determined that someone was willing to stand up for themselves, the initial aggressor generally retreated and/or moved to another target. Whilst such withdrawal would avoid physical injury, the exchange would still shape power dynamics and social interactions. The newcomers—as in the case of Finlay—were also drawing their own conclusions about who was 'all mouth' and who was a potential threat to them. Forcing someone to walk away—as Finlay had done—gave them a psychological and social advantage.

Perpetrators

Typically, these 'perpetrators' were one of the 'lads,' but the longevity of their victimising behaviour could vary, as could their status within the prisoner hierarchy, the visibility of their behaviour, the function of the victimisation, and their receptivity to external controls or incentives. There were occasions where young men would threaten, verbally abuse,

[4] 'Burn' was prison slang for tobacco.

or fight others on an isolated occasion and only when they saw no alternative. However, there were others who were more persistently involved in violence, victimisation, and exploitation, and where such actions 'can be interpreted 'as judicious public relations and investment in one's human capital development' (Bourgois, 2003: 24).

The King of the Wing

Aran was a large, stocky, full bearded, Asian Muslim who had a boisterous, brash, and imposing manner. At the time I first met him, he was convicted of driving offences. During the research, he would be released and return just as quickly. Aran also had a history of violent, firearms- and drug-related offences, and his family and friends were linked with a range of cash businesses (e.g. fast food, shisha bars, gyms, and supplement stores). The National Crime Agency subsequently claimed that this 'property portfolio' had allowed the group to launder £17 million from drug enterprise. Quite unbeknown to prison officers, Aran had already established his own foothold in criminal enterprises stretching as far as Bangladesh and Pakistan. In prison, he wanted for nothing. However, unlike others, he was not prone to flashy consumeristic displays with items from the prison catalogue. Typically dressed in his green donkey jacket and work boots, Aran was more understated in his attire than those who preferred the 'fat pads' and designer clothes. Instead, and still enjoying some of the proceeds from his criminal enterprises, Aran preferred to financially provide for his family regarding himself as their protector and defender in the absence of his father.

Within prison, Aran's reputation—and criminal credentials—had preceded him (also see Crewe, 2009: 261–262). His height and weight also had the advantage of putting him physically head and shoulders above the rest. As one of those overseeing the illicit economy, Aran gained economic and social power:

> You get a lot of respect, like the people who sell drugs in here. Everyone respects people who are selling [Mamba[5]] and have got it. (Sam)

[5] Prison slang for psychoactive substances (see Chap. 4).

His status as 'King of the Wing' was quickly apparent even to the uninformed observer. His associates would gravitate towards him during association, and he was a central figure in Friday's 'Muslim prayers' service. Those young men who were not in his good graces kept a safe distance. Some admired him, most feared him, and all were deferential. During his reign, 'nobody would say anything to him' and none would attempt to overthrow him. His position was accepted, or at least tolerated, by those on the wing.

The leadership style of the 'King of the Wing' primarily rested on self-interest, power, control, domination, and fear. Jermaine, for example, explained that:

> Everyone wants to be the bad wolf.
>
> *Why do people want to be the bad wolf?*
>
> It's because you can control people. You can tell them to do things. Even your friends, close friends. They respect you. I think you get more respect.

Any respect that Aran and others like him attracted was a mixture of a reverence for his coolness and entrepreneurial skill and a healthy recognition that he was 'not to be fucked with.' Aran was merciless with those he deemed contemptible. Harry, like others, described how Aran targeted new people:

> *So, what kind of things would he do to new people?*
>
> He'll tell them to sing at their door: 'Sing at your door or we'll kick shit out of you tomorrow'. They were shitting themselves. First time in prison, he starts chanting it, 'Oh, I've killed five people.' 'I heard he might kill you.' That shit scared the crap out of them; they're absolutely bricking it.
>
> *Had he killed five people?*
>
> No, he'd killed no one. Maybe that's why the wing's so shit, but he just told them, and they'd be shitting themselves, because they don't know who he is. He's the boss, though.
>
> *Do the rest of the wing listen as it's happening?*

> They don't say nothing. Then they just start picking fights, heckling each other, talking about people's mums and that, and then you get people at the doors laughing.

For Aran and those like him, they were 'the artisan[s] of violence' who 'derived satisfaction from the suffering of others' (Toch, 1992: 202). They experienced 'the fear that they provoke in their enemies as a kind of ersatz form of respect' (Gilligan, 2003: 1151).

Largely self-interested, the 'King of the Wings' were unconcerned about the greater good or collective solidarity (cf. Sykes, 1958). Prison officers varied in their assessment of Aran; some saw him as immature and a 'pain in the backside.' Others—particularly those whom he had threatened—preferred to give him a wide berth. Unlike some who preferred to gain their 'Enhanced status' (and the maximum freedoms and privileges the prison could offer), Aran fluctuated between Standard and Basic regime but avoided the full weight of the State's punitive sanctions for misconduct. To prison officers he seemed stubbornly resistant, but this was a less a protest than a judgment on Aran's part that 'the system' simply did not matter to him. Confinement was a temporary occupational hazard and he would soon be re-released. Far from adopting a world view that is confined to the prison (c.f. the 'State raised youths' in Irwin's account, see Irwin, 1970), he was orientated towards, and had an identity, that was very much located in the streets. At the time of writing, Aran was sought by the police for a serious assault that will no doubt result in a substantial prison sentence if he is caught and is not, as rumoured, in Pakistan. With contacts throughout the UK, and internationally, multiple police appeals have thus far proved unsuccessful.

Aran was just one of a small number of young men referred to or known as the 'King of the Wing.' With only a small number of wings, this number would always be small. The 'King of the wing,' sometimes referred to as the 'Top Dog,' sat at the apex of the prisoner hierarchy. They were the prisoner leaders, comfortable amongst 'the lads' but typically exercising influence and power over them. Such influence extended as far as: dictating the distribution of food, who played pool, who was permitted to use the telephone (or was required to forgo their place in the line), setting prices (e.g. for drugs, haircuts, for mobile phones), putting contracts out, and issuing instructions as to who would collect and hold contraband on their behalf. Thus, the 'King of the Wing' held both social, distributive, and economic power. Some of this power was partly driven by the fact that 'Dealing was high risk activity that required nerve, contracts, organisation, and a level of entrepreneurialism that many prisoners admire' (Crewe, 2009: 265). They would—as Tyrone put it—'set things' on the wing. If someone came into the prison with drugs, they were prepared to rob them to maintain their control of the economy. The King of the Wing would both create social order by providing a degree of 'extra-legal governance' (Skarbek, 2014; Gooch & Treadwell, 2023, 2025) and dictating when perceived 'violations' were punished. He also contributed to the insecurity of those who he deemed weak and fragile.

Unlike adult prisoner's disavowal of the 'powder power' of dealers in the heroin-based prison drug economy (Crewe, 2006), contemporary prison drug dealers were able to convert their economic capital into social capital and symbolic power (Bourdieu, 1986). Operating a 'business' within prison demonstrated an ability to meaningfully resist economic marginalisation and 'profit' from imprisonment. For example:

> You ask about what goes on in here, you know, money is made, there is more money in this jail than outside. I am a man. I do what I do here. I do what I do out there. I have responsibilities, I am a family man. I do what I do because it puts food on the table, because I must survive. It's business. … The business is how I keep a roof on my mother's house, the business is how I put food on the table. (Aran)

As in Aran's case, the 'business' typically involved selling drugs and mobile phones (and associated paraphernalia). It also appealed to a vision of masculinity that was both heavily paternalistic (demonstrating the ability to earn and graft) and highly consumeristic (demonstrating the ability to acquire the 'right' status symbols). Economic inequality and precarity, unemployment on the streets (Hall et al., 2013; Maguire, 2021), and low wage work within the prison rendered this form of masculinity particularly distinctive and 'virtuous.'

Violent Assailants

Tyrone was a charismatic young man who—amongst his peers—appeared to be relatively mature. He had already served time in adult prisons and felt just as comfortable amongst adult prisoners as his younger peers. In the community, he had perpetrated a string of knife robberies for mobile phones—unsophisticated violent offending that had seen some of his victims frog marched at knife point to a cash point, but had mostly resulted in very little material gain and a substantial custodial sentence. This was not, however, his first prison sentence. Having spent time in 'juvie' (child penal custody), he had long adopted a survival strategy that primarily rested on visible violence:

> The way I've gone about it I've just come out fighting, fight as many people as I can, win as many fights as I can so then I have proved what I needed to prove. Then I can go to someone and say, 'Stop talking too loud at night because you are doing my head in,' and they will stop. Not for fear of repercussions, but you know what I mean, but because they will know I have been around the block and have done what I need to do, so there is that respect. There is a hierarchy that has arisen. In any workplace or even amongst the staff, governors and whatnot, there's a hierarchy, so it is the same everywhere. Prisoners do whatever they need to do.

Tyrone valued violence for its ability to establish and prove himself, and he took pride in this violent reputation. He could be relatively calculating and commented: 'I know what I am doing. I can always calm.' He knew that there was wisdom in 'biting his lip' but acknowledged that this was harder to do when 'pride's digging at you on the inside.' Whilst he admitted he could get 'angry quickly,' his violence also held precision and control. He explained: 'if you can keep a cool head while all of those around you are losing theirs—very often that is an important attribute.'

Although he was a cleaner at the time of the interview, this had been interrupted by several periods in segregation. That said, prison officers would rely on Tyrone to stabilise the wing as much as they would punish him for infractions. For Tyrone, there was some utility in assisting prison officers in keeping an orderly wing:

> The staff came to me yesterday and said some guy was getting a bit of grief because he was new and that, so I stopped his grief and then three weeks down the line, like today, I need my haircut, boss remembers something I have done for them and then I will get that.

This sort of reciprocal 'mutual accommodation' (Liebling et al., 2011a: 54) was relatively common amongst those young men deemed 'leaders' amongst their peers and capable of 'stepping in' at the behest of staff. The ability to 'stop the grief' rested on an assumption that Tyrone's commands would be obeyed, or would be enforced, and therefore had the effect of perpetuating a culture of violence and intimidation. Tyrone had come to learn that violence was as important in controlling prison officers as it was controlling his peers.

> Even the staff have got respect for me because they have seen me fighting. And I don't involve them… And as soon as they come to twist me, it is done. The staff don't [twist me up]. Because I have set it on the staff as well, do you know what I mean, so you have got to have a bit of respect for someone who you know won't just talk—because when I am mad at the staff I don't shout at them, I don't do anything like that because then they will put you on three man unlock or they won't unlock you. You just sit there quiet, don't say nothing. Staff know that when I say I'm going to do it [assault them].

Although Tyrone was frequently mentioned in incident reports and morning meetings, he was not regarded as a loose cannon by his peers. He maintained his social status, masculine credentials, and position as one of the more influential 'lads.' However, Tyrone was learning that fear was a useful tool, and that he could manipulate and control others. He was one of several young men who did not directly bully others but were violent with sufficient frequency that they could intimidate others into doing what they wanted. There were others like him –Rhys, Ryan, Damien, Joseph, Toby—for whom violence was a useful resource and although it sometimes meant periods in 'the block,' they were willing to 'ride' segregation. For Tyrone, though, he stayed somewhat clear of the drug trade, neither using nor dealing.

Enforcers and Middlemen

Yasir was one of the young men for hire. An unimposing, slight, short Black Somali lad, Yasir was always in Shadow's orbit. Yasir was boyish in appearance, whilst Shadow was tall and broad. Shadow would set the terms; Yasir would follow them. Yasir had fled civil war after witnessing his family killed in front of him. Settling in the U.K., Yasir excelled at athletics and became a keen runner. His athletics career would abruptly end after he was apprehended for a series of street robberies conducted with a 'burner'[6] whilst riding his bicycle and stealing several thousand pounds worth of property. Despite his diminutive stature, Yasir was indiscriminate in the use of violence. He was quiet but stealthy. Largely indifferent to whether he was assaulting staff or fellow prisoners, or to any size disparity, Yasir would quickly escalate to serious acts of violence. He would take a knife to a fist fight. Inflicting serious violence did not trouble him; and most assumed that he lacked any empathy, remorse, or guilt. He was also for hire. As an 'enforcer,' violence was a marketable asset (Winlow, 2001). Yasir would take payment from Somalian and Asian prisoners. He was loyal to 'the lads' and they kept him close. Not long after his release, he was wanted by the police for this suspected involvement in an attempted murder committed with a firearm.

Whilst violence served an important regulatory function in the illicit economy, it could draw unwanted attention (Hobbs, 1998; Kotzé et al., 2022). Co-ordinating the sale and distribution of contraband within prison necessitated activities such as collecting contraband, concealing contraband, distributing it, collecting payment, maintaining debt lists, ensuring financial transactions were made in the community, the warding off of competitors, compelling payment from those who had reneged on their obligations, and, threatening debtors and/or their family members. These young men were keenly aware of the risks of being caught with contraband or debt lists in their possession and would—if they could—use the enforcers and middlemen to do their 'dirty work.' For the enforcers, they remained in the good graces of the 'King of the Wing' and would come under their protection. Their involvement solidified their

---

[6] Slang for firearm.

social capital and made them visibly part of the 'mandem,' but their instrumental violence was also profitable on its own terms. As Kotzé et al. note, 'enforcement has become a commodified illegal activity within the criminal labour market that can be sold for profit' (Kotzé et al., 2022: 5). The emergence of these enforcers within the young prisoner hierarchy is illustrative of the shift towards entrepreneurial crime both within the prison estate (Gooch & Treadwell, 2021, 2025) and by young men in the community (Densley, 2014).

Victim-Perpetrator and the Turbulence of Victimisation

Stood within the segregation unit, the shouts of the young men accommodated there for the 'Good Order and Discipline' (GOAD) of the YOI are especially loud. At the far end of the segregation unit, Greg is (ineffectively) replying to accusations that he is a 'pussy,' 'victim' and 'could never get a girl'; shouts that only elicit further abuse. Greg is a gaunt, shaven headed, medium build White man clad in a grey prison tracksuit. In recent weeks, he has variously assaulted staff, self-harmed, flooded cells, damaged property (including breaking multiple observation glasses, much to the irritation of prison officers), and set fire to his cell. This behaviour had isolated him from most prisoners—a problem now compounded by the fact that he was taking every opportunity to call other prisoners any racial slur that might elicit a reaction. Whilst on 'normal location,' Greg had been assaulted several times, partly because he spent his evenings championing Combat 18 and the English Defence League (both far-right groups, for further discussion see Winlow et al., 2017), stirring an incensed reaction. Prison officers, however, sensed that the source of conflict was also tied to an outstanding debt.

Greg was a heavy drug user who had over time moved from being one of the 'lads' on the wing to being assaulted quite badly at the pool table. Tyrone was suspected of being one of the aggressors, as was Luke, another frequently violent prisoner and accomplice. Both Tyrone and Luke were held in cells at the opposite end of the segregation unit from Greg.

Together, Tyrone and Luke were largely occupying their time in segregation by either conversing with one another or shouting insults at Greg, reminding him of their intended violent punishment, telling him how inadequate his parents and brothers were, that he should commit suicide, and that his heterosexuality was doubtful. Greg would periodically shout insults or make bizarre animal noises. He would then threaten to beat Tyrone and Luke up. Neither Tyrone nor Luke seemed to tire of these exchanges, nor did they see themselves as a victim even though objectively they were on the receiving end of as much abuse as they dispensed. At times they would shout, 'you're a full-grown man!' or 'Do you think your daughter is proud of you?' Greg was no threat to them—socially, psychologically, or physically. He was contemptible.

As O'Donnell and Edgar (1999: 98) argue, 'much victimisation is mutual': reciprocal threats and verbal abuse often preceded physical violence. Whilst there were young men who failed to recover or shed the 'victim' label, a larger group of young men moved between being the victim and perpetrator without the 'victim' label becoming their primary identity. Equally, there were situations where the primary aggressor could become the victim if, for example, they had miscalculated the relative strength of their intended target and were overcome or suffered more serious injury. There were also occasions where the victim of one incident became the perpetrator of a later incident:

> When I was first in here, one of my mates actually got rushed in the showers, like got stamped all over and that, but he never—he was asked if he wanted to move off the wing for his safety and he said, 'No,' and he waited for one of them to go in the showers and he went in there and he fucked his [the original perpetrator's] shit up, went into the office and goes, 'Now you can get me off the wing.' My mate punched him, he [the original perpetrator] slipped over and then obviously that's when he stamped all over him basically, kicking him in the face and that. But my mate had a lot worse, he had about six of them run in the shower, took him to the floor, jumping on him. (Ollie)

Lewis, for example, was assaulted by a group of young men but did not fear he would suffer a permanent loss of status:

> Nothing, just starting for no reason. 'Yo, you need to cut your hair, brother, innit you need to cut your hair.' I said, 'I don't, I wanna grow it, know what I mean bro? I wanna grow my hair so what's it to do with you, innit?' Then I said, 'Just fuck off and leave me alone.' So he's there, he's come at me now, he's gone, 'You want it? You wanna get banged?' I said, 'Try and bang me innit', I stood there. I said, 'Try and bang me. I used to do boxing and that, but if you wanna try it we'll have it, innit?'
>
> And he's—then he's got his mates involved. I said, 'I ain't fighting three or four of you. I'll have a one-on-one but not three or four of you, innit?' And then they're there now outside talking shit, whispering and that, 'Let's get him, let's get him on the way back.' I thought nothing of it, know what I mean. As I've got through this gate here 'Bang!' [makes slap sound] 'Bang!' [makes slap sound] 'Bang!' [makes slap sound] 'Bang!' [makes slap sound] about seven or eight of them. Straight in my face, know what I mean? They've knocked me out, know what I mean? I took it. Got curled up like that.

Whilst the relationship between the two separate assaults can be easily traced, this was sometimes missed by prison officers who recorded incidents in isolation and did not always have the time, curiosity, or information to draw the links between the various incidents.

The victim-perpetrator dynamic not only accounts for the mutuality of victimisation, or how roles could change within a single encounter, but how some young men drifted between being victimised and victimising others. Adam, for example, felt that he had 'a lot of issues' in the YOI. He was both quick to distance himself from the 'nerds' and 'muppets,' whilst also falling victim to robbery and violence himself. Speaking of those who had been robbed of their trainers, Adam explained:

> I don't see it as bullying. Certain lads can't say no, like with their trainers. They can't really say no because they try it but they just get battered and I mean get their heads absolutely smashed in. … We call them the muppets, they are the people who don't really say nothing. Then you have got the mandem and that's like the lads and that's the circle. There are two different circles. You are either with the nerds or you are with the mandem.

Despite this, one of Adam's three pairs of trainers were sold by someone on the wing to another individual without his knowledge. The seller then came to the cell and successfully removed the trainers from Adam's feet to complete the transaction:

> As I walked out [of the cell], that's when they dived on me and dragged me in the pad. Basically, took me off my feet because it was a bit of a fight at first, but they couldn't do nothing. They are only a pair of trainers though, so I'm not that arsed about it. I look at it like they are that broke arsed about having anything, and they are going to try that. I am not going to break into your house and come take a pair of your trainers. It is just the same now. I think it's just stupid.

Verbally, Adam is able to reconcile the robbery by belittling his aggressors. He did not accept that they gained anything in terms of power, status or superiority over him. Nor did he feel himself to be a 'nerd' or a 'muppet,' even though he would partly satisfy his own criteria for such labels. Such distancing from inferior social positions was partly achieved by Adam's own involvement in exploitation and robbery and his claims to wider forms of economic and social capital:

> I don't smoke [Mamba][7] at all. I have had a bit of it, trying it and that, but it is a big thing in here. People get addicted to it. That other circle, they will come to us. That's who we target to sell it to. They have got money coming in from their family, but that's our money. We are making money. Like people on the out come to us, that's our money to be made. … I have robbed people because like I said it's the lads who have the nice pads are the ones that are earning it. That's our circle kind of thing. We won't rob each other. But if someone comes in and they have nice shower gels, we will offer to buy them off them first, but if they don't want to sell then we will rob them.

Adam struggled to control his temper if he felt disrespected or poorly treated by prison officers. He was not averse to 'squaring up' to officers, taking them 'head on' or 'putting them in their place.' He had regularly

[7] Prison slang for psychoactive substances, see Chap. 4.

assaulted officers, and his constant aggression had resulted in him being 'ghosted' between YOIs on more than one occasion. Undoubtedly, Adam enjoyed the 'excitement' of violence, but equally, he was willing to sacrifice his own liberty and freedoms within the YOI to preserve 'face and honour' (also see Winlow, 2001: 44–45). Whilst Adam was also capable of violence towards his peers, he failed to reach the esteemed status of 'Top Dog' of 'King of the Wing'. He was 'one of the lads' and comfortably mixed in the conversations with those who had more power and status.

The 'Bandits' and the 'Foot Soldiers' Acting Under Duress

Bertie has been at it again. 'There must come a point when tough action is taken,' says the Security Custodial Manager. The security staff want to see Bertie prosecuted and receive a consecutive custodial sentence, but the police make the decision not to charge Bertie. The security team are frustrated. There had been a series of prison videos posted to internet and social media sites, and they believed it was only a matter of time before they faced the embarrassment of a video filmed within the YOI appearing in the national press. They complained that the forensic analysis of any confiscated phones was not being done, that the whole system regarded mobile phone use as an inconvenience rather than a threat, and that simply, 'Nobody seems to give a shit.' James asks, 'What did you find?' 'Three phones, two charger cables (no plugs), a couple of USBs, all in a single pad.'[8] Bertie is hardly a criminal mastermind, and regularly gained adjudications for tagging his own name around the prison. 'A total regular pain in the arse,' says one officer. Another officer on the search team chips in, 'When we caught him, you know the first thing he says to me is, 'Oh well boss, no worries, we got more phones in here than Carphone warehouse.' James and I laugh, because sometimes that is all you can do, and the security staff laugh too, still frustrated by the futility of it all. 'A pain in the arse is right,' says the officer, 'because I reckon he is right. We are

[8] Prison slang for cell.

like their warehouse. About two thirds of them phones are up his fucking backside!'

In Bertie's case, his possession of mobile telephone was voluntary. He was not coerced to hold them for others, nor was he necessarily forced to hand them over. Not all who were passing or storing contraband were the 'owners' of the items. It was not unusual, for example, for young men to be pressured or coerced into storing items for the benefit of more controlling individuals. This had the effect of passing the risk of extra days in prison or criminal charges from the owner to the steward of the property. There were others who were pressured and coerced to hold contraband:

> And they tried to make me hold phones … And that was after everyone found out my little brother died and stuff. They just seemed to put more pressure on me—I just had enough of it, the little threats and stuff.
>
> I am still having difficulties with them now. Like they send threatening messages over. … They told a couple of the lads to tell me, 'He is getting rushed,' and all this. 'We can put money on his head.' (Peter)

The recording of prison violence and victimisation was relatively unsophisticated in this respect and often failed to account for the role of those co-ordinating assaults and/or coercing others to perform a variety of roles and services for them (e.g. assaulting others, holding contraband, punishing non re-payment of debt, or cleaning their cell). There was very little grace or sympathy for the loss of items to security seizures or interruption (e.g. if a 'throwover' was intercepted by security and did not get collected as expected) and such losses were punished. In addition, some young men felt that others should go so far as protecting their interests and warning them about the arrival of the dedicated search teams or security teams. For example, Paul was assaulted for failing to warn others on the wing that the security team had arrived:

> I've seen security go downstairs. I knew I had to do summat 'cause obviously it's your instinct when you're in jail 'cause obviously you're an inmate, you have to do something to protect your other inmates. So I've banged up someone else who was on the ledge and I've told him to get out there and shout out 'Pass bins!' and I was like, 'Pass bins, pass bins' to shout to all the

> lads downstairs and obviously they've got caught with phones and Mamba and weed.[9] Them two lads who punched me up done it 'cause they're pissed that everything's gone and they're not getting nothing. The second lad jumped over and hit me. Obviously I swung back and he's followed him and says to him, 'Fucking come over,' and I've hit him and I've grabbed him like that and like as we're on the floor. I'm hitting him and he's hitting me in the head the other lad jumps over and started kicking me in the head. (Paul)

In this case, Paul was believed to be responsible for the loss of the contraband despite his attempts to warn his peers. However, such justifications could serve as a pretext with young men taking advantage of an opportunity to assault an individual deemed irritating. Assaults could also represent an attempt to direct and expunge anger and frustration where the people truly responsible for the grievance (e.g. the security staff) could not be punished.

Victims

Victimisation was such a pervasive feature of prison life that nearly everyone had at one point been tested, threatened, robbed, or assaulted. No one was immune. At any one time, only two or three young men (e.g. Aran, Luke and Shadow) were sufficiently well-respected (or more accurately feared) that none dared to threaten them or challenge their authority. These young men still could not fully 'let their guard down'—the possibility of a usurper or a misdirected assault always remained. There was a recognition that 'even donuts [those who are weak] can get brave,' and that violence was a perennial problem. It was not the assault that rendered them a victim, but their tolerance of it. As Christie argues (1986: 18), 'being a victim is not a thing, an objective phenomenon. It will not be the same to all people in all situations.' Some young men recovered quickly from any psychological and physical injury and, since sparring was so readily a part of everyday life, the 'victim' label did not

[9] Slang for cannabis.

become a permanent stain on their reputation. Instead, they took pride in their ability to defend themselves, face their aggressor, and even take a beating with dignity (especially if they were outnumbered, hit from behind or cornered).

Conversely, labels such as 'fraggles,' 'nerds,' 'fragile people,' 'tramps' and 'paigons' were reserved for those who had little or no capacity to defend themselves, lacked 'character,' were unable to manage their financial resources, disintegrated rather than 'doing their time,' were poorly presented, and/or were believed to be 'fake.' These labels conveyed 'disrespect' (Crewe, 2009: 250), disapproval and contempt. Being a 'victim' was not determined by someone's relative contribution to an assault but served as a label denoting incompetence and vulnerability:

> You don't want to get labelled as a victim, because if you do then that is all you will be for the whole time of your sentence. If you labelled as a victim, people don't want to make friends with you, they just see you as a victim. (Joseph)

> He is a nerd, a full on victim. (Steven)

As noted by Crewe (2009: 251), 'some prisoners despised weakness as a thing in itself, punishing others for representing the fears that they fought to suppress.' Such young men used violence as psychological defence work to reassure themselves that they were nothing like those weak prisoners. Those young men deemed 'victims' was socially excluded but also thought to have brought the victimisation upon themselves. Young men were not denying that victims were harmed and humiliated—thus there was no 'denial of injury' (Sykes & Matza, 1957) or a denial that such actions might constitute rule violations, rather they argued that any moral failing was not theirs but the victim's. As Toch (1977: 150) describes: 'The man is on trial and he is fatefully examined. The penalty for failure is accelerated victimisation. If a man acquits himself fully, he ensures his immunity from attack.' Being marked as a vulnerable prisoner or a 'victim' was a 'permanent marker of subordinate status' (Maguire, 2021: 153). For those who were victimised frequently, prison time was 'hard time' (Johnson et al., 2017). Even routine acts such as collecting meals, making a telephone call, taking a shower or attending work and education meant running the gauntlet amongst those who were prepared to mercilessly insult, threaten, or take things from them.

The responses of those labelled as victims varied. Some sought the protection of prison officers hoping that they would not reveal their disclosures to the aggressors. Some self-harmed. A minority simply segregated themselves within their cells and withdraw from prison life entirely, preferring to go without a meal, a shower or a telephone call. When I met Stuart, this was precisely what he was doing, seemingly unnoticed by prison officers. He had survived by living off what little food and drink he had in his cell. As the cell door was unlocked for us to speak to him, the pungent smell took my breath away. Stuart was facing many years in prison for raping family members. This combined with his dishevelled state, chubbiness, low intelligence and inability to make eye contact or interact with any confidence had clearly marked him out as a target. Stuart did not deny that he had committed the offences but discussed them with a childish naivety ('sex things, bad things'). Stuart was assaulted several times, including on one occasion where high-status prisoners manipulated another sex offender to fight as entertainment. As Taff was heard to say, he was almost the perfect 'Mamba Muppet' and they could 'test the strain on him' (a practice that was uncommon compared to adult prisons, see Gooch & Treadwell, 2020). Initially, in interview, Stuart said that the threats of violence bothered him little, partly because he concluded that he had 'lost everything' and because he was used to being beaten and assaulted. However, he had been hiding in his cell for two weeks prior to my interview with him. Prison officers had largely concluded that he would have to 'man up to survive' and discounted the possibility that there was any risk of suicide. One officer described him as 'too dull or inadequate to hurt himself.' Prison officers had—after 'dragging' him away from a group of prisoners who were punching him—ensured that he had medical treatment, but they could not eradicate the threat.

Unlike adult prisons, YOI's do not have vulnerable prisoner units. However, for those who were in crisis, respite could be found in the Supported Living Unit (or the 'victim's wing' as it was dubbed by some of the young men). The wing housed a mixture of people: those who needed some form of sanctuary, the mentors and the 'stabilisers.' It was thought that a combination of good role modelling, a calm environment, peer support and the presence of those who were able to resolve conflict and head off potential problems would provide the context for improved 'coping' by the young men who were seeking an escape from the other residential units. The unit was created at the opposite end of the YOI to the notoriously more volatile wings, shielding 'the cubs from the lions.' This did not always insulate victims from continued aggression and intimidation: notes could still be passed and a 'contract put on someone's head.' Moreover, it was not uncommon for some young men—in the relative safety of the Supported Living Unit—to begin exploiting or threatening others. However, such victimisation was quickly identified, partly because it was so unsophisticated. Curtis—one of the 'stabilisers'—was quick to squash what he perceived to be childish, petty, and unnecessary behaviour. Gold toothed, 'hench,' and widely known to be serving a long sentence (10 years) for a domestic robbery with a machete, Curtis was not to be trifled with. He was well respected and well-liked by the 'lads.' He avoided being labelled a 'screw boy' (also see Gooch & Treadwell, 2023) by maintaining a careful relationship with prison officers—one that straddled a line between conviviality but not being a 'grass.' Equally, his wider capital and respect within the YOI was such that he was not marred by being associated with the 'weak' and vulnerable. Under his stewardship, the Supported Living Unit often created a place of sanctuary and safety for the most vulnerable and victimised, and restrained those trying to be a 'big fish in a small pond.'

Not Involved in Prison Victimisation

At first glance, those who were 'not involved' in prison victimisation were the largest number. Amongst them were the prisoners like Bertie (the 'bandits') who were mischievous or violated security rules, but largely did so without embroiling themselves in violent incidents. There were also the men who were distressed and injuring themselves (who were often seen as 'fragile,' 'weak,' 'fraggles,' and 'nerds'). Others were Enhanced prisoners who had either earned positions of responsibility or transferred to the Enhanced Wing and enjoyed extra 'comforts' (e.g. in-cell showers).

The peer representatives and Enhanced prisoners could remain 'one of the lads,' especially if they could sustain the appearance of loyalty to their peers and did not absorb the priorities of prison staff or (obviously) pass information. Some Enhanced prisoners stayed connected to the bigger 'players' and were tuned into the gossip and politics of the wider prison, but obtained social prestige through a combination of advertised capacity to protect themselves, the ability to acquire material goods *and* through alternatives form of masculinity (such as fatherhood and legitimate prison employment). The Enhanced prisoners with trusted positions were careful not to lose their positions, and often straddled the line between demonstrating 'good behaviour' to prison staff and navigating possible threats and assaults that continued to be a part of prison life. Essentially, they had to hold the horizontal relationships with their peers with the vertical relationships with prison officers (and the State) in a—sometimes uneasy—balance. Those who were threatened would respond in kind and hope that the other person conceded defeat. When violence seemed inevitable, they would fight in places where detection was less likely (e.g. cells) and assume the victim would not report the incident since it would mean declaring their contributory involvement (e.g. by robbing someone, threatening someone, or using a mobile phone) and risk their position as an Enhanced prisoner (especially if also residing on the Enhanced wing).

Those who were neither distressed nor disruptive and had not obtained positions of trust and responsibility as mentors or peer representatives, were dubbed by senior managers as the 'grey men.' Their lives within the YOI were a repetitive ordering of work or education, domestics, gym, meals, association and, when such opportunities were available, family visits. These young men preferred to avoid, as far as possible, victimisation, choosing to 'keep their head down' and 'get on with their time.' They accepted that they were ultimately 'on their ones' when it came to surviving prison. Should the need arise, some would use violence, but most had sufficiently safeguarded their reputation (and could do so again), did not use drugs routinely, avoided the politics of drug violence and economic activities, and/or were motivated to secure the rewards, freedoms, and privileges offered by the State (for further analysis, see Chap. 8). In this way, they reduced the likelihood of further victimisation.

Conclusion

Although the 'deprivation of security' (Sykes, 1958) is a universal feature of imprisonment, both the nature and extent of that deprivation can vary, even within the same YOI. This deprivation may be felt more keenly by the 'nerds,' 'fraggles,' 'muppets' and 'wrong 'uns' who are systematically targeted and find it difficult to rise about their subordinate position. By contrast, the higher ranking 'Kings of the Wing' did not fear that they would be routinely robbed, exploited, or threatened, but their nefarious activity may always put them at risk of being overthrown, being 'violated' (when debts were not repaid), and being ignored as their power lapsed. That said, the 'victim' label represented something more than a legal distinction between who was responsible for violence and those who suffered it—if indeed such binary depictions were particularly useful given the frequent mutuality of victimisation (Edgar & O'Donnell, 1998). Being a 'victim' was a contemptible label for those who were deemed weak, incapable, and unable to defend themselves. Someone could technically be the victim of an assault without being defined by it, whilst others not only failed to shed the label but also became consumed by fear. The extent to which young men absorbed the logic of violence or admitted defeat was structured by life-course. The next chapter (Chap. 6) therefore interrogates the relationship between behaviour within prison and experiences of tragedy and trauma.

Irwin (1970) identified the 'state raised youth' as a particular identity adopted by men in adult prisons who had earlier experience of State care and penal institutions. Within the YOI, though, a stratification existed amongst these State-raised youths that mirrored adult prisoner society. However, there were two important differences. First, the most severe forms of criminal activity within prison—such as terrorism, extreme fatal violence, and organised crime—were far less pronounced within the YOI with the effect that there were few concerns about extremism and coercive conversions to Islam (c.f. High Security prisons, Liebling et al., 2011b). Secondly, whilst many young men wanted to 'do their time and get out' (Carrabine, 2003: 103), the need to demonstrate suitability for release was—whilst in the YOI—either an irrelevant or distant concern.

The vast majority of young men had determinate release dates and those who were serving indeterminate sentences were often several years away from their first parole hearing. Thus, young prisoner society was less influenced by the demands of the penal power and the need to evidence their rehabilitation. In Chap. 7, these orientations are better contextualised by young men's adaptations to imprisonment and the extent to which their experience of youth imprisonment was easing their transitions to adult prisons.

The argot roles reveal what behaviours were common, but also what was not. Consistent with the finding that sexual violence is uncommon (see Chap. 3), there were few references to sexualised behaviour and the 'queens,' 'wolves,' 'punks,' 'booty bandits' and 'fish' described in adult and youth institutions were absent (c.f. Bartollas et al., 1976; Bowker, 1980; Clemmer, 1940; Donaldson, 2001; Hensley et al., 2003; Lockwood, 1980; Polsky, 1962; Sykes, 1958). Equally, and in contrast to other jurisdictions and the myths about youth prison violence, the 'gang' failed to structure or define young prisoner society (c.f. Jacobs, 1974; Symkovych, 2017). However, the behaviours associated with the illicit economy mirrored patterns of organised crime in the community, albeit with less severity. Any 'hits' that were ordered may lack the extremity and severity observed elsewhere in the prison estate and in the community, but the young men in the YOI did put 'contracts' on people's heads and the more powerful young men did—as noted above—instruct and coerce 'enforcers,' 'middlemen,' and 'foot soldiers.' It is here that the shift in the dynamics of prison violence is most notable. Edgar et al. (2003: 103–104) found few incidents were related to disputes over material items (such as drugs), yet within the YOI, enforcement activities (and disputes over debt) were common.

Few were yet immersed within criminal networks that had a more international reach, or the sophistication shown by some adult prisoners, but certainly some were connected through family ties and/or were at the peripheries of more organised criminal networks. What was evident, though, was that young men were beginning to adopt roles similar to those in the community criminal networks and in adult prisons (for further analysis, see Gooch & Treadwell, 2021, 2025; Hobbs, 2013; Pearson & Hobbs, 2001, 2003). For these young men, they were not necessarily learning how to desist from offending but easing their way into the criminal networks and becoming more sophisticated in their criminal activities. Learning to navigate the prison system involved not only learning how to 'play the game' or 'work with the prison,' but also how to both secure legitimate 'rewards' for good behaviour and avoid detection for any illegitimate enterprise. These key formative lessons are discussed in Chap. 7. Notably, as individualised adaptations to prisoner life had become sharper, exploitation, and extortion was not necessarily seen as a violation of the prisoner normative code (c.f. Sykes, 1958)—a theme taken up in Chap. 8.

References

Anderson, E. (1999). *Code of the street: Decency, violence and the moral life of the inner city*. W.W. Norton and Company.

Bartollas, C., Miller, S. J., & Dinitz, S. (1976). *Juvenile victimisation – The institutional paradox*. Halstead Press.

Bottoms, A. E. (1999). Interpersonal violence and social order in prisons. *Crime and Justice, 26*, 205–281.

Bourdieu, P. (1986). The forms of capital. In J. Richardson (Ed.), *Handbook of theory and research for the sociology of education* (pp. 241–258). Greenwood.

Bourgois, P. (2003). *In search of respect: Selling crack in El Barrio*. Cambridge University Press.

Bowker, L. H. (1980). *Prison victimisation*. Elsevier.

Carrabine, E. (2003). *Power, discourse and resistance*. Ashgate.

Christie, N. (1986). The ideal victim. In E. A. Fattah (Ed.), *From crime policy to victim policy: Reorienting the justice system* (pp. 17–30). Palgrave Macmillan UK.

Clemmer, D. (1940). *The prison community*. Holt, Reinhart and Winston.

Connell, A. E., & Farrington, D. P. (1996). Bullying among incarcerated young offenders: Developing an interview schedule and some preliminary results. *Journal of Adolescence, 19*(1), 75–93.

Crewe, B. (2006). Prison drug dealing and the ethnographic lens. *The Howard Journal of Criminal Justice, 45*(4), 347–368.

Crewe, B. (2009). *Prisoner society: Power, adaptation and social life in an English prison*. Oxford University Press.

Densley, J. A. (2014). It's gang life, but not as we know it: The evolution of gang business. *Crime & Delinquency, 60*(4), 517–546.

Donaldson, S. (2001). A million jockers, punks, and queens. In D. Sabo, T. A. Kupers, & W. London (Eds.), *Prison masculinities* (pp. 118–126). Temple University Press.

Edgar, K., & O'Donnell, I. (1998). Assault in prison: The 'victim's' contribution. *British Journal of Criminology, 38*(4), 635–650.

Edgar, K., O'Donnell, I., & Martin, C. (2003). *Prison violence: The dynamics of conflict, fear and power*. Willan.

Gambetta, D. (2009). *Codes of the underworld: How criminals communicate*. Princeton University Press.

Gilligan, J. (2003). Shame, guilt, and violence. *Social Research: An International Quarterly, 70*(4), 1149–1180.

Gooch, K., & Treadwell, J. (2020). Prisoner society in an era of psychoactive substances, organized crime, new drug markets and austerity. *British Journal of Criminology, 60*(5), 1260–1281.

Gooch, K., & Treadwell, J. (2021). 'It doesn't stop at the prison gate': Understanding organised crime in prison. *Prison Service Journal, 252*, 15–30.

Gooch, K., & Treadwell, J. (2023). The 'screw boys' and the 'businessmen': Re-negotiating penal power, governance and legitimate authority through a prison violence reduction scheme. *The British Journal of Criminology, 63*(4), 1219–1236.

Gooch, K., & Treadwell, J. (2025). The prison firm: The 'transportation' of organised crime, the evolution of criminal markets and contemporary prisoner society. *Criminology and Criminal Justice, 25*(1), 245–264.

Grapendaal, M. (1990). The inmate subculture in Dutch prisons. *The British Journal of Criminology, 30*(3), 341–357.

Hall, S., Winlow, S., & Ancrum, C. (2013). *Criminal identities and consumer culture*. Willan.

Hensley, C., Wright, J., Tewksbury, R., & Castle, T. (2003). The evolving nature of prison argot and sexual hierarchies. *The Prison Journal, 83*(3), 289–300.

Hobbs, D. (1998). Going down the glocal: The local context of organised crime. *The Howard Journal of Criminal Justice, 37*(4), 407–422.

Hobbs, D. (2013). *Lush life*. Oxford University Press.

Ireland, J. L. (2000). Bullying among prisoners: A review of the research. *Aggression and Violent Behavior, 5*(2), 201–215.

Ireland, C. A., & Ireland, J. L. (2000). Descriptive analysis of the nature and extent of bullying behavior in a maximum-security prison. *Aggressive Behavior, 26*(3), 213–223.

Ireland, J. L., Archer, J., & Power, C. L. (2007). Characteristics of male and female prisoners involved in bullying behavior. *Aggressive Behavior, 33*(3), 220–229.
Irwin, J. (1970). *The felon*. Prentice-Hall.
Jacobs, J. B. (1974). Street gangs behind bars. *Social Problems, 21*(3), 395–409.
Jacobs, B. A., & Wright, R. (2006). *Street justice: Retaliation in the criminal underworld*. Cambridge University Press.
Johnson, R., Roucheleau, A. M., Martin, A. B., Cullen, F. T., & Liebling, A. (2017). *Hard time: A fresh look at understanding and reforming the prison*. Wiley-Blackwell.
Kaminski, M. M. (2004). *Games prisoners play: The tragicomic worlds of polish prison*. Princeton University Press.
Kotzé, J., Antonopoulos, G. A., & Rahman, M. (2022). The processes, logics and economies of violence in organised crime. *Trends in Organized Crime, 25*(1), 1–7.
Liebling, A., Price, D., & Shefer, G. (2011a). *The prison officer*. Willan.
Liebling, A., Arnold, H., & Straub, C. (2011b). *An exploration of staff-prisoner relationships at Whitemoor: 12 years on*. Ministry of Justice.
Lockwood, D. (1980). *Prison sexual violence*. Elsevier.
Maguire, D. (2021). *Male, failed and jailed: Masculinities and the 'revolving door' imprisonment in the UK*. Palgrave Macmillan.
McGurk, B. J., & McDougall, C. (1991). The prevention of bullying among incarcerated delinquents. In P. K. Smith & D. Thompson (Eds.), *Practical approaches to bullying*. Fulton.
Mercan, B. A. (2022). The transmission of crime as work in Turkey: Identification and strategic mutuality. *Criminology & Criminal Justice, 22*(4), 542–558.
O'Donnell, I., & Edgar, K. (1999). Fear in prison. *The Prison Journal, 79*(1), 90–99.
Pearson, G., & Hobbs, D. (2001). *Middle market drug distribution*. Home Office.
Pearson, G., & Hobbs, D. (2003). King pin? A case study of a middle market drug broker. *The Howard Journal of Criminal Justice, 42*(4), 335–347.
Polsky, H. W. (1962). *Cottage six: The social system of delinquent boys in residential treatment*. Robert E Krieger Publishing.
Sandberg, S. (2008). Street capital. *Theoretical Criminology, 12*(2), 153–171.
Sandberg, S., & Pedersen, W. (2009). *Street capital*. Bristol University Press.
Shammas, V. L., & Sandberg, S. (2016). Habitus, capital, and conflict: Bringing Bourdieusian field theory to criminology. *Criminology & Criminal Justice, 16*(2), 195–213.

Skarbek, D. (2014). *The social order of the underworld: How prison gangs govern the American penal system*. Oxford University Press.
South, C. R., & Wood, J. (2006). Bullying in prisons: The importance of perceived social status, prisonization, and moral disengagement. *Aggressive Behavior, 32*(5), 490–501.
Sykes, G. (1958). *The society of captives*. Princeton University Press.
Sykes, G. M., & Matza, D. (1957). Techniques of neutralization: A theory of delinquency. *American Sociological Review, 22*(6), 664–670.
Symkovych, A. (2017). The Ukrainian response to Sykes: Prisoner hierarchy and self-rule—Power, legitimacy, and dynamics. *The British Journal of Criminology, 58*(5), 1087–1106.
Toch, H. (1977). *Living in prison: The ecology of survival*. The Free Press.
Toch, H. (1992). *Violent men: An inquiry into the psychology of violence*. Penguin.
Winlow, S. (2001). *Badfellas: Crime, tradition and new masculinities*. Berg.
Winlow, S., Hall, S., & Treadwell, J. (2017). *The rise of the right: English nationalism and the transformation of working-class politics*. Policy Press.
Wolff, N., & Shi, J. (2009). Feelings of safety among male inmates: The safety paradox. *Criminal Justice Review, 34*(3), 404–427.

6

'Everyone in Prison Has Scars': Tragedy, Vulnerability, Masculinity, and Prison Violence

Craig's arrival did not go unnoticed. Shortly after being moved into the holding room in Reception, Craig forced his head through a reinforced glass window and did so with such force that the glass shattered and he sustained two black eyes and cuts to his face. Prior to his arrival, Craig had consumed a considerable amount of 'Mamba,'[1] leaving him incapable of rational judgement. To subdue him, prison officers hit him with batons. Eventually, Craig ended his protest; sweating, bloody, and bruised. Held in painful 'locks,' he was then carried to a cell. In the following days, he flooded the landing (much to the displeasure of other young men), smashed up his cell and threatened staff with a broom. He was then 'moved' (whilst restrained) to the segregation unit, where he was again restrained for fighting with prison officers.

Within a few hours after his arrival in segregation, a 'code blue' radio message sounded (indicating that he was experiencing breathing difficulties) and ambulance called; Craig had attempted to hang himself and pressed the cell bell shortly before doing so. It was a high-risk strategy: there was no guarantee that an officer would respond in sufficient time to

[1] Prison slang for psychoactive substances, see Chap. 4.

K. Gooch, *Prison Violence*, Palgrave Studies in Prisons and Penology,
https://doi.org/10.1007/978-3-031-91365-5_6

prevent death or life changing injuries. In this instance, it was fortuitous that Craig was in a segregation unit where officers were responsive. On other residential units, it was not atypical for bells to go ignored for long periods[2] and for officers to complain that the alarm board was 'lit up like a Christmas tree.' By the afternoon, Craig had been moved to the First Night Centre, partly due to the risks of placing a suicidal prisoner in segregation (Bonner, 2006; Brown, 2020; Kaba et al., 2014; Prison and Probation Ombudsman, 2015) and partly to offer respite.

When we encountered him at midday, Craig was banging his head against a wall and the metal cell door, but with new faces and no uniforms, the arrival of James and I gave him sufficient pause and he shouted out to us. Tears rolled down his cheeks as he lamented that he had nothing to lose or live for. His body bore the scars and injuries of just a few short days in custody and the weight of a short life exposed to frequent hardships. The marks of a ligature pulled tight around his neck were pink and visible—a haunting reminder of how close he had come to death. He pulled up his sleeves to show us where he had scratched his arm, seemingly trying to convey something of the depths of his despair. Craig was keen to tell us he had only fought harder when officers had tried to restrain him but complained that his thumb was still throbbing. Handcuffs had been used and he rubbed his wrists as he was talking, but as he shrugged off the pain he added, 'I've been tortured and felt worse pain.' Being restrained had stirred an incensed reaction from Craig. For all his claims of hardness and physical prowess, and his attempts to impress upon us that 'he didn't show emotion,' Craig frequently became overwhelmed and struggled to contain his distress. Prison staff were faced with the difficult task of deciding where to hold, and what to *do,* with a young man who might both seriously assault someone and attempt suicide.

As James and I stood at the cell door, the Duty Governor walked up and abruptly said, 'Have you calmed down yet?' Although not intended as a challenge, the question provoked Craig, partly because he was frustrated that his distress was observed but not 'seen' or understood. Hadn't the Duty Governor noticed his sheer desperation? Was her question

[2] Cell bells should be answered within 5 minutes, but it was not unusual for them to be sounding for anything between 10–30 minutes.

driven by a desire to reinforce firm boundaries and curtail his erratic behaviour? To calm down, Craig needed something more than a demand to do so. The Duty Governor simply walked away when her questions were met with yet another emotional and noisy outburst. Two prison officers quickly took her place outside the cell door, attempting to reassure Craig and put him at ease by explaining when he would be able to shower, telephone his solicitor, and have his property returned to him. After sleeping off his ordeal in the afternoon, Craig threw a blue plastic plate covered in pasta at a prison officer.

Craig's chaotic and outwardly aggressive behaviour reflected significant inner turmoil. This was Craig's first spell in custody. He was from a Traveller community but was now homeless and living rough on the streets of a large city. He had been in local authority care. Although he still had a social worker, it was unclear how present the social worker now was in his life—an absence that revealed the failings of a state 'care' system that had long stopped 'caring' (also see Gooch et al., 2022). Craig had no access to financial resources beyond what he could earn or access within the prison. Before he could begin adjusting to prison life, he was released. The total futility of his brief period of incarceration is difficult to deny. Craig had been remanded to custody for a racially aggravated public disorder offence after he had fallen asleep in MacDonald's. When woken by a security guard, he responded aggressively. Craig disputed that the verbal abuse was racist in content and anticipated that he would be released at his next court hearing—an accurate prediction. He did not return to prison before Christmas, but James would meet Craig several months later on the city streets and outside a MacDonald's still homeless and sleeping rough. I could only wonder what lay in store for a homeless young man without any familial or economic support, and already in the grip of addictions.

Craig's circumstances might seem unique: there were relatively few young men who were serving such short periods of time in prison. However, the interconnection of vulnerability and violence in Craig's biography is indicative of a much wider pattern—one that is often overlooked in policy, practice, and research. Contemporary prison policy distinguishes between the violent and the vulnerable, managing those who harm others separately to those who harm themselves.[3] Violence was rarely understood by prison staff as a possible manifestation of crisis, distress, or tragedy; rather it was seen as disorderly and recalcitrant. Equally, and with no case management system that recognises duality of harm (Slade et al., 2020), it was more common to respond to prisoner's most recent behaviour rather than recognising patterns, underlying causes, and the likelihood that vulnerability could simultaneously manifest in harm to self *and* others.

As an ethnographer, I was confronted with three empirical realities. First, binary categorisations of young men as either vulnerable *or* violent did not hold and were unduly simplistic. Second, behaviour could change rapidly in response to changing circumstances, such as declining health, the politics of prison life, and notable anniversaries. Third, harmful behaviour *within* prison—whether to themselves or others—could not be understood without first appreciating the experiences, tragedies, and losses experienced *before* arriving at the YOI, whether these experiences were in the community, in local authority care, and/or in custodial institutions for children. It was these connections between their 'inner lives' and their 'outer lives' (Ellis, 2016: 13) that were poorly understood as violence was narrowly viewed as an isolated incident confined to the prison. However, as Gilligan notes (1996: 7), 'the tragedy of violence involves not just victims, but victimisers … The whole story of violence includes, inescapably, the lives of the victimisers, and the moment we realise that, we are in the territory of tragedy.'

This chapter contextualises prison violence by integrating an analysis of the lives of young men. It illustrates how 'prisoners identities and relations in prisons are inherently shaped by biographical patterns' (Phillips, 2012: 132). One of the challenges is that almost all young prisoners have experienced adverse or traumatic events, but few would describe themselves as 'traumatised.' Yet, their behaviour often testified to that reality. Harmful behaviour within prison (whether turned on themselves or others) both revealed and left the 'traces' of 'traumatic experiences' (van der

[3] Violent and disruptive men may have a 'Challenge, Support and Intervention Plan' (CSIP) or be placed in segregation whilst those who are suicidal, low in mood, and self-harming might be cared for through an ACCT (Assessment, Care in Custody and Teamwork) process or under 'constant supervision.'

Kolk, 2014: 1). As Joshua would remind us: 'everyone in prison has scars.' Prior and continuing experiences of victimisation, loss, neglect, and rejection inevitably shaped young men's social expectations, demeanours, attitudes, and judgements that constitute the visceral habitus of violent and victimised men (Ellis et al., 2017; Winlow & Hall, 2009). Here we do not posit that prior 'victimisation *causes* an individual to be violent and to victimise others; nor that victimisation precludes perpetration ... Nevertheless, it is inescapable that these men are both harmful and harmed, and we must address analytically this complexity' (Ellis, 2016: 127). Equally, not all young men convicted of violence in the community were violent in custody. This chapter offers a fivefold typology that clarifies the relationship between negative life experiences prior to prison and harmful behaviour within prison. Specifically, the chapter distinguishes between: (1) those for whom tragedy manifests in violence; (2) those who are violent but showing emerging psychopathic traits and personality disorder; (3) those who are victimised but still perceive themselves as retaining the requisite strength, social skill and competency; (4) those—like Craig—who are violent but also harm themselves—a phenomenon described as 'dual harm' (Slade et al., 2020); and (5) those who turn the violence on themselves (but might also be victimised).

The Tragedy and Violence of the Victimisers

'It's been a long week,' he quietly admitted. Exhaling as If he had lost track of how long he had been holding his breath for. Seconds, possibly years. Callum was sat before the Adjudicating Governor In the segregation unit charged with seriously assaulting Perry. Callum, and four others, had entered his cell, threatened to slash Perry's face with a 'shank,'[4] and badly beaten him. The consistent account of all five assailants was that the beating was provoked by an earlier argument between Perry and Callum. Perry was perceived to be 'disrespectful' and 'arrogant,' refusing to apologise for the perceived violation, and thought to have been 'taking the mick out' of Callum. The others—Liam, Niall, Kieran, and

[4] An improvised weapon.

Carter—had joined the argument, angered by the fact that Perry was 'giving it the big 'un,' seemingly undeterred by their threats to stab him. Attempts by Niall to persuade Perry to apologise went unheeded, inflaming matters further still. For his part, Callum explained, 'I thought fuck that, I'll bang him out. It was a fair excuse to hit him. He can't say that to me without me losing face. I ain't going to get a nicking for nothing so I grabbed my shank. It ended up going badly for him. I lost my temper.'

After hearing the charges read by the prison officer, and listening to Callum's account, the Adjudicating Governor remanded the case for the Independent Adjudicator (a District Judge) when he visited in 2 weeks' time. Callum's fate—and that of the other four young men—was uncertain, but it was difficult to imagine how they would avoid extra time in prison. The adjudication seemed all but concluded but Callum did not move. Quietly he said, 'It's been a long week.' No one reacted. 'It's been a long week' he said for a second time, slightly louder so the Adjudicating Governor would notice. The second time, the Governor looked up from the paperwork and ceased writing. Callum continued, 'I didn't want it to go like that. I lost my temper. My son died yesterday, and my other son—they were both born prematurely—is fighting for his life. My mum is due to have an operation in a couple of hours.' Everyone paused, stunned.

It transpired that shortly before the assault, Callum had learned that his mother had been involved in a car accident with his two children. Still in shock himself, this had been the first time that Callum had summoned the courage to mention the tragedies. In making this disclosure, Callum did not make any explicit connection between the tragedy and his own contemporaneous violence. He was not even trying to excuse or explain his behaviour; rather, it seemed that it was only when before the Adjudicating Governor and with nothing to lose had he explained what had happened. If he had made the connection, or if the Adjudicating Governor had, no one mentioned it.

Seemingly bereft of any possible suggestions and searching for the right words to respond, the Adjudicating Governor warmly instructed, 'Go to the judge. Clear your head. Speak to your solicitor. I've got no concerns with your behaviour on the wing. I don't know what will happen to your job, but I can't have someone punch someone else in the face. Go to the judge and hopefully things will go well.' Callum nodded and stood. The prison officer mirrored him, preparing to escort him back to the segregation cell. Prison life would go on. Other than prison officers checking he was 'okay' and 'keeping an eye out for him,' there was little in the way of additional support. Despite the obvious ramifications of this tragedy, Callum was expected to be compliant and avoid any further outbursts. There was little scope to acknowledge his loss; like others, he was expected to process traumatic events in isolation, quietly, and stoically. The relationship between his violence acts and the loss of his son, coupled with ongoing worries about the health of his family, was obvious to all but destined to remain unaddressed and unresolved. Worse still, little was done to promote alternative strategies for resolving emotional pain—indeed, any obvious distress and help seeking would make him look and feel too vulnerable. Callum might receive punitive sanctions for the assault, but he would still be seen as a 'man.'

The relationship between tragic events and violent outcomes did not end with Callum. Nor did the ways in which violence had simply become an established way of resolving shame, humiliation, loss, rage, and pain (also see Ellis, 2016; Ellis et al., 2017; Gilligan, 1996, 2003; Winlow & Hall, 2009). Joshua, for example, was convicted of grievous bodily harm with intent after biting a man's ear off. His offence had been committed on the anniversary of his son's death—a son who had been stillborn and whose loss continued to haunt him several years later. He disclosed his grief to me whilst he quietly swept the office just an hour after having engaged in a verbal sparring match with Dean regarding their scars, tattoos, injuries, sexual and violent conquests.

Joshua and Dean were mentors whom James and I were in regular conversation with as we went to and from the office temporarily assigned to us. James was known to them as someone who was interested in boxing and martial arts. On this occasion, a conversation about boxing shifted to the scars gained and the various 'scraps' they had been in, each trying to better the other. Joshua described throwing his brother down a flight of stairs and, on another occasion, swinging his brother around by the legs until he accidentally hit his head on a wooden chair. Fearing his brother was dead, he ran to find his father at the pub to tell him that he had killed his brother, only to discover, on running back to the house, that his brother was conscious.

Dean, a willing sparring partner in this 'competitive one-upmanship' (De Viggiani, 2012: 278), complained about having a brick thrown at the back of his head. They compared 'six packs' and joked about whether they could undo a bra singlehandedly. They discussed their sexual conquests and their shared desire for a 'good woman.' Joshua relished in describing his father applauding him for having a sexual encounter with a woman older than himself. Trouser legs were pulled up to where bones had been broken. Trousers were also pulled down to reveal scars on thighs. Arms and hands were turned over to reveal other scars and tattoos. These were the scars of those who had 'stood their ground, who had backed up their words with their body and paid the price'; scars that were 'borne with pride' (Ugelvik, 2014: 187). They became 'trophies' and 'visual aids' (Ugelvik, 2014: 187) providing hard evidence of physical strength and courage. Joshua's 'Dad' tattoo was a source of pride and was offered as further proof of his 'manhood.' He was not alone in that respect. Many young men had tattoos emblazoned on their bodies to 'stand-out' and express who *they* were whilst simultaneously rendering them more easily identifiable to law enforcement agencies. As with Joshua and Dean, the scars were symbolic and easily narrated by the young men, communicating something about who they were, how much pain they could tolerate, and their masculine credentials.

When Joshua concluded the discussion by explaining 'everyone in prison has scars,' the truth and veracity of the statement was not fully appreciated even by him. Whilst the scars on his skin were accompanied by braggadocio, deeper wounds inspired greater introspection:

> I lost my little boy. Remember I told you before? I think like all the anger from that is probably why I am in prison because I never let it go. We was young weren't we? We were only 17. I just never let none of my emotions out and just kept them all to meself because I don't really like letting other people offloading problems onto others innit. Everyone has their own trouble don't they so? I wouldn't use that as an excuse as to why I am in prison because it wouldn't be fair on my little boy, would it, using him as an excuse.

In recounting the detail of his offence that brought him into prison, Joshua seemed somewhat indifferent to severity of the violence he had inflicted:

> I was having some problems with this bloke. He was harassing my missus. … I went up to the nightclubs, clubbing and dancing. I saw the bloke and he kept staring at me and smiling at me. I went to the geezer and said, 'If you go near my missus again, I'll kill you.' Obviously, I wouldn't do that, it's just a figure of speech. But I punched him. He hit me. I got him in a headlock and tore his ear off and that was that.

Joshua later confided to James that he had retained the severed ear in his pocket as a trophy and to prevent the injured party having the ear re-attached.

This was Joshua's first time in prison. He was universally popular and deemed trustworthy by prison officers who considered him a 'good lad really.' On the outside, Joshua had 'grafted' in manual labour, reflecting the cultural norms that dominated the tight-knit working-class estate from which he hailed. Throughout his sentence, Joshua's family consistently offered support, visiting regularly and, on occasion, bringing Joshua's daughter with them. His parents had created a stable home for Joshua, but he had still faced adversity:

> When I was a kid growing up, my uncle used to be a heroin addict and because where we live it is like a little estate, and everyone knows everyone. Like when I was in school and that, because everyone knows everyone, they knew what he was and obviously I didn't like it. I used to get picked on at school for it and I used to get hit and that and I never used to hit anyone back. And then I just started hitting people back. … I had to look after myself. I had no older brother or anything to look after me. I had to do it all myself. I had to learn it myself. That's why I know my younger brothers and sister won't end up in prison because they have watched me make my mistakes and they will learn from them. My mum and dad were never violent towards each other growing up. Just the estate I lived on everyone was fighting all the time. There was a lot of drugs around when I was a kid.

'Transformative violence' (Ellis, 2016; Halsey, 2018) need not always be 'brutal' (Ellis, 2016: 15). Nor must it involve persistent physical abuse (Gilligan, 1996). Rather, transformative violence affects the individual's construction of self and how he or she relates to others, effecting identity and altering the trajectory of the life-course. In Joshua's case, his early experience of victimisation, and the apparent shame he felt regarding his uncle's drug addiction, led him to conclude that injury and weakness could only be avoided If he learned to 'look after himself.' For Joshua, future shameful events could be avoided if he deployed the forms of restorative, retributive, and preventative violence that form part of the vague but powerful behavioural repertoire found within the visceral habitus of the post-industrial working class (Winlow, 2001).

Joshua's eventual imprisonment at age 18 reinforced a 'deep subjective commitment to aggression and violence in adulthood' (Ellis et al., 2017: 699). The corrosive effects of shame, and the guilt that inevitably accompanies it, were far more damaging than mere physical injuries. Real and presentational violence could strategically forestall shame whilst dissuading the sea of instrumental others determined to strip away his dignity. Gradually, his confidence grew:

> Like when I first come prison, people were asking me to do stuff for them and that, but I was like, 'No! Never.' They were like: 'We are going to bang you out'. And I just used to say, 'Alright then.' Then they say, 'Come in my pad,' and I say, 'Not a problem' and then they just don't do nothing to you. So it's all mouth really. It's if someone says to you, they are going to knock you out and you stay quiet in their head then they have won. They are more dominant than you. It's weird. It's like we are animals. Everyone fights to become the alpha male. All full of testosterone. … You always have to be violent. Everything is resolved with violence.

It was not immediately obvious that Callum and Joshua were still coming to terms with loss, pain, and grief. They had both learned to contain and control their emotions, and readily understood the utility of doing so. These were not highly emotional young men who were quick to describe their trauma to others. Nor did they oscillate between suppressed emotion and explosive violence (c.f. Laws, 2019). Their aggression could be controlled. It often had an aim and clear underpinning motive. Violence could be deployed with precision and care and was intelligible by the social audience.

Despite the calculating nature of some of the violence that occurred in the prison, for many of our respondents, tragedy tended to follow tragedy (Gilligan, 1996: 7). Violence polluted aspects of their lives that were broadly positive and which they hoped to defend. Our respondents were still very young, but their young lives were already overshadowed by grave events, the portent of which they struggled to fully understand. Callum and Joshua did not see themselves as *traumatised*, because to be traumatised was to be weak. For reasons they themselves were only beginning to recognise, violence had become a protective response to perceived threats. Violence was comforting in its familiarity. Fear was still present, but it could be managed and utilised.

Of course, many young men within the prison had experienced tragic events during their formative years, but not all sought to employ violence in the way that Joshua and Callum had. As Ellis et al. note (2017: 712): 'Traumatic experience by itself is not enough to drive the individual towards violence. The individual must be subjected to a gendered socialisation that stresses toughness, stoicism, and physicality. The traumatised individual must be encouraged to *value* violence.' For these young men, this socialisation to a normative code that stressed toughness, strength, bravery, and courage began at home, continued on the streets, and was consolidated within prison (also see Maguire, 2021).

The experience of transformative violence and insecurity ensured that some men would immediately step forward to meet the violent challenges ubiquitous to the prison social world. Others sought to avoid confrontation or would resort to violence only when no other options presented themselves. Peter, for example, attempted to distance himself from fights and conflict with his peers. On the streets, he reported regular involvement in violent conflict:

> Because they sell drugs and that, they get people coming to her [his former girlfriend's] door and giving her shit and then I would end up fighting these lads and that and then they would encourage me to do it more. Used to get me into trouble all of the time. They was getting me off my head and

> that and then… I think they used to do it on purpose get me absolutely smashed, spliffed up and that, get me smoking their weed (cannabis). I think they used to know people were coming after them and when they were coming to the door, I would go fucking mad! I used to get me into a lot of trouble.

Peter had both witnessed and experienced violence in the home:

> I watched my Mom stab my Dad when I was younger. When I was about five, my Mom stabbed my Dad. I don't know why but she ended up stabbing him with six different knives. I don't know. She got arrested. I just remember her getting arrested for stabbing him. A bit of madness really, wasn't it? He nearly died, my Dad. She stabbed him here, here, here and here. Six different knives she started with. They had an argument and that, I think he went off with some other woman and he tried coming back that night and my Mom lost it and stabbed him.
>
> My old lady's Mom used to attack me all of the time; she attacked me with dumbbells, weight bars and stuff. That's why I try and stay away from her now. I let her hit me with it. I just let her attack me. I would never hit her back. She attacked me loads of times and I never hit her back. Never got her arrested for it either.

Peter lacked the will and perhaps the capacity to defend himself whilst in prison. He explained that: 'I'm not a violent person; I don't like violence.' He sought to distance himself from prisoner politics but was unsuccessful. He found it difficult to 'stand up' to threats and intimidation from his peers. On one occasion, a 'contract was put on his head,' and he was moved to another residential unit and kept away from normal activities that might bring him into contact with his peers. He attributed his violence on the streets to his cocaine use, describing it as his 'downfall.' In Peter's case, as with some others, early experience of victimisation was not predictive of violent potential within custody.

Violence and Emerging Psychopathy and Personality Disorder

Unlike adult prisons, and partly due to the absence of forensic psychologists, psychopathy and personality disorder was far from the consciousness of most prison officers and young men. Typically, incidents of extreme or brutal violence confirmed to prison officers that these young men were volatile and dangerous, and they too could not 'let their guard down.' Few young men gained sadistic pleasure from prison violence, even amongst the group of violent offenders (Miller, 1991). Within the YOI, James and I interviewed three men—Daniel, Rambo,[5] and Steven—where concerns had specifically been raised about possible personality disorder and psychopathic traits. A larger number of young men could also be described as demonstrating callousness, lack of empathy, and a lack of remorse (for further discussion, see Kerig et al., 2012). Daniel, Rambo, and Steven demonstrated quite complex relationships with prison violence and their peers. Steven seriously sexually assaulted his 'pad mate'[6] (see Chap. 3 for discussion) and was largely feared and seen as 'dangerous' by his peers and prison officers. Conversely, Daniel and Rambo were both victims and perpetrators but failed to achieve social recognition.

Daniel had been assaulted by groups of young men within the prison on multiple occasions, primarily because of his status as a sex offender. At the time Daniel was serving a 16-year sentence for several counts of rape (of his girlfriend) and grievous bodily harm with intent (caused when defending his girlfriend). In the latter case, he had fractured the spine, eye socket and nose of the male victim. Daniel did not dispute the rape charges but alleged that his girlfriend had lied about her age and claimed she 'only got him arrested because I cheated on her.' The truth, however, was that the victim had repeatedly endured violent rapes whilst Daniel mocked her to family members. Conversely, Daniel tried to present himself as his girlfriend's protector, portraying both her parents as incapable and uncaring. His relationship with women was complex and based on control, power, and ownership, but also a sense of his own masculine

[5] This pseudonym was chosen by the young man.

[6] The person they share a cell with.

virtues as protector, provider, and caregiver. However, the excessive force used to defend his girlfriend was less chivalrous than an anxiety driven response to another man's approaches. At face value, violence might mark his superiority and proprietary 'rights,' but at its core, it was indicative of insecurity, his fears about further abandonment, and a futile attempt to chase away fears about his own inadequacy.

Daniel's parents had severed contact and, due to child protection concerns, he was no longer able contact his siblings. He had been living alone for many years prior to imprisonment and then, more latterly, with his girlfriend. His teenage years were characterised by instability, chaos, and strain, and his experiences would consolidate both his own vulnerability and his fascination with fire, destruction, and violence:

> I got suspended [from school]. I ended up starting fires and fighting more, and then, I started getting fascinated with knives. [At age 13] I got robbed once and erm, he put the knife up to my neck and then, erm, I don't know, something snapped and like I grabbed it and sort of like stuck it in his shoulder and, like, I ran off and then after that I thought, well if someone will do that to me, then what's the point in me not doing it to someone else?

> I've been kicked out a few times. I think it was about three weeks, I lived [names location]. Then like that sort of opened up my eyes a bit. Like there was an old lady who'd not long moved in and there was this lad, like Asian lad, called himself Spider, he wasn't all there, and he'd done stuff to the old lady. Then there was this geezer and like just, you know like a claw hammer, like he smashed that into his head and like that sort of like made me realise like [pause] stuff happens, shit happens, doesn't it?

In amidst his own destructive and violent tendencies were events that clearly shaped a sense of 'omnipresent threat' (Toch, 1992: 205) but also induced a perceived entitlement to use violence. Later adolescence had provided further proof of vulnerability and inadequacy, not his fortitude. Daniel reported that his girlfriend had been pregnant, attempted suicide, engaged in serious self-harm, and 'come at [him] with knives and stuff.' Daniel blamed himself for his girlfriend's self-harm and struggled with both frequently witnessing his girlfriend's serious self-harm and managing the pressure created by her 'demands for money.' He too was self-harming ('getting lighters to my arm and melting my skin'), misusing drugs (initially cannabis and then cocaine) and accruing large drug debts (e.g. £2500).

Daniel's sexual violence featured within a wider range of offences for violence, burglary, and drug dealing. His 'master status' (Becker, 1963) within the prison remained that of a 'nonce,'[7] and he was targeted as a result. Prior to the interview, another prisoner had booted him in the face and then started jumping on his head and ribs. This was not the first time that he had been assaulted, and he had not only come to accept it as 'normal' but had determined to 'keep his mouth shut' believing 'it's more in the wrong to be a snitch.' Daniel was, however, just as likely to perpetrate very serious assaults and had been warned that any further violent acts on his part would mean a 'ship out'[8] to another prison. The incident that would attract clinical intervention was one where he 'smashed' someone over the head with a plug socket and wrapped a kettle electrical cord around the victim's neck, only releasing his grip when an officer 'dragged [him] off.' The victim had—according to Daniel—'tried to embarrass [him] in front of everyone.' He explained:

> They've been doing these tests on me and that and they said, I'm showing traits of psychopath or something. It's something about being detached from people. Like the fact that they say you've got lack of empathy, lack of remorse, you don't take responsibility for stuff, you know so like, they've—they've put my risk up.
>
> I know I don't have empathy. I've always been like that. There was a kid that was picking on my brother and like, I've picked up a rusty nail and I've put that in the side of his head. And then, erm, everyone else was like 'Ah, look what you've done,' and like, I couldn't see what was wrong with it. Like, I've looked at him as he was bullying my brother, so like he deserved it.

Daniel's use of violence was never sufficient to ward off potential threats or challenges since the hatred of sex offenders was deeply engrained and

[7] A phrase that is said to originate from HMP Wakefield where those who could not be unlocked for daily exercise due to fears for their safety were marked as 'not on normal courtyard exercise' ('nonce'). The term is often now used to describe sex offenders or those who commit offences against children and the elderly.

[8] Slang for a transfer to another prison.

seen to not just legitimise, but require, physical punishment. Equally, whilst his self-harm had reduced in frequency, partly due to the separation from his girlfriend (and the associated weight of having to 'perform' as a man), he would continue to harm himself. Yet, Daniel—like Steve and Rambo—was also prone to extreme, indiscriminate violence that not only lacked any sense of boundary but would prove a source of pleasure and fantasy.

Lee revelled in telling James and I he wanted to be known as 'Rambo.' Unlike many of those who held status and gravitas, Rambo did not wear designer clothes. Instead, he had turned his prison issue grey tracksuit trousers inside out and drawn a Nike logo on the left leg of the trousers, much to the amusement of the trusted mentors. Despite his self-identity as a 'gangsta in my hood,' he was generally considered to be an oddball and was being held separately from other young men in the First Night Centre. Rambo describing enjoying violence:

> I like violence, for me it's not violent enough. … It makes me happy. I don't see it as a crime. My hobby is that I stab and shoot people. If I stab someone, I honestly feel like I've done a good deed. … Basically, I don't know what happened but, you see, me, yeah, when it comes to kidnapping, stabbing people, and shooting them, I like it. Like, it turns me on sexually, so I just started kidnapping people, stabbing people, shooting people. … When I do it, I feel like I've done a good deed, like I'm one step closer to heaven.

The persistent violence meant that Rambo was quickly excluded from school. At an early age, he had been involved in selling 'burners' (firearms) and drugs, and regularly used knives and firearms in robberies and physical assaults. His accounts of violent offences in the community were both testament to his paranoia, hypersensitivity to perceived disrespect, and inability to restrain himself. These accounts were deliberately laced with sexualised references. For example, when describing his arrest at a party, he added that he had 'a spliff in my left hand, I've got a gun in my right hand, the girl's got my dick in her hand.' At the end of the interview, when discussing his future, Rambo explained that he 'liked [violence] too much to stop,' but this not only illustrated something about his own life expectations (about returning to custody) but also his lack of restraint. He suggested that, from the age of eight, he had been involved in incidents that could have been life-threatening (e.g. 'smashing someone's head' and attempting 'to drown someone,' and numerous violent incidents involving bladed weapons).

When I met him, Rambo was serving an 11-year sentence for false imprisonment, grievous bodily harm with intent and possession of a firearm. He had already been to a secure training centre and two other YOIs (including the segregation units of those YOIs). Rambo thought that prison was 'easy' and met people whom he knew from the streets of London. He was quickly involved in prison violence, but he was keen to separate himself from those who bullied the 'vulnerable' and those 'not built like me with this street life.' The incident that had prompted concerns about his mental health was a serious assault of the young man in the neighbouring cell:

> I would assault people for no reason. I don't think you'll believe me, but my wall [young man in the neighbouring cell] told me to do it. I didn't know what he was capable of doing to me if I didn't do it, so I kind of did it out of fear.
>
> Basically, the wall in my bedroom, I chat to all the time. It's cool, but the last few months, our relationship has changed, anything can turn to an argument. It's like treading on eggshells. He has to be careful not to wind me up and same with me. He had been badgering me for weeks to assault someone. He was moving like he was going to bang me. One day, I thought I'm not playing with you anymore, and I banged him.
>
> I called him into my cell. I was punching him. I stopped, went outside my cell, put my steel cap boots on, came back in my cell, and then went back in and was stamping on him. I stood over him, he was curled up next to the bed, and I stamped all over him. One of my friends came in and said, 'You've filled him in now, stop now.' 'Cause I don't have those boundaries. I'd have happily carried on all day, until he stopped moving. That's no problem to me. I said, 'Look, I'm going to do it a little bit more.' My friend pulled me and looked me in the eyes and said, 'You will stand here and beat him until he stops moving, you will kill him.' He slapped him. I was angry at him too. He said, 'Don't get angry with me.' I respected what he was saying.

The victim required hospitalisation, and Rambo was sent for a mental health assessment. He later admitted that he knew he would have killed him, adding: 'I don't feel sorry, I haven't got it in me. I can say sorry but there's nothing there. I don't mean it.' For his part, Rambo attributed his serious violence to the murder of his friend:

> I think one of the things that has affected me the most was when I was 13, my boy died in my arms, innit. There was no one around. He was in my arms and the last thing he said, 'It's not your fault, I'll always love you.' I remember the moment when the life drained from his eyes, and I knew he was dead. He got rushed. He got stabbed like bare times. The people who rushed us weren't letting me get to him. We got rushed, they were punching me but stabbing him. I think I changed then. He was like my brother. The thing that hurt the most was that I was looking into his eyes, and one minute he was talking, and then the life just disappeared. One minute it was there, then one minute there was nothing. We had known each other a long time. All the shit that we had done together, it felt like we were older than we was, so it felt like we had known each other for a long time.

The intense trauma experienced by the murder of his best friend was not the singular cause of his defensive and pre-emptive violence, but any emerging evidence of his psychopathic traits cannot be adequately understood without accounting for the psychosocial effects of trauma. Scholars increasingly point to the ways that violence in adulthood can represent a manifestation of earlier 'shadow events' (Gilligan, 2003; Stein, 2013; Winlow & Hall, 2009). However, this relationship between trauma, psychopathy and prison violence as (young) adults remains poorly understood and contested (see Baskin-Sommers & Baskin, 2016; Golier et al., 2003; Långström & Grann, 2002; Pietrek et al., 2013; Yakeley, 2022). The generalised assumption that young men were inevitably 'violent, immature and impulsive' was preventing better identification of those whose extreme violence in the YOI might suggest the need for more substantial, careful support (Halsey & Deegan, 2015). The primary challenge remained that even if diagnostically useful, pathologising and labelling young men as 'psychopathic' or as having personality disorders did little to attract additional therapeutic support or address the underlying trauma. It did not achieve a greater understanding of the prison violence, nor the individuals involved, but it perpetuated a sense that these young men were 'other' and inherently dangerous. These 'correctional diagnoses and labels … undermine hope' (Miller, 1991: 5) and, inevitably, prison staff would rely on separation and containment—coercion that would only further inculcate them to violence.

Violent, Victimised, but Not 'Weak'

Young men reacted differently to victimisation. Some suffered fear and distress, were persistently targeted and found themselves permanently relegated to the lowest positions of the prisoner hierarchy. Others moved easily between being violent and victimised (also see Chap. 5), with defeats serving to reinforce, rather than negate, the internal logic and utility of violence (Toch, 1992).

Jack had recently been recalled for breaching his (electronically monitored) tag. His release had lasted less than 3 weeks. Yet, in the few weeks since his return, Jack had been punched by Tyrone, one of the more influential characters on the wing, leaving him with a 'fucked up lip pissing with blood.' The assault served as retribution for Jack's failure to concede to Tyrone's demands to handover 'burn.'[9] Jack was neither cowed nor distressed by the demands or the assault, largely shrugging off the assault with:

> He punched me once and then went straight into the sports hall. I was like that: Dick. I didn't have a chance to hit him back. Wish I had though. I seen him the same day. He looked at me and he put his head to the floor. He didn't eyeball me or nothing man. Because I walked past him and scratched my lip like that because it was fucked up, but it weren't nothing it was just a punch. It wasn't even a good dig. I have gotten worse digs off my ex than I have off him.

[9] Slang for tobacco.

Jack did not see himself as someone who couldn't 'hack it,' and challenged Tyrone's skill and competence.

> If you look in a man's eyes and you look at him, then that means then that you are on it. If you come in fearful, then he owns you and that's it then. It's done. I'm not the sort of person who would fucking harm myself. I am the sort of person who would try and rise above it and do something about it. If I can't do something about it, then shit is going to happen. I don't care if I have to fight. Not like cut themselves or something because that's the easy way out.

Although he talked of being 'on edge,' he lamented the lack of 'straighteners' and the tendency towards 'unmanly' violence where some were assaulted from behind. This was—to Jack's mind—'a violation':

> If someone was to stand there on a level with you. I'm telling you this. If someone was to stand there, boom, fist to fist like that, yeah, after they hit me, then that's fair enough, but I would respect someone more coming up to me, yeah, going, 'Listen, speaking about you, I think you've taken the piss out of me, yeah. I want a straightener. Bro, let's have you, okay?' No, not when someone comes up to me, 'You took the piss out of me, rah rah rah,' you get a bang. That is a piss-take. That's a violation, okay? You [should] come up to me as a man.

On 'road,' Jack lived in a violent world where violence and victimisation went hand in hand:

> I started getting into a phase where I could just think, 'Fuck it,' you know, when you start becoming a geezer. Then my mate he switched on me when I was about 16 and I got stabbed in the back. I got stabbed and it just fixed me up, to be honest with you. I started sticking up for myself. He poked from behind in the back. It was about here. [Jack points to scar] But the scar has half faded.
>
> That was a turning point for me because you think anything like that can happen. It weren't your fault and you are getting stabbed, then God knows what life is going to bring to you. It just changed my mentality. I was a little shit. Mugging everyone off, doing anything to anyone. I ended up with a

> name for myself. You are waking up in the morning and looking for ways to fuck up really and become known to people. It's just how my mind works. [After I] got stabbed and shit, it all just unravels from then. You start robbing shit. You start selling shit. Everything. It brings you into the stage of being an adult, being someone.

In becoming 'someone,' Jack was searching for ways to prevent a recurrence of the physical pain, humiliation, and inability to act. He had learnt to defend himself primarily by going on the offensive. In this way, the unprovoked stabbing at 16 is transformed into 'a mere learning process or staging post on the journey towards ultimate self-becoming' (Winlow & Hall, 2009: 294).

Despite the expressed desire to become 'someone,' Jack would later concede that he just wanted 'help, just wanted someone to listen.' Although he pinpointed a single event that he described as a 'turning point,' his 'drift' (Matza, 2018) into crime began at the age of 12 as he became involved in drug-related and violent offences. He described himself as a 'little shit' who used to 'mug everyone off' and made a 'little name' for himself. Jack's father had been absent and in prison for long periods of his childhood. The fatherly advice Jack remembered was the injunction: 'Don't let anyone fuck about with you, and if they do, knock them the fuck out.' He described his family home as one of 'struggles' and 'strife.' He simply stopped attending secondary school to spend his time 'doing nothing, sitting around and smoking weed.'[10] By age 16, he was 'shotting[11] crack' and other class A drugs. Jack had served custodial sentences as a child and arrived at the YOI as a 19-year-old already familiar with prisoner hierarchies and norms. To Jack, his reputation was a critical source of self-respect and self-worth. As he said, 'if you haven't got a name then you ain't mattering.' Having already been stabbed in the community, Jack's hyper-vigilance to threat and use of pre-emptive violence would continue in prison: 'The only worry you've got is looking around the corner at who's going to jump you.'

[10] Slang for cannabis.

[11] A term used for drug dealing.

Jack regularly 'butted heads' with prison officers, was easily antagonised, and frequently involved in violence. He was prone to what he described as 'random outbursts.' Jack was not particularly concerned with rule compliance, nor was he motivated by the 'rewards' or opportunities afforded trusted young men. Prison officers described him as a 'drain on resources,' but Jack felt persecuted. To prison officers, Jack was difficult to reason with and would unnecessarily provoke or escalate conflict. However, what was not apparent was that Jack's frustration stemmed from the inattentiveness of prison officers to cell bells, which he perceived not just making 'the difference between life and death' if he or his pad-mate had 'strung themselves up,' but also reinforcing intense feelings of worthlessness, inferiority, and shame. This humiliation did not 'fade away' but led an anticipatory strategy that involved 'being ready to fight and trump' the perceived disregard with violence (Winlow & Hall, 2009: 296). His craving for 'respect' was not just about simply ensuring that they recognised who he was, but that he was worthy of their care, compassion, and attention. He wanted to know that someone cared enough to rescue him, or his pad-mate, and that they were not forgotten. His desire for his 'personhood' (Liebling et al., 2020)—and sense of injustice when it was not recognised—was coupled with a commitment to a normative code that prized individual status, power, control and violent potential.

Young men—such as Jack—adopted an orientation to violence that Toch describes in reference to a 'violence prone individual' (1992: 141):

> In every setting in which [he] demonstrates his worth through violence, he reinforces the premise that the road to self-esteem must be paved with defeated challengers. Curiously enough, this premise is strengthened by both success and failure; success indicates that violence works; failure signifies the need for further violence to achieve redemption; both assumptions are based on (and feedback into) the fundamental premise that violence commands respect and that respect is the measure of personal worth.

These 'violence prone individuals' did not see themselves as weak or incapable; victimisation might physically harm them, but they did not socially distance themselves from peers. Rather they remained 'one of the lads,' close to the action without controlling it or holding court amongst their peers. Verbally, these individuals agreed with the central tenants of the normative prison code. Whilst this might be dismissed as sheer bravado, for individuals such as Jack, it embodied a commitment to violence capable of encompassing occasional defeats. It also represented a continuity and familiarity with the turbulent nature of violence, which sometimes left them the victim and other times the victor.

'My Head Was Starting to Go': The Violence Young Men Inflict on Themselves

Some young men in the YOI neither assaulted prison staff nor assaulted their peers, but instead they retreated from the tumult of daily prison life and directed negative emotions inward, harming themselves rather than others. Between 2009 and 2019, and despite the decrease in the number of young adults in prison, self-harm among young men aged 18–20 years old increased each year, from 2463 to 3764 incidents (Ministry of Justice, 2025). At the YOI, there was an average of 23 self-harm incidents per month (Ministry of Justice, 2025). Whilst some young men persistently struggled to endure prison life and self-harmed with relative frequency, others would have periods of 'coping' that were disrupted by bad news, victimisation, false accusations, the seemingly uncaring responses of prison officers, notable anniversaries, relationship breakdown and/or grief and loss. Thus, any 'equilibrium achieved by these men [was] one of their inner battles lost and renewed' (Toch, 1975: 95).

Young men suffered greatly at their own hand. During our research, five young men set fire to themselves and/or their cells. Fire-setting within prison is poorly understand (Tyler et al., 2019) and merits far greater research. For these young men, self-immolation rarely represented an act of political protest and resistance (c.f. Bargu, 2014; Biggs, 2005; Sweeney, 2004), and typically represented severe distress and/or a suicide attempt. In one notable instance, a young man wrapped toilet paper around his head and set fire to it. Officers extinguished the fire before opening a cell door to effect a rescue, meaning that an evacuation did not immediately follow the discovery of a fire. Other young men would visibly wear the pain, loss, shame, emotional turmoil, guilt, and hopelessness on their arms. The white bandages, raw pink lines, and fading pink and white scars on their arms would be haunting reminders of their pain. Some attempted to conceal their scars by cutting themselves on their legs or torso, but most had given up on any attempt to hide their injuries. If the body was a 'resource' (Ugelvik, 2014: 185) for practising and performing masculinity, it was here that the body failed them. These young men were 'acutely aware of the costs of failing to live up to the accepted masculine ideals' (Maguire, 2021: 139) but could not mask, 'front' or suppress distress. The distress became all-consuming and impossible to contain; they 'declared their bankruptcy' (Liebling, 1992: 232). Their collapse would be evident in their withdrawal, isolation, poor personal hygiene, sullen faces, and tears. Self-harm also extended to swallowing batteries, inserting razors or pens into or under the skin, and even eating their own flesh. Some self-harm incidents were serious enough to require hospital attendance, but it was the use of ligatures that carried real risks.

Punching and headbutting walls or cell doors was rarely regarded as a form of self-harm, seemingly because the act of punching or headbutting a wall or door mirrored physical assaults (and acceptable ways of emotional discharge). Young men would admit to such acts even if they were critical of those who self-harmed in other ways. For example, Lewis explained, 'I've just gone like that, headbutted the fucking thing [door], caught me right there, sparked myself out.' Such acts were undoubtedly a way of discharging anger, frustration, and distress but without the same social costs. Conversely, those young men who accepted the logic of violence saw self-harm as cowardly or short-sighted behaviour. It was considered futile and an 'easy way out':

> You'll see lots of people in here with scars up their arm, or their neck sometimes, but I don't see the point. No point in self-harming, like. It's not going to solve anything. It's just going to leave scars on your arms. It's stupid. You're just ruining your arms. You're going to get your arms out when you're older and you'll have big purple and blue scars. (Martin)

Not only were some young men who self-harmed seen as 'weak' and 'fragile,' but they could find themselves victimised with greater frequency or intensity. For example, Alistair would often find himself the target of abuse from other prisoners because he had visibly self-harmed. He noted:

> Other people were aware that I was a self-harmer and they'd be tormenting me and shouting out the windows all night, you know, 'Tie a bed sheet around your neck and fucking get it over with, your mum don't love you, your dad don't love you, you're a fuck up.'

The link between victimisation and suicide has been frequently reported (Blaauw et al., 2002; Goldson, 2005; Harris, 2015; Prison and Probation Ombudsman, 2011, 2013, 2014). Lord Harris concluded that bullying was 'one of the most frequently identified causes of vulnerability' amongst 18–24-year-olds in prison (Lord Harris 2015: 103). The Prison and Probation Ombudsman reported that one fifth (20%) of young adults who had died through suicide were bullied in the month before their death, compared to 13% of prisoners (Prison and Probation Ombudsman 2014). As Alastair reveals, not only does victimisation leads to suicide attempts, but such victimisation may interact with and compound earlier self-harm and suicide attempts. It also illustrates how devastating verbal abuse can be and why it should be taken more seriously (also see Chap. 3).

Suicide attempts occurred regularly. It was clear that the young men who tried to hang themselves would, for example, press their cell bell before doing so or alert others in neighbouring cells to press their cell bell. This was a high-risk strategy since cell bells were rarely answered within 5 minutes (the required amount of time). However, none of the suicide attempts resulted in death. Lives were routinely saved through the intervention of both staff and young men, and it was impossible to accurately identify the number of deaths that were narrowly avoided. For example, Carl hung himself in a segregation cell following a 'cell spin'[12] earlier that day. The Custodial Manager who had 'cut him down' explained that he had 'gasped for air' and the prison officer who had answered the

[12] A cell search.

cell bell kept repeating 'he was blue' and 'just one more minute.' She was visibly shaken, partly because she realised just how close they had come to losing Carl. She nearly ignored the cell bell—a deeply engrained habit across the prison—telling James and I that the Imam had visited Carl earlier that morning and concluding that he was okay and 'only wanted some forms.' Content with the Iman's assessment, she had decided to ignore the cell bell and complete other tasks. The precise reasons why she changed her mind and decided to answer the cell bell were unclear to both her and us. However, the decision had undoubtedly saved Carl's life.

The suicide attempts of individuals in shared cells placed incredible burdens on other young men. Peter for example, had considered suicide after his young brother died and conceded his 'head was fried … just a bit of a mess,' but ultimately decided against suicide because he thought 'I have got to be out there for my family.' For Peter, though, it was the experience of trying to save a former 'pad mate' on two separate occasions that had proven too difficult to bear:

> I was asleep and I just heard a big bang and I woke up. I said, 'What the fuck are you doing?' And I heard him gargling and choking. I rolled over and I thought shit! I jumped up and I didn't know what to do, hit the buzzer and grabbed hold of him.
>
> The next time I think he had planned it more. He had put something over the observation flap. All of a sudden, about an hour and a half after I fell asleep, the boss is kicking the door in. 'If you don't move that I am going to smash the glass.' And as I have got up, he has jumped. I've ended up catching him and shouting out to the boss. And he's [the officer] shouting, 'What is going on?' and I am shouting, 'He's trying to hang himself again!'
>
> It was a shock really because he just seems like a normal lad, like everything was all right. And after the first time that he did it he explained why he had done it and I said if you ever need to talk to me just wake me up and will have a chat. I don't know. His head was just a bit of a mess wasn't it. The lads were bullying him on the wing. When he came on the wing, he ended up passing them £300 worth of stuff. And I was like, 'What are you doing?' And he was like 'They just keep …' They ended up putting that much pressure on him.

Peter's 'pad mate' was a good example of young men who 'omit a cry for help and proceed directly to a pathway to suicide.' (Liebling, 1992: 233). Peter was referred to the mental health team but felt they 'just wanted to feed [him] tablets' and soon abandoned the prescribed medication. Her Majesty's Inspectorate of Prisons (1999: 30) has previously noted that prisoners may suffer 'acute post-incident trauma and can be affected by what the death means to them individually by confronting them with their own pain and the possibility of escaping in this way.' There is some suggestion that witnessing suicide attempts might elevate the risk of self-harm (Hales et al., 2003); whilst this was not true in Peter's case, there was some lower level 'copycat behaviour' on the Supported Living Unit.

Conclusions

All the young men were scarred, either by their experiences coming to prison and/or their experiences within it. Depending on their form, visible scars and injuries to the body were either proof of masculine credentials or evidence of their absence. Whilst those injuries and scars that could testify to battles fought and won might commend them to other men, the injuries, and scars of self-harm (particularly cuts) were stigmatising and signified failure and ineptitude. However, binary distinctions between the violent and the vulnerable, between violence and self-harm, or between 'coping' and 'distressed' were unduly simplistic and failed to capture the complex, nuanced, and multifaceted behaviour of these young men. Although young men would never use the word 'trauma,' the blurry and difficult memories, the tragedies experienced, the sense of lives lost to never be fully recovered, and the ongoing hurt and harm that would continue during their confinement (e.g. the suicide of family members, the death of loved ones, the loss of children to local authority care, the violence endured, the attempted suicide witnessed) all shaped their identity, influenced their social interactions with others and informed the survival strategies they would develop (also see Winlow & Hall, 2009). Notably, the hyper-vigilance to threat was not only explained by their attentiveness to questions of respect but their prior and ongoing experiences of harm and trauma.

For some, their deep fear, pain, humiliation, shame, guilt, and grief would only reveal itself in the violence they would inflict on others. There would be no emotional distress and no outburst; simply, at times, the casual, callous, extreme, or excessive use of violence. As Ellis notes (2016: 128), a 'complex paradox lies at the core of the lives' of these young men, one where possible 'dangerousness' co-exists with simultaneous 'vulnerability.' Fewer young men valued violence for the pleasure, control, and power it offered (although certainly there were some who did); for most, though, it was not violence that the valued 'but the ability to retain some sense of dignity and respect' (Winlow & Hall, 2009: 288). Equally, there were some who would oscillate between serious violence and serious harm to themselves, and yet others too who would accept (or at least fail to contest) the targeted ongoing victimisation from others and/or turn on themselves. Self-harm was an alternative form of violence and although it was not as widespread as interpersonal violence, it occurred with concerning frequency and arose from the same causes as interpersonal violence. Notably, attempts to identify those 'at risk' of self-harm and suicide were as problematic as those designed to identify violence-prone individuals since it was the environmental and situational factors that had greatest influence on the propensity to self-harm or contemplate suicide.

In adopting a life-course perspective, it is possible to overcome the limitations of the established literature on prison violence and explain why earlier research has failed to conclusively demonstrate a consistent relationship between prior violent offending in the community and prison violence (Delisi et al., 2004; McGuire, 2018; Steiner & Wooldredge, 2008; Teasdale et al., 2016; Tewksbury et al., 2014). Prior experience of violence and victimisation—either as a victim or as a perpetrator—had a range of effects within prison. Tangled within such behaviour were emotions such as rejection, abandonment, humiliation, grief, shame, fear, anger and powerlessness. As other have noted (Winlow & Hall, 2009: 296), these young men 'seemed to be experiencing emotionally driven psychosocial processes that are far more complex than peer-group pressure or an injunction to follow the scripts that guide the 'doing' of some suppositious 'hegemonic masculinity.'

Our understanding of prison violence (and other forms of harm in prison) is incomplete if we fail to consider how violence, abandonment, and tragedy has already irreversibly structured young men's lives, and how daily prison life itself would leave more scars. Within prison, identifying these scars, and then knowing how to bind wounds that had lain raw and unattended for years, was not just complex but simply not done. There was little in the way of 'social and psychological recovery' (Halsey & Deegan, 2015: 27). Exposure to self-harm, suicide attempts, fire-setting, victimisation, and the use of force—either directly or vicariously—shaped these young men. It finely tuned their instincts. It taught them to be wary and distrustful. It heightened their reactions. It made them intolerant of slights, disrespect, and perceived threats to self. It framed their attitudes, perspectives, and expectations. This was not without cost or consequence to the young men themselves, to prison staff or to society more broadly. Recognising the harms, losses, and tragedies that contextualise prison violence is not to deny young men's agency or responsibility. As Billingham and Irwin-Rogers note (2022: 1), 'Explanation is not exoneration.' However, prison violence cannot be effectively prevented if we fail to appreciate the meaning(s) attached to violence and the way tragedy, violence, and loss continues to feature within these young men's lives. Chapter 7 extends this analysis by considering the formative lessons learnt during youth imprisonment, and how such experiences reinforced the utility of violence.

References

Bargu, B. (2014). *Starve and immolate: The politics of human weapons*. Columbia University Press.

Baskin-Sommers, A. R., & Baskin, D. (2016). Psychopathic traits mediate the relationship between exposure to violence and violent juvenile offending. *Journal of Psychopathology and Behavioral Assessment, 38*(3), 341–349.

Becker, H. (1963). *Outsiders*. Free Press.

Biggs, D. (2005). Dying without killing: Self-immolations, 1963–2002. In D. Gambetta (Ed.), *Making sense of suicide missions* (pp. 173–208). Oxford University Press.

Billingham, L., & Irwin-Rogers, K. (2022). *Against youth violence: A social harm perspective*. Bristol University Press.
Blaauw, E., Arensman, E., Kraaij, V., Winkel, F. W., & Bout, R. (2002). Traumatic life events and suicide risk among jail inmates: The influence of types of events, time period and significant others. *Journal of Traumatic Stress, 15*(1), 9–16.
Bonner, R. L. (2006). Stressful segregation housing and psychosocial vulnerability in prison suicide ideators. *Suicide and Life-threatening Behavior, 36*(2), 250–254.
Brown, E. (2020). A systematic review of the effects of prison segregation. *Aggression and Violent Behavior, 52*, 101389.
De Viggiani, N. (2012). Trying to be something you are not. *Men and Masculinities, 15*(3), 271–291.
Delisi, M., Berg, M. T., & Hochstetler, A. (2004). Gang members, career criminals and prison violence: Further specification of the importation model of inmate behavior. *Criminal Justice Studies, 17*(4), 369–383.
Ellis, A. (2016). *Men, masculinities and violence: An ethnographic study*. Routledge.
Ellis, A., Winlow, S., & Hall, S. (2017). 'Throughout my life I've had people walk all over me': Trauma in the lives of violent men. *The Sociological Review, 65*(4), 699–713.
Gilligan, J. (1996). *Violence: Reflections on our deadliest epidemic*. G.P. Putnam's Sons.
Gilligan, J. (2003). Shame, guilt, and violence. *Social Research: An International Quarterly, 70*(4), 1149–1180.
Goldson, B. (2005). Child imprisonment: A case for abolition. *Youth Justice, 5*(2), 77–90.
Golier, J. A., Yehuda, R., Bierer, L. M., Mitropoulou, V., New, A. S., Schmeidler, J., Silverman, J. M., & Siever, L. J. (2003). The relationship of borderline personality disorder to posttraumatic stress disorder and traumatic events. *American Journal of Psychiatry, 160*(11), 2018–2024.
Gooch, K., Masson, I., Owens, A., & Waddington, E. (2022). After care, after thought: The invisibility of care experienced men and women in prison. *Prison Service Journal, 258*, 4–12.
Hales, H., Davison, S., Misch, P., & Taylor, P. J. (2003). Young male prisoners in a Young Offenders' Institution: Their contact with suicidal behaviour by others. *Journal of Adolescence, 26*(6), 667–685.
Halsey, M. (2018). Child victims as adult offenders: Foregrounding the criminogenic effects of (unresolved) trauma and loss. *British Journal of Criminology, 58*(1), 17–36.

Halsey, M., & Deegan, S. (2015). *Young offenders: Crime, prison and struggles for desistance*. Palgrave.

Harris, L. (2015). *Changing prisons, saving lives: Report of the independent review into self-inflicted deaths in custody of 18–24 year olds, Cm 9087*. Her Majesty's Stationery Office.

Her Majesty's Inspectorate of Prisons. (1999). *Suicide is everyone's concern: A thematic report by HM Chief Inspector of England and Wales*. Her Majesty's Inspectorate of Prisons.

Kaba, F., Lewis, A., Glowa-Kollisch, S., Hadler, J., Lee, D., Alper, H., Selling, D., Macdonald, R., Solimo, A., Parsons, A., & Venters, H. (2014). Solitary confinement and risk of self-harm among jail inmates. *American Journal of Public Health, 104*(3), 442–447.

Kerig, P. K., Bennett, D. C., Thompson, M., & Becker, S. P. (2012). "Nothing really matters": Emotional numbing as a link between trauma exposure and callousness in delinquent youth. *Journal of Traumatic Stress, 25*(3), 272–279.

Långström, N., & Grann, M. (2002). Psychopathy and violent recidivism among young criminal offenders. *Acta Psychiatrica Scandinavica, 106*(s412), 86–92.

Laws, B. (2019). The return of the suppressed: Exploring how emotional suppression reappears as violence and pain among male and female prisoners. *Punishment & Society, 21*(5), 560–577.

Liebling, A. (1992). *Suicides in prison*. Routledge.

Liebling, A., Williams, R., & Lieber, E. (2020). More mind games: How 'the action' and 'the odds' have changed in prison. *British Journal of Criminology, 60*(6), 1648–1666.

Maguire, D. (2021). *Male, failed and jailed: Masculinities and the 'revolving door' imprisonment in the UK*. Palgrave Macmillan.

Matza, D. (2018). *Delinquency and drift*. 2nd Edn. Routledge.

McGuire, J. (2018). *Understanding prison violence: A rapid evidence assessment*. Her Majesty's Prison and Probation Service.

Miller, J. (1991). *Last one over the wall: The Massachusetts experiment in closing reform schools*. Ohio State University Press.

Ministry of Justice. (2025). *Safety in custody statistics: Quarterly update to September 2024*. Ministry of Justice.

Phillips, C. (2012). *The multicultural prison: Ethnicity, masculinity and social relations among prisoners*. Oxford University Press.

Pietrek, C., Elbert, T., Weierstall, R., Müller, O., & Rockstroh, B. (2013). Childhood adversities in relation to psychiatric disorders. *Psychiatry Research, 206*(1), 103–110.

Prison and Probation Ombudsman. (2011). *Learning from PPO investigations: Violence reduction, bullying and safety*. Prison and Probation Ombudsman.
Prison and Probation Ombudsman. (2013). *Learning lessons bulletin: Child deaths*. Prison and Probation Ombudsman.
Prison and Probation Ombudsman. (2014). *Learning lessons bulletin: Young adult prisoners*. Prison and Probation Ombudsman.
Prison and Probation Ombudsman. (2015). *Segregation: Learning lessons bulletin*. Prison and Probation Ombudsman.
Slade, K., Forrester, A., & Baguley, T. (2020). Coexisting violence and self-harm: Dual harm in an early-stage male prison population. *Legal and Criminological Psychology, 25*(2), 182–198.
Stein, A. (2013). *Prologue to violence: Child abuse, dissociation and crime*. Routledge.
Steiner, B., & Wooldredge, J. (2008). Inmate versus environmental effects on prison rule violations. *Criminal Justice and Behavior, 35*(4), 438–456.
Sweeney, G. (2004). Self-immolative martyrdom: Explaining the Irish hunger-strike tradition. *Studies: An Irish Quarterly Review, 93*(371), 337–348.
Teasdale, B., Daigle, L. E., Hawk, S. R., & Daquin, J. C. (2016). Violent victimization in the prison context. *International Journal of Offender Therapy and Comparative Criminology, 60*(9), 995–1015.
Tewksbury, R., Connor, D. P., & Denney, A. S. (2014). Disciplinary infractions behind bars. *Criminal Justice Review, 39*(2), 201–218.
Toch, H. (1975). *Men in crisis: Human breakdowns in prison*. Aldine Publishing Co.
Toch, H. (1992). *Violent men: An inquiry into the psychology of violence*. Penguin.
Tyler, N., Gannon, T. A., Ciardha, C. Ó., Ogloff, J. R., & Stadolnik, R. (2019). Deliberate firesetting: An international public health issue. *The Lancet Public Health, 4*(8), e371–e372.
Ugelvik, T. (2014). *Power and resistance in prison: Doing time, doing freedom*. Palgrave Macmillan.
van der Kolk, B. (2014). *The body keeps the score: Brain, mind and body in the process of healing of trauma*. Penguin.
Winlow, S. (2001). *Badfellas: Crime, tradition and new masculinities*. Berg.
Winlow, S., & Hall, S. (2009). Retaliate first: Memory, humiliation and male violence. *Crime, Media, Culture: An International Journal, 5*(3), 285–304.
Yakeley, J. (2022). *Psychoanalytic perspectives on psychopathy* (pp. 381–412). Springer International Publishing.

7

Learning to 'Jail': Young Men's Adaptations to Prison Life

Imprisonment during the critical formative years of young adulthood was life altering. For a small number of young men, their imprisonment was an aberration in the context of a stable, secure, and generally law-abiding life. For the vast majority, though, their journey to prison had started in early childhood, and was marked by experiences of local authority care, child penal custody, life on 'the road' in impoverished communities, and disrupted or strained family life (also see Maguire, 2021). Adam was one such example. At 19 years old, Adam was a stocky, cheeky, and likeable 'lad' who continually featured in violent incidents. He was restless and walked with a bounce in his step—a bounce that could quickly turn into verbal or physical sparring. His behaviour ranged from mischievously hiding from staff (much to their irritation) and playful 'banter,' to assaulting prison officers and robbing other young men of their property. These assaults meant he was often restrained, 'blocked off,'[1] getting 'nickings'[2] and being awarded 'extra days' in prison by the District Judge. He

[1] Slang for spending a period of time in segregation.

[2] A 'nicking' is when a prison officer reports a violation of Prison/YOI Rules (see Prison Act 1952, Prison Rules 1999 and Young Offender Institution Rules 2000). The person who is alleged to have committed the offence is required to attend an Adjudication where a Governor Grade will either accept a guilty plea or, in the event of a not guilty plea, determine whether the charge has been proved. Sanctions can be imposed if the charge is proven.

K. Gooch, *Prison Violence*, Palgrave Studies in Prisons and Penology,
https://doi.org/10.1007/978-3-031-91365-5_7

was banned from another YOI due to his assaults against prison officers. Adam was himself also 'rushed and jumped' by other young men, occupying a precarious position amongst the 'lads' and never attaining the social standing of the 'Top Dog.' Being in prison was draining for him. He described the prison as 'getting to him;' his chief complaints being the 'disgusting' conditions, the 'horseshit' regime, and the 'bollockings' from prison officers when time out of cell was cut short and he was unwillingly 'banging up.' This was not Adam's first in custody, nor would it be his last.

Adam began offending at age 12 when his mother was diagnosed with cancer. Although his mother would recover, her illness created a 'turning point' (Wheaton & Gotlib, 1997). Adam described himself as 'growing up fast,' feeling compelled to 'look after the family' and engaging in 'spur of the moment' assaults and burglaries. His father appeared to hold a peripheral role in family life, with Adam dismissing him as a 'crackhead' and someone he was 'embarrassed to be with.' By age 13, Adam was in a secure children's home, and by 15, in a YOI for children. When I first met him, it was his second time at the young adult YOI. He was serving a two-year sentence for assaulting the mother of his son with a knife—an incident he blamed on her phoning him whilst his was 'in town on a night out' and on her being 'chatted up' by his close friend. Adam felt 'disrespected' and claimed he had 'lost it a bit.' These admissions revealed the fragility of his own sense of self, his hyper-vigilance to perceived threat, and a desire for control—traits that framed his interactions with his peers and prison officers. He admitted that another former partner alleged he raped her—a prosecution that collapsed because the 'girl' withdrew (as is the case in 70% of rape cases, see Ministry of Justice, 2023a). Adam suggested she had only pressed charges because her father forced her to do so—a 'neutralisation strategy' (Sykes & Matza, 1957) that was particularly useful in a context where sex offenders were social pariahs. However, his casual regard for women continued in the YOI; Adam alleged he had been in a sexual relationship with a prison officer who had since left but whom he described as 'a bit of a slag.' Both his children had already been taken into the care of the local authority—a loss he grieved, leaving him clinging to the hope that his mother might gain custody of his children.

For want of other opportunities to provide for himself and his family, Adam became involved in drug dealing in the community and in the prison: 'money needs to be made.' He took pride in his ability to provide for himself within prison by selling (but not using) psychoactive substances and anabolic steroids. He had long learnt to target those who were likely to become reliant on the drugs. During his time in the YOI, his connections to criminal networks were still developing, but they would be later solidified on his subsequent release. In the months that followed, Adam would become embroiled in a large conspiracy to supply drugs into multiple prisons across the county. His early grafting in the YOI served as an apprenticeship for far more sophisticated, organised, and large-scale drug trafficking, actions that would ultimately see him serving another 3.5 years in prison. During a chance encounter in another prison, it became apparent that his 'survival strategies' and propensity for violence remained unchanged. Even as he has aged, he continued to fight officers and challenge authority. He had simply concluded that he had 'nothing to lose' and imprisonment simply amounted to 'psychological warfare,' a war that was best fought—to his mind—with fists. On one hand, he was unable to free himself from the use of violence in response to threat but felt a degree of hopelessness and helplessness in the face of its life-depleting consequences. In his mid-twenties, he was no closer to release, and ostensibly no more mature, than when I first met him. Imprisonment had simply created a developmental 'deep freeze' (Zamble & Porporino, 1988). Even after our re-encounter, Adam's self-defeating attempts to resist 'the system' would continue. He was later released but soon recalled to prison.

Being held in prisons with high rates of violence is known to 'reduce the odds of successful re-entry' into the community (Meyers et al., 2023) and those who frequently participate in prison violence are more likely to re-offend (Listwan et al., 2013; Eichenthal & Blatchford, 1997). Not all would re-offend, but the odds were that at least 30% would do so with the first year following their release (Ministry of Justice, 2025a). The likelihood of reoffending was higher for those who had already served custodial sentences, increasing to between 50–75% (Ministry of Justice, 2025a). This is just in the first year and only reflects detected crime; more would re-offend in the years that followed, and as time passed news of police searches and/or further convictions came to my attention or I would meet them in adult prisons as my research continued. The notion that prisons should be especially punishing and punitive to deter future crime is attractive but unsupported by the evidence (Cullen et al., 2011)—indeed the greater the strain and more negative the 'moral climate,' the more likely the risk of offending (Listwan et al., 2013; Auty & Liebling, 2020).

None of the young men wanted to return to prison post-release, but having been imprisoned, the experience would be more familiar and predictable—as it had already proved to be for those who were on their second, third, or fourth sentence. I did not attempt to trace the trajectory of these young men's lives on their release, but they were able to describe the formative lessons they had learnt about navigating a custodial sentence. This chapter describes these lessons, including: how young men learnt to negotiate threats to self ('learning to fight'), how they developed or extended entrepreneurial-based criminality ('learning to graft'), and how they conceived and navigated the demands of penal power ('learning to play the system' or 'keep your head down'). Such survival strategies would—in any other context—be deemed harmful and detrimental rather than functional and adaptive. By exploring the specific formative lessons that these young men were learning within the YOI, this chapter expands Maguire's thesis that imprisonment in child and young adulthood aids young men's transitions to adult prisons, and 'played a significant role in trapping many of them in an enduring and costly cycle of revolving door incarceration' (2021: 198–199). Young men adopted strategies of resistance, violence, and exploitation because the educational, community, and institutional spaces they had navigated had not only taught them that this was a route to 'manhood' but had typically closed down opportunities for secure attachment, financial stability, and legitimate employment. Young men's engagement in prison violence and the illicit economy must be understood within this wider social, penal, and cultural context.

Imprisoning Young Men

When this research began, the number of young adult men (aged 18–21 years old) in prison was already in decline. In 2011, there were 8000 young adults; within 10 years, the number was as few as 3000 (Ministry of Justice, 2013a, 2022a). Young adults now represent less than 4% of the general prison population (Ministry of Justice, 2025b). Thus, the growth of the 'prison industrial complex' (Wacquant, 2010) has been primarily focused on prisoners over the age of 21 years old and reflects a myriad of compounding factors, including: the prosecution of historic sex offenders in the wake of Operation Yewtree (House of Commons Justice Committee, 2020); the lengthening of prison sentences (Ministry of Justice, 2022a; Crewe et al., 2020); the legacy of the problematic 'imprisonment for public protection' (IPP) sentence which keeps prisoners in custody many years post-tariff (Ministry of Justice, 2022a, 2025b; House of Commons Justice Committee, 2022); difficulties demonstrating suitability for release (Jarman & Vince, 2022); more people being recalled to prison (Ministry of Justice, 2022a); and, substantial court delays (Ministry of Justice, 2023b, 2025b).

Quite why there are now fewer young men in prison is difficult to explain. It cannot be attributed to a fall in the overall number of young men in the general population (Office for National Statistics, 2022) nor deliberate policy initiatives. Moreover, young men have been just as affected by the judicial tendency to impose longer life sentences (see Crewe et al., 2020). It is possible that the trend towards 'decarceration' (Goldson, 2005) is an indirect product of successful efforts to reduce the number of children in penal custody during the late 2000s and early 2010s (Ministry of Justice, 2022b; Taylor, 2016)—a natural consequence of which is fewer young men graduating to prison custody and fewer exposed to the deleterious effects of contact with the criminal justice system at an early and formative age (McAra & McVie, 2007). It is likely that young adults have also benefitted from the 'depoliticization of youth crime' (Bateman, 2012, 2014) at a time when Government attention was diverted from youth crime to other political and economic crises, such as the aftermath of the aftermath of the wars in Afghanistan and Iraq, the global economic crash of 2008, the Scottish Referendum, Brexit, the multiple Prime Ministerial (and Government Cabinet) changes and more latterly the COVID-19 pandemic. In addition, there have been few exceptional incidents of the magnitude of James Bulger's murder and the 2011 riots to renew anxiety about youth crime and inspire excessive incarceration (Lightowlers & Quirk, 2015; Goldson, 2000).

The most notable shift—and one that was quickly apparent during this research—has been in the very nature of youth crime itself. Over the last 30 years, the images of youth crime have variously included: the 'twockers'[3] (those taking a motor vehicle and driving away with it) and 'joyriders'; the burglars; the anti-social generation loitering in public spaces; youth gangs; and, knife crime (for an analysis, see Muncie, 2021). Throughout the 2010s, though, the proportion of children and young men receiving immediate custodial sentences for violence increased whilst custodial sentences for acquisitory offences (such as theft, burglary, and handling stolen goods) decreased. Although legislative changes to address knife crime have also caused more children and young men to be received into custody for possession of weapons (Ministry of Justice, 2021), there was an overall reduction in violence in the community (Billingham & Irwin-Rogers, 2022). By contrast, the number of immediate custodial sentences for fraud and motoring offences remained almost negligible, and custodial sentences for drugs and sexual offences remained broadly consistent over time (ibid.).

Whilst the nature of youth offending has changed, those YOIs have consistently been drawn from backgrounds of social, economic, and educational disadvantage (Goldson, 2008). Young prisoners are far more likely to have been excluded from school, experienced local authority care, experienced abuse or neglect, experienced the loss or death of family members (including to imprisonment), have alcohol and substance misuse problems, demonstrate neurodiversity, have experienced traumatic brain injury, and/or have mental health needs (Maschi et al., 2011; Williams et al., 2012; Hosser et al., 2007, Weeks & Widom, 1998; Prison Reform Trust, 2004). The interviewees in the YOI were no different. The

[3] A term used to describe those committing the offence of taking a motor vehicle without consent, contrary to section 12 of the Theft Act 1968.

youthful age, ongoing maturation and development, complex needs of young adult prisoners and the stark differences between children's and adult custodial institutions gives rise to powerful arguments to both hold young adult men separately from adults and provide distinct provision (Barrow Cadbury Trust, 2005; Liebling, 2012; House of Commons Justice Committee, 2016, 2018).

For over 100 years, the need to accommodate young men separately from adult prisoners remained a fundamental penal principle.[4] The 1895 Gladstone Committee first recognised the specific needs of older, adolescent young men and suggested that there ought to be dedicated provision. Until then, legislation only distinguished between children (under the age of 16) and adult offenders, holding the former in philanthropic reformatory schools and the latter in the gaols, prison Hulks and Houses of Corrections (later consolidated into prisons). The impetus for discreet custodial institutions for young adults arose from the belief that the adult prisons had become 'Universities of Crime' where impressionable young men were encouraged to become more sophisticated criminals. The Gladstone Committee were persuaded that the years 16–21 years old was the period when 'criminal habits' were formed but where there is a 'degree of plasticity that might be put to good use in the right direction' (Prisons Committee, 1895: 30). Whilst recognising that young men in prison can be 'quite as difficult' as older men, they concluded that, 'the importance of saving them from a life of crime is not diminished, and it is all the more necessary to make the most strenuous efforts to reclaim them' (ibid.).

The Committee proposed the development of a 'penal reformatory'—'a half-way house between the prison and the reformatory' (ibid.), seeking to bridge the gap between adult institutions and the ostensibly welfare orientated reformatories for children under 16. The Committee were persuaded that the existing arrangements were so inadequate that even a 'moderate percentage of success would justify much effort and expense' (ibid.). These conclusions, and the subsequent creation of the Borstals, marked the 'discovery of adolescence' (Muncie 2015: 64). The

[4] Specific provision for girls and young women was slower to appear and harder to sustain. Young adult women are held in prisons alongside adult women.

'experiment' with young adult custody began with Borstals (1902–1982), and then was repeated with Detention Centres (1948–1988) and Youth Custody Centres (1982–1988), before evolving into YOIs. In addition, the original sentence of 'detention under penal discipline in a Borstal'[5] was renamed 'detention in a young offender institution'[6]—a specific sentence only available for those aged 18–21 years old.[7] Over time, YOI have become increasingly 'adult like,' lacking the resources and distinctiveness that the penal reformers considered most necessary (Maguire, 2021; Barrow Cadbury Trust, 2005; Lösel et al., 2012; Her Majesty's Inspectorate of Prisons, 2021). The recycling of institutions from Borstals to YOIs has seen a dilution in imagination and intention. Compared to its predecessors which sought to operate with 'firm and exact discipline' (Hood, 1965: 15–18) or as a 'short sharp shock,' it is hard to locate the penal philosophy underpinning YOIs (also see Her Majesty's Inspectorate of Prisons, 1997, 2021). Indeed, it now appears to be a foreshadow of the adult prison estate.

The State Raised Youth

Of the interviewees, more than two thirds had served time in 'juvie' (either a secure training centre and/or a YOI) and were 'State Raised Youth' (Irwin, 1970). Some would transfer from these facilities to the young adult YOI as part of a sentence, but the vast majority had a brief period of freedom between sentences. As young adults, they lamented the loss of their childhoods (also see Gooch, 2016) and felt compelled to 'grow up fast':

> I've had all my childhood in prison, you know what I mean? Always in custody. (Ethan)

> I've grew up in jail and I've learnt a lot. (Paul)

[5] Prevention of Crime Act 1908 section 1

[6] Criminal Justice Act 1998

[7] This sentence is not used when other provisions take precedence (e.g. the mandatory life sentence for murder).

Like custodial institutions for young adults, rates of violence within child penal custody[8] are disproportionately high (for an analysis, see Gooch, 2019). Alarmingly, as the number of children within child custody has decreased, the rate of violence increased (Ministry of Justice, 2020, 2024). As many as 89% of children in custody had been bullied or victimised by their peers, and 79% reported being bullied or victimised by staff (Her Majesty's Inspectorate of Prisons, 2024). For our interviewees, imprisonment during childhood would consistently form 'one of their most memorable and significant life changing experiences' (Maguire, 2021: 138). Notably, those who had been in child custody had already been schooled in the need to rebuff any 'testing' by their peers, to respond violently to perceived 'violations,' and the consequence of failing to live up to masculine scripts (also see Gooch, 2019). Crucially, therefore, violence as a feature of prison life had been normalised well before many arrived in the young adult YOI.

Ryan, for example, had served his first custodial sentence for armed robbery in a children's YOI. He would subsequently be imprisoned twice more for armed robbery (related to drug dealing), and it was on the third occasion that James and I met him. For Ryan, 'grafting' had started at an early age and he believed he had 'big rankings' in the street drug economy—a reputation that he prized and was prepared to violently defend. On entering child custody, he met others he knew, and quickly learned that his survival was predicated on this willingness to 'fight' his way out of conflict—a strategy he willingly embraced:

> I come out the next day and I smack a couple of kids up. That's how it was. First time I come out, any time I come to jail, I fight with someone. Because as soon as someone sees that they've got an advantage, they take you for a victim. Everybody's going to take you for a victim. That's how it's going to be, always, in jail. Any jail. If they think you're a push over and you show them once that you're a push-over, they're going to do it again, do it again, do it again. What are you going to do?

---

[8] Child penal custody has been labelled by the Ministry of Justice as the 'Youth Custody Service,' overlooking the status of those within such institutions as children.

Ryan enjoyed violence, describing it as 'nice' and appreciating its 'quality, ferocity, cunning and cool conduct' (Winlow, 2001: 171). In the child YOI, he spent four periods in segregation. When I met him, Ryan had already been involved in 23 fights during his current sentence, including breaking someone's jaw. When James and I interviewed him, Ryan had just returned from 'the block' after punching two officers. Although Ryan had successfully established a 'name' for himself, he was keenly aware that this reputation was situational—people knew who he was and what he could do, but he conceded that if he moved to another prison, he would need to re-establish himself by 'going for the hardest man, find[ing] the hardest fuck' and then 'just bang[ing] him.' With his father and step-father in prison, and the belief that his 'boys' had done stretches for him, Ryan (like others) had a fatalistic attitude towards future imprisonment Graduating to young adult YOIs caused Ryan to adopt 'more intensified versions of violent masculine performances in order to survive' (Maguire, 2021: 158).

By the time this young cohort of prisoners transferred or arrived in young adult institutions as young adults, many were already scarred by imprisonment. Perversely these scars would serve to suggest that they had a degree of 'carceral capital' (see Chap. 8)—that they had proven themselves, that they were 'known,' that they had been provoked or attacked and held their own (even if they had been hurt or injured). It was proof that they could stand. For example, Isaac had been imprisoned in a YOI for 15–18-year-olds after being caught with large quantities of cocaine and heroin. His drug dealing began at an early age, as did the burglaries, and as he grew older, he would undertake 'more and more serious crime.' Whilst his transition into child custody was made smoother by his familiarity with other teenage boys from the streets of one of the local, large cities (also see Maguire, 2021), he still came into conflict with others:

> There's a big scar there, as well. Whilst I was in [Children's YOI], there was another situation. I got a scar [shows James and I the back of the head] when I was on the landing. I did not expect this at all. I just turned my back. I got hit, looked straight around. Straightaway the govs[9] got both of

[9] Slang for prison officers.

> us straightaway and then, obviously, all of a sudden, from what other people said anyway, the blood was coming out. I put my head down like that and I saw all the blood dripping. It was a bar [the weapon]. To my surprise, it didn't even hurt me, like. It didn't hurt. The thing that hurt me the most was fucking getting it glued though cah, you know, it hurt fucking bad.

The most notable difference between the child and young adult YOIs was that the opportunity for violence had increased, partly because these young men were allowed freer access to cells. Isaac acquired more scars as a young adult in the YOI, scars that he wanted to show us and explain:

> I got slit twice with a razor blade. That's one. That's a light slice, and then there's one here. [showing the scars on his face and head] I was in that shower, there, just normal showering. A couple of lads came through. Obviously, I just told the screws that I slipped and fell, but the guy that came through was, like, three times, four times bigger than me and he came through first, showed me the razor blade. I was like, 'Fucking hell!' I kicked back and straightaway went bang and then that's hit me and then must have hit me twice with it, as well. I didn't even realise that he hit me with a razor blade until I saw other lads ran in. I got a little beating, as well. Other lads ran in, looked at my face and just went … I must have been covered in my blood. I got taken to the hospital.

What was most telling about Isaac's descriptions was how matter of fact he was, but within the account was the sense that violent assaults could take you by surprise when you were simply undertaking normal activities such as showering or walking around the prison. Isaac was not unique in bearing scars from child penal custody; others had scars on their body where they too had been stabbed or hit. Such peer violence was typically met with painful forms of physical restraint, segregation (sometimes euphemistically described as separation), and more time locked in cells. The 'multiple and intersection expressions of violence perpetuate fear, damage and harm for all child prisoners,' the cumulative effects of such can become 'too much to bear' (Goldson, 2013: 14). Whilst there were some who adopted pre-emptive and defensive strategies, others—like Alistair—started to self-harm as—to use his words—a 'cry for help.'

Learning to Fight and Survive

Prisons and YOIs are 'hypermasculine' or 'ultra-masculine' worlds (Toch, 1998) in which the 'normal values and behaviour patterns of powerful men take on an extreme form in the face of powerlessness against the institution' (Jewkes, 2005: 61–62). 'Manliness' was predicated on the advertised capacity, threat, and willingness to use violence (Michalski, 2017; Sloan, 2016; Newton, 1994; Sykes, 1958; De Viggiani, 2012). As described later (in Chap. 8), what qualified as 'manly' violence and victimisation was rooted in notions of strength, courage, and bravery, rather than indiscriminate or 'sneaky' acts. Young men were still forging their identities and, unlike adult prisoners, were less likely to have alternative markers of masculinity such as fatherhood, long-term sexual relationships, employment and/or highly established criminal careers and carceral journeys that would solidify social status without the need for further proof of their ability to defend themselves. Prison mentoring, education and work provided some with alternative forms of 'respectable masculinities' but largely 'official prison learning and training … was clearly wholly inadequate for this purpose' (Maguire, 2021: 199). This not only intensified the importance of peer social esteem during a life-stage when peer groups are already more salient (Brown, 2004), but rendered prisoner politics, social prestige and other people's estimations of their strength more critical.

Although many would import norms and attitudes that were conducive to the use of violence (Ricciardelli, 2015; Jewkes, 2005; Newton, 1994; Maguire, 2021), those who did not often became inculcated in the logic and rationality of violence and victimisation within the YOI. Perpetrators often minimised their behaviour by explaining 'I don't see it as bullying' or 'I'm just using my authority' (see Chap. 8). Young men who would have preferred to avoid violence sometimes felt compelled to decisively respond to any threat. Keve (1980) describes as the 'quicksand effect' of prisons, i.e. 'the prison's talent for drawing many of its prisoners deeper and deeper into a round of misbehaviours.' Whatever their orientations before prison, young men learned that violence was a socially acceptable response—something that was reinforced by the State's reliance on coercive force to respond to violence (see Chap. 9).

Prison violence and victimisation was a 'taken for granted' and anticipated feature of prison life by young men who often dismissed the significance of violence as 'it's prison'—a normalisation that prison officers often found difficult to accept (Sim, 1994). Darren, a Supervising Officer, described an assault that had impacted him:

> There was blood everywhere. There was a lot of blood on the floor. There was blood on me, because the lad rushed towards me, and we had to restrain the victim, which wasn't nice especially as he had been assaulted and all the lads were around him. … So I'm telling the lads to calm down, talking to them, laughing with them and joking, and then, within seconds, it was back to normality. I got someone to clean the blood up, and then it was back to normal again. It was good, but kind of eerie, because the guys on the left, they were playing pool as if nothing had happened.

The seeming ease with which the young men continued to play pool, and how easily blood could be washed away, troubled Darren. Even with 22 years' experience, the apparent normalisation of violence generated concern, not because Darren necessarily feared he would be seriously assaulted, but because the young men appeared to be unmoved by the considerable loss of blood. Of course, all these incidents were noticed by the young men even if they did not visibly react. The assaults became the backdrop against which young men made assessments about the likely survivability of the YOI. In the example Darren gave, playing pool—rather than intervening or become embroiled in a fight—was a prudent response by the on-lookers who knew better than to intervene. The appearance of 'returning to normal' did not mean that these young men were unaffected. The fact that young men maintained a hyper-vigilance to threat and could 'never let your guard down' created an intense but also damaging environment. It is difficult to fully establish the trauma associated with direct and vicarious experience of prison violence, or indeed the long-term ramifications of living in a volatile, turbulent, and frightening environment, but clearly some were changed by their experiences and were hardened by them.

Young men not only learned the utility of violence in establishing respect but also learned how to avoid detection. Assaults occurred 'on-sight' (where CCTV cameras were in operation and where they would be seen by staff) and 'off-sight.' Prisoners were keenly aware of the locations that were not covered by CCTV, such as showers, cells, and spaces near wing offices. The decision to fight on or off sight largely depended on the purpose of the incident, any possible risk that the aggressor themselves might be attacked, and whether the aggressor had 'time to get them.' Thus, 'changes in the visibility of violence are not random or aimless' (Durán-Martinez, 2018: 6). It is often assumed that young men are impulsive and less able to engage in consequential thinking. Some violent incidents were undoubtedly opportunistic and spontaneous. On other occasions, young men deliberately assaulted the victim(s) in locations where speedy staff intervention was guaranteed and the perpetrator could minimise the likelihood of serious harm whilst also visibly addressing their grievances and moral injuries (also see Gooch, 2019). Other would not only ruminate, but, and much like some adult prisoners, would bide their time waiting for the best opportunity to act. For example, Kade explained:

> The only thing we've got is time, innit? And, obviously, we've got a lot of it, and honestly, we ain't got much to do. So, well certain ones of us anyway, we start learning language and how officers are. We monitor how officers act in situations. So, then after a month or two of watching a set of say 12 officers on a shift, we know what shifts going to happen now. So, we know, right, at the weekend, these 12 officers are going to be on. Then we know, out of them 12 officers, these six officers act in a certain way in this situation. So, if a fight was to kick off, we'd know, these six officers will let the fight continue, instead of these six officers who would stop the fight straight away. Or, we'd know, them four officers would probably let us in the shower, and fight with that kid. Or we'd probably know them officers wouldn't, you know what I mean? So, we know them better than they know themselves in a sense.

Some—like Kade—were skilful readers and keen observers of others, including prison officers—a characteristic that would serve them well both on the streets and in prison. It allowed them to 'better calibrate their fighting decisions' (Gambetta, 2009: 85) but also better avoid the penalties associated with violence.

Learning to 'Graft': The Connection Between the Streets and the Prison

Whilst the illicit economy provides relief from the material deprivation that is an intrinsic feature of imprisonment (Sykes, 1958, also see Chap. 4), 'grafting' as an adaptation was not unique to imprisonment. When faced with the inability to secure resources the 'legal way,' some young men had learnt that surviving the streets meant finding ways to secure illegitimate income by grafting (typically drug dealing)—street based criminal behaviour that continued or was refined in prison. Whilst an individual might refer to grafting as legitimate employment and income, it was far more common for 'grafting' to refer to illegitimate employment. Within prison, grafting included dealing, trading, exploitation, and extortion. Even within prison, money remained a key concern:

> Money. It always comes down to money problems. (Cory)

Similarly, Lewis reported: 'I love grafting.' Luke went so far as to say that: 'The only thing that makes us feel we are on road again is doing what we usually do.' For young men like Luke and Lewis, grafting was such a familiar part of everyday life on the streets that continuing such activities and earning money within prison restored a sense of normality. More fundamentally, they could distance themselves from the infantilising tendencies of the prison and find ways to carve out agency, generate income, and restore a sense of pride through the acquisition of designer clothes, toiletries, and small comforts. For those who prized consumer artefacts, grafting provided further proof of masculinity.

Grafting clearly had 'seductive appeal' (Katz, 1988: 4). On the streets, these young men took pride in their ability to generate financial income and purchase high value, high status items such as expensive clothes, electronic gadgets, and cars. Drawn from poverty and with few economic or social advantages, it was common for young men to steal or earn the money through low level drug dealing. Not all young men were poor; some were drawn from affluence but had come into contact with low-level drug trading and taken advantage of an opportunity to earn money. As Anderson notes (1999: 111), 'The drug trade is certainly illegal, but it is the most lucrative and accessible element of the underground economy and has become a way of life in numerous inner-city communities.' Notably, grafting was also seen as an honourable occupation by young men such as Steven: 'I was earning money, grafting, dealing drugs. I don't rob houses; I don't agree with it. I don't need to nick [steal] TVs.'

It might be assumed that these young men could—with sufficient resolve, hard work and better judgement—pursue and sustain legitimate employment. This is to pre-suppose a level of choice that few thought they had. For example:

> I deal. Money needs to be made. I don't know how to make money any other way. I don't feel like I am going to get a job. I want to be a youth worker but because of my offending, it's not going to help because I have assaults against young people. Drug dealing is the only way young people can make money. There are no jobs out there. I have never signed on in my life. I don't like it. (Adam)

The vast majority of young men articulated a desire for legitimate work and to pursue what they thought was a successful life: a house, car, partner, and children (also see Maguire, 2021). However, they simply could not conceive how they could secure this stability and lacked the 'self-determination,' optimism, opportunities and plans for the future deemed critical for 'redemption scripts' (Maruna, 2001: 147).

Few young men had remained in secondary school long enough to complete their GCSEs[10] at age 16.[11] Somewhere between year 7 (age 11–12) and year 10 (age 14–15), they had been excluded from school, or

[10] A 'General Certificate in Secondary Education' is awarded typical at age 16.

[11] Only two of the 53 interviewees had gained a GCSE qualification.

been to a Pupil Referral Unit (PRU)[12] or alternate educational provision. Any alternative education provision was rarely sustained over time. For those who had spent periods of their childhood in local authority care, disruption to their educational career was perpetuated by frequent changes in placement, chaotic experiences of residential care homes or a tendency to run away (Gooch et al., 2022; Maguire, 2021). With few, if any, academic qualifications, these young men were unable to secure the well-paid jobs that earned the sums that they aspired to. As these young men began securing convictions, as many had done, they became increasingly 'fatalistic about their chances of prolonged employment' (Winlow, 2001: 64). These difficulties were exacerbated by de-industrialisation and wider market shifts from manual labour to 'feminised work' in the care and hospitality sector (Maguire, 2021; Winlow, 2001; Winlow & Hall, 2006; Hobbs, 2013)—work that they regarded as 'shit,' subservient and only for 'mugs.'

Faced with few opportunities for legitimate employment, it was relatively easy to slip into low-level drug dealing. As Decker and Townsend Chapman note (2008: 5), drug markets 'were characterised by entry and succession that was less formal, less structured and with fewer barriers than might be suspected.' As these young men gradually ceased formal school education, many began or had friends already involved in riskier activities and gradually became acquainted with older young men involved in drug dealing or more serious criminal activity. It was common to hear young men describe low level criminal damage escalated over time, leading to custodial sentences for robbery, burglary and violence offences (also see Marsh, 2020). The 'drift' (Matza, 1964) happened subconsciously. For example:

> Before I came in here I wasn't living at home, so I was living by myself, and I just had to fend for myself, so I was doing the wrong things, so robberies, silly stuff like that, selling drugs. It's one of those things. You have to do it to get by, because when I wasn't living at home, I wasn't getting money off my mum and I wasn't really interested in working. I just wanted quick, easy

[12] Pupil Referral Units are places of alternative school provision with much shorter hours of schooling. Young men were often referred to Pupil Referral Units due to poor behaviour (e.g. fighting), truancy, and school exclusion.

> money, which was selling drugs because I didn't really want to rob anybody, but then, as you get older, you get into that group and you don't want to look like the odd one out. You want to impress your friends and then you do what your friends do, and then it's hard to get out of it. (Cory)

Often, these young men were low level drug dealers rather than the high status 'criminal entrepreneurs' (Winlow, 2001) reaping the more lucrative financial rewards. However, the shift towards entrepreneurial crime created an opportunity to financially gain from crime and violence, an opportunity that was 'grasped by a growing number of young men' (Winlow, 2001: 162).

Structural impediments were only half the story. Some young men simply wanted 'fast money' and greater sums of money than they could hope to generate from low-paid but legitimate employment. Of course, it was risky business, but it was just that—business. It was hard to imagine how prison and probation officers could persuade young men that low paid employment was an appealing alternative to the 'fast money' that could be earned through criminal enterprise. As Hall et al. note (2013: 45), most young men 'were not willing to condemn themselves to the drudgeries of welfare, job-seeking, and just getting by.' Ryan reported, 'I love money more than anything.' Hussain was convicted of conspiracy to supply class A drugs and had previous convictions for kidnapping and witness intimidation:

> Nowadays, boss, you know I've applied for jobs but nobody wanted to give me a job. If you've got a criminal record, you can't get a job. The easy way is to sell drugs, do you know what I mean? It's quick money, easy money, but, obviously, there are consequences to it, as well, aren't there? It's ridiculous money, man. You don't even want to know. They make, like, £2,000 a day and that. £2,000 or £4,000 a day, honestly. You're probably thinking, 'What the hell?' the line is just too good. It's too much good money, you know, in class A drugs. There are too many junkies out there, man, and too much skinning, man.

Involvement in criminal enterprise led a range of other offences beyond possession and supply offences, including robbery, armed robbery, kidnapping (false imprisonment), grievous bodily harm, threats to kill, and murder.

In the prison, it was in the engagement with the illicit economy where there was yet further stratification of the young men. The more sophisticated young men were learning to graft to secure both legitimate and illegitimate rewards. Others lacked any financial resources, were too naïve to successfully navigate or rebuff attempts by others to extort or steal from there, and others still were simply willing to accept their inferior status for the 'quick hit' provided by drugs. For those who were able and willing to graft, it brought reputation, status, and a 'name.' Ryan explained:

> Dad comes from a respectable home. He's done quite a long time in jail for selling drugs, but obviously, me, mom and that come from a respectable family and that. You get me? I was in the game and obviously, you ask any other person from [names area] who knows me, I had big rankings in my place.

Whilst some young men were connected and familiar with drug dealing in the community, they had not yet fully developed their criminal networks to the extent that criminal activity within the prison could yet be described as fully 'organised crime.' Dealing within the prison could be naïve, haphazard and chaotic (Hobbs, 2013), but it was also 'crime that was organised' (Densley, 2012; Gooch & Treadwell, 2025).

Grafting within prison necessarily required networks of associates, acquaintances, and/or family members within and beyond the prison, including individuals who could: manufacture or access drugs in the community, transport to the prison, arrange payments, transfer money, convey drugs across the wall and fence, collect packages from the prison grounds, pass goods between prisoners, hold goods in cell, enforce repayment or punish non-repayment. For example:

> Then they are getting the drugs in and then they are repaying their mates on the outside, splitting the profits with their mates. So they are making money even though they are in jail. Their mates are making money from the jail. Ridiculous amounts really. (Peter)

Consequently, for many young men, imprisonment was serving to consolidate and provide useful lessons about how to earn, to network and organise, and navigate security measures. For those who had not yet engaged in drug dealing prior to imprisonment, they would learn much about the profitability of illicit economies. For those more sophisticated, entrepreneurial, and well-connected individuals, this behaviour represented an entry point into more serious, organised criminal activity, and consolidated criminal skills and competencies that would aid them in more successful and sophisticated criminal activity post prison. Thus, patterns of behaviour within the YOI prepared young men for the everyday realities of adult prisons where ongoing, serious, and organised crime was taking root and becoming increasingly well embedded (Gooch & Treadwell, 2020, 2021, 2025). As in the example of Adam and Hussain, some would enter prison with prior experience of drug dealing, continue such activity within prison, and then become part of wider regional and international criminal networks worth millions of pounds.

Learning to 'Play the System' or 'Keep Your Head Down'

Will is due to be released after serving a long sentence and is one of the few prisoners trusted to work in the community on release on temporary licence (ROTL). Most of the staff are congratulating themselves and him on a job well done. Will has—everyone agrees—transformed himself. Having worked hard during his sentence, he had been offered employment on release. He proudly returns from his final work placement beaming with pride. As a mark of appreciation and respect, his co-workers have clubbed together to purchase an expensive designer watch. The card that accompanies it sings his praises. He shows James the watch, 'Nice that,' James says, 'it's worth some cash and shows that they must have really liked you.' Will beams. 'I have turned a corner,' he says, 'I'm not coming back somewhere like here, I've learned.' As he walks to reception on his last day in the YOI, Will says his goodbyes as he goes. He is closely followed by the Security Custodial Manager (CM) who remarks, 'If only

I had a quid,' shaking his head. The CM is not celebrating Will's transformation. The Security CM catches James in the corridor, 'You see Jones [Will's surname] has gone?' he asks. James nods. 'What do you reckon?' he asks James, but he doesn't give him time to answer. 'Don't buy what all these are saying,' the CM tells James, 'I know he was bringing stuff [drugs] in. I know it and I tried every way to catch him. Every way. We watched him like a bloody hawk trying to get him, while everyone else in here thought the sun shone out of his arse. It pisses me right off.' In the week following Will's release, the smell of psychoactive substances (a burning plastic smell) declines significantly in the Residential Unit for the trusted and enhanced prisoners.

Most young men could predict when they would be released and did not suffer the 'pain of uncertainty and indeterminacy' (Crewe, 2011). Those young men who were serving life and indeterminate sentences had not yet turned their attention to how and when they would be released—that prospect was too distant and the route to release was impossible to discern with too many more hurdles and transitions yet to occur (also see Crewe et al., 2020). Consequently, they typically turned their attention to the present, often becoming quickly absorbed in the immediacy of prison politics. Few interventions were available to specifically support *young* men, thus, the offending behaviour programmes were only available for a small number of individuals and rarely featured in young people's accounts of what was important and what they needed to *do* whilst in prison. Psychologists were distant figures, and most young men did not have any need to meet one. Rather, it was the discretionary power of prison officers that was of most importance (c.f. Crewe, 2009). Prison officers determined who was on what level of the Incentives and Earned Privileges (IEP) Scheme, and therefore how much time out of cell they could have, whether they were entitled to extra gym sessions, how much money they could spend, whether they had access to family visits days, who qualified for a move to the Enhanced wing, who could be given trusted jobs, and who would potentially qualify for Release on Temporary Licence (ROTL). Whilst decisions such as ROTL and the possibility of earlier release on Home Detention Curfew (HDC) were decisions made in the backstage offices far removed from the prison landings (Crewe, 2009), what was recorded about the young men, whether they were seen as a 'good' and trustworthy 'lad,' and whether they were on 'Enhanced' were the most critical decisions for these young men. Thus, the full weight of penal power was felt in the decisions made by prison officers on the landings and in the everyday social life of the prison (c.f. Crewe, 2009, also see Chap. 9).

Prison officers primarily demanded compliance and obedience from the young men, rather than anything more paternalistic, moral, or rehabilitative. They were not necessarily demanding 'personal transformation' (Crewe, 2009: 137); rather they were seeking a safe, easy, calm, and violence free day. Those who were seen to be proactively engaged in employment, courses or in trusted prisoner roles were praised and recognised by prison officers (principally by maintaining them on Enhanced regime and giving a little more latitude when they made requests). There were some young men—such as Ryan, Aran, Adam, Steven, Shadow and Luke—who saw little legitimacy in prison officer authority, even if prison officers used their power appropriately. These young men were less likely to assault officers when prison officers used their power judiciously (primarily because there were fewer obvious reasons for direct conflict), but they remained active in their resistance of prison officers and the demands that they behave in particular ways (and avoid behaviour such as grafting). For those who were compliant, the motivations varied from 'instrumental compliance' (Crewe, 2009), a pragmatic acceptance of or 'dull compulsion' to the rules (O'Donnell, 2023; Carrabine, 2003), a desire to become better versions of themselves, or the enduring difficulties adjusting to prison life made prison officer's expectations somewhat obsolete and unachievable.

Some young men—such as Dean, Joseph and Finley—recognised that the appearance of compliant behaviour served their interests. To use their words, they wore a 'mask' with officers whilst trying to 'fly under the radar.' To facilitate illicit activities, they would seek jobs that afforded greater time out of their cells (e.g. cleaner, gym orderly, severy worker) and/or greater freedom around the prison as a whole and close to the perimeter fences (e.g. being a 'Red Band'[13]). This created the means to

[13] Red Bands were given more freedom to enter different areas of the prison and were typically given more trusted roles.

'wheel and deal' (Tompkins, 2016), collect or move contraband, enforce demands for repayment, and/or pass messages. For example:

> Landing cleaners, they can go wherever they want. They can go over to that side, B wing, get whatever they want, pass it through the door, under your door, bring it over here and pass it.
>
> When the people who are working on recycling and Red Bands, especially Red Bands, it means they can walk around the prison unescorted and they bring the drugs in and take them around. It's very, very easy. (Sam)

Charismatic young men who appeared helpful and could create convivial relationships with prison officers were often more likely to be rewarded with the highly prized jobs. Paradoxically, it was the ability to 'play the game' that united the 'King of the Wing' and the most enhanced prisoners who remained largely uninvolved in victimisation. Both groups of prisoners had learned how to navigate the system and benefit from a degree of status, freedom, and agency. Whilst a 'King of the Wing' might be on Basic regime, some learnt to continue their nefarious activities whilst also remaining on Enhanced regime by using others to do their 'dirty work.' Crucially, young men engaged in criminal enterprise believed that their control of the wing was not only tolerated by prison officers but also useful to them. For example:

> Like, they [the prison officers] would prefer, in a sense, someone they could get on with to control the wing, rather than find people they don't get on with, to control the wing. … He's [the prisoner is] making the officers' lives a bit easier [and] they're going to lay off him a bit more. But, when the wing starts going downhill, and he starts losing respect from prisoners and that, then them officers take him out because he's no good no more.
>
> It's never verbal. They know, I know. That's how it goes with everybody like. If you take the piss, you know what the consequences are going to be. If you just keep it down, and whatever not, then you'll be alright. But, obviously, again, it's with certain officers. Certain officers won't have none of it, like. Won't have none of it. They'll just shut the operation down there and then. (Matthew)

This tolerance of 'extra-legal' or 'illegitimate' governance (Skarbek, 2004; Gooch & Treadwell, 2023) was a Faustian pact. The outcomes of such unspoken agreements were unpredictable and could be catastrophic if too much power was ceded (ibid.). However, unlike our experiences of some adult prisons, these implicit agreements never reached the point of creating 'no go' areas unpoliced by prison officers or the reconfiguring of penal power (see Crewe & Liebling, 2017).

Some young men—such as Cory, Jack, Thomas, Paul, and Chris—accepted that resisting the State, or engaging in prisoner politics, was self-defeating. They concluded that their individual interests were better served not through illicit gain but through compliance, however, performative. For example:

> Keep your head down and not get involved when other people have an argument. If you get yourself involved, it just brings more trouble for yourself. If you want to just get your time down and get out of here, the best thing to do is keep your mouth closed, keep your head down, and do what you've got to do to get out. (Cory)

For Cory, and others like him, his compliance was more pragmatic than normative (see Crewe, 2009). They did not accept that they were in want of personal transformation—indeed, many felt trapped in a set of circumstances that made imprisonment an inevitable outcome rather than a personal failing. They retained a desire for a law-abiding life, even if they could not conceive of the route to that life. Within prison, it was the futility of resistance and the conclusion that their time in prison would be easier if they simply kept their head down that meant they avoided conflict with staff and prisoners. They were not immune from the excesses of prison officer behaviour, but less likely to experience its capricious effects because they were largely compliant and caused few problems with officers. This did not mean they did not grow frustrated with prison officers or the arbitrary nature of the IEP scheme, and often gave examples of perceived injustices, but they would tolerate grievances rather than confront officers.

Others—such as Aidan and Robert—were motivated not by the futility of their resistance but by their desire to be better fathers and role models for their children or, in Robert's case, by the desire to remain in the community and care for his mother:

> When I was on the phone, I was in education and they got me and I picked up the phone and my mom was on there and she said, 'You'd better sit down, are you sitting down? I have got cancer again.' 'That's it,' I said, 'Mom, I am never coming back to jail. I am not just doing it for you, I am going to do it for myself.' (Robert)

These external imperatives re-orientated young men and reminded them of what was important to them.

> I am feeling nervous [about being a father] but I am excited too. But I want to be a good dad, I don't want my son to grow up and think, 'My dad is a crackhead, my dad is just a druggie, getting into trouble all of the time. He is a burglar. He is a jail head.' I don't want that. I want him to know what I have been through. If it is a girl or a boy, I want them to know that I can change. And it is time to change now. The tables are turning now. (Aidan)

The organisation of family days, which allowed for more engagement between young men and their children, was particularly productive in both encouraging young men to invest in relationships with their children but also to remove themselves from activities that might jeopardise their entitlement to the family days.

For others living on the Enhanced Unit with Aidan and Joshua, their compliance was more instrumental and predicated on an assumption that 'doing more for the prison' was prudent, permitted more freedom, and ultimately eased the burdens of imprisonment:

> Obviously the more you do for the prison, the more the prison will do for you. If you want to just keep your head down and play it by the book and then everything comes your way. I mean I've got my board next week for my ROTL[14] so I've just been working for that since the day I come in prison. I've been doing that for nearly 18 months now. It's just a waiting

[14] An abbreviation for Release on Temporary Licence.

> game, it's stressful. Sometimes you can do loads of work and get no recognition for it. (Joshua)

At first glance, Joshua seemed to have absorbed the logic of the system. It was however a very strategic approach reflecting an ability to 'read' social situations and determine the best ways to 'play the game.' The inherent danger in demanding that young men demonstrate their moral worth and (at least performatively) their compliance with the rules set by the system (however arbitrary) was that young men could become frustrated and disenfranchised when their attempts to satisfy prison officers went unnoticed.

In discerning the priorities of the 'system,' young men also learned that the best ways to secure their interests could mean acting in incredibly harmful ways. Somewhat perversely, the efficiency with which prisons had designed its policies and practices meant that young men could predict that a response would be more, rather than less, forthcoming if they assaulted an officer, set fires, self-harmed, or attempted suicide. Assaulting an officer would guarantee a move to segregation, something that could provide sanctuary for any young men who felt unsafe. Equally, young men could predict that serious violence was likely to get a reaction from staff. For example, one young adult assaulted his pad mate and when asked for an explanation in an adjudication said:

> I had been asking for three weeks to move out of the cell and no one listened. He was smelly and stinking the cell out. I told the staff to move him or I would smash him, and so I did.

On other occasions, self-harm and arson was an effort to compel staff to comply with their wishes or to recognise the extent of their frustration, distress, or fear. Such actions were variously described as manipulative and whilst it was certainly instrumental behaviour, it was high stakes behaviour that sought to communicate psychological pain and emotional distress. However, self-harm (whether as a threat or in actuality) to access a television was a source of frustration for prisoners and prison officers. For example:

> I'm sitting in my cell with no telly yeah for smacking a server worker but there's another kid on this landing right now who has a TV in his cell. The rule is in this jail if you smash your tv then you don't get a new one yeah. A couple of nights ago, he smashed his TV his [cell door] panel. Every single thing in his cell, his clothes, his papers, he threw it all out the window and set it all on fire. He burnt the whole floor and his door is burnt and he is sitting in his cell now with a TV because they give him another TV. All I do is tick up for myself [trade] and I have got no TV for 28 days. He cuts himself. This geezer is lost. He doesn't come out of his cell anyway. All the officers know that he is a marked man. He just stays behind his door. (Luke)

In most cases, the television would be given, appearing to 'reward bad behaviour' and give the impression to others that the 'ACCT[15] gets things done.' In some cases, young men made deliberate decisions to self-harm or tie a ligature rather than risk being implicated in a violent encounter with their peers or carry the penalties associated with assaulting a member of staff. In this way, violence—whether turned on themselves or others—was a to 'get things done.' It attuned young men to strategies that could prove functional but exacerbated the propensity towards harm. In other cases, self-harm, suicide attempts, isolation in their cells and fire-setting was the manifestation of profound and enduring fear and distress. For these young people—such as Alistair, Stuart, Daniel, Lewis, Ollie, and Chris—the demands of penal power were a distant concern and paled into insignificance compared to the enduring effort to simply survive.

Conclusion

After reviewing self-inflicted deaths amongst young adults in custody, Lord Harris (2015, 5) concluded that young adult prisoners were 'young, vulnerable and still developing individuals who need to be nurtured and supported safely to navigate through the complexities of their lives into

[15] The Assessment, Care, Custody and Treatment is used to assess and support prisoners who at risk of self-harm and suicide.

purposeful, mature adulthood.' The YOI was wholly ill-equipped for this task. With little to distinguish the YOI from provision in adult prisons, there were neither the resources, specialist services nor dedicated provision to support the multifaceted needs of this young population. Although the prison leadership team sought to minimise the worst excesses of State power and re-establish the moral foundations of the YOI (see Chap. 9), they were doing so against a backdrop of ineffective policies, system (in) efficiencies, and economic (ir)rationality where the appetite was to dilute the principles of separate and distinct treatment for young adult men (Ministry of Justice, 2013b). Whilst I argue that young men should continue to be held in dedicated facilities, those institutions also need to be well-resourced, specifically designed (in provision, structure, activity and architecture), carefully led, staffed with well-trained, well-supported and dedicated teams, and give due regard to the needs of individual young men (and the harms experienced not just inflicted). The considerable efforts by individual senior leaders and prison officers to support individual young men was often only the 'tip of the iceberg' in terms of who needed that support and could not withstand the tide of disadvantage, hopelessness, lack of recognition and tragedy that had characterised the lives of so many for so long.

Not only was the YOI ill equipped and resourced to challenge masculine strategies that valorised violence (Maguire, 2021: 138), but it reinforced them. There was little to 'encourage or open up alternative avenues to manhood' (Maguire, 2021: 138). To be 'manly,' these young men had to contain enduring tragedy, loss and pain with stoicism and emotional fortitude. Indeed, violence was seen to be a more prudent solution than advertised distress or emotional collapse, or even disclosing and describing their concerns to prison staff. If these young men were learning anything about how to be 'real men' or to navigate custodial sentences, they were learning how to navigate a system that prioritised compliance, however performative. There was little that supported personal growth, promoted 'redemption' (Maruna, 2001), or created opportunities for young men to find or solidify interests and skills (rather than simply complete a course for the sake of performance metrics). This is a systemic problem: the primary focus of penal power is control and compliance, and the pursuit of such goals is often done in the most counter-productive ways. Set against this backdrop, these young men were finding alternatives form of capital that were of value in the unique social 'habitus' (Bourdieu, 1977) of the prison, a theme taken up in Chap. 8.

References

Anderson, E. (1999). *Code of the street: Decency, violence and the moral life of the inner city*. W.W. Norton and Company.

Auty, K. M., & Liebling, A. (2020). Exploring the relationship between prison social climate and reoffending. *Justice Quarterly, 37*(2), 358–381.

Barrow Cadbury Trust. (2005). *Lost in transition*. Barrow Cadbury Trust.

Bateman, T. (2012). Who pulled the plug? Towards an explanation of the fall in child imprisonment in England and Wales. *Youth Justice, 12*(1), 36–52.

Bateman, T. (2014). Where has all the youth crime gone? Youth justice in an age of austerity. *Children & Society, 28*(5), 416–424.

Bourdieu, P. (1977). *Outline of a theory of practice*. Cambridge University Pres.

Brown, B. B. (2004). Adolescents' relationships with peers. In M. Lerner & L. Steinberg (Eds.), *Handbook of adolescent psychology* (pp. 363–394). Wiley.

Billingham, L., & Irwin-Rogers, K. (2022). *Against youth violence: A social harm perspective*. Bristol University Press.

Carrabine, E. (2003). *Power, discourse and resistance*. Ashgate.

Crewe, B. (2009). *Prisoner society: Power, adaptation and social life in an English prison*. Oxford University Press.

Crewe, B., & Liebling, A. (2017). Reconfiguring penal power. In A. Liebling, S. Maruna, & L. Mcara (Eds.), *Oxford handbook of criminology* (pp. 889–913). Oxford University Press.

Crewe, B., Hulley, S., & Wright, S. (2020). *Life imprisonment from young adulthood: Adaptation, identity and time*. Palgrave Macmillan.

Cullen, F. T., Jonson, C. L., & Nagin, D. S. (2011). Prisons do not reduce recidivism: The high cost of ignoring science. *The Prison Journal, 91*(3), 48S–65S.

De Viggiani, N. (2012). Trying to be something you are not. *Men and Masculinities, 15*(3), 271–291.

Decker, S. H., & Townsend Chapman, M. (2008). *Drug smugglers on drug smuggling: Lessons from the inside*. Temple University Press.

Densley, J. A. (2012). The organisation of London's street gangs. *Global Crime, 13*(1), 42–64.

Durán-Martinez, A. (2018). *The politics of drug violence: Criminals, cops, and politicians in Colombia and Mexico*. Oxford University Press.
Eichenthal, D. R., & Blatchford, L. (1997). Prison crime in New York state. *The Prison Journal, 77*(4), 456–466.
Gambetta, D. (2009). *Codes of the underworld: How criminals communicate*. Princeton University Press.
Goldson, B. (2000). 'Children in need' or 'young offenders' hardening ideology, organizational change and new challenges for social work with children in trouble. *Child and Family Social Work, 5*, 255–265.
Goldson, B. (2005). Child imprisonment: A case for abolition. *Youth Justice, 5*(2), 77–90.
Goldson, B. (2008). Child incarceration: Institutional abuse, the violent state and the politics of impunity. In P. Scarton & J. McCulloch (Eds.), *The violence of incarceration* (pp. 86–105). Routledge.
Goldson, B. (2013). Violence, child prisoners and institutionalised impunity. *Criminal Justice Matters, 98*, 14–15.
Gooch, K. (2016). A childhood cut short: Child deaths in penal custody and the pains of child imprisonment. *The Howard Journal of Crime and Justice, 55*(3), 278–294.
Gooch, K. (2019). 'Kidulthood': Ethnography, juvenile prison violence and the transition from 'boys' to 'men'. *Criminology & Criminal Justice, 19*(1), 80–97.
Gooch, K., & Treadwell, J. (2020). Prisoner society in an era of psychoactive substances, organized crime, new drug markets and austerity. *British Journal of Criminology, 60*(5), 1260–1281.
Gooch, K., & Treadwell, J. (2021). 'It doesn't stop at the prison gate': Understanding organised crime in prison. *Prison Service Journal, 252*, 15–30.
Gooch, K., & Treadwell, J. (2023). The 'screw boys' and the 'businessmen': Re-negotiating penal power, governance and legitimate authority through a prison violence reduction scheme. *British Journal of Criminology, 63*(4), 1219–1237.
Gooch, K., & Treadwell, J. (2025). The prison firm: The 'transportation' of organised crime, the evolution of criminal markets and contemporary prisoner society. *Criminology and Criminal Justice, 25*(1), 245–264.
Gooch, K., Masson, I., Owens, A., & Waddington, E. (2022). After care, after thought: The invisibility of care experienced men and women in prison. *Prison Service Journal, 258*, 4–12.
Hall, S., Winlow, S., & Ancrum, C. (2013). *Criminal identities and consumer culture*. Willan.

Harris, L. (2015). *Changing prisons, saving lives: Report of the independent review into self-inflicted deaths in custody of 18–24 year olds*. Her Majesty's Stationery Office.

Her Majesty's Inspectorate of Prisons. (1997). *Young prisoners*. Her Majesty's Inspectorate of Prisons.

Her Majesty's Inspectorate of Prisons. (2021). *Outcomes for young adults in custody*. Her Majesty's Inspectorate of Prisons.

Her Majesty's Inspectorate of Prisons. (2024). *Children in custody 2023–2024*. Her Majesty's Inspectorate of Prisons.

Hobbs, D. (2013). *Lush life*. Oxford University Press.

Hood, R. (1965). *Borstal re-assessed*. Heinemann.

Hosser, D., Raddatz, S., & Windzio, M. (2007). Child maltreatment, revictimization, and violent behavior. *Violence & Victims, 3*, 318–333.

House of Commons Justice Committee. (2016). *The treatment of young adults in the criminal justice system*. House of Commons Justice Committee.

House of Commons Justice Committee. (2018). *Young adults in the criminal justice system*. House of Commons Justice Committee.

House of Commons Justice Committee. (2020). *Ageing prison population*. House of Commons Justice Committee.

House of Commons Justice Committee. (2022). *IPP sentences*. House of Commons Justice Committee.

Irwin, J. (1970). *The felon*. Prentice-Hall.

Jarman, B., & Vince, C. (2022). *Making progress? What progression means for people serving the longest sentences*. Prison Reform Trust.

Jewkes, Y. (2005). Men behind bars. *Men and Masculinities, 8*(1), 44–63.

Katz, J. (1988). *Seductions of crime: A chilling exploration of the criminal mind - from juvenile delinquency to cold-blooded murder*. BasicBooks.

Keve, P. E. (1980). The quicksand prison. *The Prison Journal, 63*(1), 47–58.

Liebling, A. (2012). Young adult offenders in custodial institutions. In F. Lösel, A. E. Bottoms, & D. P. Farrington (Eds.), *Young adult offenders: Lost in transition* (pp. 65–73). Willan.

Lightowlers, C., & Quirk, H. (2015). The 2011 English 'riots': Prosecutorial zeal and judicial abandon. *British Journal of Criminology, 55*(1), 65–85.

Listwan, S. J., Sullivan, C. J., Agnew, R., Cullen, F. T., & Colvin, M. (2013). The pains of imprisonment revisited: The impact of strain on inmate recidivism. *Justice Quarterly, 30*(1), 144–168.

Lösel, F., Bottoms, A. E., & Farrington, D. P. (2012). *Young adult offenders: Lost in transition*. Willan.

Maguire, D. (2021). *Male, failed and jailed: Masculinities and the 'revolving door' imprisonment in the UK.* Palgrave Macmillan.
Marsh, B. (2020). *The logic of violence: An ethnography of Dublin's illegal drug trade* (Routledge advances in ethnography). Routledge.
Maruna, S. (2001). *Making good: How ex-convicts reform and rebuild their lives.* American Psychological Association.
Maschi, T., Gibson, S., Zgoba, K. M., & Morgen, K. (2011). Trauma and life event stressors among young and older adult prisoners. *Journal of Correctional Health Care, 17*(2), 160–172.
Matza, D. (1964). *Delinquency and drift.* Wiley.
McAra, L., & McVie, S. (2007). Youth justice?: The impact of system contact on patterns of desistance from offending. *European Journal of Criminology, 4*(3), 315–345.
Meyers, T. J., Testa, A., & Wright, K. A. (2023). Managing violence: In-prison behavior associated with placement in an alternative disciplinary segregation program. *American Journal of Criminal Justice, 48*(1), 250–272.
Michalski, J. H. (2017). Status hierarchies and hegemonic masculinity: A general theory of prison violence. *British Journal of Criminology, 57*(1), 40–60.
Ministry of Justice. (2013a). *Offender management statistics quarterly—April 2010—September 2012.* Ministry of Justice.
Ministry of Justice. (2013b). *Transforming the management of young adults in custody.* Ministry of Justice.
Ministry of Justice. (2020). *Youth justice statistics 2018–2019: Behaviour management in the youth secure estate.* Ministry of Justice.
Ministry of Justice. (2021). *Offender management statistics quarterly: July to September 2020.* Ministry of Justice.
Ministry of Justice. (2022a). *Offender management statistics quarterly: January to March 2022.* Ministry of Justice.
Ministry of Justice. (2022b). *Youth custody data.* Ministry of Justice.
Ministry of Justice. (2023a). *Criminal justice system overview—adult rape.* Ministry of Justice.
Ministry of Justice. (2023b). *Prison population projections 2022 to 2027, England and Wales.* Ministry of Justice.
Ministry of Justice. (2024). *Youth justice statistics 2022–2023: Behaviour management in the youth secure estate.* Ministry of Justice.
Ministry of Justice. (2025a). *Proven reoffending statistics: January to March 2023.* Ministry of Justice.

Ministry of Justice. (2025b). *Offender management statistics quarterly: July to September 2024*. Ministry of Justice.
Muncie, J. (2021). *Youth and crime* (5th ed.). Sage.
Newton, C. (1994). Gender theory and prison sociology: Using theories of masculinities to interpret the sociology of prisons for men. *The Howard Journal of Crime and Justice, 33*(3), 193–202.
O'Donnell, I. (2023). *Prison life: Pain, resistance and purpose*. New York University Press.
Office for National Statistics. (2022). *Labour market statistics time series*. Office for National Statistics.
Prison Reform Trust. (2004). *A lost generation: The experiences of young people in prison*. Prison Reform Trust.
Prisons Committee. (1895). *Report from the Departmental Committee on Prisons (the Gladstone report)*. Her Majesty's Stationery Office.
Ricciardelli, R. (2015). Establishing and asserting masculinity in Canadian penitentiaries. *Journal of Gender Studies, 24*(2), 170–191.
Sim, J. (1994). Tougher than the rest? Men in prison. In T. Newburn & E. A. Stanko (Eds.), *Just boys doing business? Men, masculinities and crime* (pp. 100–177). Routledge.
Skarbek, D. (2004). *The social order of the underworld: How prison gangs govern the American penal system*. Oxford University Press.
Sloan, J. (2016). *Masculinities and the adult male prison experience*. Palgrave Macmillan.
Sykes, G. (1958). *The society of captives*. Princeton University Press.
Sykes, G. M., & Matza, D. (1957). Techniques of neutralization: A theory of delinquency. *American Sociological Review, 22*(6), 664–670.
Taylor, C. (2016). *Review of the youth justice system*. Ministry of Justice.
Toch, H. (1998). Hypermasculinity and prison violence. In L. Bowker (Ed.), *Masculinities and crime* (pp. 168–178). Sage.
Tompkins, C. N. E. (2016). There's that many people selling it': Exploring the nature, organisation and maintenance of prison drug markets in England. *Drugs: Education, Prevention and Policy, 23*(2), 144–153.
Wacquant, L. (2010). Prisoner reentry as myth and ceremony. *Dialectical Anthropology, 34*(4), 605–620.
Weeks, R., & Widom, C. S. (1998). Self-reports of early childhood victimization among incarcerated adult male felons. *Journal of Interpersonal Violence, 13*(3), 346–361.

Wheaton, B., & Gotlib, I. H. (1997). Trajectories and turning points over the life course: Concepts and themes. In I. H. Gotlib & B. Wheaton (Eds.), *Stress and adversity over the life course: Trajectories and turning points* (pp. 1–28). Cambridge University Press.

Williams, K., Papadopoulou, V., & Booth, N. (2012). *Prisoners' childhood and family backgrounds: Results from the Surveying Prisoner Crime Reduction (SPCR) longitudinal cohort study of prisoners*. Ministry of Justice.

Winlow, S. (2001). *Badfellas: Crime, tradition and new masculinities*. Berg.

Winlow, S., & Hall, S. (2006). *Violent night: Urban leisure and contemporary culture*. Berg.

Zamble, E., & Porporino, F. (1988). *Coping, behaviour and adaptation in prison inmates*. Springer.

8

'They Want Ratings!': Carceral Capital, the Prison Code, and the Rationality of Prison Violence and Victimisation

The sun was still rising on a bleak November day as officers arrived for their shifts. Some smiled and joked with each other as they walked from the car park to the gate with their kit, bags, and water bottles in hand. As James and I stood in the car park about to repeat the same routine, our attention was drawn to the conspicuous fleet of luxury cars (including Bentleys) parked in the slip road opposite the prison. The symphony of the morning birdsong was punctuated by loud cheerful voices, laughter, and the sound of rap music as a cluster of men and women waited for Charlie's release. The entourage accompanying the vehicles looked dressed for the city's nightspots. Men were clad in Moncler, Moose Knuckles, Canada Goose jackets, off white and Gucci jeans, Balenciaga and Prada trainers. Despite the cold morning, the women wore styled hair, Mulberry, short white and black designer dresses, spray tan and fur coats. An abundance of heavy gold jewellery adorned the men and women alike. The crowd shouted between one another, swore, laughed, shrieked, and passed drinks. They seemed utterly oblivious to the hard stares, tuts, and perplexed looks of the passing prison staff. Bottles of Champaign and Cognac had already been opened. The smell of skunk cannabis, cigars, and cigarettes floated across the dawn vista.

K. Gooch, *Prison Violence*, Palgrave Studies in Prisons and Penology,
https://doi.org/10.1007/978-3-031-91365-5_8

Although the cars were ceremoniously parked outside the prison gate and some distance from the double fence line, young men and prison officers in the residential units would discuss the arrival of the Bentleys later that morning. The young men on the wings would never see what was happening outside the gate, but they did not need to see the cars to understand their meaning. The 'conspicuous consumption' (Bourgois, 2003) exhibited in the slip road was readily understood by the young men as a mark of social distinction, success and '[triumph] in the continual battle to acquire, display and experience all the consumer universe has to offer' (Hall et al., 2013: 45). Within the YOI, Charlie had developed a form of 'carceral capital' which rested on his violent potential, his ability to 'hold himself,' his social dexterity and skill, and the acquisition of highly desired consumer items. Charlie had no record of prison violence (the same was not true in the community), but those young men with the most respect and power within the YOI often did not need to use overt physical violence themselves. The ostentatious display and 'ornamental consumerism' (Hall et al., 2013: 45) at the prison gate further consolidated Charlie's reputation. This social and economic capital was of little value in 'going legit,' but grafting had allowed Charlie to acquire more wealth and culturally valid status symbols than could be gained through legitimate employment—work that was much harder to obtain and retain (Hall et al., 2013; Maguire, 2021). Collecting material goods provided incontrovertible evidence of an ability to graft, avoid theft and robbery, and earn as real *men* against a background of material deprivation. It was the combination of entrepreneurial skill and a capacity for violence that was crucial, not violent potential in isolation.

This chapter focuses on the logic of prison violence and victimisation. Quite from being disorderly and unpredictable, this chapter illustrates how deeply functional prison victimisation can be. Such logic is—as noted in studies of street violence (Anderson, 1999; Bourgois, 2003; Ellis, 2016; Hobbs, 1995; Jacobs & Wright, 2006; Marsh, 2020; Winlow, 2001; Winlow & Hall, 2006)—grounded in structural, social, cultural, political and economic context. Fiske and Rai (2015: xxii) argue, 'When people hurt or kill someone, they usually do so because they feel they ought to: they feel it is morally right or even obligatory to be violent.' Here, Fiske and Rai's thesis is extended to the prison context to argue that prison victimisation occurs within a social world where violence and victimisation is often viewed as rational, logical, and moral (in the sense that it was viewed as the right thing to do in the peculiar circumstances of the prison even if prohibited and/or unlawful). As Joseph remarked: 'You're not going to smack someone for no reason. Like you've always got a reason do it.' Violence was not senseless and mindless but 'always deeply meaningful' (Billingham & Irwin-Rogers, 2022: 118).

This chapter addresses the question of *why* young men are violent and for what purpose. It is argued that the rationality of prison violence was rooted in the desire for social recognition, the pursuit of justice, the prisoner normative code, and the functionality of prison violence in navigating the pressures, strains, and challenges inherent in prison life. Typically, it is assumed that the rationality of violence is primarily derived from the desire to (re)assert and perform masculinity. Masculinity is—it is rightly argued—'under siege' within prison (Newton, 1994: 198) due to the infantilising, largely single sex, impoverishing and isolating nature of the prison that threatens traditional routes to the performance of masculinity when it is most needed (Sykes, 1958). Yet, too often, the performance of masculinity is narrowly tied to the *use* of violence (Michalski, 2017; Toch, 1998; Sloan, 2016; Sim, 1994). However, victimising others did not in and of itself guarantee that an individual was seen as 'manly' or deserving of respect and esteem. Indeed, those young men with the most respect and power often did not need to use violence at all. Threats could prove sufficient for controlling others, or need not be issued at all, but only if the individual was seen as credible. For this, and for the 'enforcers,' carceral capital was crucial. For those who possess it, carceral capital is a form of social distinction. It confers power and status on some at the expense of others. This chapter therefore develops Bourdieu's notion of social capital (Bourdieu, 1986) for a prison context to broaden our understanding of prisoner society. Whilst the conceptualisation of carceral capital is closely bound to the performance of masculinity, it has at its core the 'search for social recognition' (Honneth, 1995) and respect that goes beyond gender to critical issues of human dignity and moral worth.

Carceral Capital, Social Recognition, and Respect

Young men desired social recognition and respect (Billingham & Irwin-Rogers, 2022). However, this social approval was dependant on others (Honneth, 1995; Sandberg & Pedersen, 2009) and constantly under threat. For young prisoners, certain forms of recognition were denied due to their 'exclusion from mainstream society' (Bourgois, 2003), their impoverishment, their drug use and/or dealing, the denial of opportunities for personal growth, the absence of desirable jobs in and out of prison, the relational terms set by prison officers (see Chap. 9) and their 'lack of faith' in State authorities (Anderson, 1999). Most had deduced that traditional indicators of manhood (e.g. employment, houses, cars, 'nice holidays,' consumer items) were difficult to obtain through legal means. However, their desires for the 'good life' (not just a 'fast life') and to be free men with means, partners, and children were no less apparent despite their seemingly 'rebellious practices' (Bourgois, 2003: 8). Like the streets (Anderson, 1999; Bourgois, 2003; Ilan & Sandberg, 2019; Sandberg, 2008; Shammas & Sandberg, 2016), young men developed alternative forms of 'capital' (Bourdieu, 1973, 1984, 1986) within the context of the prison's 'violent … subculture and underground economy' (Sandberg & Pedersen, 2009: 43). This 'carceral capital' and oppositional culture offered an 'alternative forum for personal dignity' (Bourgois, 2003: 8) and 'symbolic power' (Bourdieu, 1973, 1984, 1986) in a context where middle-class values, culture, and capital appeared not just unobtainable but also unrewarding (Willis, 1978).

For Bourdieu, there were three forms of symbolic capital that explained the reproduction of social structures, including the intergenerational continuation of class-based social groups. These included: 'cultural capital' (education qualifications, cultural goods such as paintings, books, monuments, attendance at museums, theatres, and concerts), 'economic capital' (money, property rights, nobility rights) and 'social capital' (networks, connections and relationships) (Bourdieu, 1986). It was Bourdieu's contention that cultural and social capital could be converted into economic capital, but also that these various forms of capital conferred symbolic power and explained why class structures were maintained. Bourdieu argued that the distribution of cultural capital was uneven between the classes, but the children of the upper and middle classes not only benefitted from more cultural capital but also the means to realise that capital. Although Criminologists have somewhat belatedly developed the notion of 'street capital' (Anderson, 1999; Bourgois, 2003; Ilan & Sandberg, 2019; Sandberg, 2008; Shammas & Sandberg, 2016) and the 'street field' (where street capital is produced) (see Fraser, 2013; Sandberg & Fleetwood, 2017; Fraser & Matthews, 2021), far less attention has been focused on the forms of capital developed within the unique 'carceral habitus' of the prison (although note by way of exception Caputo-Levine (2013) and Schlosser (2013)). Notably, although 'violence was one way of establishing cultural authority' (Hobbs, 1994: 120) within prison, the 'lads' achieved social status and domination because of a much wider set of credentials.

Carceral capital was a combination of social capital, cultural capital, and economic capital but these forms of capital were different in kind to those described by Bourdieu (1973, 1986) and were accompanied by forms of physical capital and gravitas. Carceral capital was an imprecise mix of: physical presence, heterosexuality, a willingness and capability to defend himself and his interests, carceral experience, cultural awareness, a credible criminal identity, and economic capital. It could be accentuated when young men demonstrated: a proven ability to attract women (e.g. a long-term partner, details of sexual conquests, being a father); control the illicit economy; a calm and confident demeanour with prison officers (especially if this involved controlling officers or failing to take any 'shit') and the ability to stoically 'do your time.' As Paul noted, 'you've got to show character.' In the context of street culture, Anderson (1999: 134) argues:

> Once mastered the savoir faire of the street world—knowing how to deal coolly with people, how to move, look, act, dress—is a form of capital, not a form middle class people would respect, but capital that can nonetheless be cashed in.

Within the YOI, knowing how to move, look, act, speak, and dress was of equal value. Carceral capital was essentially 'masculine in its essence' (Sandberg & Pedersen, 2009: 43), but what was gained through carceral capital was something more than simply being 'manly.' Like street capital, carceral capital was a 'form of legitimate power' amongst their peers and had 'the capacity to generate profit' (Sandberg & Pedersen, 2009: 42). It also gave people a 'name' and distinguished them from their peers, enhancing social recognition and respect. As Jack explained, 'If you haven't got a name then you ain't mattering.' Carceral capital was a 'viable and vital source of identity, status, recognition, reputation and power' (Barry, 2006: 40) within a context of social marginalisation, personal indignity and economic precarity.

The embodiment of carceral capital was a key safeguard against persistent and targeted victimisation, particularly robbery, demands for cell rent, demands for the repayment of inherited debt, sustained verbal abuse and social exclusion. Those who held the most carceral capital did not need to use violence at all. Real power lay with those whose commands were followed without threat or force. It was not that these young men would or could not use violence, they just simply did not need to. For example:

> Some of the most dangerous people in this place will never lift a finger, and that is real power. They do not have to go splash[1] a man in man's cell, they can have man go splash a man in his cell with a word. (Nibbs)

Those young men who were controlling others were rarely identified by prison officers since any assaults were narrowly viewed in terms of the parties visibly and immediately involved. It was easy, therefore, for the dynamics of prison victimisation to be overlooked, and those controlling individuals to continue with impunity. Whilst the desire to avoid detection was often compelling, some also derived psychological gratification form controlling others. For example:

[1] Slang for 'stabbing' an individual.

> Half of the kids on this wing can't come out for their dinner because as soon as they step out of their door it's game over. The officers have to get their food for them, they can't even have showers. That's going on right now on this wing. I can name off more than five people, no hope. It goes on every single wing in this prison. Sometimes yeah, especially with one person, the satisfaction of knowing that I'm keeping that behind their door, stopping them from getting their own meals. The satisfaction of me knowing that is better than having the burn [tobacco]. In some cases, the satisfaction is so much better for me. (Luke)

These psychological gains illustrate that it is not 'all about the money' (Hobbs, 2012) and financial losses did not always lead to the diminution of an individual's status. Remarkably, the most domineering young men could also influence the behaviour of prison officers. Young men—such as Tyrone—knew that their reputation and willingness to confront, and if needed assault, officers had saved them from needless hassle:

> Like a kid the other day didn't bang up, he had his food and said, 'I'm going to smack one of you in the face.' They just dropped him [restrained him] because they were thinking, 'No you are not.' Do you know what I mean? But if I said it, they would want to talk more. 'What can we do for you? What do you want? You have been doing so well.' Sometimes you have got to let them think they have had that win. It is bad saying that you manipulate it, but when you are in jail, you have got to do what you have got to do.

For Tyrone, and those like him, assaulting or confronting an officer risked sanctions and segregation in the short-term, but once their 'name' and capital was established, the young men benefitted from greater flexibility from prison officers. The treatment of young men was therefore uneven. Arguably, de-escalating a situation without recourse to coercive physical force could be a better use of authority, but when officers were quicker to restrain prisoners who were already judged 'weak' by their peers, they reinforced social inequalities and hierarchies.

Those who had less capital were those young men who: struggled to competently navigate often-buoyant social interactions; who sold or lost all their property (and lived in bare cells); who wore prison issue clothes;

who were homosexual, transgender, or effeminate; the 'nonces;'[2] those with poor physical hygiene; and those who were unable to negotiate with prison officers or advocate for their own interests. Equally, distress signalling behaviours, such as self-harm, setting fire to themselves or their cell, flooding a landing or self-isolating attracted little empathy. Such behaviour was regarded as 'fucking shameful' and served to indicate that the young men were 'not about this life.' Those with little capital were rarely 'one of the mandem,' and either failed to achieve any social standing or retreated (Cohen & Taylor, 1972; Toch, 1975, 1977). Their fear was contemptible. Dale commented that you could not only 'smell fear,' but could also see it. Jake explained:

> If you look in a man's eyes and you look at him, then that means then that you are on it. If you come in fearful, then he owns you and that's it then. It's done. You can tell from their characteristics and their body language and all that sort of stuff. I reckon some of the screws put on fronts as well. Some of the screws have been put in their place a few times and they don't know what to do.

Rather than acknowledging that imprisonment is stressful for all (as most young men would privately concede), fear was viewed as a personal failing. It rendered the fearful individual subservient—he was 'owned'—and an easy target. Toch (1997: 150–151) argues, 'The person who shows fear under fire from practised diagnosticians of fear, is classified as 'unmanly'; [t]o show fear is to invite further threatening or testing.' In this way, young men were able to justify the victimisation that often resulted and young men were—as it was described to us—'eaten alive' and 'terrorised.'

Carceral capital manifested in a mixture of bodily, physical, and consumer symbols. Young men made snap judgements about their peers based on facial expressions, body language, size, tattoos, scars, posture and personal hygiene—what Bourdieu (1984) describes as 'body hexis.' For example:

---

[2] 'Nonces' was an abbreviation for 'not on normal criminal exercises' and was largely used as a slur for sex offenders and/or those who committed offences against children and the elderly.

> People who don't shower, people who don't keep their cells clean. If you see how they come out and they look tramp-ish and stuff, people tend to get bullied man. All people who are just nittsing you for drugs, drug nitties really. Some crackheads. (Aidan)

Physical 'presence' was not the same as physical size. Whilst young men thought that 'the law of the big' generally meant bigger was better, much depended on how an individual conducted themselves:

> You can't come in if you've got sloppy feet, and shit, looking at the floor. You have to hold your head on your shoulders. You speak when you're spoken to. You speak loudly and clearly. You get the point across. (Jack)

Whilst many young men wanted to enhance their physique in the gym, sculpting their bodies did not guarantee enhanced social status. Juno, for example, was a gym orderly who was of muscular build and stood well over six foot tall. He was imprisoned for an alcohol fuelled serious violent offence. Inside the YOI, he had won several bench-pressing and running challenges set by the 'PEI's.'[3] Juno was clearly skilled in physical violence and prepared to fight if needed. Consequently, some young men would avoid conflict with Juno since they were unlikely to leave unscathed, but Juno was not deemed worthy of respect by all. Jack and Cardiff, for example, were less impressed:

> He looks like a big, hard cunt, he probably is, but that counts for fuck all to me, you can look all that, big tree trunk arms and a massive puffed out chest, and that counts for nothing nowadays does it? Being a big, hard fucker, oh well, you won't be that big when you turn your back you get a shank in your kidney or spleen, bag you up,[4] fuck man. Nowadays, me I don't fuck about man. I've kweffed[5] plenty of man, I don't give a fuck. (Jack)

---

[3] An abbreviation of 'Physical Education Instructor.'

[4] 'Bagging up' referred to the act of being stabbed in the buttocks so that the victim needs a stoma bag.

[5] 'Kweffed' referred to stabbing or shooting someone.

Although this conversation could be dismissed as essentially performative, it illustrated the somewhat contradictory attitudes towards weapon carrying among imprisoned youths. Weapon use altered the odds in favour of the weapon carrier and could greatly increase the risk of serious injury. Whilst for some this undermined the weapon carrier's violent credentials, for others it meant that physical size was less important and could be easily overcome.

Social capital was predicated on a 'network of connections' (Bourdieu, 1986: 21), with these connections being forged with young men in shared communities (typically working class and local authority estates), in local authority care, and/or in earlier periods of imprisonment. Equally, some young men were associated with higher profile offenders and/or family members (sometimes in other prisons). Within prison, the 'credibility of former identities is enhanced rather than erased' (Hobbs, 1995: 7) although some would enhance their network with alliances in other YOI's and prisons, giving greater geographical reach to their network. When young men were transferred to or withing the YOI, being 'known' not only increased their credibility and social capital but also made access to goods easier to obtain (and at better prices). It also secured a degree of protection from victimisation:

> I knew a few people so no-one could say anything, know what I mean, at the end of it I was alright man, everyone was looking after me. (Lewis)

> Because that is my local jail, there was a whole wing just full of all of my boys and there are new people coming onto the wing and we are saying 'this is our wing.' And it starts off like that. (Robert)

Much could be judged from who was prepared to 'vouch' for them or include them in their 'circle.' Damien, for example, explained:

> Obviously, I am known around the floor. I have done knife crime, robbery, I have done burglaries, I have done armed robberies, thefts, stolen cars—but don't normally drive cars I drive motorbikes now. I have done cars. Like jewellery, money, everything. Shops, everything. I have done everything. From the petty thefts, like when I was younger, snatching things to robberies. It is just the way I am.

For young men such as Damien, the transition from child to young adult custody, and the increasing severity of his criminal offending, was a marker of growing criminal competency and growing familiarity with the carceral social world. Being 'known' also had the effect of eliminating concerns that an individual was a 'nonce' or otherwise discreditable.

The cultural capital of the YOI was not that of the cultural goods such as books, art, and education qualifications, but the familiarity with prisoner culture, prison daily life, and the 'system' (also see Neuber, 2011). Paralleling the inheritance of 'cultural wealth' amongst the upper and middle classes alluded to by Bourdieu (1986), some of these young men inherited prison cultural awareness from imprisoned fathers, step-fathers, mothers, siblings and cousins. For example, Ryan was deeply immersed within the criminal and prison sub-culture. His attributed his antagonistic approach to prison staff, and the readiness with which he used violence, to the received wisdom of his father and step-father:

> My dad always said to me when I was younger, 'Trust nobody. Trust nobody.' And, that's what I've always done and I've always got by. No matter what, I've always got by. See these screws in jail, wankers, trust me, proper horrible bastards.

At the time of interview, Ryan's father had already spent 23 years in prison for a range of violent and drug-related offences. Ryan's stepfather was also involved in 'the game,' something that Ryan would become involved with at an early age: 'I hang around with my old man and his mates. People know not to fuck with us.' Whilst he was somewhat unusual in his overt hostility and readiness to assault prison officers, he carried his 'big rankings' and experience of youth custody within him into the prison. He readily understood what made the difference between inferiority and superiority in the prison subculture. Despite the normal frustrations with being confined and having limited agency, he adjusted relatively easily to the terms of prisoner society. He explained: 'I don't mind jail or on road, it's all part the same, there are things I cannot do in here, sure, but it is not that bad.'

Whilst Gambetta (2009) argues that criminal credentials can serve as 'signals' as to who might be prepared to carry out criminal activities in the community, criminal credentials—such as index offence—were not sufficient proof of the capacity for *prison* violence nor a guarantee of social esteem. Being remanded, convicted, or sentenced for violent, kidnapping, and homicide offences did not guarantee power, status or reputation. Indeed, index offence had become a less critical criterion in securing elevated positions within the prisoner hierarchy than it was in previous decades. There were undoubtedly young men such as 'Shadow' whose conviction for murder, connections to London, and gang associations were well known, but his social status was also derived from his ability to control, threaten, and manipulate those around him. He quickly became 'King of the Wing' and faced few attempts to overthrow him or contest his power and status. As a young Black man who lurked at the side-lines controlling and orchestrating the economy, fights, and assaults, 'Shadow' was regarded by other young men as an apt name for an individual who intimidated them, threatened them, and could easily arrange his 'foot soldiers' to assault them. Shadow's self-assured presentation was, however, a sharp contrast to Danny's.

Danny was remanded for a murder allegedly committed with his older cousin. It was Danny's first time in prison, an experience he was enduring alone since his cousin had been sent to an adult prison. Danny had accompanied his cousin to a pre-arranged meeting with a drug dealer to buy a small quantity of cannabis. Rather than paying the dealer, Danny's cousin had stabbed the dealer five times, with a wound to the heart proving fatal. Danny was adamant that he had not inflicted the fatal injury nor been involved in the prior disagreement with the dealer. His presence at the scene meant that he was caught by the Criminal Law doctrine of joint enterprise (for discussion, see Green & McGourlay, 2015; Hulley et al., 2019; Omerond & Laird, 2016) which would allow him to be prosecuted alongside his cousin. When James and I met Danny in the First Night Centre, he relayed his innocence through tears. He was struggling to sleep and declining meals. Danny was terrified of living in prison and the possibility of receiving a life sentence. He was tall, but his gaunt presentation and blood shot eyes suggested vulnerability, further signalled by the bright orange 'ACCT'[6] document that had been 'opened' out of concern that he might attempt suicide. The mentors' advice to Danny was to 'shape up,' impressing upon him the importance of 'fronting it,' 'of staying away from Mamba,' and 'not getting into debt.' Dean, a serial armed robber and one of the mentors, somewhat exasperated, imparted some very simply advice:

> Man, start to fucking play the role man. If these [young men] think you are a pussy, they will fuck you. All that is on you. 'Cause you can walk onto the wing some terrified fucking pussy or you can walk on like a man and do whatever time you have easy. It is on you.

Two days later, James passed Danny as he moved to C wing. There was less redness in his eyes, but he was sullen and silent. He nodded to James as he passed, carrying a plastic bag of his limited possessions to begin life on a wing. Eighteen months later, Danny was cleared of the murder, but lived at the margins of prisoner society throughout his time in prison. 'Capital takes time to accumulate' (Bourdieu, 1986), but young men such as Danny simply did not gain it and adopted a survival strategy that rested on social distance rather than social esteem.

Violence 'was one way of establishing cultural authority' (Hobbs, 1994: 120), but form mattered. Violence alone was insufficient to be deemed 'manly' or deserving of honour. Those young men who were 'loose cannons' were described as 'crackheads,' 'fraggles' and 'wasters.' Here the violence was seen to be excessive, unreasonable, and unmanly (also see Jewkes, 2005; Sykes, 1958). Those individuals shouting out their windows were often dismissed by staff and other young men as 'windows warriors'—a derogatory term to suggest that they were 'all mouth and no trousers,' lacking the requisite courage or capacity to confront the person physically or face to face. 'Tough talk' was insufficient (McCorkle, 1992: 166) unless the instigator was also prepared to 'front' it out the following day:

[6] 'ACCT' stands for Assessment, Care in Custody and Treatment and is the process used to manage prisoners who are self-harming and/or considering or attempting suicide.

> We were arguing. They was saying stuff out the window and started shouting, 'White bastard,' and stuff like that. And these were like Somali lads and I just shouted stuff like, 'Shut the fuck up you dickheads,' and then they started saying, 'Suck your mum, suck your mum,' and I just said, 'Fucking hell lads I hear that when I was at primary school have you not grown up yet?' and they were like, 'Fuck you fuck you.' … Then one of his little cronies come with a metal bar and was trying to hit me with it and I said, 'Come on then fucking hit me with it,' and then they never did nothing like because the other lads stopped it and then I walked out and that was it. Window warriors. (Joshua)

> It's because they're frightened face-to-face. They shout out the window, and then half of them won't come out their cell the next day. So, they stir it up, and then they just don't come out. (Toby)

Verbal abuse was not 'cheap' (c.f. Gambetta, 2009). It could incur greater losses to one's reputation if the abuser was not prepared to face their victim and convincingly defend themselves should the victim retaliate. Thus, verbal abuse shouted out the windows did little for bolstering their reputations as 'real men'—and could endanger it—unless it was fortified by a convincing, confident, and visible willingness to use violence.

Cowardly violence was also condemned. It was always possible to overcome someone who was 'big' or 'hard' by using weapons, involving associates, or assaulting them from behind, but such behaviour was resented by those who preferred man-to-man contest ('straighteners'). For example:

> They want ratings. If they put me out, they've got me rating. You know it. I don't think they'll do that. I've had fights with big men. They'll have fights with pool balls anything [laughs]. I was just standing there. Man come up to me out of nowhere. [Makes smacking sound]. Never spoke to me or nothing. Judas! The little prick, man. No way man, what a crackhead. That man had mental issues. He stabbed some geezer on the phone. He ran up to him and stabbed him for no reason. This guy's just loopy. I don't know where the fuck he is now. I caught him. [laughs] (Ryan)

Cowards did not gain social esteem, but the disavowal of 'Judas' assaults also represented an attempt to minimise any possible loss in social standing. In this case, Ryan punished the assault, neutralising any long-term damage to his reputation and reinforcing his relative power and status. Thus, it was not the challenge or attempt to gain 'ratings' that was decisive, but the failure to answer the challenge.

Central to the concept of carceral capital, and the performance of masculinity, was economic power and capital. The 'conspicuous consumption' (Bourgois, 2003) of property, goods, and seemingly innocuous items such as toiletries and food achieved something more than simply alleviating the depriving nature of the prison. It demonstrated an ability 'to have and to hold.' For example, Joshua explained that he smoked to:

> … signify you have it. If people think you haven't got it, they think you cannot get it, if you follow me, for a long time I didn't want people thinking he hasn't got none because, well it doesn't make you look good.

The significance of this was best illustrated when meeting 'Darwin.' As I walked through the First Night Centre, Darwin was leaning over his crutches outside his cell and engaging in easy conversation with the mentors. He had moved to the First Night Centre whilst he recovered from the broken leg. Darwin was a likeable character but lacked some of the gravitas held by the mentors. He had adopted a strategy of trying to blend in with 'the lads' and was neither motivated to claim power from his peers nor motivated to curry the favour of staff. As I stood talking with Darwin, his cell door lay wide open. Neat rows of food and toiletries were carefully displayed in full view of anyone who happened to walk past the cell or peer into it. As I glanced over, I noticed amongst the stacks of shower gels, deodorants, and noodles, about 12 boxes of Jaffa Cakes.[7] 'You like Jaffa Cakes then?' I asked. 'No, I hate them,' came the reply. The food was not for consumption, but exhibition. The cell was a stage.

Cells on every wing were adorned with excessive quantities of toiletries, food items and even religious texts such as Bibles displayed in neat, carefully orchestrated, and regimented lines (according to colour, brand, and item). These items were 'key consumer artefacts' (Hall et al., 2013: 62). Those cells with the most items were the 'fat pads' and 'penthouses'

---

[7] Jaffa Cakes are small chocolate cakes sold in boxes.

of the wing and a source of pride, often prompting invitations from young men to view their cells. Luke, for example, bragged:

> After this interview, I want you to take a stroll down to my pad and take a look at my cell. That's all I want you to do. And then tell me who is living comfortably out here. You look at my pad and you tell me what a fat pad is. These kids are living in crack dens and I am living in the penthouse suite.

The careful 'line by line' storage of items meant that any cell theft was easily noticed, but the performative display of one's belongings also served a crucial communicative function. Whilst the closing of the cell door might isolate the prisoner from any immediate physical threats, the cell is still visible when locking and unlocking prisoners, and at other periods of the day such as mealtimes, association[8] or 'domestics.'[9] Thus, what happens within the cell, and what is on show, is as important as what happens out of the cell.

Some items had more currency than others and young men could further distinguish themselves with the visible acquisition of scarce items. The more 'exclusive' the items, the more status and distinction gained. For example:

> My pad's fat. I love it. Foreign [shower] gels, exclusive. Paid top prices for them. You can only get shit gels here. I've got a stereo, had a PlayStation, got my clothes, my food. I never go without. (Steven)

Foreign' or 'exclusive' toiletries were likened to 'gold' and were typically those that could not be bought within the YOI but had been acquired in other prisons or YOIs. Thus, possessing such items emphasised custodial experience and enhanced their carceral capital. The 'fat pads' were a marked contrast to the cells that were barely softened with prison issue bedding and curtains (if at all), and were lacking in any goods, food, toiletries, or clothing. Those who were persistently victimised were often left bereft of any comforts, clothes, or trainers they had, and/or were

[8] 'Association' is an unstructured period when prisoners can use the telephone, use the exercise yard, play pool, listen to Prison Radio from a TV, and socialise with their peers.

[9] 'Domestics' is the period in the prison timetable ('regime') when prisoners are unlocked to shower, access cleaning products and use the telephone).

required to sell all they had to repay ever accumulating debts. The fat pad was a visible manifestation of the form and structure of the social hierarchy:

> You can see who the bullies are. They are always the ones with loads of stuff in their cells. That's from getting it from other people and bullying other people for their canteen and stuff. (Sam)

The young men who robbed, confiscated goods, or profited from exploiting and extorting others not only achieved social standing, but visibly gained at the expense of others. The sharper the economic scarcity, the more important and more valuable the economic capital (Winlow, 2014; Winlow & Hall, 2009).

The Prisoner Code, Personal Dignity, and Social Recognition

Central to the notion of carceral capital and the pursuit of social recognition was a 'set of informal rules governing interpersonal public behaviour, particularly violence' (Anderson, 1999). What constituted capital and how much capital was acquired was assessed against a set of widely understood norms. Equally, young men's own sense of pride, personal integrity and personal dignity was often tied up in their adherence to the prisoner code. Although prisoner society has always been guided by an informal, unwritten code of norms, values, and expected behaviours (Sykes, 1958: 143), recent research suggests that the prisoner code has been weakened due to the growth of prison drug economies (Crewe, 2005; Jewkes, 2005), the bloating of the prison population (Skarbek, 2014), the intensification of penal power (Liebling, 2004: 486); the emergence of faith based allegiances (Hamm, 2013; Jacobs, 1977; Liebling et al., 2011), and—in the United States—the dominance of prison gangs (Jacobs, 1977; Pyrooz & Decker, 2019; Skarbek, 2012). However, the prison code has not been rendered obsolete. Rather than indicate its absence, the seemingly individualistic responses were symptomatic of how the normative code has evolved. Within the YOI, there were six tenants that remained central: (1) don't grass; (2) pay your debts; (3) don't steal; (4) don't weaken or lose your head, but instead be tough and be a man; (5) don't bully (to be distinguished from extorting others which was permitted); and, (6) do your own time.

The injunction against 'grassing' and 'snitching' remains the 'cornerstone of the prison value system' (Crewe, 2009: 394). Those young men who were more immersed in street and prison cultures were more likely to avoid grassing on principle: being a snitch was simply not *who they were.* Others would tolerate victimisation from their peers rather than seek support from officers because they thought it was 'worse to be a snitch.' There were occasions when young men were seriously injured for grassing (e.g. being stabbed). However, the maxim 'snitches get stitches' was so deeply engrained that young men would refrain from snitching of their own volition. In other cases, the threat of punishment was sufficient. That said, young men were prepared to grass in the right circumstances. Young men would often concede that there were a 'lot of snitches.' It is not that the principle of inmate solidarity had been totally jettisoned; but young men prioritised their own self-interest. Those young men who had reached the point of overwhelming fear and desperation would turn to prison staff for protection. Some would give names, but others would simply speak in slightly generic terms about what was happening or urge officers to 'check the cameras.' Other breaches might occur when, for example, prisoners feared serious violence and they wanted to prevent serious harm to themselves or others (also see Crewe, 2012). Rarely would prisoners warn a prison officer that a member of staff would be assaulted, but it was not unheard of.

Snitching was sometimes a very deliberate action designed to punish the contemptible. For example, Paul and Alex (his pad mate) stole three mobile phones. To avoid any immediate physical repercussions, both Paul and Alex had moved wings, taking the mobile phones with them. The goods now lost, the bereft young men snitched knowing that not only would the goods be seized from Paul and Alex, but they would also both be required to appear before the District Judge and would face additional time in prison (to a maximum of 42 extra days). A £200 contract was put 'on [Paul's] head to get [him] punched up.' In this instance, Paul was not assaulted because he was one of 'Frankie's boys' and Frankie issued orders for other young men on the wing to 'look after [him].'

There were, however, no reprisals or punishment for the snitching and the behaviour would be excused on the grounds that stealing was dishonourable.

The clearest breach of the norm against 'grassing' was illustrated by the very small number of individuals who were persuaded to act as a CHIS (covert human intelligence source) and field information and intelligence to the authorities. Of course, their effectiveness as CHIS relied on secrecy by them and those to whom they divulged information. Other young men were unaware of their flagrant breaches of the code and the violations went unpunished. The CHIS typically derived some benefits from their services, even if only a degree of protection within the prison. Typically, the CHIS was someone who was somewhat unassuming but able to 'keep their ear to the ground.'

A 'taken for granted' aspect of the prisoner normative code was: 'do not weaken or lose your head.' No one wanted to be seen as 'weak' even if they could not summon the resources to be viewed as anything else by their peers (and by officers). Young prisoners did not consider victimisation of the weak as morally questionable. They acknowledged that young men would 'prey on weakness' but concluded that the victim had attracted such behaviour through their own moral and social failings (Edgar & O'Donnell, 1998). Very little compassion was extended to victims; victimisation was largely seen as a personal choice:

> People who allow themselves to get bullied. People who don't stand up for themselves. If you allow yourself to be victimised, then you are going to be victimised. (Jake)

Even those who were victims would concede that they misjudged their interactions with others or had in some way communicated weakness. For example, Sam explained:

> I had footprints all over my head, basically cracked open blood everywhere.
>
> *Why did they do that to you?*
>
> Because I showed a sign of weakness. Because I showed that I was a victim and I was talking to other people who had been victimised. I showed vulnerability. I showed the vulnerable side of me and I spoke to other people who were being victimised.

Like other victims, Sam's explanation of his own victimisation validated, rather than contested, the normative code. Although Sam's rationalisation appears surprising for its essential toleration of predatory behaviour, for him and other victims the ability to explain an assault mitigated unpredictability and fear (although rarely extinguished it).

There was a strong cultural imperative to dismiss bullying as immature behaviour (also see Edgar et al., 2003; Gooch, 2019). For most young men, the mark of maturation was conferred on the 'lads' who could fight 'man-to-man.' Consequently, the term 'bullying' had largely passed away from their everyday usage and was largely seen as childish, school-like behaviour:

> I don't get involved in that game, that's something I don't get in. See now, I don't agree with bullying. … I used to be one in high school and that, but fuck that. I just realised obviously. See me on road, obviously, when I used to hang around with all the youngers and that like, they don't care, but when I hanged around with the elders and mature people, you see. It's not that about that kind of game. (Ryan)

Although the underlying behaviour was similar, bullying was distinguished from enforcement and extortion activities with the latter seen as a natural and acceptable extension of criminal enterprise. Those young men who were most prone to relentlessly victimise others, were quick to state that they were not bullying:

> That's one thing I disagree with. I mean I know you can class little things as bullying like walking into someone's pad and taking something. That's not bullying. That's just using my authority. These officers can come in our cell if we have a picture of a bird with their tits out, they can take it down because of their authority but I wouldn't class that as bullying. Bullying is like a big thing in here. (Luke)

Luke was revered because he could, should he so desire, take on someone his own size. That Luke would compare his persistent robbery, extortion, and degradation of his peers to the use of State authority illustrated something of his own self-aggrandising tendencies, the perverse moral rationalisation, and his psychological separation from those he judged inferior.

A new tenet of the prisoner code was to 'pay your debts.' By engaging in the illicit economy, prisoners were seen to have agreed to a 'social contract' (Shortland, 2019), one that required timely repayment. To Damien, it was simple: 'you know how the game works, they know how the game works.' Prisoners could not appeal to staff in order to resolve a dispute, party since this could often mean admitting their own rule violations (also see Skarbek, 2014, 2020) and partly because officers had no authority in the illicit economy. Young men would insist on repayment even when circumstances were beyond the debtor's control, mirroring the attitudes of 'predatory capitalists' of the street drug dealing world (Marsh, 2020: 61). The injunction 'don't exploit inmates' (Sykes, 1958; Sykes & Messinger, 1960) was not mentioned. It was not those who extorted others who were condemned, but the 'debt heads' who could not meet their financial obligations. This emergence of this new norm constituted the most significant evolution of the prison code. Skarbek argues (2014: 7) that norms 'emerge and change to help people co-ordinate social interactions.' In this case, the evolution of the code was prompted by the deterioration in prison conditions, greater impoverishment within prison, the inability to maintain personal hygiene standards (especially in the beginning of the research), greater individualisation, the increasingly consumeristic street cultures, the demand for contraband, the growing democratisation of entrepreneurial crime and the legitimisation of grafting.

Whilst lapses in repayment might appear benign at first, to ignore such violations was to be 'mugged off' and have 'the piss taken out of you,' risking more critical losses to the perceived strength, character, and fortitude of the lender. Thus, 'even small debts were worth chasing because of what was at stake in terms of authority and reputation' (Crewe, 2009: 383). For example:

> I cornered one guy on free flow and said where is my money? He didn't have it so I banged him in the face. Put him out, down, and dusted and walked off. He owed me money. He just kept ducking back and he thought

> I was never going to catch him. So I caught him, banged him and just left him on the floor. They had to put him in healthcare. (Mark)

Non repayment of debt was consistently punished. These young men would go to some lengths to recover debts or punish non-repayment, including: trying to get on to the wrong wing; deliberately trying to get locked in the wrong cell to threaten or assault a debtor; issuing a 'contract on someone's head'; sending messages across wings; coercing others to assault the debtor; and, assaulting people even when the likelihood of detection was high. Such violence was performative and communicative. Too much was at stake to excuse indebtedness. Even if the debt was never repaid, the act of enforcing the debt and punishing non-repayment was sufficient to salvage the dealer's reputation and to mitigate any perceived social losses.

Instead of directly assaulting a debtor, the lender might also benefit by making a demand for the debtor to assault another prisoner or a prison officer whom they found contemptible. Such acts would expunge the debt. For example:

> That's where a lot of fights can come as well, because obviously, if you owe someone, like, a hefty debt and that person you owe it to don't like your pad-mate, he can shout up to you through the window saying, 'Bang your pad-mate out and we'll allow the debt,' or, 'Bang this person out for me, and we'll allow the debt. It happened to me. [It's] just doing their dirty work, so that they're not the ones that are getting nickings.[10] (Luke)

If threats and demands failed and a lender preferred to avoid physical confrontation or lacked the power to require others to do so, they may simply steal any items that considered would satisfy the debt. Such actions were not seen as a violation of the normative code against stealing because the goods were seen as rightly theirs to take and justifiable recompense for the non-repayment of debts.

Young prisoners believed that you had to do 'your *own* time.' It was necessarily a personal pursuit but also seen as the most prudent way to

[10] 'Nicking' was prison slang for an adjudication, a formal hearing with a Governor where penalties could be imposed for any proven rule violations.

navigate 'the system' and the mark of manly stoicism and fortitude. Of course, this atomisation of prisoner society has been very deliberately created by prison policy, particularly in relation to the Incentives and Earned Privileges (IEP) Scheme, indeterminate sentences that rely on proof of reduced risk in order to secure release or transfer to open conditions, mandatory drug testing, enhanced physical and digital security measures, and the recording of (normally negative) reports and intelligence that was often inaccessible and incontestable to these young men (Crewe, 2009, 2012; Liebling, 2004). This was not the only reason for individualised adaptations. Faced with the precarity of street life, these young men had long learned that they had to be self-reliant and independent.

The Functions of Violence and Victimisation

Prison violence and victimisation were functional and typically had an aim and objective. It was rare for violence to be senseless, with assaults typically being intelligible to those who inflicted them and often to their victims. Beyond the enforcement of the normative code, violence served the purposes of: (1) punishment for perceived wrongs; (2) the pursuit of justice; (3) retaliation; (4) revenge; (5) defence of self and property; (6) the negotiation of power; and, (7) expunging or communicating frustration with the illegitimacy of the State.

Mirroring the cultural habitus of the streets, respect was 'viewed as almost an external entity, one that is hard-won and easily lost—and so must be constantly guarded' (Anderson, 1999: 33). Young men were highly sensitised to, and greatly angered by slights, 'violations' and being 'mugged off.' What they feared was public shame and humiliation (Gilligan, 1996, 2003) and the associated diminution in their power and status. Disrespect was a 'denial of social recognition' and represented an injustice to those who considered themselves worthy of respect (Honneth, 1995). In this sense, disrespect was a moral injury and violence served to repair the injustice (ibid.). There was nothing trivial about a 'violation' and young men considered their reactions to be not only proportionate, but a 'social obligation' (Toch, 1992: 189) and fundamentally 'right.' It is not the severity of the affront that necessarily matters, but the fact that an individual dared challenge or question the individual at all. For example:

> It was like, 'Excuse me, please.' 'Fuck off, I'm on the phone.' He got sliced in the face, for telling one lad to suck his Ma. The lad that actually done it, went in the showers, done it, and walked back out. Walked in the showers, kicked the crap out of the geezer, sliced him in the face, and walked out, and left him on the floor bleeding. He was terrorising him [with a] razor blade mounted on a toothbrush. (Harry)

Disrespect extended beyond verbal abuse and threats to include attempts to circumvent the queue for the telephone or the serving of smaller meals. For example:

> You know the servery there, me and my friend jumped over smacked up the servery workers because they were trying to give us small meals. That can't happen. (Luke)

> It was those little square pieces of cake - you usually get two or three and he has put one on there. The boss is right there, so I can't really talk, you know what I mean, so I just looked at him as if to say, 'What is going on?' And he said, 'That is all I can give out today'. And I said so you are not going to put any more cake on there? And he said 'no'. So I jumped over there, smacked him and then my friend has jumped over and started joining in. I am not stupid enough to do things on sight in front of everybody like that all the time. But that time that example needed to be made. People saw it and I was chuffed. (Tyrone)

Respect was relative, i.e. what young people thought they were 'owed' varied. Not all of the young men considered themselves entitled to larger portions (often at the expense of others who would have to accept more meagre portions) even if they remain highly sensitised to antagonising verbal threats, gestures and stares. For Luke and Tyrone, assaulting those who had dared to give them 'small meals' was symbolic and communicative. The potential penalties for assaulting the servery worker were outweighed by the long-term benefits associated with consolidating their power and position, ensuring that no further challenges ensued, and indicating what would happen to anyone who dared question their 'authority.'

This hyper-vigilance to the disrespect extended to young men's evaluations of their treatment of prison officers. Young men with more carceral capital not only thought they were owed, but also gained, differential treatment by prison staff. For example, Steven believed prison officers were more likely to verbally persuade him to comply with their wishes:

> I'm not cheeky to staff. I've got no reason to be. I don't let them talk shit to me though. I saw some staff swing for a kid. Nah, they'd never do that to me. They wouldn't twist me up, they know I'll chin them. They say, 'Come on Steven, walk to your cell.' They have twisted me up a couple of times when I've been out of control.

Carceral capital was seen to justify a set of 'perks' that sat outside the formal IEP Scheme, the loss of which would be then perceived as an open challenge. Equally, any attempt by a prison officer to reinstitute the fair distribution of meals was regarded as disrespect by young men such as Tyrone and Luke who had grown accustomed to such deference. Thus, the perceived legitimacy of prison officer authority was influenced by how some young men felt they ought to be recognised, which did not always sit neatly against the espoused prison rules. For example, Tyrone explained:

> Every time I go to servery I get a nice, nice meal, yeah? And I went there the other day and there was a new boss, he didn't know me or whatever and he said, 'You can't have that, you have what everyone else is having.' So I just put my plate down and walked over to the old boss and said, 'Listen, I am going to have to fight him. I mean, he is taking the piss, he is not giving me the right food. And he is telling them I can't.' I can't go mad at the servery lads because he has told them that. My problem is with this boss directly. So they sat us both down in the office and they said some shit about, 'Oh we are trying to work with Tyrone, he is a good lad. He just gets angry quick.' He understood. I got my food.

He was quick to add:

> It's not bullying [the officer]. I have done things to get the perks. Look, I have had my fights with staff, the lads—I have done everything. I have done it all though when I go to the servery the lads respect that. Because I don't need to say 'put some more chips on there' because they are anyway. Do you know what I'm saying? There wouldn't be a talking thing. If they tried to stitch up my plate we would have it off there and then.

Although the YOI attempted to create an IEP scheme that leveraged rewards for positive (i.e. non-violent) behaviour, young men such as Luke, Tyrone, Steven and others like them felt that they had gained their 'perks' through proof of their violent capabilities. They did not seek respect from prison officers through compliance but believed that such recognition and respect was owed because of their carceral capital. They had—to their minds—proved themselves, and their superior status justified differential treatment. Thus the legitimacy of prison officer behaviour and what constituted 'authority used rightfully' (Liebling, 2011) was subjective and influenced by the respect and regard that young people thought they were individually owed.

Violence not only functioned to preserve an individual's sense of recognition, but also discredit those who were deemed unworthy of respect. This was symbolic, communicating a commitment to the normative code and a lack of association with those deemed contemptible. The routine punishment of sex offenders was universally accepted as not just as legitimate, but praiseworthy. Sex offenders had little or no social status, were ostracised, and endured far greater suffering than any other group within the YOI. Those who were not *known* sex offenders were unwavering in their commitment to physical violence to punish those they believed to be sex offenders. Sex offenders who were assaulted were simply not seen as victims by their peers. Rather, the various forms of victimisations that were inflicted upon them were seen as just punishment. For example:

> Rape or paedos or any of that sort of thing will get you bullied in here. I will kill them. I will happily do it. All day man, all day. Sick and twisted individuals, that's why. (Jack)

> I'll bang out any nonce, I don't give a fuck. I'll smash their face. That's why they get put in jail, they need it. Done it to loads of nonces, don't give a

> fuck. I'm living here and my next door neighbour is fucking kids. Disgusting. We shouldn't have to mix with nonces, gays and stuff. They are all lost. They should go on the same wing. (Steven)

Whilst those young men convicted of sex offences experienced profound 'disintegrative shame' (for a detailed analysis, see Ievins, 2023), it was considered appropriate by the other young men (and by prison staff). The antagonism towards sex offenders was justified by personalising the offending and suggesting that the victim of an offence wholly unrelated to them could have been 'my girlfriend, sister, daughter':

> Obviously that's just horrible. I don't like people like that. It's just horrible. I have got a missus, it could have been my missus. If you play with children, then that could have been my son. I am not having that. I don't want you in my wing. I don't want it. I could be having a shower on domestics and my pad could be open and you could be in my pad looking at pictures of my kid. I don't want you anywhere near me—just go away. (Jake)

Whilst young men were quick to recognise the profound impact of sexual assault—'you've traumatised her now for her whole life'—they were less concerned about the impact of robbery, violent crime, threats to kill, threats with a firearm or knife, or their own violence within the family or towards their partner. There was, therefore, an unevenness to their moral evaluations and their assessments about what constituted dignified behaviour. Some young men went so far as to say that believed that sex offenders came to prison specifically for the purpose of being assaulted, representing a skewed conceptualisation of justice and punishment. Isaac went as far as saying, 'You don't deserve to come out of jail.' The 'denial of the victim' was such that any physical assault was seen as 'rightful punishment' (Sykes & Matza, 1957) and generated little moral indignation from their peers (or some prison officers). Indeed, these young men considered that there was dignity in punishing sex offenders. Thus, it's not just that victimisation caused 'no serious damage to their self-worth' (Sykes & Matza, 1957), but their self-worth and social standing may be enhanced.

In some cases, violence was vengeful. During the inspection week, for example, 'Terror' was stabbed in the leg by Ciaran as he left the family visits room using a flick-knife that had been thrown over the double fence line. Terror had allegedly kidnapped Ciaran's sister prior to coming into prison. Terror was seemingly unmoved by his own stabbing, nonchalantly explaining that he would, 'sort it out on the outside [the YOI].' This was not the only example. Cody had stabbed Mukobo on the streets, causing him to lose a kidney. As soon as Mukobo saw Cody on 'freeflow,'[11] he assaulted Cody. Staff intervention prevented a more serious or prolonged assault, but Mukobo remained dissatisfied 'If I see him again, I'll do my thing.' However, after more problems with staff on the wing, Mukobo proceeded to flood the landing. He then threatened to kill himself and was found by staff with a noose around his neck. His peers were so angered by the flooding that he was moved to the Care and Supervision unit (segregation unit). Although young men were often described by practitioners and policy makers as impulsive, some held grudges, ruminated, and were prepared to bide their time. Prison violence was not always contained within the prison walls. As Mukobo and Ciaran illustrate, some conflicts were imported from the community and would remain unresolved at the point of release.

These young men generally believed that they had a legal right to defend themselves, however, self-defence was rarely accepted as a defence for prison rule violations. Acting in self-defence was, however, a functional response to threat, preventing them from physical injury and the loss of prized items such as trainers and canteen.

> I don't know, if someone has fucking hit me, I'm not just gonna stay and stand there, I'm obviously gonna fight back. (Thomas)

> If someone hits me then I am hitting them back. I don't care who they are. But I'm allowed to do that anyway it's self-defence. (Joshua)

Defence of self or property was normalised and deemed appropriate, even if the violence appeared excessive, disproportionate, or continued long

[11] 'Freeflow' took place at the beginning and end of each morning and afternoon in the working week to allow young men to move from the residential units to work, education, the gym, visits, the chapel and healthcare.

after the threat had been removed (and therefore had gone beyond what was permitted as a defence). Indeed, it was those who failed to defend themselves who were seen to lack credibility. Assaults and fights could backfire if the initial perpetrator was overcome or more badly injured, as was sometimes the case.

> I got jumped two weeks ago. Some guy ran his mouth, said my girlfriend's a slag, I told them to 'Shut the fuck up,' and he didn't like it, so he come in my pad, with all my mates in the pad, stupidly, and then I just swished and bombed him in the jaw—and he looked like a twat. So, his mates from sosh[12] decided we are going to wrap me, at least six of them. I got a broken nose and everything.

That said, most felt that the attempt itself (however unsuccessful) was virtuous. For example, Cory explained that young men should 'Stick up for yourself, even if it means that you're going to get punched up.' Equally, for people such as Chris, an assault or fight in prison could never be as bad as the abuse suffered as a child:

> If they try to take something off me, I would punch them up. My dad used to beat me up you know what I mean. If I can take being beaten by a 36-year-old bloke when I am 10 years old then no one in here is going to hurt me.

In this way, prison violence could represent a 'shadow event' (Winlow & Hall, 2009) where young men sought to overcome the shame and humiliation associated with earlier incidents of victimisation by decisively dealing with aggression within prison.

Violence was one way to negotiate and resolve the balance of power between prisoners. Both parties believed that they had to intimidate the other to protect themselves from victimisation, and in this sense the conflict was a power contest not just a physical altercation (also see Edgar et al., 2003). Incidents involving pad-mates were often cited as examples:

---

[12] Prison slang used to refer to 'association,' the period in the day when young men could socialise or use the exercise yards.

> I'm eating my noodles and watching TV and he's come in my pad. This was like about nine o'clock. We were talking and he's just like, 'Oh, I'm going to sleep, turn the TV off.' I said, 'Yo, are you mad? You just come in my pad and you think I'm turning the TV off, mate? I'm eating my noodles, you get me, and I'm watching TV, you get me.' He goes, 'Ah yeah, say no more, say no more,' jumped off the bed, went, 'Turn the TV off.' I've put my noodles down, got up, smacked him, he's dropped and I was just stamping on him and that. Turning my TV off, yeah man, no one does that, that's a violation now he's in jail. Everyone would do that, anyone would. (Finley)

Several pairings appeared to reach some compromise in their shared cells, but it was not unusual to find one pad-mate occupying, or claiming, a more dominant role in the cell. In situations such as those outlined by Finley, violence was both the acquisition and a symbolic expression of power; it also served to reinforce hierarchical relationships and communicated norms about appropriate behaviour. The most marked attempts to navigate the imbalance of power were between prisoners and prison officers. In such circumstances, assaults on staff were often a response to perceived disrespect, 'violations,' and frustrations either with the prison itself (e.g. delayed or reduced time out of cell), the specific actions of an individual officers, or the seemingly rigid and inflexible application of the rules (see Chap. 9 for further analysis). Young prisoners were expressing their frustration, anger, and resentment at their relative powerlessness as well as the careless use of power by prison officers or the prison itself (see Chap. 9). Of course, the State could respond with as much, if not more, power and coercive force—a form of legitimised violence that had to be subject to careful moral constraints to avoid exacerbating the problem of interpersonal prison violence.

Conclusion

Victimisation—including violence, threats, control, extortion and robbery—was a productive way to gain power, control, social significance and physical safety. However, only the 'right' forms of victimisation were honourable. Conversely, victimisation that involved bullying, cowardly assaults, verbal abuse without a willingness for physical violence, and/or 'out of control' violence was condemned. Equally, symbolic power and social recognition were conferred on those who not only demonstrated bravery and courage, but also entrepreneurial skill and the ability to graft and collect consumer goods. The desire for social recognition was accentuated during the early phases of the research where conditions were especially poor, and officers adopted more punitive and less compassionate approaches (see Chap. 9). Notably, the less prison officers trusted young men, recognised their claim to dignity and recognition, or acknowledged their potential, the more important social recognition amongst their peers became. This illustrates how the perceived morality of prison officer behaviour and the 'moral performance' (Liebling, 2004) of the prison as a whole influences the apparent utility and logic of prison violence—a theme taken up in Chap. 9.

The prisoner normative code provided predictability. It explained why violence happens, and although young men never felt that they could truly relax or 'let their guard down,' the fact that violence was rational meant that it lessened the 'probability of random violence' (Anderson, 1999: 27). This explained why, despite the regularity of violence and victimisation, most young men paradoxically felt safe (also see Bottoms, 1999). This is not to say that young men no longer needed to remain vigilant about changes to their surroundings (or to the people within it), but that they were able to tolerate and navigate the volatility and brutality with some confidence that they were exempt from the predictable victimisation of the 'nerds,' 'nonces' and homosexual or transgender prisoners. Victimisation conforms to cultural norms and codes in such a way that even to the victims themselves, it was explicable even if unwelcome. Thus, the logic of prison victimisation was accepted not only by perpetrators but also by the wider 'collective' (Wacquant, 2014: 126). Whilst aspects of the normative code were informed by prior experiences of the 'streets' and child penal custody,—it was a logic that was taught, learned and performed with and for others. Luke, for example, complained: 'I'm sick of giving these kids life lessons.' Young men were keen observers of each other, and although not all violations of the code were punished, the contempt of the weak, the informer, the debtor, and sex offenders created a moral and cultural context that was quickly learnt and readily understood. Rather than vilifying violence, the young prisoner normative code permitted and valorised it; thus, 'social controls' that should deter violence were 'rendered inoperative' (Sykes & Matza, 1957). Crucially, it was the ability to coolly control others (sometimes very charismatically) that attracted social esteem, therefore putting an emphasis on relatively narcissistic and negative behavioural tendencies.

The pursuit of justice explained why non repayment of debt was inexcusable, why disrespect and violations could not be tolerated, why provocation could not be ignored, why illegitimate treatment could produce sufficient frustration and humiliation that it warranted reprisal against officers (even if personally costly), why some believed they were entitled to other people's belongings, and why some young men ought to be excluded, ignored, and ostracised. This sense of justice was underpinned by—objectively viewed—relatively distorted constructions of who was worthy or deserving, where power should lie, who was to be respected, and, in some cases, overinflated and narcissistic senses of self. That said, the conceptualisation of justice amongst this young prisoner population was connected to the YOI's organisational culture and practice of justice. In assessing the legitimacy of their treatment, young men were making assessments about how justly they were treated by the State, but also whether there was an investigation into any victimisation, the quality of any investigation, whether inappropriate behaviour was tolerated, the way reward mechanisms functioned, the penalties applied for rule violations, the way the suicidal and distressed were treated, the evenness of their treatment (i.e. whether prison officers were held to account), whether the treatment was fair, and fundamentally, whether they were listened to (or indeed heard at all). Indeed, it was clearly the case that where the moral performance of a prison slips, and injustice abounds, prisoner solutions were brought into sharp relief. Equally, as the 'law*ful*ness' (not law*less*ness) and justice of the prison improved, prison victimisation (both in frequency and severity) reduced. It is this organisation culture and context that is analysed in Chap. 9.

Whilst these young men would become immersed in a culture and code that might enable their survival in prison, it also trapped them. The search for personal dignity, social recognition, and respect through carceral capital ultimately served to inculcate them to strategies, norms, and behaviours that made imprisonment more, not less, likely. What appears deeply functional is also deeply ruinous. As Bourgois notes (2003: 9), 'although street culture emerges out of a personal search for dignity and a rejection of racism and subjugation, it ultimately becomes an active agent in personal degradation and community ruin.' Whilst 'carceral capital' held a symbolism and currency that was of utility in YOIs and prisons, and when returning to the streets (Hobbs, 1995), it was of little advantage in securing legitimate employment (Maguire, 2021) or in helping them become partners and fathers who did not demand power and control. Even if they were willing to work or find a 'normal life, their 'masculine strategies' were likely to 'continue to be a major barrier for them on release' (Maguire, 2021: 125).

References

Anderson, E. (1999). *Code of the street: Decency, violence and the moral life of the inner city*. W.W. Norton and Company.

Barry, M. (2006). *Youth offending in transition: The search for social recognition*. Routledge.

Billingham, L., & Irwin-Rogers, K. (2022). *Against youth violence: A social harm perspective*. Bristol University Press.

Bottoms, A. E. (1999). Interpersonal violence and social order in prisons. *Crime and Justice, 26*, 205–281.

Bourdieu, P. (1973). Cultural and social reproduction. In R. Brown (Ed.), *Knowledge, education, and cultural change* (pp. 71–112). Tavistock.

Bourdieu, P. (1984). *Distinction: A social critique of the judgement of taste*. Routledge, Kegan and Paul.

Bourdieu, P. (1986). The forms of capital. In J. Richardson (Ed.), *Handbook of theory and research for the sociology of education* (pp. 241–258). Greenwood.

Bourgois, P. (2003). *In search of respect: Selling crack in El Barrio*. Cambridge University Press.

Caputo-Levine, D. D. (2013). The yard face: The contributions of inmate interpersonal violence to the carceral habitus. *Ethnography, 14*(2), 165–185.

Cohen, S., & Taylor, L. (1972). *Psychological survival: The experience of long-term imprisonment*. Penguin.

Crewe, B. (2005). Prisoner society in the era of hard drugs. *Punishment & Society, 7*(4), 457–481.

Crewe, B. (2009). *Prisoner society: Power, adaptation and social life in an English prison*. Oxford University Press.

Crewe, B. (2012). Prison culture and prisoner society. In B. Crewe & J. Bennett (Eds.), *The prisoner* (pp. 27–39). Routledge.

Edgar, K., & O'Donnell, I. (1998). Assault in prison: The 'victim's' contribution. *British Journal of Criminology, 38*(4), 635–650.

Edgar, K., O'Donnell, I., & Martin, C. (2003). *Prison violence: The dynamics of conflict, fear and power*. Willan.

Ellis, A. (2016). *Men, masculinities and violence: An ethnographic study*. Routledge.

Fiske, A. P., & Rai, T. S. (2015). *Virtuous violence: Hurting and killing to create, sustain, end and honor social relationships*. Cambridge University Press.

Fraser, A. (2013). Street habitus: Gangs, territorialism and social change in Glasgow. *Journal of Youth Studies, 16*(8), 970–985.

Fraser, A., & Matthews, D. (2021). Towards a criminology of atmospheres: Law, affect and the codes of the street. *Criminology & Criminal Justice, 21*(4), 455–471.

Gambetta, D. (2009). *Codes of the underworld: How criminals communicate*. Princeton University Press.

Gilligan, J. (1996). *Violence: Reflections on our deadliest epidemic*. G.P. Putnam's Sons.

Gilligan, J. (2003). Shame, guilt, and violence. *Social Research: An International Quarterly, 70*(4), 1149–1180.

Gooch, K. (2019). 'Kidulthood': Ethnography, juvenile prison violence and the transition from 'boys' to 'men'. *Criminology & Criminal Justice, 19*(1), 80–97.

Green, A., & McGourlay, C. (2015). The wolf packs in our midst and other products of criminal joint Enterprise prosecutions. *The Journal of Criminal Law, 79*(4), 280–297.

Hall, S., Winlow, S., & Ancrum, C. (2013). *Criminal identities and consumer culture*. Willan.

Hamm, M. S. (2013). *The spectacular few: Prisoner radicalization and the evolving terrorist threat*. New York University Press.

Hobbs, D. (1994). Mannish boys: Danny, Chris, crime, masculinity an business. In T. Newburn & E. A. Stanko (Eds.), *Just boys doing business?: Men, masculinities and crime* (pp. 118–134). Routledge.

Hobbs, D. (1995). *Bad Business*. Oxford University Press.

Hobbs, D. (2012). 'It was never about the money': Market society, organised crime and U.K. criminology. In S. Hall & S. Winlow (Eds.), *New directions in criminological theory* (pp. 257–275). Routledge.

Honneth, A. (1995). *The struggle for recognition: The moral grammar of social conflicts*. Polity Press.

Hulley, S., Crewe, B., & Wright, S. (2019). Making sense of 'joint enterprise' for murder: Legal legitimacy or instrumental acquiescence? *British Journal of Criminology, 59*(6), 1328–1346.

Ievins, A. (2023). *The strains of imprisonment: Moral communication and men convicted of sex offences*. University of California Press.

Ilan, J., & Sandberg, S. (2019). How 'gangsters' become jihadists: Bourdieu, criminology and the crime–terrorism nexus. *European Journal of Criminology, 16*(3), 278–294.

Jacobs, J. B. (1977). *Stateville*. University of Chicago Press.

Jacobs, B. A., & Wright, R. (2006). *Street justice: Retaliation in the criminal underworld*. Cambridge University Press.

Jewkes, Y. (2005). Men behind bars. *Men and Masculinities, 8*(1), 44–63.

Liebling, A. (2004). *Prisons and their moral performance*. Oxford University Press.

Liebling, A. (2011). Distinctions and distinctiveness in the work of prison officers: Legitimacy and authority revisited. *European Journal of Criminology, 8*(6), 484–499.

Liebling, A., Arnold, H., & Straub, C. (2011). *An exploration of staff-prisoner relationships at Whitemoor: 12 years on*. Ministry of Justice.

Maguire, D. (2021). *Male, failed and jailed: Masculinities and the 'revolving door' imprisonment in the UK*. Palgrave Macmillan.

Marsh, B. (2020). *The logic of violence: An ethnography of Dublin's illegal drug trade*. Routledge.

McCorkle, R. (1992). Personal precautions to violence in prison. *Criminal Justice and Behavior, 19*(2), 160–173.

Michalski, J. H. (2017). Status hierarchies and hegemonic masculinity: A general theory of prison violence. *British Journal of Criminology, 57*(1), 40–60.

Neuber, A. (2011). Understanding violence in the 'society of captives': Sykes meets Bourdieu in prison. *Howard Journal of Criminal Justice, 50*(1), 1–16.

Newton, C. (1994). Gender theory and prison sociology: Using theories of masculinities to interpret the sociology of prisons for men. *Howard Journal of Crime and Justice, 33*(3), 193–202.

Omerond, D., & Laird, K. (2016). Jogee: Not the end of a legal saga but the start of one? *Criminal Law Review, 8*, 539–552.

Pyrooz, D. C., & Decker, S. H. (2019). *Competing for control: Gangs and the social order of prisons*. Cambridge University Press.
Sandberg, S. (2008). Street capital. *Theoretical Criminology, 12*(2), 153–171.
Sandberg, S., & Fleetwood, J. (2017). Street talk and Bourdieusian criminology: Bringing narrative to field theory. *Criminology & Criminal Justice, 17*(4), 365–381.
Sandberg, S., & Pedersen, W. (2009). *Street capital*. Bristol University Press.
Schlosser, J. A. (2013). Bourdieu and Foucault: A conceptual integration toward an empirical sociology of prisons. *Critical Criminology, 21*, 31–46.
Shammas, V. L., & Sandberg, S. (2016). Habitus, capital, and conflict: Bringing Bourdieusian field theory to criminology. *Criminology & Criminal Justice, 16*(2), 195–213.
Shortland, A. (2019). *Kidnap: Inside the ransom business*. Oxford University Press.
Sim, J. (1994). Tougher than the rest? Men in prison. In T. Newburn & E. A. Stanko (Eds.), *Just boys doing business? Men, masculinities and crime* (pp. 100–177). Routledge.
Skarbek, D. (2012). Prison gangs, norms, and organizations. *Journal of Economic Behavior & Organization, 82*(1), 96–109.
Skarbek, D. (2014). *The social order of the underworld: How prison gangs govern the American penal system*. Oxford University Press.
Skarbek, D. (2020). *The puzzle of prison order: Why life behind bars varies across the world*. Oxford University Press.
Sloan, J. (2016). *Masculinities and the adult male prison experience*. Palgrave Macmillan.
Sykes, G. (1958). *The society of captives*. Princeton University Press.
Sykes, G. M., & Matza, D. (1957). Techniques of neutralization: A theory of delinquency. *American Sociological Review, 22*(6), 664–670.
Sykes, G. M., & Messinger, S. L. (1960). The inmate social system. In R. A. Cloward (Ed.), *Theoretical studies in social organisation of the prison* (pp. 5–14). Social Research Council.
Toch, H. (1975). *Men in crisis: Human breakdowns in prison*. Aldine Publishing.
Toch, H. (1977). *Living in prison: The ecology of survival*. The Free Press.
Toch, H. (1992). *Violent men: An inquiry into the psychology of violence*. Penguin.
Toch, H. (1997). *Corrections: A humanistic approach*. Harrow and Heston.
Toch, H. (1998). Hypermasculinity and prison violence. In L. H. Bowker (Ed.), *Masculinities and crime* (pp. 168–178). Sage.
Willis, P. (1978). *Learning to labour: How working class kids get working class jobs*. Saxon House.

Winlow, S. (2001). *Badfellas: Crime, tradition and new masculinities*. Berg.

Winlow, S. (2014). Trauma, guilt and the unconscious: Some theoretical notes on violent subjectivity. *The Sociological Review, 62*(2 suppl), 32–49.

Winlow, S., & Hall, S. (2006). *Violent night: Urban leisure and contemporary culture*. Berg.

Winlow, S., & Hall, S. (2009). Retaliate first: Memory, humiliation and male violence. *Crime, Media, Culture: An International Journal, 5*(3), 285–304.

9

Loosening the Screws: Leadership, Conditions, Culture, and Morality

The prison officer's account was clearly a lie. The Adjudicating Governor[1] had caught Clive in the lie, and having done so, Clive was now struggling to amend his account to make his evidence plausible. Prison adjudications are 'a particular form of justice' focused on 'behaviours that disrupt prison order' (Fernandez, 2015: 117) not just criminal conduct. In this case, the charge was disobeying a direct order[2] and Oliver was sat in front of the Adjudicating Governor listening to Clive explain the 'nicking.' Clive alleged that Oliver had refused to leave the showers when told to do so and then 'dragged his heels' when returning to his cell. He claimed that Oliver had been given the allotted period for 'domestics'[3] (30 minutes), had sufficient time to shower, and it was therefore reasonable to expect him to return to his cell when asked to do so. If the charge was proved,

[1] A 'governor grade' senior manager (e.g. a Head of Security, Head of Safety or Head of Residence) typically perform the role of adjudicating Governor. The 'Governing Governor' or Deputy Governor can preside over such hearings, but it is unusual for this to be the case.

[2] An offence under section 55(25) of the Young Offender Institution Rules 2000.

[3] 'Domestics' was the allotted period in the daily prison regime where young men could shower and clean their cells.

K. Gooch, *Prison Violence*, Palgrave Studies in Prisons and Penology,
https://doi.org/10.1007/978-3-031-91365-5_9

Oliver could lose entitlements such as gym access, association,[4] his television and/or the ability to order canteen.[5] Oliver's defence was that he had not been unlocked at the proper time and was given less than 5 minutes to shower before Clive ordered him out. Oliver had tried to reason with Clive, and when reason failed, had refused to leave the shower. Another prison officer was called as a corroborating witness for Clive but gave an account that matched Oliver's version of events. As the Adjudicating Governor's questions continued, Clive struggled to explain the inconsistencies in his account, becoming flustered and red faced. Oliver was incensed.

Adjudications brought justice, integrity, and the 'moral quality of prison life' (Liebling, 2004) into sharp relief. Justice was, however, a contested concept. To prison officers, the adjudication was a key test of senior management support. Claims that senior management were unsupportive quickly followed any decision to 'throw out' an adjudication or award penalties considered unduly lenient. For prison officers, justice was served when prison officers were unquestionably believed, and punitive sanctions awarded to the young men. Prison officers did not always feel as powerful as they sometimes appeared (Sparks et al., 1996: 42), which meant that they were highly sensitised to the responses of senior managers to any perceived wrongdoing by young prisoners. To Clive, the affront to his authority and non-compliance by Oliver was the greater wrong; not the failure to follow the 'regime,'[6] nor the failure to allow young men to shower, nor the misleading information about how long the young men had been given to shower. The seemingly intractable problem was that whilst prisoners desired justice, the prison system primarily sought compliance, not justice. In fact, compliance was still demanded even in the face of injustice, unfairness, indignity, and inhumanity. Normal human reactions such as anger, frustration, grief, distress, or anxiety had to be contained even when faced with unbearable tragedy, indignity, and immorality. Rather prison officers held an unfailing belief in the need for

[4] 'Association' was a period of unstructured activity where young men could inter alia play pool, socialise, go into the exercise yard, and make telephone calls.

[5] 'Canteen' consisted of toiletries, food, stationery, and other goods. It could be ordered on a weekly basis.

[6] Prison slang for the daily schedule of activities.

prompt obedience, particularly from those they regarded as aggressive, disruptive, or recalcitrant.

In this 'kangaroo court,' young men wanted due process, distributive justice, fair and even treatment, to be believed, and—crucially—not to be 'stitched up' by prison officers with petty charges. To Oliver, Clive had erred in three critical ways. First, Oliver considered it an 'absolute fucking liberty' for prison officers to lie. He had, as he tried to impress upon the Adjudicating Governor, 'entitlements and rights.' Secondly, to Oliver, Clive was a hypocrite. To Oliver's mind, prison officers should follow the rules and if officers couldn't follow the rules, why should he? Third, Clive had not only failed to facilitate a shower, but had also proved incapable of compromise and continued his punitive approach by 'nicking' Oliver—an excessive use of discretionary power. In a context where prison officer's relational capital was severely depleted, 'nickings' had become one way for prison officers to penalise young men for (often minor) non-compliance. This method for re-asserting moral authority was rarely effective and often divisive. Clive was not well liked by prisoners and was variously called a 'fat prick' or 'that cunt.' The feeling was mutual. When James and I were first introduced to Clive, one of his opening statements was: 'I can tell they [the young men] are lying because their lips are moving.' Unsurprisingly given his combative approach, he would feature in several physical restraint incidents. Disillusioned and cynical, Clive was one of few officers who remained resistant to the reforming efforts of the senior leadership team.

Having heard the evidence, the Adjudicating Governor directed her gaze at Oliver and concluded, 'I find the charge against you proven.' After consulting the list of possible punishments, the Adjudicating Governor announced that the 'losses' would be suspended. A pragmatic solution had been found: in refusing to leave the shower room, Oliver had technically refused to obey a direct order, but the lenient punishment reflected a sympathy with Oliver's frustration at the officer's tardiness. For Adjudicating Governors, there were obvious 'moral tensions' (Fernandez, 2015: 123) in not wanting to suggest misbehaviour was acceptable, or jeopardise the good will of prison officers, but in also seeking to ensure that prisoners were fairly treated (Bennett, 2016). Some Adjudicating Governors asked more inquisitive questions about what had led up to the alleged conduct; others aimed for something more 'rehabilitative' (Howard & Wakeling, 2020), asking what young men could do differently in future. In some cases, this created an opportunity for young men to confide in the Adjudicating Governor. On other occasions, though, such questions were polarising, especially when young men felt bereft of alternative choices, when they felt the 'nicking' was unjustified, or where prison staff had contributed to the situation. Following Oliver's adjudication, the Adjudicating Governor confided in us that she thought Clive was 'clearly lying,' adding, 'I'll be going to check that they're [the young men] getting showers now.'

Gilligan argues (1996: 11) that 'All violence is an attempt to achieve justice, or what the violent person perceives as justice.' By this, Gilligan means that the violent person is seeking retribution or compensation for what is owed to him or someone else. Young men typically believed that they were worthy of moral and social recognition by the State and its agents, and the difference between what they thought was 'owed' and what they received constituted an injustice (Honneth, 1995). This chapter extends this argument by accounting for the ways in which the prison's own claim to justice influenced the logic, visibility, and frequency of prison victimisation. Justice can appear to be an abstract normative value, but it is empirically experienced and evaluated (Liebling, 2013, 2015). For prisoners, 'justice' was multi-dimensional, incorporating notions of fairness, humanity, respect, and dignity. This was consistent with Woolf's (1991) definition of justice, which collapses notions of humanity, fairness, interpersonal treatment and preparedness for their return to the community.

In re-asserting the importance of justice to the fabric, operation, and culture of the prison, I move away from the overly procedural emphasis that has come to dominate scholarly and practitioners' conceptualisations of justice within prison (see, for example, Beijersbergen et al., 2015; Bierie, 2013; Brunton-Smith & McCarthy, 2016; Fitzalan Howard & Wakeling, 2019; Reisig & Mesko, 2009). This literature is based on Tyler's (2006) study on why people obey the law (and accept the decisions of the police and judiciary)—research that suggests that people are more likely to comply with State authority if they have a 'voice' (have their views considered), are treated with 'respect' (being treated politely, having respect for their rights, and for them as people) and 'neutrality' (i.e. honest and unbiased), and have 'trust in authority' (i.e. that they are willing to help and protect them). However, there are critical differences between prisons and policing, not least of all because prison officers are in continuous contact with prisoners, because prison officers have more power over prisoners, because the enforcement of 'rules' goes well beyond criminal conduct and extends to matters of domestic and personal life, and because prisoners rely on prison officers for very basic necessities and functions (Hulley et al., 2012; Liebling et al., 2011). The primary problem with the literature on procedural justice is that it is orientated to questions about compliance, but this instrumental reading of prisoner behaviour overlooks the need for social 'recognition and justice as a condition for human flourishing and wellbeing' (Liebling, 2011b: 534) and violence prevention.

In the account above, Oliver—like others in similar circumstances—clearly objected to the perceived lack of due process, but what was considered 'right,' 'fair,' and 'just' was a much more widely drawn concept. It was bound up in everyday practices and interactions. Due process mattered, but it was more than a legalistic sense of whether rules were followed. Outcomes mattered, and it wasn't necessarily the case that young men would accept a penalty simply because a policy was followed. Just outcomes also included 'receiving an answer to one's question, as well as gaining a favourable response,' thus the distinction between 'procedure' and 'outcomes' was less clear cut (Hulley et al., 2012: 20). Evaluations of 'justice' were just as much tied up in: what officers didn't do (e.g. whether cell bells were answered or toilet roll supplied); how they spoke to the young men; whether it was even 'fair' to use a particular process in the first place (e.g. 'why did they even give me a nicking if I've already apologised?'); whether prison staff appeared indifferent to their distress; whether they were given opportunities to progress; whether prison staff could admit fault or acknowledge how their behaviour or decisions had contributed to a prisoner's (mis)behaviour; how and when young men were restrained (and whether it was done capriciously or excessively); and, how power was used (e.g. simply refusing to unlock someone).

It is well established that the 'moral quality' of a prison is linked to prisoner suicide and distress (Liebling, 2011b)—moral quality is also linked to prison violence. Within the YOI, high levels of prison violence were a symptom of the 'moral neglect' (Liebling, 2004). In this case, the failure of the YOI to 'persuade these prisoners that it was treating them fairly' (Woolf, 1991) led not to collective disorder, but to increased interpersonal violence. The subsequent reduction in prison violence was achieved by repairing the moral, physical, cultural, and social foundations of the YOI. Crucially, there were no changes to *who* was sent to the YOI—thus the importation factors did not change, illustrating that the most productive way to reduce high levels of prison violence is to improve the moral, cultural, social, and relational quality of the prison, not search for 'rotten apples.' The YOI had to be lawful (and therefore inappropriate behaviour could not be ignored), but as the Governing Governor stated, 'you can't punish your way out of violence.'

The very deliberate efforts made by the prison leadership team to improve the experience of imprisonment and regain their claim to moral authority reveals four crucial findings about the prevention of prison violence: (1) that you cannot rely on punishment and control to reduce prison violence whilst the prison remains immoral, inhumane, and unjust; (2) that social order begins with moral order and the consistent practice of justice, integrity, respect, fairness; (3) focusing on improving the environmental, cultural, and relational factors is more productive than trying to increase restrictions, controls, and punitive measures (indeed, this may simply generate prison violence); and (4) that prisoners need to feel an individual sense of significance, respect, recognition and to mitigate the propensity towards violence. As May (1998: 37) argues, 'it is the lack of significance, and the struggle for it, that underlines much violence.' Young men wanted their human moral worth and dignity to be recognised and respected, and the absence of this was an intolerable injustice and moral injury. It endangered their 'positive understanding of themselves' (Honneth, 1995: 168).

Mending the Broken Windows

With alarming uniformity, 'It's a shithole!' were the first words uttered by young men describing the YOI. Such refrains are common when conducting prison research, but these young men were not simply repeating the general claim that prison life is 'shit' but pointing to the brutalising effects of 'ritual uncleanness' (Douglas, 1966). Paul remarked: 'It was a fucking shithole man. I went into a pad[7] and I lay down in my bed and I thought this is really prison.' Poor prison conditions led the young men to conclude they had been catapulted into 'prison,' rather than being held in an institution specifically designed for *young* men. Here the 'depth of imprisonment' (Crewe, 2021; Downes, 1988) was not felt in the distance from release (Crewe, 2011; King & McDermott, 1995), but being buried in an institution that neglected their needs and disregarded their worth. It was a form of 'moral depth'[8] not just penal depth. None of the young men expected imprisonment to be an easy experience (also see Calavita & Jenness, 2015; Useem & Kimball, 1991), but they did expect that they would be better cared for and that their status as *young* men would be better recognised. Fundamentally, dirty and impoverished conditions represented a devastating assault to self and a form of 'slow violence' (Billingham & Irwin-Rogers, 2022; Gilligan, 1996; Nixon, 2013)—it was neither banal nor innocuous, and nor was it simply a 'background feature' (Billingham & Irwin-Rogers, 2022: 107). Rather, these structural harms become part of young men's 'inner worlds' (Bakkali, 2019) and 'psychological architecture,' undermining the social recognition and respect they desired. Squalor created unrest and generated heightened vigilance; '[d]irt is essentially disorder' (Douglas, 1966: 2). The effects were pervasive, not only contributing to hopelessness, distress, and self-harm, but also fostering interpersonal violence.

The relationship between prison conditions and prison victimisation is subtle but nonetheless important, arising from: (1) the need to borrow, steal, or rob items the State had failed to provide; (2) the defence of property in limited supply; (3) the use of drugs to psychologically manage the

[7] Prison slang for a cell.

[8] Many thanks to Professor Ben Crewe, University of Cambridge, for his helpful suggestion here.

problem of 'doing time'; and, (4) the creation of a unique psycho-social context where the 'feeling I count for something' is achieved 'through different types of violence' (Billingham & Irwin-Rogers, 2022: 122). Moreover, poor prison conditions were symptomatic of a chaotic and haphazard approach by prison officers, an approach that also created a permissiveness about interpersonal violence. These young men did not protest their treatment through collective disorder, partly because prison staff retained the 'ability to contain disturbances' (Useem & Kimball, 1991: 218), partly because there was no 'seemingly small event' (Boin & Rattray, 2004: 53) to stimulate collective protest, and partly because young prisoner society was atomised, lacking the sort of collective will to resist the State (also see Murray, 2023). This is not to say that young men passively accepted poor conditions; they were still drawing 'cues' (Wortley, 2002) about the morality of the prison and their punishment.

For these young men, 'doing their time' meant avoiding the contamination of other people's dirt, excrement, hair, bodily fluids, and rotten food. For young men who paid careful attention to their physical appearance, the ritual uncleanliness was particularly threatening to their personal dignity and self-confidence. The inability to rid oneself of clinging physical contagions, particularly from those deemed contemptible, only added to their horror. Whilst some simply lived in the filth, others made rigorous attempts to purge their cell of impurities and attached agentic importance to such acts:

> Shit conditions. I hate this place. This prison is dirty man. It's nasty. I hate being in this prison. It is unhygienic man, I hate it. You can go into some dirty cells but I wouldn't put myself in a dirty cell. I had to clean it up. (Jermaine)

For young men like Jermaine, their resistance to the routine uncleanliness bolstered their masculine performances, asserting that they could still be neat, well presented and resourceful men despite their impoverished conditions. For others, the squalid conditions contributed to psychological collapse. For example, Chris swallowed an excessive amount of prescription medication when placed in a filthy cell:

> I walked in there and there was no mattress on the top bunk. I was padding up with someone and there was one mattress. So, we couldn't stay in that pad. All the other cells had been smashed up. There was a little drawer thing, like a little cabinet, and that had been ripped off the wall. The floor was all wet. There was all food on the floor and everything. All the ceiling was burnt. All graffiti all over the walls. Just trampy man it was. They [the officers] said they will sort it out, but nothing happened. It sent me into a state of depression and I tried to top myself because of the state of the pad.

Prison suicide attempts rarely have a single cause (for further analysis, see: Liebling, 1992), and in this case, Chris' distress and depression was exacerbated by the apparent indifference of prison officers and their decision to place him on a wing with young men who presented a threat (something he had alerted officers to before the move). However, the example illustrates the psychological harm caused by inhumane prison conditions.

Poor prison conditions were the physical manifestation of moral malaise. Officers were aware that they were placing young men in filthy, soiled, and poorly equipped cells covered in offensive graffiti and exposed to the elements. To do so repeatedly required a degree of: (1) desensitisation—where what is incongruent with personal values becomes less shocking; (2) distraction—where staff focus on other tasks; (3) distance—by, for example, remaining in staff offices rather than being present on the landings and actively responding to prisoners' needs; (4) dissociation—seeing prisoners as undeserving, 'other' and in need of punishment; (5) disregard—where humane conditions are unimportant; and, (6) defeat—where '[p]ast experience has instilled a sense of powerlessness and they do not act even when they could do so effectively' (O'Donnell, 2023: 24). This form of defeat has been described as 'learned helplessness' (O'Donnell, 2023), but is also linked to hopelessness. In a very conventional sense—prison officer work was 'dirty work' (Ashforth & Kreiner, 1999; Hughes, 1958). Prison officers were creating a situation (either through wilful neglect, structural impediment, or an inability to effect change) that trapped them in a 'shared misery' with the young men and threatened their dignity too.

These problems were not recent or unknown. The Inspectorate of Prisons (HMIP) had repeated their concerns about poor conditions in three separate inspections of the YOI prior to the damning inspection that finally prompted financial investment. Whilst prison officers might have been the ones locking young men in squalid cells, senior managers within and beyond the prison were complicit. It might be true that senior managers had 'stopped seeing things,' but as those in control of financial resources, they were not 'passive bystanders' (Cohen, 2001)—a point that was not lost on prison officers:

> We were in a terrible, terrible place. We tried to address this with the last Governor on various occasions, and the one before, but it just fell on deaf ears and then when HMIP [HM Inspectorate of Prisons] came, it wasn't a shock to any member of staff here, but it was a massive shock to [the then Director of Public Sector Prisons]. He actually said to John [a prison officer] after his tour, 'I can't believe it, I'm shocked at the state of the windows,' and John said, 'Well I find it hard to believe you're shocked when the Governor knows, the Area Manager knows. We've told everybody. It's been going for years.' And it boils down to cash, to money. (Dave, Supervising Officer)

Prison staff—both within and beyond the prison—seemed to absorb the political rhetoric and adopt a 'scarcity mindset.' This was a moral, not a financial, decision. It was more than a failure to order enough underwear or fix the broken windows, but represented a decision that these young men were not worth more—that they did not *deserve* their own clean underwear or to sleep in clean cells, that the young men did not *matter*. In so doing, prison staff were not implementing prison policy, they were creating it (Fassin, 2015: 5). The incoming Governing Governor gave short shrift to any suggestion that the budget could not extend to supplying personal necessities:

> When I got here it was no toilet roll, it was no boxer shorts. I met lads who had been locked up, no showers, had not had a kit change. They [the young men] were told there isn't any [kit]. They could not get clean underwear. I said to staff, 'Is this real?' and they said, 'Yes, we have been told there is no money, it's austerity.' I would not have that. Austerity does not mean we

> cannot buy boxer shorts, but there had become this sort of negative culture. Everything was, 'No, we can't have it,' even if the question had never been asked. The assumption was there was no money for, and that had been accepted. But decency is not expecting young men to wear the same unwashed boxershorts for two weeks. I had my new finance manager on it. His first day, his first job was: get me 1000 pairs of boxer shorts here this afternoon.

Such decisions were symbolic, communicating the importance of humane treatment in a context where prison staff routinely neglected young men's needs. A programme of refurbishment was quickly instituted, taking more than a year to complete and costing more than £1 million. The refurbishment programme was a necessary first step to creating social order and re-establishing a moral benchmark amongst prison officers. As Douglas (1966: 2) argues, '[d]irt offends against order. Eliminating it is not a negative moment, but a positive effort to organise the environment.'

Cleanliness remained a relentless pursuit; it was also a moral practice. To the young men, the poverty and impurity of the conditions created a sense of *injustice* not just indecency. Many prison staff acknowledged that humane prison conditions were the 'basics' without which all other aspects of prison life collapse. However, the morality of improved conditions was contested. Early in the research, for example, a prison officer complained about the emphasis on decency, stating 'decency needs justice too.' Here, the demand for justice represented a desire for greater punishment, ostensibly out of regard for the victims but largely because these young men were still regarded as undeserving and in need of authoritarian, harsh treatment. Even simple acts such as ensuring that young men had sufficient clean clothes were often framed as a 'zero sum games'—some prison officers felt that they were losing something (although it was not always clear what that was) and that the essential aspects of punishment were diluted. Prison officers could also stymie reforming efforts by simply declining to supply any necessities:

> It's not a problem getting hold of spice [psychoactive substances] in here, but if you want a bog [toilet] roll off the staff boss, it's a different matter. (Freddie)

> If I need one of them, 'Boss, can I have this? Boss, can I have that?' You know, just the little things that you ask for, and they say, 'No,' like that. I've seen bosses come to you, look at you and just [imitates a stare] like that, and walk off, and then you feel like, fuck this. You're on your (cell) bell[9] now. You're pressing your bell. They look at you and they think, 'No, I don't want to entertain him. I don't even want to waste my breath.' [They say] 'No, because I don't have to.' That's what you get. 'Because I don't have to. I don't have to answer to what you say. Close your flap.' (Jack)

There was a general thoughtlessness to what it might mean to be 'desperate for a shit' and shouting out to prison officers to bring toilet roll. On one occasion, rather than simply handing the toilet roll to the young man, the officer removed individual sheets of toilet paper one by one and then handed them over. She then turned and walked away, taking the toilet roll with her, and proudly saying to her colleagues, 'It's Christmas!' before giggling. What could have been an act of care became spiteful. It was a careless use of power that generated more work for the wing officers who were later responding to further requests for a toilet roll (something officers also bemoaned). It is not the material deprivation alone that causes frustration, nor solely the inability to 'get things done,' but the lack of 'respect.' This form of respect has been described as 'organisational respect' (Hulley et al., 2012) but it was something more than simply the ability to 'get things done' (Hulley et al., 2012: 15)—it was a critical factor in indicating 'recognition' (Honneth, 1995), dignity and worth.

Set against this background, it was those prison officers who reliably acquired highly prized items—such as toilet rolls, toilet brushes, bedding, or plastic cutlery—who were deemed trustworthy. Responsivity was an act of care and respect (Hulley et al., 2012). Crucially, those prison officers who were effective in answering requests gained considerable social capital with the young men and were less likely to be assaulted (also see Tait, 2008). If young men were frightened and/or in need of urgent

[9] Cell bells can be pressed within the cell by prisoners alerting prison officers that they need attention. Prison officers were keen that the bells were only pressed in a genuine emergency.

help, they reported their concerns to those officers who had proven responsive to their material needs:

> You pick out certain officers that are genuine and are good and everything. You basically stick with them. You build your trust and bonds with them and then if you have any problems or issues you go to them. They will help you. (Sam)

Demonstrable respect created the foundations for trust. In the prevention of prison violence, self-harm, and suicide attempts, questions of trust became crucial. Liebling and Arnold (2012: 421) argue '[t]he difference between 'a little' trust, and 'even less' was small (statistically speaking) in a prison setting, but had major sociological implications.' Mirroring the need to carefully assess the character of their peers (see Chaps. 5 and 8), misjudging officers also carried risks. For example:

> I've walked into the one lad's pad that's called me over and he's slapped me in the face and jabbed me there, and I've come out the pad and [the officer] goes, 'What was that about?' And obviously, because the last time when he weren't very discreet, I felt like I couldn't tell him, so I turned round and goes, 'Ah nothing. Me and my boy having a laugh.' And I left him at that. (Ollie)

Young men needed prison officers to take their practical, emotional, and interpersonal needs seriously (Hulley et al., 2012: 17). The carelessness of some communicated indifference but also contributed to physical assaults. Young men believed that only a few officers could be trusted with the effect that some chose not to confide in officers at all, either tolerating the victimisation, attempting to defend themselves, relying on their peers for personal safety (and assaulting others in groups), crafting and stockpiling weapons (Brennan, 2019), or using drugs to manage distress (in some cases leading to assaults due to indebtedness).

Relationships and Recognition

A prison can appear cleaner, but staff-prisoner relationships remain transactional, distant, and hostile. As it was aptly put to us: 'you can buy new windows, but you can't buy good relationships.' Violence is inherently relational, it is therefore not surprising that the causes of assaults against staff included perceived disrespect, frustration, and the misuse of power and authority (for further analysis, see Doolin & Gooch, 2022). For staff, violence was threatening, unjustifiable, and illegal. For the young men, it was an attempt to find agency and express their resentment, disapproval, and frustration at the actions of the State or select individuals. How staff-prisoner relationships are framed has a bearing not only on the likelihood and severity of staff assaults, but also on the number and severity of assaults between prisoners. For example, Sparks et al. (1996: 317–318) found that the light, relaxed, and unobtrusive style of supervision by prison officers at HMP Long Lartin meant that riots were avoided, and there were fewer staff assaults, but there was a degree of 'backstage' violence. Laxity and indifference can leave the vulnerable unprotected, victims unsupported, and give freedom to perpetrators to act with impunity. Within the YOI, re-establishing respect and improving the quality of staff-prisoner relationship was a key priority for the senior leadership team.

Nearly all of the young men could cite examples of good prison officer work or name officers whom they thought were 'good,' 'safe,' 'funny,' or 'firm but fair.' When asked to describe good prison officer work, or why a certain officer stood out, most young men described an officer's willingness to help, be 'supportive,' have a 'joke,' answer cell bells in a timely manner, respond to their requests and needs, and understand that they were young men who were still maturing. Some young men preferred a much more relaxed form of authority, partly because they resisted the rigid enforcement of rules or the assertion of authority by prison officers:

> Some of them [prison officers], God, they live for this. It just irritates me. Obviously, I understand you have got to do your job but if it is not harming anyone, and you are not stepping out of line, it is all right. (Tyler)

Herein lay the difficulty: there was a difference between 'good' and 'right' relationships (Liebling, 2011a). 'Right' relationships required a consistency in the rules and regime that neither veered towards undue laxity (which could feel unpredictable and generate insecurity) or an excessive and over-bearing enforcement of the rules at all costs (Liebling, 2011a). Whilst many young men appreciated 'jokes' and 'banter,' and would also drift into slightly juvenile 'messing around' and 'piss taking,' such behaviour by prison officers risked being offensive or distressing. Young men would have no choice but to go along with any joking at their expense by prison officers. James and I observed countless examples of kind, compassionate care by prison officers, but such positive experiences were easily overshadowed by more negative interactions and attitudes.

Prison officer behaviour attracted emotionally charged reactions. Young men were polarised in their descriptions of prison officers, either describing them as 'good' or with expletives and insults ('tossers,' 'proper idiots,' 'cunts,' 'pricks,' 'wankers,' 'horrible bastards' 'job's worths'). Physical assaults on prisoners by officers were neither seen nor reported, but prison officers did not need to physically assault these young men for the experience of imprisonment to be brutalising. The arbitrary, heavy handed and clumsy use of discretionary power created friction and conflict as well as intensifying distress, frustration, and a sense of injustice. It 'drained' (Miller, 2022: 206) young men physical, emotionally, and psychologically. The inherent power balance was keenly felt and frequently reinforced:

> If you're a dickhead to them, they're going to be a dickhead to you and they can do a whole lot worse. They're screws. They've got more powers over you, definitely. They could twist you up,[10] turn all the electrics off, twist you, know what I mean? Give you a nicking, IEPs,[11] put you on basic so you lose your telly, and everything like that, your canteens. I mean, the bare minimum of the things they can do. They've got authority over you. (Martin)

---

[10] Being 'twisted up' referred to the use of control and restraint techniques (C&R) which included the use of painful 'locks' on, for example, thumbs and wrists to gain co-operation.

[11] 'IEP' refers to the Incentive and Earned Privileges (IEP) Scheme. Young men could receive 'IEP' warnings and if too many accrued, could lose freedoms and privileges. Alternatively, they could receive positive reports, which would also be considered in reviews of their IEP status (and whether they should be basic, standard, or enhanced).

Prison officers were inevitably contributing to the 'moral life of the State' (Fassin, 2015). They had the power to affirm or degrade young men. Compared to their descriptions of peer violence, questions regarding prison officer relationships were met with equal (and often more) anger, frustration, distress and helplessness. Peer violence and victimisation had a logic and rationality, but the poor, rude, and antagonistic behaviour of prison officers did not. In fact, many young men struggled to explain or understand why 'grown men' and women would create conflict and render the task of 'doing time' so much harder. Such behaviour was simply 'morally unintelligible' (Auty & Liebling, 2020).

Officers typically demanded respect, which primarily meant immediate compliance to their instructions and polite, courteous behaviour. Young people subscribed to a normative culture that cherished respect as an 'entity' that must be 'constantly guarded' (Anderson, 1999: 33), but prison officers reinforced the necessity of demonstrable respect. Officers typically expected young men to prove that they were worthy of respectful treatment from officers—a premise that was not accepted by young men:

> Between helpful officers brilliant. Between officers who treat you like they are above you and that you are worthless, then it's not good. They need to show you respect. They demand respect but they aren't going to get it. You can't demand respect off someone because they are in prison. … It doesn't work like that. Just because you get a wage slip doesn't mean that you are a much better person than someone else. (Jake)

To them, it was for the prison officers to behave consistently, fairly, and respectfully. Young men wanted to be 'recognised' (Honneth, 1995) and receive 'respect as esteem' (Hulley et al., 2012) simply because they were human beings not because they had proven their worth. They did not accept the moral superiority of officers or consent to their authority over them simply because they were prison officers.

> They're just a human being, got blood running through them the same. You get me? If they give me shit, I give it to them back. If they swing and punch me, I swing back. Don't make a difference. (Ryan)

Conversely, prison officers typically believed that they were worthy of respect and obedience by virtue of their position and irrespective of how they expressed or conducted themselves. That said, the best officers understood that the day would be 'smoother' and they were less likely to be assaulted, if they kept their word, refrained from rude or capricious behaviour, were fair in the use of authority, and adopted a calm, confident and relaxed approach with young men.

Situational Controls

The accepted wisdom amongst prison officers was that high levels of prison violence could only be quelled with the intensification of control, that to prevent violence meant limiting opportunities for violence by restricting young men's freedom. Disproportionate situational controls can, however, 'chafe and vex and arouse frustration and annoyance' (Sparks et al., 1996: 323). The Governing Governor was resistant to the idea that 'screwing everything down' would reduce prison violence. Instead, they sought to introduce a more proportionate approach to physical security, believing that this would communicate a belief that that these young men were capable of acting in non-violent ways and that most desired such. As an example, non-essential gates were removed to allow young men to move more easily to and from the residential units. This move was designed to eradicate the 'self-fulfilling message that violent and destructive behaviour is expected' (Wortley, 2002: 73). This was met with some disquiet and trepidation by prison staff, partly because it was feared that this would only increase the number of violent incidents on 'free flow.' No increase in incidents did occur. Symbolically, the removal of the gates conveyed greater faith and trust that young men would not fight—something they responded to.

This did not mean that an unduly relaxed or laissez-faire approach to security concerns was adopted. The senior management team were simultaneously seeking to address the punitive approach of prison officer whilst also ensuring that there was a resilience regarding procedural and dynamic security—the latter typically defined in relation to *inter alia* observational skill, knowledge of prisoners, and an awareness of interpersonal and prison dynamics. In one instance, a senior manager caught a young man and his female visitor copulating in a visits room, a fact that had been missed by staff. The act was widely reported amongst staff but there were serious lessons. This was an example of lax security, and whilst the Governing Governor would eventually (after 'hitting the fucking roof') come to see the amusing side, that only happened after supervising staff had been warned about lax performance. The senior management team were rightly highly critical of the selective use of security, as one senior manager remarked:

> Staff were keen to tell me that piled bags of rubbish and junk—that could become improvised weapons or a fire hazard—were fine and good, but that prisoners could not be trusted to make their way from a wing to healthcare on camera all the time, because that was a security issue. They seemed to be selective in what a security issue was. I sort of lost count of pointing out that a clean, tidy prison is also about security.

As one of the senior managers explained, 'that we had an escape here once like 10 years ago cannot be used as a reason to continually do the wrong things, or not do the right thing and say 'it's security'.'

Prison officers often attributed the poor 'lines of sight'—a term used to describe the ability of prison officers to scan, observe, and oversee the wing—as a contributory factor to the frequency of prison violence. The architecture undoubtedly made policing the wing a disjointed exercise. Despite the YOIs relatively recent design, it was impossible to stand on the wing and see both spurs in full view at the same time. The problem of poor 'lines of sight' had also been identified in earlier Independent Monitoring Board and HM Inspectorate of Prisons reports, but it was a red herring. Although prison officers at the YOI were ill served by the design, it was doubtful whether this was significantly contributing to the problem of prison violence. The problem was not that they couldn't see the landings, but that they weren't always on the landings. The temptation during lulls in the day was always to drift back to the central staff offices that joined one wing to another (or on the Enhanced Residential Unit, an office that was positioned near to the entrance) where they could sit, chat with colleagues, eat, and make hot drinks (even if cell bells were going unanswered). Consequently, the Supervising Officers and Custodial Managers sought to find the balance between encouraging the prison officers to be more present and proactive whilst also allowing for appropriate respite.

The most easily available situational control was the prison cell. For some prison officers, 'happiness was door shaped.' As one officers suggested: 'if you unlock them, the incidents go up. But if you curtail the regime, and unlock them less, the incidents go down.' This desire to contain the young men was driven by fear and/or the belief that this would deter poor behaviour. Long periods in the cell fostered boredom, resentment, and frustration, especially for these adolescent men who found it difficult to expend their youthful energy. Crucially, it did not stop victimisation since some young men simply threatened or abused others whilst in their cell (also see Chap. 3), and in some cases, caused greater violence because young men were so frustrated. To reduce prison violence, the time out of cell and spent in well supervised and meaningful activity had to increase, not decrease. This was more than an administrative act. Facilitating opportunities to engage in, to grow, and to learn communicated that they were not prisoners to be contained but young men with potential.

Law*full*ness and Law*less*ness: Putting 'the Law Back into the Place'

Immediately after the 'full staff briefing,'[12] an officer approached me to explain why he did not 'nick' or 'confront' young people about their behaviour anymore. On the first point, he complained that the Adjudicating Governors did not find young men guilty of the charges that were accused of or, if they did, only gave a suspended sentence and did not move young men to other wings or prisons afterwards. To the second point, the officer explained that other officers did not confront

[12] The 'full staff briefing' is a meeting of all prison staff (including health and education colleagues), typically involving an address from the Governor and/or presentations. At the YOI, the full staff briefings were held in the chapel.

prisoners for fear of retaliation or disciplinary investigation, particularly in relation to the use of physical restraint. This was surprising since the Governor had taken a very firm view that they could not 'sack your way out of a problem.' When probed, the officer said that prison staff feared being investigated and dismissed because a particular Governing Governor had been zealous in disciplining staff when they restrained young men. Surprisingly, that Governing Governor's tenure had ended several years earlier and there had been two successors since. The officer had not even worked in the YOI at the time, but a Governor's actions many years before had become part of the organisational memory. Other such stories loomed large in the minds of prison officers and were seen to provide further proof as to why the young men were dangerous and untrustworthy. For example, earlier prison riots and the notable attempt of a young man to escape through the window in the Governing Governor's office had all formed part of narrative that perversely justified the under use of power to enforce appropriate boundaries, but did not actually prevent the overuse of physical restraint, segregation, or—as the officer conceded—other informal punishments (including locking young men in their cells for long periods of time without the governance and oversight associated with segregation use). It had fuelled both laxity and punitiveness.

It is difficult to pinpoint the exact moment a prison becomes disordered and approaches lawlessness, but it is palpable and tangible. As the young men themselves described and as I observed, signs were found in seemingly innocuous details such as 'loud music constantly, shouting out the doors, shouting out the windows' as well as scattered clothes, piles of litter, and unclean cells and landings. Prisons officers were prone to retreat to their offices. When James and I first arrived at the YOI, prison officers were fatalistic and complacent about their ability to prevent violence and victimisation concluding, 'you'll always get bullying,' 'you get bullying wherever you go' and 'it's prison!' However, prison officers were both staging violence and tolerating victimisation between prisoners. One Custodial Manager described a situation where the YOI needed to 'ship out'[13] an individual. Two young men were told by prison officers to fight

[13] Prison slang for transferring prisoners between prisons.

to determine who would be the one to leave. The individual who won the fight was told that he was being shipped out and refused to do so on the grounds that he had won the fight and should be allowed to stay, as per the rules set out by the prison officers. The officers then nicked the person refusing to go on the grounds that he was refusing a direct order. The young man's defence was: 'I won the fight, I shouldn't be the one to go.' Not only were there 'no consequences for unlawful behaviour,' and officers were routinely ignoring the 'black eyes and blooded noses,' but they were actively encouraging fights and assaults. As John Locke once said, 'When law ends, tyranny begins.'

To address the high rates of prison violence and victimisation, the Governing Governor had to 'put the law back into the place.' At the time, it would have been easier to conflate 'lawfulness' with an overtly punitive and authoritarian approach. Indeed, the Prisons Minister of the day had declared that the 'full weight of the law will come down upon them [prisoners] if they dare assault a prison officer or another prisoner.' However, the leadership team believed that the overzealous use of harsh punishments was futile and ineffective. Even if swift and predictable—which is often considered more effective (Apel & Nagin, 2011; Ashworth, 2019; von Hirsch et al., 1999)—excessive punishments would only further disenfranchise the young men. Whilst the senior leadership team were keen to ensure that there were penalties for serious assaults, the view was simply that 'you can't punish your way out of violence.' These core beliefs were partly based on the prevailing evidence that increasing sentence severity would not deter criminal behaviour (ibid.), and that these young men were still impulsive, maturing, and developing their consequential thinking. Thus, the emphasis was on recognising and rewarding positive behaviour. This is not to say that they were not prepared to hold young men to account for their behaviour. The senior leadership team sought to instil a culture where violence and victimisation was noticed and reported, where action was taken to support and protect victims, and where there were consequences for misconduct, but where those consequences were also coupled with efforts to recognise human potential, promote desistance and create second chances.

Creating a lawful prison also rested on the 'sweet spot' between neither under-enforcing the rules nor overusing power. More skilful prison officers garnered trust, respect, and social capital from young men through the 'selective non-enforcement' of rules (Haggerty & Bucerius, 2021: 1; Liebling, 2011a: 131), but this only created moral and social order when it represented a proportionate response to wrongdoing (rather than wilful neglect or corruption). These young men wanted a 'secure and legally ordered environment' (Calavita & Jenness, 2015: 94) and wanted prison officers to keep them safe. One of the reasons why some chose to fight or assault someone in highly visible locations was because they were relying on prison officers to intervene and prevent them succumbing to very serious injury. Young men generally wanted the structural and physical security provided by the appropriate, judicious and competent use of power and authority by prison officers. Young men wanted to know where the boundaries were, even if they would 'bounce' up against them regularly and were largely resistant to authority. They did not want to be 'walking on eggshells' (also see Crewe, 2011). Although the use of power by the State can often be regarded by scholars as capricious, arbitrary, and excessive, the under-use of power was just as dangerous (Crewe & Liebling, 2017; Gooch & Treadwell, 2023).

State Sanctioned Violence and Notions of Justice

'Explain to me the policy, how officers can put their hands on me.' Desperation and frustration in his voice, Kyle was sat in front of the Adjudicating Governor imploring him to explain what he should have done differently in the circumstances. He was charged with an offence of threatening to kill an officer during a C&R ('control and restraint') incident, and another of leaning into an officer's arm, which was interpreted as being 'threatening and abusive.'[14] Kyle's account was that he had gone to the cell three doors down to borrow tissues. He craned his head around the cell door, but an officer put his arm up to block his path. Kyle said he then leant on the officer's arm so he could still see into the cell and was 'C&R'ed. (restrained). At that point, he was angry and could not recall

[14] Contrary to Young Offender Institution Rules 2000 s55(22)

threatening the officer but did recall that he had 'said to take your hands off me.' Although he had quickly apologised for threatening the officer, one of the officers was injured in the restraint, needing medical attention for two 'cracked' ribs. Later that same day, Kyle went to the staff office and pushed the door open. The prison officer had then said, 'Don't push my door.' Kyle's account—which wasn't disputed—was that the officer then stood an inch away from this face. Kyle took a step back, but the officers then 'jumped' on him (restraining him again).

Kyle is now pleading with the Adjudicating Governor: 'I don't understand. If officers are trying to twist me up[15] and I say I don't want to and put my hands up, and they are still running at me, what can I do to take myself out of the situation?' He continued, 'I apologised to the officer—what was the point of the nicking?' As the hearing continues, the Adjudicating Governor hears the conduct report which reveals that he had 15 previous adjudications. Kyle grumbled, 'it doesn't mention anything about stopping fights, positive IEPs, or cleaning graffiti, it just mentions the bad things.' Little is said about Kyle threats to kill himself, or that he had tied a sheet around his neck and when that was removed, had been banging his observation glass. Having pleaded guilty to the charges, Kyle was given 5 days losses of the gym. As he stands to leave the adjudication room, with his questions about the use of coercive force or how to avoid conflict with prison officers unanswered, he simply says, 'How can I ever win?'

The State holds the monopoly on the legitimate use of violence (Weber, 1947). The inescapable truth was that young men's lives within the prison were structured by coercive force (also see Scraton et al., 1991: 61); violence and control were written into the fabric and nature of the prison. May (1999: 134) goes so far as to say that prisons *teach* violence, that 'prisons teach *control* as a means of achieving ends. The control is most often achieved through aggression, power, strength and intimidation.' Physical restraint is often perceived by prison staff to be causally related to prisoner behaviour—the argument being that such measures would not be needed if prisoners were not 'recalcitrant,' aggressive, or violent. However, this underestimates the extent to which force is used simply to

[15] Being 'twisted up' was prison slang for being physically restrained.

secure 'compliance' with prison officer's orders—requests that may range in seriousness from being asked to return to their cell to a direct order to end a protest or riot.[16] Within the YOI, the Inspectorate had criticised the frequent sustained use of physical restraint and the under-use of 'de-escalation techniques.'

Young men's experiences of, and attitudes towards, prison violence could not be divorced from their experiences of physical restraint. The use of physical restraint was divisive and emotive. It was never a benign or neutral act, and few regarded the use of force as necessary even if the prison officer might be able to legally justify the act. Physical restraint—often dubbed as being 'twisted up'—reinforced the imbalance of power:

> There's all screws like that in here that try and take the piss out of you. When [the officers] twist up somebody, and they just twist them up and put them in, like, one position, the screws[17] start kneeing you, and everything. They're kneeing me and they pushed my arm, like, all the way back, and I'm going, 'You're going to break my arm.'

> Honestly, my pad mate got twisted up because he was waiting for a phone call and they go to him, 'Oh, your basics are over. You can't have a phone call, so you have to get banged up.' Obviously, he goes, like, 'I want to wait a minute and a half for the phone,' so he could make a phone call. The bosses twisted him up. They come to the pad, and put him in the pad. They twisted me up, as well. Like, I was at the door. They go to me, 'Come out.' I wasn't coming out of the pad, so they twisted me up, you get me, and when they twisted me up, they dragged me from here all the way to block.[18] Like that [demonstrating restraint positions] but bending your wrists and fucking you up. It hurts, like, you know, man. (Hussain)

The deliberate infliction of pain was violent, but it was also demeaning. When it occurred against the context of uneven treatment, the punitive use of sanctions, and authoritarian styles of prison officer work, it amplified perceptions of injustice and indignity. Prison officers could quickly lose the 'moral high ground,' especially when physical restraint was used

[16] A direct order is needed before prisoners can be charged with prison mutiny.

[17] 'Screws' was used to refer to prison officers.

[18] The term 'block' was used to refer to the Care and Supervision Unit (segregation unit).

simply to compel compliance. It also undermined any suggestion by prison staff that violence did not have utility in controlling others.

The segregation of young men in the 16 bed 'block'—or the 'care and separation unit' as it was euphemistically called—could occur in three situations. First, to segregate young men for their own interests.[19] However, this sanctuary seeking behaviour (Toch, 1977) also represented a lack of confidence in prison officers to keep them safe. The need for such segregation dissipated over time, particularly as staff-prisoner relationships improved and the 'Supported Living Unit'[20] became available. Second, young men could also be held in segregation for the 'good order and discipline of the prison,' including in the aftermath of an assault, whilst pending an adjudication, after a hostage incident or following disorder. Not all fights or assaults against other young men would lead to an individual being moved to segregation, but this was almost certainly the case if a young man assaulted a member of staff. Third, young men could be required by the Adjudicating Governor to spend 7 days in segregation[21] in 'cellular confinement' as a penalty for rule violations. The use of segregation does not, however, reduce the likelihood of further serious violence (Meyers et al., 2023), and the isolation can exacerbate psychological distress and mental ill-health (Brown, 2020; Haney, 2003, 2017, 2018; Miller & Young, 1997). Segregation may have an incapacitation effect, but violent incidents also occurred in the segregation unit. At best, segregation could create an opportunity to prevent more serious imminent harm or 'put a hold on' until a longer-term plan could be established. It was common to find, though, that young men who had repeated periods of segregation were somewhat willing to 'ride it out' rather than recognise the attempt to curb their violence behaviour. In some cases, time spent in segregation cemented an individual's reputation and carceral capital.

The segregation unit of any prison is a 'barometer' for the rest of the prison. Much can be revealed about the state of the wider prison by the segregation unit. Who is there. Why they are there. How long they are

[19] Young Offender Institution Rules 2000, Rule 49(1)

[20] A unit for those who were especially distressed, unwell, or being victimised.

[21] Young Offender Institution Rules 2000 section 60 (as amended)

there. How clean the unit. How responsive the staff. Whether prison officers can see humanity in those whose actions they may find abhorrent. Whether prison officers exact their own punishment. All these things bring into sharp relief the culture, morality, relational quality and penal philosophy of the prison. During the first inspection, and much like the rest of the YOI, conditions within the segregation unit were poor and young men could only shower or make telephone calls sporadically. Senior leaders appeared to have opted out of the governance role, neither opting to review nor opting to track segregation use. Reflective of the punitive bias, segregation was overused. In a six-month period, over 400 young men had been held in segregation, almost the entirety of the YOI. Worse still, young men who were believed to be at risk of self-harm and suicide were being held in the segregation unit for reasons that were not justified.

To reduce prison violence, the incoming Governing Governor had to re-set how segregation was used, for what purpose and with what governance. There were three noticeable changes in policy. First, cellular confinement was removed as a penalty for rule violations, as another reminder to staff that you could not 'punish your way out of violence.' Second, the two 'special accommodation' cells were taken out of use. These cells have no furniture or facilities, bar a plug in the floor. They are 'an extreme and isolating form of custody' (Prison and Probation Ombudsman, 2015). Third, those who were on an ACCT document,[22] and were therefore thought to be at risk of self-harm and suicide, would not be held in segregation. Any attempts to do so had to be discussed with the Governing Governor (or Deputy Governor in their absence). This decision was based on the evidence that holding a suicidal individual in a segregation cell could greatly increase the risk of suicide (Bonner, 2006; Brown, 2020; Kaba et al., 2014; Prison and Probation Ombudsman, 2015). In addition, the very clear message was that segregation should be a 'last resort' and only used for the shortest time.

These changes were not welcomed by all prison staff. Like the use of adjudications, some prison officers interpreted segregation decisions as an

[22] Assessment, Care in Custody and Teamwork document is opened when there are concerns that a prisoner may self-harm and attempt suicide.

indicator of management support. This was not simply about length of stay but whether perpetrators (particularly perpetrators of staff assaults) were returned to the unit or not. Prison officers were vehement in the belief that perpetrators should be moved to another unit or transferred out of the establishment altogether. Even if this was posited in terms of the best interests of the prisoner, it was premised by fear, anxiety, and a belief that just punishment required such action.

> I get assaulted by a prisoner. He goes to the segregation unit, and within two hours, he's back on the same landing as me, and I've got to act in a professional manner with him. That can go the opposite. The next time he comes anywhere near me, my guard's going to be up because I think I'm going to get assaulted again.

In these instances, prison officers keenly felt the power imbalance between them and senior managers, but crucially, between them and prisoners—seeing prisoners as gaining more 'rights' than they were. Herein lies one of the challenges with prison reform: instilling moral practices requires an approach that recognises the rights, worth, and interests of prisoners, but this can be a zero-sum game for prison officers who feel neglected, unsupported, or forgotten. In this case, the impulse to redress the use of segregation was not misplaced, but 'taking staff with you' was a precarious act and by no means straightforward.

Conclusions

It is axiomatic to conclude that it is the interaction between the individual and the environment that best explains the causes of prison violence. As Toch argues (Toch, 1997: 1), 'We love to preach and teach it, but we often ignore it in practice.' Equally there has very little research on what to *do* to reduce and prevent prison violence (Wooldredge, 2020), or indeed where to start when faced with a chaotic, violent, and inhumane prison. It is instructive that the reduction in violence within the YOI was achieved without any changes to the importation factors—the YOI continued to receive young men with the same backgrounds, legal status, and criminal convictions as before. It was their environment that changed, and in time, the extent to which they were violent towards others or themselves.

The logic of prison violence stems not only from individual experience (Chaps. 6 and 7), social norms between peers (Chap. 8), but also the environmental context—specifically, how power is used, how coercive force is used, how prison policy is interpreted and created, when formal punishment is used, prison conditions, the underpinning values, and the extent to which the prison succeeds in creating a sense of 'justice' and 'lawfulness.' Fundamental notions of humanity, fairness, respect, and recognition were collapsed into a wider concept of 'justice,' and the extent to which prisoners felt that they were treated with justice made the difference between what was viewed as a 'survivable' or 'catastrophic prison' (Liebling, 2015). These young men were 'powerfully alert to matters of justice and moral treatment' (Liebling, 2013: 206) and were making and revising their 'moral evaluations' (Fernandez, 2015) on an ongoing basis. The quality of their treatment structured their perceptions of the legitimacy of the State's power to punish. It was a matter of principle. They believed that the State should not prove itself hypocritical in demanding responsible and pro-social behaviour from them whilst disregarding their humanity, discarding their worth, abusing their power, and failing to uphold their rights.

The demand for moral treatment was common to all young men, irrespective of their own behaviour (also see Liebling, 2013: 206). Crucially, it illustrates the importance of social recognition and respect in the prevention of prison violence. When social recognition is withheld by the State—either through the 'slow violence' of poor conditions, the failure to meet basic needs, the 'othering' of young men and assumption that they are 'undeserving,' overly restrictive situational control, the humiliation of physical restraint, and the denial of opportunities to improve and realise their potential—it not only strengthens the value of carceral capital (described in Chap. 8), intensifies the appeal of the illicit economy, can cause conflict with staff, but threatens the State's rehabilitative goals. Young men could not align themselves with the State's rehabilitative demands when the State's own moral performance was in doubt. In this

YOI, had the senior management team not instituted moral reform, frequent violence, extortion, and exploitation would have continued.

It is impossible to neatly extrapolate and isolate the impact of specific decisions or actions, or say which changes had the greatest impact on the propensity and texture of prison violence. Indeed, it is the cumulative effect of the changes made, and the principles and values that underpinned them, that contributed to improvements in social order and prisoner wellbeing. It illustrates why the importation-deprivation model has reached something of a 'stalemate' (Crewe, 2009; Wooldredge, 2020). Having concluded that the interaction between the individual and institution is most important, the 'inextricable link' has proved 'hard to study' (Toch, 1997: 1), primarily because there has been an overestimation of the power of quantitative research to extrapolate correlations, and a dearth of ethnographic and qualitative research. Equally, this chapter illustrates that what 'matters' is a wider set of factors than those captured by the deprivation model alone (Sykes, 1958), including culture, leadership, values, forms of power, styles of prison officer governance—i.e. it is not just about what is taken away, but what is created, instilled, and practised.

References

Anderson, E. (1999). *Code of the street: Decency, violence and the moral life of the inner city*. W.W. Norton and Company.

Apel, R., & Nagin, D. S. (2011). General deterrence: A review of recent evidence. *Crime and Public Policy, 4*, 411–436.

Ashforth, B. E., & Kreiner, G. E. (1999). "How can you do it?": Dirty work and the challenge of constructing a positive identity. *The Academy of Management Review, 24*(3), 413–434.

Ashworth, A. (2019). The common sense and complications of general deterrent sentencing. *Criminal Law Review, 7*, 564–578.

Auty, K. M., & Liebling, A. (2020). Exploring the relationship between prison social climate and reoffending*. *Justice Quarterly, 37*(2), 358–381.

Bakkali, Y. (2019). Dying to live: Youth violence and the munpain. *The Sociological Review, 67*(6), 1317–1332.

Beijersbergen, K. A., Dirkzwager, A. J. E., Eichelsheim, V. I., Van der Laan, P. H., & Nieuwbeerta, P. (2015). Procedural justice, anger, and prisoners' misconduct: A longitudinal study. *Criminal Justice and Behavior, 42*(2), 196–218.

Bennett, J. (2016). *The working lives of prison managers*. Palgrave Macmillan.

Bierie, D. M. (2013). Procedural justice and prison violence: Examining complaints among federal inmates (2000–2007). *Psychology, Public Policy & Law, 19*(1), 15–29.

Boin, A., & Rattray, W. A. R. (2004). Understanding prison riots: Towards a threshold theory. *Punishment & Society, 6*(1), 47–65.

Bonner, R. L. (2006). Stressful segregation housing and psychosocial vulnerability in prison suicide ideators. *Suicide and Life-threatening Behavior, 36*(2), 250–254.

Brennan, I. R. (2019). Weapon-carrying and the reduction of violent harm. *British Journal of Criminology, 59*(3), 571–593.

Brown, E. (2020). A systematic review of the effects of prison segregation. *Aggression and Violent Behavior, 52*, 101389.

Brunton-Smith, I., & McCarthy, D. J. (2016). Prison legitimacy and procedural fairness: A multilevel examination of prisoners in England and Wales. *Justice Quarterly, 33*(6), 1029–1054.

Billingham, L., & Irwin-Rogers, K. (2022). *Against youth violence: A social harm perspective*. Bristol University Press.

Calavita, K., & Jenness, V. (2015). *Appealing to justice: Prisoner grievances, rights and carceral logic*. University of California Press.

Cohen, S. (2001). *States of denial: Knowing about atrocities and suffering*. Polity Press.

Crewe, B. (2009). *Prisoner society: Power, adaptation and social life in an English prison*. Oxford University Press.

Crewe, B. (2011). Depth, weight, tightness: Revisiting the pains of imprisonment. *Punishment & Society, 13*(5), 509–529.

Crewe, B. (2021). The depth of imprisonment. *Punishment & Society, 23*(3), 335–354.

Crewe, B., & Liebling, A. (2017). Reconfiguring penal power. In A. Liebling, S. Maruna, & L. Mcara (Eds.), *Oxford handbook of criminology* (pp. 889–913). Oxford University Press.

Doolin, K., & Gooch, K. (2022). Preventing staff assaults. *Prison Service Journal, 260*, 14–21.

Douglas. (1966). *Purity and danger: An analysis of concept of pollution and taboo.* Routledge.

Downes, D. (1988). *Contrasts in tolerance.* Oxford University Press.

Fassin, D. (2015). *At the heart of the state: The moral world of institutions.* Pluto Press.

Fernandez, F. (2015). Sanctioning behind bars: The humanization of retribution in prisons. In D. Fassin (Ed.), *At the heart of the state: The moral world of institutions* (pp. 117–143). Pluto Press.

Fitzalan Howard, F., & Wakeling, H. (2019). *Prisoner and staff perceptions of procedural justice in English and welsh prisons.* HM Prison and Probation Service.

Gilligan, J. (1996). *Violence: Reflections on our deadliest epidemic.* G.P. Putnam's Sons.

Gooch, K., & Treadwell, J. (2023). The 'screw boys' and the 'businessmen': Re-negotiating penal power, governance and legitimate authority through a prison violence reduction scheme. *The British Journal of Criminology, 63*(4), 1219–1236.

Haggerty, K. D., & Bucerius, S. M. (2021). Picking battles: Correctional officers, rules, and discretion in prison. *Criminology, 59*(1), 137–157.

Haney, C. (2003). Mental health issues in long-term solitary and "supermax" confinement. *Crime & Delinquency, 49*(1), 124–156.

Haney, C. (2017). "Madness" and penal confinement: Some observations on mental illness and prison pain. *Punishment & Society, 19*(3), 310–326.

Haney, C. (2018). The psychological effects of solitary confinement: A systematic critique. *Crime and Justice, 47*, 365–416.

Honneth, A. (1995). *The struggle for recognition: The moral grammar of social conflicts.* Polity Press.

Howard, F., & Wakeling, H. (2020). *Evaluating rehabilitative adjudications in four English prisons.* Her Majesty's Prison and Probation Service.

Hughes, E. C. (1958). *Men and their work.* Free Press.

Hulley, S., Liebling, A., & Crewe, B. (2012). Respect in prisons: Prisoners' experiences of respect in public and private sector prisons. *Criminology & Criminal Justice, 12*(1), 3–23.

Kaba, F., Lewis, A., Glowa-Kollisch, S., Hadler, J., Lee, D., Alper, H., Selling, D., Macdonald, R., Solimo, A., Parsons, A., & Venters, H. (2014). Solitary confinement and risk of self-harm among jail inmates. *American Journal of Public Health, 104*(3), 442–447.

King, R. D., & McDermott, K. (1995). *The state of our prisons.* Oxford University Press.

Liebling, A. (1992). *Suicides in prison*. Routledge.
Liebling, A. (2004). *Prisons and their moral performance*. Oxford University Press.
Liebling, A. (2011a). Distinctions and distinctiveness in the work of prison officers: Legitimacy and authority revisited. *European Journal of Criminology, 8*(6), 484–499.
Liebling, A. (2011b). Moral performance, inhuman and degrading treatment and prison pain. *Punishment & Society, 13*(5), 530–550.
Liebling, A. (2013). Legitimacy under pressure. In J. Tankebe & A. Liebling (Eds.), *Legitimacy and criminal justice: An international exploration* (pp. 206–226). Oxford University Press.
Liebling, A. (2015). Appreciative Inquiry, generative theory, and the failed state prison. In A. Miller & W. R. Palacious (Eds.), *Qualitative research in criminology* (pp. 251–269). Routledge.
Liebling, A., & Arnold, H. (2012). Social relationships between prisoners in a maximum security prison: Violence, faith, and the declining nature of trust. *Journal of Criminal Justice, 40*(5), 413–424.
Liebling, A., Price, D., & Shefer, G. (2011). *The prison officer*. Willan.
May, R. (1998). *Power and innocence*. W.W. Norton and Company.
May, J. P. (1999). Feeding a public health epidemic. In J. P. May & K. R. Pitts (Eds.), *Building violence: How America's rush to incarcerate creates more violence* (pp. 132–137). Sage.
Meyers, T. J., Testa, A., & Wright, K. A. (2023). Managing violence: In-prison behavior associated with placement in an alternative disciplinary segregation program. *American Journal of Criminal Justice, 48*(1), 250–272.
Miller, R. J. (2022). *Halfway home: Race, punishment and the afterlife of mass incarceration*. Little, Brown and Company.
Miller, H. A., & Young, G. R. (1997). Prison segregation: Administrative detention remedy or mental health problem? *Criminal Behaviour and Mental Health, 7*(1), 85–94.
Murray, C. (2023). *Young men, masculinities and imprisonment: An ethnographic study in Northern Ireland*. Palgrave.
Nixon, R. (2013). *Slow violence and the environmentalism of the poor*. Harvard University Press.
O'Donnell, I. (2023). *Prison life: Pain, resistance and purpose*. New York University Press.
Prison and Probation Ombudsman. (2015). *Segregation: Learning lessons bulletin*. Prison and Probation Ombudsman.

Reisig, M. D., & Mesko, G. (2009). Procedural justice, legitimacy, and prisoner misconduct. *Psychology, Crime & Law, 15*(1), 41–59.
Scraton, P., Sim, J., & Skidmore, P. (1991). *Prisons under protest.* Open University Press.
Sparks, R., Bottoms, A. E., & Hay, W. (1996). *Prisons and the problem of order.* Oxford University Press.
Sykes, G. (1958). *The society of captives*. Princeton University Press.
Tait, S. (2008). Care and the prison officer: Beyond "Turnkeys" and "care bears". *Prison Service Journal, 180*, 3–11.
Toch, H. (1977). *Living in prison: The ecology of survival.* The Free Press.
Toch, H. (1997). *Corrections: A humanistic approach*. Harrow and Heston.
Tyler, T. R. (2006). *Why people obey the law*. Princeton University Press.
Useem, B., & Kimball, P. A. (1991). *States of siege: U.S. prison riots 1971–1986.* Oxford University Press.
von Hirsch, A., Bottoms, A. E., Burney, E., & Wikstrom, P.-O. (1999). *Criminal deterrence and sentence severity: An analysis of recent research.* University of Cambridge.
Weber, M. (1947). *The theory of social and economic organization.* Oxford University Press.
Wooldredge, J. (2020). Prison culture, management, and in-prison violence. *Annual Review of Criminology, 3*(1), 165–188.
Woolf, L. J. (1991). *Prison disturbances April 1990.* Her Majesty's Stationery Office.
Wortley, R. (2002). *Situational prison control: Crime prevention in correctional institutions.* Cambridge University Press.

10

Conclusion

The Chief Inspector swept into the chapel and took his position in the centre of a long table flanked on either side by key members of the inspection team. The leadership team and regional manager were already assembled, eagerly awaiting the results. As the Chief Inspector read the draft summary of the report, the improvements in the 'healthy prison test' quickly registered on the faces of the prison leadership team. Nervous anticipation turned to joyful relief as they listened to the comments and calculated the scores one by one. Safety was no longer rated as 'poor' (a score of 1 out of 4) but was now 'reasonably good' (a score of 3 out of 4). In recognition of the improvements in prison conditions and the relationships between staff and young men, the assessment of 'respect' had improved from 'poor' (a score of 1) to 'good' (a score of 4 out of 4). At the time, only three other prisons in the country had achieved a '4' for respect. Improvements in the other aspects of the healthy prison test were more moderate, with purposeful activity and resettlement improving from 'poor' to 'not sufficiently good' (a score of 2 out of 4). This latter had been expected: the Governing Governor's strategy prioritised creating a safe, decent, and respectful environment first, sequencing the planned changes so that the necessary reforms to offender management

K. Gooch, *Prison Violence*, Palgrave Studies in Prisons and Penology,
https://doi.org/10.1007/978-3-031-91365-5_10

and resettlement would come later—a strategy that the Inspectorate accepted. The YOI had, according to the Inspectorate, been 'transformed.' No longer was the YOI failing the healthy prison test.

Much had been achieved in 15 months, but improving the YOI was a long-term project. As the Chief Inspector noted, some changes were recent and would take time to fully embed. His encouragement that 'you are close to being the best of in the [Prison] Service' was accompanied with the 'don't go back to normal if normal is what it was 15 months ago.' Although the improvements were underpinned by a host of economic, policy, strategic, and political decisions, at its heart had been an effort to instil morality in a place where hopelessness, inhumanity, and injustice were so common as to be taken for granted. Creating and sustaining moral practices was not a single event but would require constant and continual effort (Gibbons & deBelleville Katzenbach, 2006: 67). The changes in practice were fragile, and it would have been just as easy to slip backwards as it would be to continue moving forwards. As a staunch reminder—if one was needed—on the morning of the inspection feedback, one young man stabbed someone who had kidnapped his sister and another young man climbed on the gate in healthcare, refused to come down, and was restrained and taken to the segregation unit. Governing and leading the YOI would remain a complex and difficult task—these young men were still maturing, enduring countless tragedies, hurting, grieving, testing boundaries, and learning to be 'men' in extreme circumstances. They needed care, compassion, just treatment, clear and consistent boundaries, support to desist from harm, recognition, and the encouragement and opportunities to realise their potential. They needed to 'matter' (Billingham & Irwin-Rogers, 2022; Honneth, 1995), their lives needed to matter, and their futures needed to matter.

As the inspection team left the chapel, tears were already falling down the faces of the senior managers. Ties were ceremoniously pulled off as the team began to embrace and congratulate one another. Senior leaders within HM Prison and Probation Service would send their congratulations to the Governing Governor as news reached them of the Inspectorate's conclusions. The inspection feedback was quickly followed by a full staff briefing where the Governing Governor and Regional Manager were able to relay the good news and offer their thanks and congratulations to all staff. Quite unusually, prison officers no longer stood together at the back of the chapel but moved into the seated positions to listen closely to the feedback, evidencing their commitment to the reformation of the YOI. The Governing Governor acknowledged that it was 'a team effort' and spoke of their pride in what had been achieved. The room erupted in a round of applause. Later, a prison officer who had been on patrol duty on the landings (and was unable to attend the briefing) stopped James and I to ask what the 'scores' were as he didn't dare believe that what he had heard was true. This positive inspection had, in part, validated the team's efforts of the previous 15 months and relieved them of the label 'worst prison in the country' that so many had grieved. Victimisation continued, but less frequently and with less serious injury. The difference between inspection visits was that the leadership team had a better grasp of what was happening and why, and victimisation was no longer tolerated and ignored by prison staff.

This study sought to understand the anatomy, causes, dynamics, culture, and prevention of prison violence in the YOI with the highest number of assaults. Whilst there was a practical imperative to the research—namely, enabling the senior leadership team to make a series of evidence-based decisions in preparation for re-inspection—the dearth of research on young adult prisoners and contemporary youth prison violence created a pressing need for this research. It was also undertaken at a time when the theoretical debate regarding the causes of prison violence had grown stale (Crewe, 2009; Wooldredge, 2020), when prevention research was under-developed (Maruna, 2023), and when rates of prison violence across the English and Welsh system were continually increasing (Ministry of Justice, 2025). In adopting an ethnographic and qualitative sensibility, it was possible to move beyond the limitations of testing predetermined variables and superficial explanations for the increase in prison violence, and account for the multifaceted changes that were reshaping prison life and the structure and meaning of prison victimisation. This concluding chapter summarises the overarching findings and considers their implications for policy, practice, and future research.

The Problem of Prison Violence and Victimisation

The problem of prison violence is, and has always been, prescient. This study has shown that the 'dark figure' of prison victimisation is far darker than official statistical data suggests. This is not simply because not all victimisation is reported or recorded, but because the threat and actuality of victimisation goes far beyond fights and assaults. Whilst the finding that victimisation is multifaceted is not new (Bowker, 1980; Edgar et al., 2003b), it is often overlooked in research that concentrates primarily on physical and/or sexual violence. Chapter 3 illustrates that physical and sexual violence is both underpinned and intimately connected to a much wider range of behaviours, including: verbal abuse, threats, exploitation, extortion, robbery, theft, and social exclusion. The assault or fight can be the 'tip of the iceberg,' and the conclusion of interactions and conflicts that have manifested over days and weeks. There was a considerable 'intelligence gap' within the YOI, with intelligent reports rarely capturing the true reason for physical violence, if it captured a reason at all, illustrating something of the dangers of relying on administrative records to analyse prison violence. This finding reinforces the need to understand the problem of prison violence from the perspective of victims and perpetrators, and in its situational context.

The Prison/Young Offender Institution Rules do not explicitly prohibit robbery or theft, and it was typical for prison officers only to challenge verbal abuse when it was directed at them. Whilst prison adjudications are ripe for reform, the unwillingness, and sometimes fatalistic attitudes, of prison officers to address all forms of prison victimisation either through adjudications or through more informal means (e.g. a conversation) led to its proliferation. Young prisoners not only took their cues from the prison environment (Wortley, 2002), but also from prison officer behaviour. Some young men exploited lapses in supervision and concluded that they can hurt, rob, or exploit others with impunity (Edgar & O'Donnell, 1998; Sparks, 1982). The extent to which prison officers leant on formal punishments, created their own informal punishments, or overlooked misbehaviour was relatively complex and tied to perceptions of management support, fear, prior victimisation, and a belief in the utility of punitive sanctions or control to deter and manage violence. Strengthening the lawfulness of a YOI required a complicated blend of what has been described as 'security' and 'harmony' values (Braithwaite, 1998b; Crewe & Liebling, 2011), i.e. a delicate combination of the rule of law, appropriate consequences for wrongdoing, and the use of authority on one hand, and a belief in the possibility of change and recognition of dignity on the other. It required the 'right' (Liebling et al., 2011b) use of power and authority, neither overzealous and punitive nor laissez-faire and lax.

This study found that the Ministerial explanations for the increase in prison violence—namely that it was young, gang-associated and drug-using men who were responsible (Ministry of Justice, 2016)—were faulty and based on an inaccurate reading of the Ministry of Justice's own data, misunderstanding about the relationship between drug use and violence, and an erroneous importation of the U.S. based and inconsistent evidence about gang association. Whilst there were several young men who were associated with urban street groups or at the peripheries of more organised entrepreneurial crime, there was little imported group conflict, and the young men did not recruit or continue group activities in the YOI. Social groups did form, often based on shared characteristics or geographies. Group assaults were common, but it was not 'gang' behaviour. This finding illustrates the hazards of importing US centric research and the need to understand violence within its geographical context and according to age and gender.

Dangerous Young Men?

Young adult prisoners are often described by policy makers and practitioners as 'risky,' 'volatile,' and 'dangerous.' This is a convenient narrative when trying to find politically palatable explanations for a deterioration in prison safety. It is a dangerous narrative. It does little to either support desistance, prevent violence, address the intense vulnerability of some young men, prompt greater and better provision, or recognise that young men are still maturing and are capable of far more than criminality. It promotes fear amongst prison officers. The tendency to focus on troublesome youth is reminiscent of wider debates on youth violence (Billingham & Irwin-Rogers, 2022) and overlooks the far greater contribution of adult prisoners (Ministry of Justice, 2025, also see Chap. 1) and the systematic deterioration in prison conditions and culture from the 2010s onwards.

None of the young men were violent all the time (Collins, 2008; Edgar et al., 2003a). Some of the most violent young men would desist when family dynamics changed (e.g. they became a father or a relative was unwell), or when prison officers encouraged them, extended trust 'intelligently' (Liebling et al., 2011a) and communicated a belief that they could be something more than violent young men. There were far more young men who would have preferred to avoid violence and whose involvement was episodic. Violence was not easy, and most were not competent fighters nor were they particularly keen to endanger themselves (Collins, 2008). That said, they still concluded that the primary strategy for long-term self-defence and preservation was to decisively rebuff any threats, verbal abuse or attempts to steal their property. Far from supporting desistance, economic precarity within the YOI, fierce competition, uneven treatment, the 'slow violence' (Nixon, 2013) of very poor conditions, and the indifferent and punitive attitudes of prison officers intensified the desire for control, power, and the use of violence to bolster social standing. If the aim was to protect the public, imprisonment was not only failing to support desistance, but it was actively creating the conditions where some who were ordinarily disinclined to use violence felt compelled to adopt strategies of violence to protect themselves. As Toch (1977: 178) argues, 'it is one thing for prisons to fail to regenerate wolves. It is another thing for prisons to make beasts of lambs.'

These findings have implications for the management and prevention of prison violence, and for the canon of importation studies on prison violence. First, you cannot reduce high levels of prison violence by solely focusing on 'violence prone' (Toch, 1978) prisoners. If a YOI or prison remains lawless, absent of moral order, inhumane, impoverished, and lacking in the competent, confident, and careful or 'right' use of power and authority (at all levels), those who accept the utility of violence are more likely not only to engage in victimisation but also 'create and mobilise' narratives (Williams & Liebling, 2023) that justify and legitimise their (violent) actions. The starting point for violence prevention is the context, not the individual. This finding does not mean that appropriate, dynamic risk assessment is not needed—indeed this can be a crucial part of violence prevention, as seen in the murder of Zahid Mubarek at HMYOI Feltham (Her Majesty's Inspectorate of Prisons, 2014; Keith, 2006)—but recognises that searching for recalcitrant youth is fruitless if a YOI or prison remains morally depleted or 'morally dangerous' (Liebling, 2004a). Even if you can identify who is most likely to be violent, importation studies often fail to explain what you then *do* with that information. Given the role of tragedy in these young men's lives, the poverty of hope and aspiration, the lack of social recognition and worth, and the situational context, it's difficult to imagine how a thinking skills or an anger management programme could have ever persuaded these young men that violence was simply a function of their impulsivity and poor emotional regulation and that they ought to just think, act, and reason better (also see Maruna, 2023).

Second, it is impossible to accurately predict who the 'violent prone' people will be with any reliability. Adaptations and responses to imprisonment are more 'idiosyncratic' (Adams, 1992) than importation studies suggest. As this study has shown, not all those young men who are violent in the community were violent in prison, and not all those who had been previously violent within custody continued to be so. Over time, some young men who had been perpetrators of violence during prior periods of imprisonment had often gained sufficient carceral capital and a 'name' that threats were sufficient, or their readiness for violence was well known, mitigating the risk of, or need for, victimisation. There were more frequent episodes of violence amongst a small cohort of young men (less than 10% of the population), but there was a degree of irregularity to such incidents and the dynamics could change quickly. Today's perpetrator could become tomorrow's victim.

Third, focusing on the actuality of violence is a poor assessment of risk and social dynamics. Perpetrators can be victims, coerced into assaulting officers and their peers, robbing others, or other acts such as collecting, passing, and holding contraband. Equally, those who were least violent might be those were directing others, issuing instructions, or encouraging their peers to engage in illicit behaviour. It was these young men who were often more controlling, more intimidating and who were the emerging 'puppet masters.' What these men were 'learning' was how to secure the best rewards of performative compliance whilst also continuing their nefarious activities. There was little in the way of normative compliance, and their time in the YOI had effectively prepared them for 'grafting' in adult prisons (as some went on to do).

Importation studies point to who might be *more likely* to assault others, leaving the precise contributory factors to a violent incident poorly understood. Violence is—as this study has explored—a complex phenomenon. It is intimately tied to political economy (within and beyond the prison), social and prison policy, the relational context (between prisoners, between prisoners and prison officers, and between prison officers and prison leaders); the moral environment and normative underpinnings of both organisational and prisoner culture; the proportionality and nature of prison security; the quality and philosophy of prison leadership; the quality, style, and construction of prison officer governance; the use of coercive force and segregation; and, crime, criminal culture and criminal identities. It must be understood in the context of life course and the meanings that young men attach to violence, which varies between individuals. This necessitates ethnographic and qualitative research, yet it is this research that is often dismissed as subjective or unscientific (Stuart, 2020; Young, 2011). Is there any utility, then, in studying importation factors? The argument here is not that quantitative research does not have value, but it has become a 'broken record,' testing and re-testing the same factors without advancing our understanding of why any relevant variables are material. Often such quantitative studies attempt 'logical' explanations for variables, but this easily leads to error. Quantitative research needs to sit alongside, and be informed, by ethnographic or qualitative research.

Transformed Prisons, Transformed Prisoner Society

Despite the extant research on prison violence, there has been little English qualitative or ethnographic research on prison violence since Edgar et al.'s (2003a) extensive study in the 1990s. Prisons are not the same institutions they once were—they are arguably less liberal, more austere, more depriving, and more demanding (Crewe & Liebling, 2011). Writing shortly after the turn of the century, Liebling notes that '[i]n most prisons still, the landing is still the same landing; … and the essential prison experience remains fully recognizable by those who have always been there. Meanwhile, the world around the prison landing has been transformed' (2004b: 4). In the time that has passed since Liebling penned these words, life on the prison landing (and in the landing offices) had also been transformed. The study has revealed that the causes of this transformation include: (1) the 'reconfiguration of penal power' (Crewe & Liebling, 2017) and prison officer governance; (2) an intensification of managerialism, centralisation, and bureaucratisation; (3) a lean prison staffing and management model; (4) a new drug economy; (5) economic scarcity, and the growing need for prisoners to rely on the illicit economy to access simple necessities; (6) the resulting debt economy; (7) the growing financial profitability of the prison illicit economy; (8) greater ease of drug supply and the diversification of contraband supply routes; (9) the availability of new technologies, facilitating criminal activities and creating new forms of victimisation (notably global humiliation and direct threats to prisoner's families); (10) political instability, perpetual change programmes and policy failures (e.g. the privatisation of probation); and, (11) a loss of dynamic security. For young men, this was also coupled with a hardening of penal policy (Ministry of Justice, 2013); post-industrial decline in working class employment (Hall et al., 2013; Maguire, 2021); and, early entry into low-level drug dealing (sometimes through exploitation).

The transformation of the prisoner social world manifests in: an evolution of the prisoner normative code (to stigmatise indebtedness not exploitation); a reshaping of the prisoner hierarchy (where the 'Top Dog' or 'King of the Wing' is the one controlling the illicit economy); the valorisation of economic gain, capital, and power; the subordination of debtors; prisoners developing drug addictions within prison; greater individualisation; vulnerable prisoners becoming even less protected; the use of violence as a 'tool' (also see Marsh, 2020; Pearson & Hobbs, 2001) in the illicit economy; and, the growth of criminal collaborations within prisons that are diffuse, informal, and highly adaptable. That said, the effects have been uneven. It is in the closed adult male prisons that organised crime has become more embedded and the excesses of financial gain from the illicit economy increasingly evident (Gooch & Treadwell, 2021, 2023, 2025). Within the YOI, young men were 'learning to graft' and some were already at the edges of more organised entrepreneurial crime. The value of the illicit economy was also more likely to be in the hundreds of pounds, rather than the thousands of pounds seen in adult male prisons. Taken together, the 'problem of prison order' (Sparks et al., 1996) is now different in kind. Across the closed male prison estate, victimisation is pervasive, normalised, and more severe. Riots continue, although rarely on the same scale as the Strangeways riots of 1991 (Woolf, 1991) or the riot of 2016 at HMP Birmingham. But crucially, prisoners are increasingly fulfilling 'governance' roles on the landings in the absence of sufficient and competent guardianship by prison officers (Gooch & Treadwell, 2023; Skarbek, 2014). It is far harder for prison officers to regain power and control when too much has already been conceded, and it is this challenge that now faces the male prison estate.

This study suggests that Sykes' 'teleological functionalism' (Sparks et al., 1996: 43) that ties prisoner behaviour so neatly to structure is problematic. The increase of violence within the YOI, or more widely across the prison estate, and the social roles and norms adopted, were not simply a function of intensified structural deprivation. Equally, the importation of street and criminal cultures is also an inadequate explanation. Both the deterioration and improvements in the YOI studied were partly the consequences of leadership style, skill, and decision making, but simply seeing prison violence through the lens of a 'management perspective' (McCorkle et al., 1995) would also have been blinkered. The prison is an 'organisation in action' (Jacobs, 1977: 5, 11)—it is dynamically affected by the wider social, economic, political, policy, and moral environment. All these elements are important, and actions have meanings within those contexts. Crucially, actions find a moral meaning within a context. The prison is a 'special moral place' (Liebling, 2004a) where virtues such as justice, integrity, dignity, respect, humanity matter for human flourishing and well-being. Conversely, moral neglect can lead to distress (Liebling, 2011), crisis and violence. Living with injustice is suffocating. Living in an environment where those who are supposed to care for you antagonise or disrespect you, and threaten your sense of moral and social recognition, is crushing. A moral vocabulary is often missing from research on prison violence. However, it is my contention that we cannot fully understand prison violence without accounting for the morality of the prison and its daily practices. Moral order leads to social order. Crucially, the perceived 'morality' and importance of prison violence and victimisation by young men were influenced by the moral environment and in particular the pursuit of social recognition, respect, and justice.

Violence and victimisation were meaningful and intelligible. Even when callous, brutal, or extreme, it was often viewed as 'right,' 'virtuous' (Fiske & Rai, 2015) or necessary. For these young men, though, violence was functional in terms of restoring order, negotiating power, avenging wrongs, retaliating against provocation, punishing reprehensible behaviour, resolving conflict, enforcing norms and rules, challenging illegitimate behaviour by prison officers, discharging emotion, and defending self. The logic of prison violence stemmed from the desire for social recognition, respect, and the pursuit of justice. Young men sought validation and social recognition from their peers and from prison staff. It was this social recognition that was protective in terms of avoiding the persistent targeting experienced by the 'nerds' and 'victims,' or the opportunistic cell theft and robbery, and it was this social recognition that enveloped them within the 'mandem' and 'lads.' Social recognition was underpinned by carceral capital and conformity to the prisoner normative code and situated within a cultural milieu where violence and victimisation held an 'economic rationale' (Marsh, 2020) and was an effective strategy for self-preservation and social recognition.

Preventing Prison Violence and Victimisation

In researching prison violence, I have never been too far away from the criticism that the enquiry was misplaced and would be better focused on structural violence, social injustice, and prison abolition. Much harm could undoubtedly be prevented by: (1) reforming social care and local authority care provision; (2) fundamentally reforming youth custody (including the abolition of YOIs for children) (Goldson, 2005); (3) investing in high quality community mental health services, youth services, community services, and housing accommodation; (4) inclusive schooling that is enriching for all (for further analysis, see Billingham & Irwin-Rogers, 2022); (5) a dramatic reduction in the overall size of the prison population and the length of custodial sentences; (6) and, greater use, and reimagination, of community disposals. As Desmond Tutu said, 'There comes a point where we need to stop pulling people out of the river. We need to go upstream and find out why they are falling in.' This study demonstrates how critical structural inequality, social harm and professional neglect are in young prisoner's lives. Any 'upstream' solutions might prevent some from entering or returning to prison but does not obfuscate the need for prison reform. To borrow Desmond Tutu's expression, there's a need to both stop the bodies falling in upstream and pull them out downstream. There will always be some people for whom imprisonment is the only means to safely protect the public, and whilst there is still a need for prisons (even if fewer and smaller in number), there is much than can be done to reduce prison violence and to support those in prison.

In the context of community violence, Billingham and Irwin Rogers argue: 'we should aim not just for less violence between young people, we should aim to be a far better and less harmful place in which to grow up. The two are inseparable' (Billingham & Irwin-Rogers, 2022). Here I extend this argument to violence between young people in secure training centres, YOIs, and adult prisons. The prevention of prison violence by young men (but especially adult prisoners) should remain a focus, but we should aim for far better and less harmful YOIs for young men to grow up in. In closely confined, male dominated spaces with scarce resources, we can anticipate that some violent incidents will occur (Sykes, 1958), but it does not follow that prisons will always collapse into disorder, chaos, or squalor. Nor should we anticipate that all institutions holding young men will necessarily be chaotic, turbulent, and volatile.

The high levels of violence within the YOI were symptomatic of a lack of operational wisdom and moral practices, including: inhumane conditions; cynical, punitive and uncaring cultures and attitudes; low staff morale; inconsistent governance; complacency and a tolerance (even expectation) of victimisation between prisoners; a lack of strategy about how to accommodate young people with different needs (and how to use healthcare, the induction unit, and segregation); disproportionate security measures; little support in the first hours and days of confinement; staff corruption; and the overuse of State sanctioned violence and segregation. To recognise 'brutal facts' (Collins, 2001) about less than satisfactory prison practices, policies, environments, cultures, and climates is often interpreted as a denial of the heroism and courage of staff, the inadequacy of their lot, and the reality that most want to do the right thing. But both things can be true: staff might be trying the best, but prisons still be morally woeful. Equally, without leadership support and investment, staff might want to do more but feel hopeless and helpless (and simply give up).

The transformation of the YOI—and the reduction in violence—was achieved through skilful moral and operational leadership, improving material conditions, recognising and rewarding pro-social behaviour by young men, promoting education and employment, proportionate security measures, understanding and responding to violence and self-harm when it occurred, and treading a careful line between the rule of law and the use of power and authority on one hand, and the promotion of redemption narratives, offering trust, and individual care. It was a sophisticated form of 'moral dualism' (Braithwaite, 1998b, also see Crewe & Liebling, 2011) that was well understood, even instinctive, for the senior leadership team but was harder for some prison officers to grasp and embody. For many officers, offering trust to gain trustworthy behaviour (Braithwaite, 1998a), or promoting 'redemption narratives' (Maruna, 2001) for those who were aggressive and disruptive, or prioritising the compassionate care of those who had little respect (e.g. sex offenders), was counter-intuitive and had been counter-cultural. Achieving the 'demanding combination of freedom and safety, or harmony and security' is extremely difficult in a prison (Crewe & Liebling, 2011; Liebling, 2004a: 211), but it is critical. Central to the reforming efforts was the belief that these young men were 'deserving'—that they were *worth* something, that they *mattered,* that they were worthy of respect, and that they should receive fair treatment. Billingham and Irwin-Rogers (2022: 123) note that 'feeling like you do not matter can play a significant role in the complex causal chains which lead to different forms of violent acts.' The prevention of prison violence, therefore, is fundamentally tied to the creation of a relational, cultural, and physical environment where young men's claims to moral worth, personal dignity, respect, and justice are not just recognised but integral to operational policies and practices. This finding runs contrary to typical prison policies and relational contexts where too often young men are expected to 'earn' respect and demonstrate moral worth—beliefs that are contrary to young men's own belief in their inherent worth. It is this gulf in expectation that undermines attempts to engage young men in desistance or paternalistic demands for rehabilitation. At worst, the immorality and injustice of the State expose young men to greater trauma, tragedy, and harm, perpetuating distress and inflicting more scars.

Broken Windows or a Broken System?

Whilst high levels of prison violence are often explained in terms of more dangerous or more violent men, they are symptomatic of the moral, social, economic, and cultural prison context. There were moments during the research where the harm caused, and the indifference to, the young men moved me to tears, as it did others. It is difficult to truly describe the horrors of the cells, or the experience of witnessing uncontained distress that I was powerless to resolve, or describe the moment where a young man nearly died in the segregation unit, or convey my largely concealed frustration at the passive response of prison officer to the desperate cries of a young man who was about to bludgeon his 'pad mate' with a TV. But the hardest thing for me to reconcile was why the

YOI had been left to crumble—morally and physically. Even a cursory glance at the inspection reports in the decade prior to this research illustrates that there was nothing new about the Inspectorate's concerns about poor prison conditions, distant staff relationships, high levels of violence, extensive segregation use and the (over)use of physical restraint. In retrospect, it's difficult to understand why HM Prison and Probation Service—in a collective sense—waited until the YOI was 'morally outrageous' (Liebling, 2004b: 477) before acting. As an external observer, I could not help but wonder: Why were earlier Inspectorate findings seemingly ignored? Why were pleas to fix the broken windows unanswered? Why wait for the YOI to be branded the worst in the country and threatened with closure before investing the necessary resources? How much harm was caused in delaying?

Of course, we could blame austerity. Healthy prisons cannot—contrary to Grayling's assertions—be run cheaply (Ministry of Justice, 2012). Centralised 'cost cutting' exercises would occur in a frequent, cyclical way throughout the 2010s and into the 2020s. Arguably, this could have made any additional expenditure on individual institutions difficult for the Prison Service to spare. We could also point to a punitive and unforgiving political climate. We could blame the distraction and instability caused by constant 'change' programmes and shifts in penal policy. We could point to a population crisis that forced Governors into placing prisoners in unsuitable accommodation (despite their protestations). But perhaps the greatest indictment of the system—as it was explained to me—was that resources did not flow to the YOI because to invest in one prison was to take money from another, and with so many prisons beginning to struggle, how could you decide which prison to invest in? It was easier, it was argued, to simply invest resources where it was most needed, one critical inspection at a time. This 'whack a mole' approach was reactive, lacked strategic thought, and has seen the Prison Service move from one crisis hit prison to another (and sometimes back again). Whilst there is some attempt to proactively invest support and resources in those public sector prisons most beset with problems, Ministerial decisions to both under-invest in prisons and over-stretch what prisons are required to do (e.g. by lengthening sentences, increasing the use of imprisonment, and under-investing in mental health services) means that the prison system is far from reaching a point of stability. Recovery is likely to take many years if such investment does come and prove impossible if it does not.

What is most tragic about the history of this YOI is not just that it was allowed to fall into such a state of physical and moral disrepair, nor that the delay in improving the YOI caused many young men to suffer untold harm, but that the YOI was neither the first nor last to attract attention for the repeated and serious failures of the healthy prison test, and many more prisoners would suffer in circumstances that were predictable and preventable. The pervasive problems within the YOI had taken root over time and continued unchecked. It is tempting to see such deterioration as an isolated problem. Yet, this 'failed State prison' (Liebling, 2015: 262) was emblematic of wider systemic decline. Concerns about the response of the Prison Service to their reports and recommendations led the Chief Inspector of Prisons to develop the 'Urgent Notification Process' with the then Secretary of State for Justice. The Chief Inspector was 'very concerned … at the way in which far too many recommendations are not achieved and in [his] mind are not taken seriously' (Clarke & Chamberlen, 2019: 7), and the Urgent Notification Process sought to prompt 'urgent' action by the Secretary of State for Justice (and by extension the Ministry of Justice and HM Prison and Probation Service), and secure wider public attention to the 'serious challenges within prisons in England and Wales' (ibid.). At the time of writing, the process has been implemented in respect of 11 prisons, including three repeated notifications (for HMPs Bedford, Bristol, and Exeter). It is striking that, to date, all the institutions that have been subject to an urgent notification have been Category B Local Prisons and institutions accommodating children and young people—two of the most complex parts of the prison system where those in custody are at a heightened state of vulnerability.

Much could have been learnt about the YOI's trajectory—both in how to prevent the crisis and in how to recover from it. In the aftermath, though, there has been a degree of organisational amnesia. I was not only asked about the veracity of the Inspectorate's finding but was told by some Governing Governors that it was 'all just smoke and mirrors.' The implication being that the Governing Governor and their senior management team had somehow 'duped' the Inspectorate and presented a false rosy picture. That this suggestion came from within HM Prison and Probation Service was perhaps the most surprising part. It is possible that such assertions reflected a misunderstanding about the Inspectorate's findings and assumed that the necessary improvements were more embedded than they were. However, the accusation revealed something of the competitive culture amongst senior leaders within the Prison Service—a culture that was partly encouraged by 'score cards,' performance metrics, the perception that a poor inspection could be 'disastrous' for careers, and suggestions by Ministers that Governors would be held accountable for any failures or poor performance within *their* prisons (Ministry of Justice, 2016, 2021). Governing Governors are typically highly responsible and highly invested individuals, but these tough punitive Ministerial messages about accountability overlooked the structural and political decisions that Governors had little influence over but would deal with the fallout from sentencing policy, constant penal policy change, the privatisation of facilities management, restricted autonomy over budgets, the removal of local organisational support (e.g. finance and HR), population pressures, and the incarceration of people with acute mental health needs for whom there were no secure beds.

The 'replicability problem' (i.e. the challenge of spreading innovation) has been noted in other public sector organisations, such as health and social care (Horton et al., 2018). In this study, the replicability problem included failure to capture and disseminate the strategic approaches and practices developed to improve a poor and failing YOI, with the effect that any Governor subsequently faced with similar challenges started afresh, relying on their own instincts and operational knowledge. So much of the art and skill of prison leadership is simply left to chance, and rests on a hope that a Governor will discern what to do. How bold Governors are very much depends on how confident they are, and how willing they are to 'put their head above the parapet' and risk their own reputation. Part of the explanation for the replicability problem is the tendency to see new innovations and improvements as personality driven (Horton et al., 2018), rather than the product of a team effort. Consequently, the focus is on the personality (and whether that person is well-regarded), rather than what is repeatable. Another explanation for the replicability problem noted in healthcare that also plagues the Prison

Service is the 'not invented here' problem (Horton et al., 2018: 43), where 'organisations reject good ideas developed elsewhere in favour of their own internally developed ideas.' Prisons have their own unique personalities, organisational memories, and cultural legacies. However, failing prisons often share common problems in their social, moral, and cultural climate. Moreover, new ideas do not become 'business as usual,' partly because it means moving away from what is familiar. There is a surprising tendency within prisons to retain the familiar even if the familiar is ineffective.

Whatever the cause, the learning about how to prevent and/or recover from a crisis has been lost as attention has turned to repairing the latest prison to fall on its knees. The prison system is cycling through crisis not reversing it. Concerns about prison performance have led to an intensification of administrative and bureaucratic control, and the pursuit of 'assurance' metrics, targets, league tables and action plans (for an analysis, see Bennett, 2020; Liebling & Crewe, 2013). The layers of management *above* the prison have increased whilst perversely reducing the number of managers available *within* a prison to effect change. Tragically, Crewe's prediction (2009: 451) that the risk that 'managerialism can too easily become an end in itself, rather than a means to humanitarian ends' has been borne out. The implicit message—whether intended or not—is that Governors cannot be trusted to lead their prisons, understand what is needed, and ensure that it is done. Indeed, the language of governor autonomy and empowerment has been shrouded in competitiveness and accompanied by threats that the Governors of the worst performing prisons would be called to meetings with the Secretary of State for Justice (Ministry of Justice, 2016, 2021). Managerialism is seductive because it *feels* like governance (in the sense of informed oversight and analysis), and it creates an industry that suggests 'something is being done.' However, very little of managerialism improves the 'moral performance' of a prison (Liebling, 2004b), engages with the complex business of culture reform, or provides the moral leadership and relational context where prison officers and prisoners feel safe, supported, secure, valued, or recognised. It is notable that in the case of the YOI, the reforms were less about technical compliance with the expectations of the Inspectorate, action plans, or 'initiative-itus' (Baroness Casey, 2023). Instead, the focus was on the values that underpinned the desired changes—not just what needed to be done, but why. Equally, improved 'performance' was sought through prioritising the 'right' actions and practices, not 'gaming the system' (Bennett, 2020). Managerialism cannot achieve what moral leadership, practices, and environments can.

Endings

The conclusion of this study marked new beginnings. The departure of the Governing Governor five months after the re-inspection necessitated temporary arrangements until a new Governing Governor could permanently take up the post. Several senior managers would move to new roles in other prisons or regional offices. There were more questions than certainties. Would the resolve of the remaining senior managers to 'continue the journey' prove sufficient? Would a new Governing Governor adopt a new approach? For the senior management team who had invested and committed themselves so wholeheartedly, would any other leadership challenge quite be the same? These departures created an opportune moment for James and I to 'leave the field,' but I remained in contact with the leadership team and continued to work with many in their new roles. I left the YOI, but it did not leave me. An ethnographic study of a prison or YOI is never just about a prison and is never just a research exercise. It is about the lives of those who inhabit and work within the prison walls. It confronts us with humanity and inhumanity, justice and injustice, tragedy and joy, and the very best and worst forms of humanity. As the people James and I met shared their stories with us—whether as staff, managers, governors, or as those imprisoned—we were changed by them. As researchers, this project has been the making of us both (Gooch, 2021; Treadwell, 2018). Since ethnographic research necessarily requires the 'full use of self' (Liebling 2001: 475), how could the research not linger with us?

Whilst this study was bookended by two inspections—one shocking and another uplifting—this was not the end of the troubles experienced by the YOI. At the time of writing, the YOI had once again received the accolade from HM Inspectorate of Prisons of being the most violent prison of its type. Over time, the physical environment had deteriorated again. Young men were locked in their cells due to fears that they were 'risky.' Use of force was high and segregation use had increased. Staff had once again retreated to the office. Management 'grip' was lacking in certain areas. The strategies, values, and priorities that had underpinned the reformation of the YOI had fallen away. In an unhappy turn of events, the YOI had gradually drifted back to the conditions that had initially given rise to the stark criticism that prompted this research. Though it has not failed all measures of the healthy prison test again, the history of the YOI is not one of continued stability, but of short bursts of improvement followed by substantial decline. The encouragement by the Chief Inspector 'don't go back to normal if normal is what it was 15 months ago' has—it seems—long been forgotten.

This begs the question: can you really transform the violent prison (and make it last)? In the case of this YOI, we will never know. Whilst abolitionists would rightly be quick to point out that prisons are structurally violent places, this research shows that that the extent of that violence, immorality, and damage is a choice. Too often the decisions made—whether economic, managerial, practical, or policy decisions—serve to increase the likelihood of harm and fail to sustain improvements. Typically, the Prison Service responds to a positive re-inspection by re-imposing financial restrictions, increasing the number of prisoners, replacing the (often promoted) Governing Governor with one whom does not share the same reforming zeal or approach, and/or focusing primarily on 'performance' rather than maintaining a focus on moral practices. The Prison Service turns its attention to the latest prison to receive a critical inspection report and moves resource and effort there. As it was succinctly put: 'the circus moves on.' Although prisons are grossly underfunded, the problem is not solely a resource issue. You cannot purchase leadership, relationships, hope, integrity, justice, dignity, or faith in the redeemability and potential of young prisoners. The prison is a 'special, fragile moral environments' (Liebling, 2004a: 213) where moral order and moral practices need constant attention. Neglect is easy, but costly.

For the young men James and I encountered, there were no neat endings. We would leave them, but they would not leave prison custody for days, weeks, months, or years. As we continued our research on prison violence across the adult prison estate, we would meet our interviewees again. Some were still serving their sentences. Some had been released and returned to prison for more serious offences. Others James met in boxing gyms or homeless on the streets. Others are (at the time of writing) 'on the run,' doing their best to avoid arrest and re-imprisonment. However effective the prison leadership team had been in reducing prison violence and improving the YOI, and whether they reoffended or not, imprisonment had dramatically and irrevocably altered these young lives as they had tried to survive—sometimes competently and sometimes barely at all—in an unforgiving and too often inhumane and unjust place. There was still too much violence, and too many young men (and prison staff) would leave scarred by their experience. However well-intentioned the leadership and staff team, they were working within a system that was increasingly failing these young men, and neither investing in their young lives nor in the places that would confine them. If anything, the knowledge that children and young people are disproportionately perpetrators of prison violence has led to the 'adulteration' of penal policy, the loss of distinct provision for young adults, and the inability to consider how prisons generate violence. It's not that 'we can forget need' (Liebling, 2012), we have forgotten it. Too many young had 'grown up in the system' and it was in the system that they would stay because too little was done to address mental health needs, the impact of trauma and tragedy, to support them to be fathers and partners, to create the 'hooks' for change (McNeill, 2012), to provide meaningful employment opportunities, or to foster human flourishing. This does little to protect the public, and it does little to prevent prison violence.

References

Adams, K. (1992). Adjusting to prison life. In M. Tonry (Ed.), *Crime and justice: A review of research.* University of Chicago Press.

Bennett, J. (2020). Against prison management. *Prison Service Journal, 247*, 4–13.

Billingham, L., & Irwin-Rogers, K. (2022). *Against youth violence: A social harm perspective.* Bristol University Press.

Bowker, L. H. (1980). *Prison victimisation*. Elsevier.
Braithwaite, V. (1998a). Institutionalising distrust, enculturating trust. In V. Braithwaite & M. Levi (Eds.), *Trust and governance* (pp. 343–375). Russell Sage Foundation.
Braithwaite, V. (1998b). The value balance model of political evaluations. *British Journal of Psychology, 89*(2), 223–247.
Casey, B. (2023). *An independent review into the standards of behaviour and internal culture of the Metropolitan Police Service*. Metropolitan Police Service.
Clarke, P., & Chamberlen, A. (2019). The Chief Inspector of Prisons, Peter Clarke reflects on recent problems in prisons. *Prison Service Journal, 243*, 6–12.
Collins, J. (2001). *Good to great*. Random House.
Collins, R. (2008). *Violence: A micro-sociological theory*. Princeton University Press.
Crewe, B. (2009). *Prisoner society: Power, adaptation and social life in an English prison*. Oxford University Press.
Crewe, B., & Liebling, A. (2011). Are liberal-humanitarian penal values and practices exceptional? In T. Ugelvik & J. Dullum (Eds.), *Penal exceptionalism? Nordic prison policy and practice* (pp. 175–198). Routledge.
Crewe, B., & Liebling, A. (2017). Reconfiguring penal power. In A. Liebling, S. Maruna, & L. Mcara (Eds.), *Oxford handbook of criminology* (pp. 889–913). Oxford University Press.
Edgar, K., & O'Donnell, I. (1998). Assault in prison: The 'victim's' contribution. *British Journal of Criminology, 38*(4), 635–650.
Edgar, K., O'Donnell, I., & Martin, C. (2003a). *Prison violence: The dynamics of conflict, fear and power*. Willan.
Edgar, K., O'Donnell, I., & Martin, C. (2003b). Violence in prison. In R. M. Lee & E. A. Stanko (Eds.), *Researching violence* (pp. 69–87). Routledge.
Fiske, A. P., & Rai, T. S. (2015). *Virtuous violence: Hurting and killing to create, sustain, end and honor social relationships*. Cambridge University Press.
Gibbons, J. J., & deBelleville Katzenbach, N. (2006). Confronting confinement: A repot of the commission on safety and abuse in America's prisons. *Washington University Journal of Law and Policy, 22*, 385–562.
Goldson, B. (2005). Child imprisonment: A case for abolition. *Youth Justice, 5*(2), 77–90.
Gooch, K. (2021). "You've got a hard edge!": The gender politics, complexities and intimacies undertaking prison research at the "edge". In J. A. Schlosser (Ed.), *Prison stories: Women scholars' experiences doing research behind bars* (pp. 173–192). Rowman and Littlefield Publishing Group.

Gooch, K., & Treadwell, J. (2021). 'It doesn't stop at the prison gate': Understanding organised crime in prison. *Prison Service Journal, 252*, 15–30.
Gooch, K., & Treadwell, J. (2023). The 'screw boys' and the 'businessmen': Re-negotiating penal power, governance and legitimate authority through a prison violence reduction scheme. *The British Journal of Criminology, 63*(4), 1219–1236.
Gooch, K., & Treadwell, J. (2025). The prison firm: The 'transportation' of organised crime, the evolution of criminal markets and contemporary prisoner society. *Criminology and Criminal Justice, 25*(1), 245–264.
Hall, S., Winlow, S., & Ancrum, C. (2013). *Criminal identities and consumer culture*. Willan.
Her Majesty's Inspectorate of Prisons. (2014). *Report of a review of the implementation of the Zahid Mubarek inquiry recommendations*. Her Majesty's Inspectorate of Prisons.
Honneth, A. (1995). *The struggle for recognition: The moral grammar of social conflicts*. Polity Press.
Horton, T., Ilingworth, J., & Warburton, W. (2018). *The spread challenge: How to support the successful uptake of innovations and improvements in health care*. The Health Foundation.
Jacobs, J. B. (1977). *Stateville*. University of Chicago Press.
Keith, B. (2006). *Report of the Zahid Mubarek inquiry*. The Stationery Office.
Liebling, A. (2004a). The late modern prison and the question of values. *Current Issues in Criminal Justice, 16*(2), 202–219.
Liebling, A. (2004b). *Prisons and their moral performance*. Oxford University Press.
Liebling, A. (2011). Moral performance, inhuman and degrading treatment and prison pain. *Punishment & Society, 13*(5), 530–550.
Liebling, A. (2012). Young adult offenders in custodial institutions. In F. Lösel, A. E. Bottoms, & D. P. Farrington (Eds.), *Young adult offenders: Lost in transition* (pp. 65–73). Willan.
Liebling, A. (2015). Appreciative inquiry, generative theory, and the failed state prison. In A. Miller & W. R. Palacious (Eds.), *Qualitative research in criminology* (pp. 251–269). Routledge.
Liebling, A., & Crewe, B. (2013). Prisons beyond the new penology: The shifting moral foundations of prison management. In J. Simon & R. Sparks (Eds.), *The SAGE handbook of punishment and society* (pp. 283–307). Sage.
Liebling, A., Arnold, H., & Straub, C. (2011a). *An exploration of staff-prisoner relationships at Whitemoor: 12 years on*. Ministry of Justice.
Liebling, A., Price, D., & Shefer, G. (2011b). *The prison officer*. Willan.

Maguire, D. (2021). *Male, failed and jailed: Masculinities and the 'revolving door' imprisonment in the UK*. Palgrave Macmillan.
Marsh, B. (2020). *The logic of violence: An ethnography of Dublin's illegal drug trade*. Routledge.
Maruna, S. (2001). *Making good: How ex-convicts reform and rebuild their lives*. American Psychological Association.
Maruna, S. (2023). Wicked problems, not wicked people. In A. J. Tamatea, A. J. Day, & D. J. Cooke (Eds.), *Preventing prison violence: An ecological perspective* (pp. xii–xiii). Routledge.
McCorkle, R. C., Miethe, T. D., & Drass, K. A. (1995). The roots of prison violence: A test of the deprivation, management, and "not-so-total" institution models. *Crime & Delinquency, 41*(3), 317–331.
McNeill, F. (2012). Four forms of 'offender' rehabilitation: Towards an interdisciplinary perspective. *Legal and Criminological Psychology, 17*(1), 18–36.
Ministry of Justice. (2012). *Rehabilitation revolution: The next steps*. Ministry of Justice.
Ministry of Justice. (2013). *Transforming the management of young adults in custody*. Ministry of Justice.
Ministry of Justice. (2016). *Prison safety and reform, cm 9350*. Ministry of Justice.
Ministry of Justice. (2021). *Prison strategy white paper*. Ministry of Justice.
Ministry of Justice. (2025). *Safety in custody statistics: Quarterly update to September 2024*. Ministry of Justice.
Nixon, R. (2013). *Slow violence and the environmentalism of the poor*. Harvard University Press.
Pearson, G., & Hobbs, D. (2001). *Middle market drug distribution*. Home Office.
Skarbek, D. (2014). *The social order of the underworld: How prison gangs govern the American penal system*. Oxford University Press.
Sparks, R. F. (1982). *Research on victims of crime: Accomplishments, issues, and new directions*. US Department of Health and Human Services, Public Health Service, Alcohol Drug Abuse, and Mental Health Administration, National Institute of Mental Health, Center for Studies of Crime and Delinquency.
Sparks, R., Bottoms, A. E., & Hay, W. (1996). *Prisons and the problem of order*. Oxford University Press.
Stuart, F. (2020). *Ballad of the bullet: Gangs, drill music and the power of online infamy*. Princeton University Press.
Sykes, G. (1958). *The society of captives*. Princeton University Press.
Toch, H. (1977). *Living in prison: The ecology of survival*. The Free Press.

Toch, H. (1978). Social climate and prison violence. *Federal Probation, 42*(4), 21–25.

Treadwell, J. (2018). Doing ultrarealist ethnography: Romanticism and running with the riotous (while buying your round). In S. K. Rice & M. D. Maltz (Eds.), *Doing ethnography in criminology: Discovery through fieldwork* (pp. 289–301). Springer International Publishing.

Williams, R., & Liebling, A. (2023). Do prisons cause radicalization? Order, leadership, political charge and violence in two maximum security prisons. *British Journal of Criminology, 63*(1), 97–114.

Wooldredge, J. (2020). Prison culture, management, and in-prison violence. *Annual Review of Criminology, 3*(1), 165–188.

Woolf, L. J. (1991). *Prison disturbances April 1990*. Her Majesty's Stationery Office.

Wortley, R. (2002). *Situational prison control: Crime prevention in correctional institutions*. Cambridge University Press.

Young, J. (2011). *The criminological imagination*. Polity Press.

Epilogue

> I'm an adult, I should be in an adult establishment. Coming to a YOI is added punishment. (Michael, adult prisoner in the YOI when re-rolled)

My departure from the YOI was short lived. I was invited to return to the YOI on several occasions, to meet with the Governing Governor(s) and their senior team(s) as they changed, and to conduct a related research study—on the experiences of care leavers within YOI[1] (see Gooch et al., 2022). Almost imperceptibly, in the time since the initial fieldwork concluded, the principle of distinct treatment for young adult prisoners has been abandoned. Whilst the specific needs of young people aged 18–25 years old are acknowledged by HM Prison and Probation Service (see House of Commons Justice Committee, 2018), young adults are no longer held in separate institutions. Gradually, each YOI for young adult men has been re-rolled, either to a Category C & YOI or to serve another

[1] I am grateful to Professor Nathan Hughes and Dr Isla Masson with whom this research was developed. We are also indebted to the efforts of Dr Kim Turner, Dr Caroline Cresswell and Georgina Barkham for their able assistance.

K. Gooch, *Prison Violence*, Palgrave Studies in Prisons and Penology,
https://doi.org/10.1007/978-3-031-91365-5

purpose. Feltham B[2] and Deerbolt retained their status as young adult YOIs until 2023, when prison population pressures (Ministry of Justice, 2023) led to an increase in the age of young men accommodated there. The YOI where James and I conducted this research was re-rolled as a Category C & YOI prison, holding adult prisoners alongside young adults. At the time of writing, there are no dedicated YOIs for young adults.

This dramatic change in policy and practice has erased the principles that compelled the Gladstone Committee (1895) to introduce Borstals for young men and removed any special or specialist consideration for the specific needs of young adult men. Young adult prisoners have become invisible, and whilst there are a very small number of dedicated wings, most young adults are mixed with adult prisoners, seemingly overlooking the extent to which this may intensify their vulnerability and/or expose them to criminal networks or behaviours that solidify rather than disrupt criminal activity. The assumption is that holding young adults with adult men reduces rates of violence. Indeed, in *Transforming the Management of Young Adults in Custody*, Jeremy Wright, then Minister for Prisons and Rehabilitation, claimed:

> When large numbers of people in this age group are held together, they can become so volatile it becomes difficult for staff to manage them. If this continues, there is a danger that the experience of young adults in custody will become more about containment and less about rehabilitation and supporting them to desist from offending. (2013: 3)

These assumptions seem to privilege statistical data as a 'true account' of prison violence, and overlook the possibility that variation might be explained by differences in the visibility and recording of violence. Adult prisoners have often learnt when, where, and what to fight over. Conversely, young men are less likely to bide their time and pick a more opportune moment (although some will), and they sometimes deliberately fight in front of prison officers in the hope that intervention will be swift and the likelihood of serious injury reduced. The accumulation of

[2] HM YOI Feltham is split into Feltham A, which holds teenage boys aged 15–18 years old, and Feltham B, which until 2023, only held young adults.

social and carceral capital (often as young men), and the development of alternative forms of masculine performance (e.g. finding a partner, having children, gaining employment or a business), may mean that adult prisoners already have a 'name' and/or feel less likely to be drawn into 'petty' victimisation (e.g. some forms of verbal abuse). Simply moving adult prisoners into YOI may—as Michael notes—feel like a punishment or retrograde step for adult men and does little to engender the accumulation of alternative forms of capital amongst young men seeking recognition and respect. Equally, assertions such as those made by Jeremy Wright do not consider the severity of the violence. The risk of homicide for adult prisoners is greater in prison than in the community (United Nations Office on Drugs and Crime, 2019)—this is not true for young adult prisoners.

It is notable that mixing young adult and adult prisoners has made very little difference to rates of prison violence, which have remained stubbornly high (Ministry of Justice, 2025). Most staggering, of course, is that the Ministry of Justice seemed to have overlooked the fact the extent to which violence and disorder was a matter of choice on the part of the State. It is—as this book has argued—the product of policy incoherence, chronic underinvestment, poor operational practice, understaffing, the over-use of imprisonment, impoverished regimes and relationships, and ultimately, the failure to hold and practice moral standards and behaviours.

The decision to remove distinct provision is morally outrageous because it is so cynical. Rather than an informed strategy to support desistance amongst young adult men, it was a move based on efficiency, economy, and an attempt to improve performance ratings. At a time of increased prison population, and with fewer young adults in prison, spaces in the YOIs were given to adult prisons to ease the capacity pressures in the Category C prisons. Of course, this was not the reason given in the consultation paper:

> We are proposing that all young adults will be accommodated in mixed institutions, where resources are targeted on their risks and rehabilitation and resettlement needs. We want to ensure that their time in custody is both safe and effective. We want to ensure they benefit from resettlement

> prisons and we feel that, for this group in particular, being supported as they move through the gate and into their local communities will enable young adults to move away from a life of crime. (Ministry of Justice, 2013)

The suggestion that young adults would be provided with better, targeted support is empty rhetoric. No such investment, support, or resources have been extended to young adults, other than to introduce a maturity screening test and 'intervention'. However, it is unclear how an intervention can accelerate maturation whilst continuing to confine young men in chaotic and underfunded settings. As Charlie Taylor, Chief Inspector of Prisons has noted (2021), 'With little provision or resource, the opportunity for custody to provide this group with structure and purpose while they matured was missed.' It is no surprise that the Inspectorate consistently finds that 'the outcomes for young adults [are] worse than for older prisoners (those aged over 25)' (Her Majesty's Inspectorate of Prisons, 2021). Worryingly, the Ministry of Justice had previously been warned that moving young adult men into the mainstream adult prison population would have little effect on re-offending and would not create places of safety and decency (Her Majesty's Inspectorate of Prisons, 2006). Indeed, HM Inspectorate of Prisons have argued that dedicated YOIs or units for young adults generally 'performed' better than sites where young adult men were held amongst adult prisoners (Her Majesty's Inspectorate of Prisons, 2006).

The loss of distinct provision for young adults is contrary to the burgeoning evidence that demonstrates that young adulthood is a period of ongoing maturation and physical, neurological emotional and psychological development. It is also a sharp contrast to the approach taken within the Appellant Courts, which have shown a greater willingness to recognise that the youth and maturity of an individual is a relevant factor when sentencing young people over the age of 18, and that maturation and development continue long after an eighteenth birthday (e.g. *R v Clarke, Andrews and Thompson*[2018] EWCA Crim 185). For the longest period, the transition from youth custody to the young adult and adult prison estate has been akin to 'falling off a cliff' in terms of the changes in resources, staffing, and the movement to more adult systems and policies (also see Price, 2020). Despite the reforming efforts of the senior management team within the YOI, what could be done to improve the lot of young prisoners was hampered by penal policies designed for adult prisoners and the need to adhere to operational principles created for Category C prisons. A longer-term view would be to reform youth custody and further develop and resource the provision for young adults in dedicated YOIs. Ultimately, the reduction in the young adult male population was a missed opportunity to radically reform and improve the provision for young adults in custody. The death of the YOI is far from an 'evidence based' or even 'evidence informed policy' (Stevens, 2024). It is impossible to predict what the long-term consequences of this missed opportunity will be, but they are likely to be particularly detrimental and generate more violence than they reduce.

References

Gooch, K., Masson, I., Owens, A., & Waddington, E. (2022). After care, after thought: The invisibility of care experienced men and women in prison. *Prison Service Journal, 258*, 4–12.

Her Majesty's Inspectorate of Prisons. (2006). *Young adult male prisoners: A short thematic report*. Her Majesty's Inspectorate of Prisons.

Her Majesty's Inspectorate of Prisons. (2021). *Outcomes for young adults in custody*. Her Majesty's Inspectorate of Prisons.

House of Commons Justice Committee. (2018). *Young adults in the criminal justice system*. House of Commons Justice Committee.

Ministry of Justice. (2013). *Transforming the management of young adults in custody*. Ministry of Justice.

Ministry of Justice. (2023). *Prison population projections 2022 to 2027, England and Wales*. Ministry of Justice.

Ministry of Justice. (2025). *Safety in custody statistics: Quarterly update to September 2024*. Ministry of Justice.

Price, J. (2020). The experience of young people transitioning between youth offending services to probation services. *Probation Journal, 67*(3), 246–263.

Prisons Committee. (1895). *Report from the Departmental Committee on Prisons (the Gladstone report)*. Her Majesty's Stationery Office.

Stevens, A. (2024). *Drug policy constellations: The role of power and morality in the making of drug policy in the UK.* Bristol University Press.
United Nations Office on Drugs and Crime. (2019). *Global study of homicide.* United Nations on Drugs and Crime.

Glossary

ACCT Assessment, Care in Custody and Teamwork—the process used to care for prisoners who are at risk of suicide and self-harm

Added days A maximum of 42 days can be added to the end of a custodial sentence by the Independent Adjudicator for a proven violation of Prison/Young Offender Institutions Rules. Those serving life sentences, imprisonment for public protection sentences, or whole life orders cannot be given added days

Adjudication A prison disciplinary hearing convened by a governor to establish whether the alleged violation of Prison/Young Offender Institutions Rules has occurred. Sanctions can be suspended or applied for admitted/proven charges, or the matter can be referred to the Independent Adjudicator if the matter is serious and/or may merit 'added days'

Association A period where prisoners are given supervised but informal time out of cell to, for example, play pool, walk around the exercise yard and, in this Young Offender Institution, use the telephones

Basic The lowest level of the Incentives and Earned Privilege scheme, normally involving the removal of a television and carrying limitations on gym access, time out of cells, canteen orders and visits

Block Slang for the Segregation Unit

Blocked off Slang for being segregated

K. Gooch, *Prison Violence*, Palgrave Studies in Prisons and Penology,
https://doi.org/10.1007/978-3-031-91365-5

Burn Slang for tobacco

C&R Control and Restraint, use of physical force

Canteen Items such as food, toiletries and stationery, and could be ordered on a weekly basis

Canteen sheets A4 forms used to order canteen distributed and returned on a weekly basis

CM Custodial manager

CSU Care and Separation Unit, another name for the segregation unit

Domestics A period when prisoners can clean their cells, shower, use the telephones and speak to prison officers about any queries

Enhanced The highest level of the Incentives and Earned Privilege scheme. Those on Enhanced have, for example, the greatest access to the gym, the greatest time out of cell, and increased access to their 'spends' (see below). Certain items are only accessible to those on Enhanced (e.g. a computer console), and some opportunities can only be given after a prolonged period on Enhanced (e.g. living on the Enhanced Unit, Release on Temporary Licence, serving as peer representative, and certain types of family visit days)

Free flow A supervised period when prisoners walk to and from the residential units to access the classrooms, workshops, gym, healthcare centre, chaplain, visits area, and library

Ghosted Being transferred to another prison/Young Offender Institution

GOAD Good order and discipline

Gov Slang for prison governor, sometimes used by young men to refer to prison operational staff in a more general sense

Governing Governor The prison governor in overall charge of the prison

HMIP Her/His Majesty's Inspectorate of Prisons

HMPPS Her Majesty's Prison and Probation Service

Hooch A fermented liquid typically brewed within a cell using items available from the kitchen or canteen (e.g. fruit, bread, sugar)

IEP Incentives and Earned Privileges Scheme

Improvised weapon Weapons fashioned within prison from items such as toothbrushes and razor blades or created by inserting pool balls and tuna cans in socks

Independent Adjudicator A District Judge who adjudicates offences against Prison/Young Offender Institutions Rules and the Criminal Law (e.g. serious assault, possession of a mobile phone, possession of a weapon)

Juvie In a general sense this refers to youth custody (for 10–17 year olds), but young men typically had secure training centres and young offender institutions in mind (not secure children's homes)

Kweffed To cut or stab or be stabbed

Mamba A psychoactive substance (i.e. synthetic cannabinoid)

Nicking A 'nicking' is when a prison officer reports a violation of Prison/YOI Rules (see Prison Act 1952, Prison Rules 1999 and Young Offender Institution Rules 2000)

NOMS National Offender Management Service

Nonce An abbreviation for 'not on normal criminal exercises' and largely used as a slur for sex offenders and/or those who had committed offences against children and the elderly

NTRG National Tactical Response Group

On road An expression used to refer to being in the community although it may be used to specifically refer to being on the streets

Orderly A prison trusted with additional responsibilities in, for example, the gym, servery, or library

Pad Slang for a prison cell

Pad mate Slang for a person with whom a cell is shared

Pagan Slang for someone who is considered fake or a liar

Plugging Slang for concealing items (typically contraband) in the anus

PRU Pupil referral unit

Red Bands Young men who had more extensive access to the prison and could remove around more freely

Regime The prison's daily timetable, sometimes referred to in an administrative way (e.g. as a schedule to adhere to) and at other times as a judgement of prisoner behaviour and rehabilitation (e.g. whether they were 'complying' or 'engaging' with the regime)

Res Residential unit

ROTL Release on temporary licence, typically permitted in the Young Offender Institution to pursue employment opportunities outside of the prison

Screws Slang for prison officer

Servery Where food is served

Shank Slang for a knife

Shipped Transferred to another prison/Young Offender Institution

Shotting Slang for drug dealing

SLU Supported Living Unit, a special unit for those who needed additional support and/or were vulnerable to victimisation and exploitation in other areas of the Young Offender Institution

SMT Senior Management Team, a group of operational and non-operational governors

SO Supervising officer, more senior than a prison officer but without line management responsibilities

Spice A psychoactive substance (i.e. synthetic cannabinoid)

Splash Slang for stabbing someone

Standard The middle level of the Incentives and Earned Privilege scheme, with neither the restrictions of 'Basic' (see above) nor all the rewards of 'Enhanced.' Access to a television is permitted on Standard but not Basic

Sweatbox Cellular escort vans used to transfer prisoners to and from court and/or to other prisons/Young Offender Institutions

Throwover A package thrown over the wall and/or fence often containing contraband

Twisted Up Slang for control and restraint (C&R), but typically referring more specifically to the use of pain compliance techniques

Volumetric control A policy that specifies how much property, and what kinds of property, a prisoner can keep within their cells. Traditionally, the contents of their cell were required to fit within two property boxes

Index[1]

[1] Note: Page numbers followed by 'n' refer to notes.

K. Gooch, *Prison Violence*, Palgrave Studies in Prisons and Penology,
https://doi.org/10.1007/978-3-031-91365-5

The manufacturer's authorised representative in the EU is Springer
Nature Customer Service Centre GmbH, Europaplatz 3, 69115 Heidelberg,
Germany. If you have any concerns regarding our products, please
contact ProductSafety@springernature.com

Printed and bound by CPI Group (UK) Ltd, Croydon, CR0 4YY
30/09/2026
02225583-0015